Wellbeing in Politics and Policy

Series Editors
Ian Bache
Department of Politics
University of Sheffield
Sheffield, UK

Karen Scott
Cornwall Campus
Exeter University
Penryn, UK

Paul Allin
Department of Mathematics
Imperial College London
London, UK

Wellbeing in Politics and Policy will bring new lenses through which to understand the significance of the dramatic rise of interest in wellbeing as a goal of public policy. While a number of academic disciplines have been influential in both shaping and seeking to explain developments, the Politics discipline has been relatively silent, leaving important theoretical and empirical insights largely absent from debates: insights that have increasing significance as political interest grows. This series will provide a distinctive addition to the field that puts politics and policy at the centre, while embracing interdisciplinary contributions. Contributions will be encouraged from various subfields of the discipline (e.g., political theory, comparative politics, governance and public policy, international relations) and from those located in other disciplines that speak to core political themes (e.g., accountability, gender, inequality, legitimacy and power). The series will seek to explore these themes through policy studies in a range of settings—international, national and local. Comparative studies—either of different policy areas and/or across different settings—will be particularly encouraged. The series will incorporate a wide range of perspectives from critical to problem-solving approaches, drawing on a variety of epistemologies and methodologies. The series welcomes Pivots, edited collections and monographs.

More information about this series at
http://www.palgrave.com/gp/series/15247

Ian Bache · Karen Scott
Editors

The Politics of Wellbeing

Theory, Policy and Practice

Editors
Ian Bache
Department of Politics
University of Sheffield
Sheffield, UK

Karen Scott
Department of Politics
University of Exeter
Penryn, Cornwall, UK

Wellbeing in Politics and Policy
ISBN 978-3-030-09630-4   ISBN 978-3-319-58394-5   (eBook)
https://doi.org/10.1007/978-3-319-58394-5

Cover illustration: JNBazinet/Getty Images

Printed on acid-free paper

This Palgrave Macmillan imprint is published by the registered company Springer International Publishing AG part of Springer Nature
The registered company address is: Gewerbestrasse 11, 6330 Cham, Switzerland

ACKNOWLEDGEMENTS

This volume draws on contributions to the ESRC seminar series on *The Politics of Wellbeing* (Grant Ref: ES/L001357/1). We would like to express our gratitude to the ESRC for their support for this project, which brought together 131 participants from academia and the policy world over six events between 2013 and 2015. We would like to thank all of those who contributed to the success of the series and, in particular, to our co-convenor, Charles Seaford.

CONTENTS

LIST OF FIGURES

CHAPTER 1

Wellbeing in Politics and Policy

Ian Bache and Karen Scott

INTRODUCTION

Why another book on wellbeing? In the past decade or so, numerous volumes have been published on this topic, signifying the dramatic rise of interest by academics, policy-makers and civil society in the concept of wellbeing. Considering the wealth of this literature, one would think there was little new to say on the subject. Our book, however, addresses an important gap in wellbeing studies: it provides new perspectives from the discipline of politics. In this chapter, we set out why we think this is important and highlight the potential contribution of the politics discipline.[1]

Wellbeing[2] has become a focus for political debate and a goal of public policy in many countries in recent decades. This focus on wellbeing has intensified in the wake of the financial crisis as politicians and policy-makers have sought new narratives and new policy frames that challenge the dominance of GDP growth as an indicator of progress and a lodestar for policy. A number of academic disciplines, economics and

I. Bache
Department of Politics, University of Sheffield, Sheffield, UK
e-mail: i.bache@sheffield.ac.uk

K. Scott
Department of Politics, University of Exeter, Penryn, Cornwall, UK
e-mail: k.e.scott@exeter.ac.uk

© The Author(s) 2018
I. Bache and K. Scott (eds.), *The Politics of Wellbeing*, Wellbeing
in Politics and Policy, https://doi.org/10.1007/978-3-319-58394-5_1

1

psychology in particular, have been influential in both shaping and seeking to explain developments in wellbeing measurement, while the disciplines of sociology and geography have provided important critical perspectives, highlighting the differentiated understandings and lived experiences of wellbeing between and within nations. However, the politics discipline has been relatively silent on developments, whether on conceptualisations of wellbeing for public policy purposes, new measures of progress, or attempts to bring wellbeing into policy. This may be understandable to the extent that developments have only relatively recently moved from a focus on concept and measurement to the policy arena. However, their emergence is the outcome of a process that has been gestating for some time, and one that has 'transformative potential' in politics and policy (Kroll 2011, p. 1). The absence of contributions from scholars of politics has left important theoretical and empirical insights largely absent from debates: an issue that this book seeks to address. In short, this book provides the first collection in the field of wellbeing that places the concerns of the politics discipline centre stage.

As Crick (1982, p. 18) observed, 'Politics arises from accepting the fact of the simultaneous existence of different groups, hence different interests and different traditions' and is the process through which such differences might be articulated, contested and reconciled. Thus, politics is concerned with the processes through which power and resources are distributed: 'who gets what, when, how' (Lasswell 1936, np). Central to understanding political processes is the interplay of the 3 'I's—ideas, interests and institutions. Ideas refer to basic values of different groups or individuals, the notion of interests identifies winners and losers from different options, and institutions are the fora through which the reconciliation of differences is sought (Weiss 2001; Rosendorff 2005).

According to Aristotle, oft-quoted in contemporary texts on wellbeing, political science is the 'ruling science' in furthering the good life, for it 'legislates what must be done and what avoided' and provides the legitimisation for all other knowledge (*Nicomachean Ethics, i2*). Such an attempt to impose a hierarchy of disciplines is inappropriate in a modern world that increasingly values interdisciplinary endeavours to understand complex issues. Moreover, the politics discipline draws on a range of other fields—economics, geography, history, law, philosophy, psychology and sociology among them—and has been described as 'an eclectic discipline' (Flinders 2013, p. 151). Yet it is clear to us that the relative dearth of commentary from politics scholars is detrimental to the study of wellbeing. The discipline can offer important perspectives on how the issue of wellbeing is framed according to different values, highlight who stands to win or lose from contrasting approaches and different policy options and deepen understanding of the institutional processes through which decisions are taken. Such themes are at the intellectual core of this volume.

While the intellectual themes of this book are located primarily in the discipline of politics, it incorporates contributions from scholars in cognate disciplines whose concerns overlap and from those whose research and practice concerns specific policy developments. It explores key themes and issues in a range of settings—international, national and subnational/substate. Through this combination of intellectual inquiry, empirically grounded research and investigation across different settings, we aim to provide fresh insights and develop new lenses through which to understand the rise and significance of the wellbeing agenda.

In the next section of this chapter, we chart the rise of wellbeing in politics and policy before outlining the nature and scale of current initiatives at both international and national levels. Following that we reflect further on the terrain of the politics discipline, before illustrating the relevance of the discipline to understanding, defining and measuring wellbeing in contemporary politics. We conclude by outlining the contributions to this volume.

WELLBEING IN POLITICS AND POLICY

Debates on the 'good life' and the role of individuals, society and the state in promoting this date back at least as far as the ancient Greeks. Similarly, attempts at measuring wellbeing 'can be traced back as far as one likes' (Allin and Hand 2014, p. 3). Our focus in this book is on contemporary political interest in wellbeing: the second of two such waves of interest since the Second World War (Bache and Reardon 2013, 2016; see also Scott 2012). In the 1960s, there was an intensified focus on the conceptualisation of objective quality of life conditions and the creation of instruments to measure them, giving rise to the so-called social indicator movement. This was driven by growing dissatisfaction with GDP as the dominant measure of progress, as post-war prosperity created conditions for materialism and inequality to increase (Offer 2000). These first-wave critiques of GDP and the legitimisation they were given by senior politicians in the USA and across Europe led to the development of new social surveys in a number of advanced industrial countries (see Bache and Reardon 2016, p. 41). However, the impact of these developments on politics and policy was limited for several reasons, including the difficulties of marshalling a vast array of diverse statistics to inform coherent policy goals; a now well-recognised challenge of bringing evidence into policy. These initiatives lost momentum in the 1970s in the context of recession and changes in the dominant political ideologies and associated social welfare discourses in key nations involved (e.g. USA, UK).

The second and current wave of political interest emerged in the 1990s, driven by environmental challenges, increased understanding of the drivers of wellbeing and growing acceptance of the value of measuring subjective wellbeing[3] for public policy purposes (Bache and Reardon 2016). In advanced liberal democracies, the idea that globalisation, hyper-consumerism and greater individual freedom are leading to social breakdown became popularised,[4] alongside a growing awareness of increasing social inequalities. Momentum gathered pace as the effects of the financial crisis gave rise to a new level of discontent with neoliberal economics, leading to protests in many countries and increasing concern about the impacts of economic inequalities and concentration of wealth (see for example Stiglitz 2012; Piketty 2013). In this context, wellbeing emerged as a new paradigm of development alongside a range of other alternatives, including the more established notion of sustainable development, bringing with it a new industry of wellbeing measurement to challenge the dominance of GDP as an indicator of progress (Scott 2012, p. 4). Initiatives within international organisations, such as the OECD, EU and UN, combined with the entrepreneurial activity of think tanks, academics and statisticians to accelerate the flow of ideas around wellbeing across and within national boundaries.

The Commission on the Measurement of Economic Performance and Social Progress (CMEPSP), established by President Sarkozy of France (2008–2009)—which is variously referred to as the CMEPSP, Sarkozy Commission, Stiglitz Commission, Stiglitz-Sen Commission or Stiglitz-Sen-Fitoussi Commission—accelerated developments in a range of places. In the context of growing economic crisis, its brief was to:

> ...identify the limits of GDP as an indicator of economic performance and social progress, including the problems with its measurement; to consider what additional information might be required for the production of more

relevant indicators of social progress, to assess the feasibility of alternative measurement tools, and to discuss how to present the statistical information in a more appropriate way (CMEPSP 2009, Executive Summary).

This commission reported in 2009 and has since been an important reference for many national wellbeing initiatives.[5] The report identified eight components of wellbeing: material living standards; health; education; personal activities including work; political voice and governance; social connections and relationships; environment; security—economic and physical (CMEPSP 2009). It argued that 'All these dimensions shape people's wellbeing, and yet many of them are missed by conventional income measures' (CMEPSP 2009, p. 15). Of particular significance was the argument that subjective wellbeing indicators should be used alongside more established objective indicators in guiding policy.

Predominantly, the second wave has manifested through the development of new frameworks for measuring wellbeing—at international, national and subnational/substate levels. At the international level, important developments include the EU's *GDP and Beyond* initiative, the OECD's *Better Life* global platform, and the UN's *Sustainable Development Goals*. National initiatives are particularly prevalent in EU and OECD countries (e.g. Australia, Canada, France, Germany, Mexico, New Zealand and the UK), but also beyond (e.g. Bhutan, Ecuador, Morocco and The Philippines). The many diverse initiatives across the world often reflect different cultural, intellectual and political drivers and traditions: a diversity that is reflected in the contributions to this book. Subnational/substate cases include Scotland and Wales in the UK, the US states of California and Vermont and the Chinese province of Guangdong, but there are numerous others. Indeed, in 2014 it was estimated that the number of new measurement frameworks at various levels was in excess of 160 (Allin and Hand 2014, p. 258). Accompanying the introduction of new measures have been various attempts to bring wellbeing into policy (for an overview of developments in measurement and policy see Bache and Reardon 2016).

Yet while there is increasing agreement that GDP growth is not fit for the purpose of measuring societal progress, different actors emphasise different themes in seeking to challenge its dominance: some are most concerned with promoting happiness or mental wellbeing (Layard 2005), for others it is social justice issues (Wilkinson and Pickett 2009) and for others it is to foreground concerns around environmental sustainability (Jackson 2011) and so on. Indeed, the CMEPSP controversially argued that sustainability and wellbeing should be measured separately; an issue that is symptomatic of an ongoing struggle to ascertain whether the development of wellbeing indicators should be regarded as an integral part of, or even a precursor to, sustainability measurement or as a separate endeavour to avoid confusion (see Michalos 2011; Scott 2012).

In short, during the last decade in particular, many governments and other organisations have made a significant investment to conceptualise, study and measure wellbeing for public policy purposes. This is matched by the rising number of academic works on the subject and the endeavours of the public, voluntary and private sectors to use the concept to promote various messages, behaviours or products. As White (2015, p. 5) states: 'the diversity, volume and velocity in references to wellbeing suggest a cultural tide that sweeps together a range of different interests and agendas'. In terms of public policy, she categorises the complexity of the field into four main approaches to wellbeing: a macro approach to widen the scope of government beyond GDP as a marker of progress; a focus on personal behaviours; a focus on life satisfaction or subjective wellbeing to evaluate policy (which may include attribution of monetary value to aspects of wellbeing); and a fundamental challenge to current political economies. Necessarily then, these different 'faces' of wellbeing and their advocates are sometimes in tension and the field of wellbeing encompasses a wide range of perspectives. In this context, the idea of wellbeing is mobilised in different ways, by different groups, to support different purposes. As such, it is crucial to explore 'what and whose values are represented, which accounts dominate, what is their impact and on whom' (Scott 2012, p. 4). Such issues put the study of politics centre stage.

The Terrain of the Politics Discipline

While it is commonplace to refer to a single discipline of politics, this masks an array of traditions and subfields[6] and contestation is at the heart of the discipline. So, while there might be broad agreement that the discipline focuses on 'how politics works', there are wide differences on what constitutes the terrain of politics. This includes the definition of 'the political' and whether this appertains to certain formal institutions and processes, or also to wider social structures and systems and to personal life, as feminist political theorists and others have argued. Similarly, while there is a common foregrounding of questions of power, this concept is understood and studied in very different ways: e.g. more or less observable 'faces' of power, 'power to' and/or 'power over', discursive power, power as an entity which is 'held', power as a relation between people, power as a complex and dynamic system and so on. Further, there is a distinction between an empiricist focus on 'what is' and normative theorising on 'what should be'. Moreover, while some variants of political science might focus on understanding the operation of political systems primarily to help solve problems, more critical perspectives might approach those problems by deconstructing those very systems to challenge problems manifest in established ways of thinking and doing and raise questions about the boundaries of legitimate action.

A number of themes and contributions that are central to disciplinary debates in politics have clear relevance for current debates on wellbeing and raise important questions. These include:

- *The political theory underpinnings of different approaches to wellbeing.* How might these provide insights into the coherence and consistency of definitions of wellbeing and the related approaches to measurement and policy? And how, therefore, might such insights be of benefit to policy-makers and civil society in taking forward the agenda?
- *Power relations in wellbeing theory, policy and practice.* How might we understand the different capabilities of various actors to access and affect developments and thus recognise how and why some interests dominate while others are marginalised?
- *Dilemmas relating to legitimacy and accountability in defining, measuring and bringing wellbeing into public policy.* How might insights on this inform debates on the appropriate role of the state, society, market and individual?
- *The nature of governance, public policy and policy change.* How might analysis help identify the barriers to policy change, the most effective policy instruments, the most relevant and appropriate mechanisms, and the challenges of implementation? How might they inform debate around the most effective governance arrangements and the potential trade-offs between accountability and effectiveness? How might they help identify the most relevant and appropriate participants in governance arrangements?

- *Systemic variables that shape the prospects for wellbeing in different contexts.* How might we understand cultural and ideological differences in the way that wellbeing is conceived, measured and brought into policy in different settings?
- *The processes by which ideas and norms relating to wellbeing flow from one place to another.* Why are some states keen to advance this agenda while others are not? What are the dynamics of international organisations, processes or networks in which the agenda is being shaped and reshaped?
- *The different framings of wellbeing that may be used to support particular regimes, groups or narratives.* How might a study of these help understand the potential for wellbeing to bring about political change?
- *The relationship between wellbeing developments and current and alternative frameworks of political economy.* How might understanding this shed light on the extent to which the wellbeing agenda can be advanced within different political economy approaches and the prospects for shifts in approaches to accommodate wellbeing more effectively?

These different foci, and their associated different methodologies, indicate the rich and diverse potential contribution of the discipline to academic research and policy debates on wellbeing and also provide the context for the chapters that follow. We cannot do justice here to the many and varied theories, questions, approaches and methodologies that comprise the discipline—or indeed in the book as a whole. Rather, in order to illustrate our general argument, in the remainder of this chapter we illustrate how contributions from politics connect with contemporary debates on how wellbeing should be understood, defined and measured for public policy purposes: issues central to the field.

POLITICAL THEORY AND WELLBEING

In contemporary debates on wellbeing in advanced Western liberal societies, traditional Western philosophy has unsurprisingly dominated. Ideas tend to be divided broadly into 'hedonic' and 'eudaimonic' accounts of the good life, which we discuss next. We then review briefly some critiques regarding the limitations of these ideas and offer some comments on how political theory can contribute further insights. While theoretical scholarship in general might draw attention to different conceptions of wellbeing, *political* theory specifically relates ideas about wellbeing (or the good life) to the nature and role of the state. Central to this is an examination of the relations between the state, society and the self. How does a theory of an individual good life, for instance, connect with political ideologies and state imaginaries, political structures and institutions, political processes and decisions?

Current discussions about wellbeing in public policy draw heavily on certain accounts of the good life that find their roots in ancient ethical theory, which focused particularly on the relationship of virtue (*arête*) and happiness (*eudaimonia*) (Annas 2002). For the ancients, *arête* did not hold quite the same meaning as contemporary ideas of virtue. It is often translated as 'excellence' and used to describe skills, good habits and the development of practical wisdom, although this does not preclude morality from being a central component. The term *eudaimonia* is strictly translated as 'blessed with a good spirit' but is more commonly translated by classicists as 'happiness' or 'the good life' (for a discussion of the meanings of these terms see Annas 1993, 1998; Rabbås et al. 2015). Across different classical schools of thought, *eudaimonia* was seen as the highest good or ultimate goal in life, but theories of how to attain this differed: for Aristotelians, *eudaimonia* was enacted (partly) through the development of character and intellectual virtues, which were constitutive of living a good life; for Epicureans, *eudaimonia* was achieved through cultivating skills and knowledge to pursue pleasure and avoid pain, and so these virtues were instrumental to a good life; for the Stoics, *eudaimonia* was underpinned by the development of resilience to life's vicissitudes, and so vital was this virtue that it could be seen as being sufficient for happiness (Annas 1998, 2002; Rabbås et al. 2015).

Aristotle's particular idea of how to achieve *eudaimonia* has been the one to define the term in contemporary discussions and is often linked to the idea of 'flourishing'. His writings in *Nicomachean Ethics* argue for a perfectionist conception of what constitutes *eudaimonia* that is, put simply, the fulfilment of a person's highest human potential through the cultivation of a number of virtues, which include courage, justice, moderation, honesty, greatness of soul, hospitality, cultivation of knowledge and perceptiveness, proper judgement and practical wisdom (Nussbaum 1993, pp. 245–246). These virtues would help ensure 'appropriate functioning' in each sphere of life (ibid., p. 250). As mentioned above, this fully flourishing account of a human life as the highest good is described in contemporary wellbeing discussions as eudaimonism and set in contrast to hedonism.

Classical hedonistic accounts date back to Aristippus and later to Epicurus, who developed the Epicurean school of philosophy. These theories place emphasis on the maximisation of pleasure and the freedom from pain (*aponia*). These are not, as oft misunderstood, unbridled attempts to satiate bodily desires, but based on an ethical theory that pleasure is the highest good and the proper aim of human life. This is achieved through the cultivation of knowledge about what makes life pleasurable for each individual and the freedom to pursue activities accordingly.

Hedonism arguably had its fullest and most influential expression in the ideas of the eighteenth-century English philosopher Jeremy Bentham (1996 [1823]):

> Nature has placed mankind under the governance of two sovereign masters, pain and pleasure. It is for them alone to point out what we ought to do, as well as to determine what we shall do. (Bentham 1.1)

Bentham identified pleasure as the ultimate goal and often synonymised this with 'happiness' (good feeling) or 'utility'. Central to his utilitarian ideas was the belief that individuals are the experts of what makes them happy, and so they should be free to exercise their own preferences in order to maximise this. He believed that 'The business of government is to promote the happiness of the society, by punishing and rewarding' (VII, i) and the state could help wayward individuals to develop better habits (which reduced pain to themselves or others), but the state had no business instructing people what their pleasures should be. John Stuart Mill,[7] whose text 'On Liberty' is considered the founding document for liberalism, took utilitarianism and, influenced by the Romantic period, extended it, 'giving richness of life and complexity of activity a place they do not have in Bentham, and giving pleasure and the absence of pain and of depression a role that Aristotle never sufficiently mapped out' (Nussbaum 2004, p. 62). He distinguished between two ideas of happiness: a feeling or state of pleasure (the Benthamite version) and a more complex one around notions of growth and development in which there was a role for learning from suffering. He is often accused of elitism, as he was keen to help the unschooled masses to appreciate higher pleasures: he wanted everyone to develop their full potential, although he believed in the freedom not to.

Utilitarianism and liberalism underpinned eighteenth/nineteenth-century classical economics, which was based on the notion that humans are rational, self-interested beings who will seek to maximise their own happiness given enough freedom and resources. Equalising opportunities to partake in a free market would provide the best mechanism to allow people to maximise their income, using that to satisfy their preferences. This concept of *homo economicus* dominated ideas of welfare, putting a high emphasis on income and therefore national economic growth and later the measurement of GNP/GDP. This idea has been the touchstone of liberal economic theory for the last century (Dolan et al. 2006) whether underpinning the 'embedded liberalism' of Keynesianism between 1945 and 1975 or the 'revolution' of neoliberalism in the late 1970s and early 1980s (Harvey 2005, pp. 11/1). The hedonic tradition is reflected in current wellbeing debates, with high-profile advocates such as the 'new utilitarian' economist (and member of the UK House of Lords) Richard Layard (2005, p. 147) suggesting that 'happiness should become the goal of policy'.

As the limitations and impacts of utilitarianism and associated economic theories came under increasing scrutiny in the latter part of the twentieth century (see Seaford, this volume, Chap. 5), Aristotle's work received renewed attention. His perfectionist view of wellbeing resonates in the contemporary work of Amartya Sen and Martha Nussbaum, among others, whose Capabilities Approach,[8] developed in the 1980s and 1990s, sets out a theory of what is necessary to enable everyone to live a good life, should they so choose it (see Austin, this volume, Chap. 3).

Capabilities theory was first proposed by Sen as a critique, on the one hand, of the traditional utilitarian approach to welfare economics and, on the other, in response to a Rawlsian theory of justice based on equitable distribution of goods (a bundle of rights and resources) important for wellbeing (Rawls 1971). As Sen and others have pointed out, a utilitarian focus on happiness (often measured as individual life satisfaction or subjective wellbeing) alone is problematic, because people have 'adaptive preferences', meaning their expectations of life are linked to their experience of life. Consequently, a poor person may be satisfied with less (Elster 1983). Sen also argued that social justice frameworks such as Rawls' should be focused on the freedoms people have to achieve quality of life, rather than on the technical possession of rights or resources (Sen 1980): he often gives the example of a disabled person needing more resources than an able-bodied person to achieve the same quality of life and therefore equal distribution of resources may miss important social justice issues. Sen proposed instead that we should take account of the freedoms people have to 'lead the kind of life he or she has reason to value' (Sen 1999, p. 87). Through its focus on freedoms and opportunities, the Capabilities Approach takes into account the different ways that individuals can be constrained in their choices by economic, social, political and cultural factors (Robyens 2005). Sen's approach has influenced development policy and its related measurement frameworks in particular, not least the development of the Human Development Index, which combines measures of GDP, life expectancy and education to compare countries across the world (see Bache and Reardon 2016, pp. 56–57). Sen was also one of the key authors of the CMEPSP report (see above).

Although seen as the two distinct camps of wellbeing theory, eudaimonic and hedonistic beliefs concerning the good life are just two strands of philosophy deriving from earlier Socratic teachings that attempted to bring ancient philosophy away from a focus on the cosmos and down into the realms of politics, combining both a theoretical and practical philosophy of life. Less well cited in contemporary wellbeing literature are the other schools of thought such as Stoicism, although this too has had an impact on contemporary debates. Founded by Zeno (333–261 BC) and later developed by Epictetus, Stoicism (as developed by Epictetus) was to live dutifully in accordance with nature and to seek freedom by training oneself to control one's reactions to life rather than trying to control life (Irvine 2009). Stoicism can be seen reflected in developments in psychology leading to the emergence of cognitive behavioural therapy (CBT), which has become such a feature of the debate and response on mental wellbeing in the UK (Evans, this volume, Chap. 2). The positive psychology movement has been influential on initiatives aimed at educating citizens to improve their wellbeing through a series of personal behaviours and ways of thinking and the teaching of personal resilience skills in schools (see Ecclestone, this volume, Chap. 10).

These philosophies echo in contemporary debates on wellbeing, particularly in relation to the conceptualisations of the good life, the appropriate role for government and on how far citizens should be responsible for their own wellbeing. The resurgence of interest in these ancient theories in late modernity may be symptomatic of a profound questioning in an increasingly precarious context of neoliberalism. However, these debates are in danger of missing two vital aspects central to a politics of wellbeing: firstly, and most obviously, a focus on the political implications of these conceptualisations of the good life and what the rise of different approaches to wellbeing in policy means to relations between the individual, society and state; secondly, the inclusion of ideas from the many and diverse traditions of thought that may have something additional or alternative to offer, for example, from the Islamic 'golden age' or from feminist political thought.

On the first aspect, the explicit inclusion of contemporary political theorists can bring abstract theoretical explorations of wellbeing into dialogue with key concepts in politics, such as the state, power, liberty and democracy. Wellbeing debates could benefit from considering contemporary political theory that, for example, investigates the effect of neoliberalism on everyday life (for instance see Brown 2015). Without considering the relationship of wellbeing to the wider economic and political context, the use of abstract wellbeing theories in policy discussions, however well-meaning, risk speaking past everyday experiences and struggles. Moreover, they do not provide guidance on how to effect political change to advance wellbeing.

On the second aspect, there is an ongoing questioning of the 'canon' of Western philosophy by feminist and post-colonial theorists (among others) that, as Stuurman (2000, p. 148) argues, is reflective of an 'ongoing debate about the broader question of the history, identity, and political future of that elusive, pseudo-geographical concept we are in the habit of calling "the West"'. In an increasingly globalised world where political, cultural and social norms are shifting rapidly, it is right to ask if these long-standing philosophical traditions offer the inclusivity and methodological robustness to understand the increasingly complex and diverse politics of wellbeing. Aristotle is often cited as the first philosopher who theorised extensively on the 'good life' in relation to political systems and advocated an involved citizenry. However, his functionalist account—that each person has a natural role in life and must fulfil that to the best of their ability in order to flourish—worked very well for the citizenry, namely the male political elite, but not so well for women, slaves and immigrants who were politically disenfranchised. This has led some political theorists to question whether this philosophy of wellbeing can sustain the inclusion of marginalised groups, or if it is inherently connected to discriminatory ways of seeing the world (for example see Okin 1979) and as such should be viewed as a theory of how to maintain the political status quo. Ahmed critiques the contemporary focus on happiness in the West for not recognising the ways in which the goal of happiness has perpetuated social norms that disadvantage women, gay and black people (Ahmed 2010). This challenge is rarely tackled in detail in contemporary policy documents on wellbeing (at least in most EU/OECD countries), which often do not engage with power relations and which tend to promote wellbeing as an unproblematic gender and culture neutral idea.[9]

In addition to the above concerns, some argue that contemporary discourses of wellbeing promote a reductionist view of wellbeing and focus attention away from the social and political basis of wellbeing onto an individual model where people are responsible for their own wellbeing (Edwards and Imrie 2008; Scott 2015). For example, in their critique of the new agendas of wellbeing in the context of disability in the UK, Edwards and Imrie argue for a wellbeing agenda that does not 'propagate the idealist ways in which we see the world but, rather, addresses the way that it is' (2008, p. 339). They give an example of why this is important, suggesting that by promoting a self-actualisation view of wellbeing these discourses signal a 'retrograde step' from the concerted attempts of disability rights lobby groups that have tried to 'shift interpretations of disability from individualised, biological, conceptions based on internal limitations, to ones situated in the socio-structural relations of an ablist society' (2008, p. 338). They are among a number of critics who claim that in current wellbeing measurement discourses and practice 'far too little attention has been devoted to theorising about how sociopolitical conditions determine quality of life' (Flavin et al. 2011, p. 265).

Thus, individual versus social or collective notions of wellbeing in current debates can be located within long-established and contemporary political debates. They are shaped by metatheoretical dispositions that not only direct attention to the issue of who has responsibility for wellbeing, but also 'what matters' for wellbeing (individual or social) and—the topic of our next section—how this should be measured.

Measuring 'What Matters'

How wellbeing is understood in different traditions of political theory necessarily shapes approaches to measurement. To illustrate, a simple distinction between wellbeing as happiness (hedonic tradition) and wellbeing as flourishing (eudaimonic tradition) leads to the search for different indicators. In current developments, those in the hedonic tradition tend towards emphasising subjective wellbeing indicators focusing on individuals' perception of their levels of happiness, anxiety, or life satisfaction (e.g. Layard 2005; O'Donnell et al. 2014). By contrast, those in the eudaimonic tradition tend towards a broader range of both objective and subjective indicators (e.g. Anand et al. 2009). Beyond this stylised distinction are more nuanced critiques of current approaches to measurement.

A growing body of work critiquing contemporary wellbeing measurement highlights the tensions between different ontological and epistemological assumptions about wellbeing in different academic and policy research communities. For example, while the authors of the CMEPSP (2009) report outlined a set of domains of wellbeing that must be fulfilled for human flourishing, critical perspectives on this approach to wellbeing, which Atkinson (2013) calls the Components Approach, argue for more awareness of the context-based, relational and dynamic nature of wellbeing (for example Scott 2012; Atkinson 2013; White and Blackmore 2015). Therefore, many critics resist these fixed views of wellbeing as applied to atomistic individuals because they fall short of understanding the detailed everyday relations in which wellbeing is negotiated by people in relations with each other. Scott (2012) critiques the dominance of certain types of evidence (experimental and quantitative studies where randomised controlled trials are seen as the 'gold standard') in the generation of wellbeing data and calls for deeper thinking at policy level for how in-depth qualitative, participatory and context-dependent research on wellbeing can also be included to inform policy. In addition, the UK wellbeing agenda, for example, has been critiqued for its focus on individual responsibility for wellbeing, rather than structural determinants, (Tomlinson and Kelly 2013), and the way that individual wellbeing is used instrumentally to promote other policy agendas (Scott 2015). Much of this critique points to ideas of participatory democracy and the public policy challenge of incorporating many ideas about wellbeing, from different groups, in different contexts, to inform one set of national measures.

In addition to the critiques on the conceptualisation and construction of measures, there are also considerable difficulties for statisticians and policy-makers who want to promote wellbeing within government and who argue for the legitimacy of wellbeing measures to be used in policy discussions or policy evaluations. Many debates remain over the technicalities of measuring wellbeing relating to: using objective or subjective indicators; the reliability and validity of data; creating multidimensional frameworks or a single indicator; and how much weight should be given to the different domains of wellbeing. As with the bigger philosophical debates, these technical debates have political and policy implications, particularly regarding the legitimacy and validity of using measures. The decision by governments to give attention to indicators creates a set of 'evidence', but how this evidence is legitimised and taken up in policy is complex. This is a well-researched area, as is the difficulty of finding a clear impact of different forms of evidence on policy (see for example Weiss 1999). Ethnographic studies of policy-making create a picture of the complex and contingent nature of the evidence/policy interface (Wilkinson 2011; Stevens 2011; Rhodes 2011). Wilkinson's (2011) study of UK government, for example, describes the way that information flows connect with policy as 'organised chaos'. Stevens (2007) argues for an 'evolutionary analogy' to understand the use of evidence in policy, and in his view it is not the survival of the fittest piece of evidence but the fittest carrier of that evidence which counts, arguing that powerful groups both 'trawl' for and 'farm' evidence. Such work by political scientists can contribute to understanding how wellbeing evidence can influence policy through theoretically informed approaches of the practical policy-making.

The drive in policy interest to 'measure what matters' and to legitimise this activity has meant that several governments have carried out consultation with the public about what matters to them.[10] This is viewed as a crucial part of the process, acknowledging that statistical indicators are not neutral either in the way they are constructed or in how they are used and so stakeholder consultation offers the potential for political legitimacy, both nationally and locally. Although there seems to be contradictory evidence on whether participatory or direct democracy may actually be constitutive of wellbeing (Dorn et al. 2007, 2008), a substantial body of evidence finds that participation in the development of measures and indicators increases commitment to them. What is clear is that including stakeholders in wellbeing measurement has implications for the skills and resources of governments to consult transparently, systematically analyse responses and effectively build the responses into decision-making around measurement. In the case of the UK Measuring National Well-being public consultation, recent work suggests this remains a challenge (Oman 2015; Jenkins, this volume, Chap. 12).

Measurements of wellbeing reflect not wellbeing per se but rather they reflect standard (and dominant) practices of academic inquiry, statistical production and policy-making processes. They reflect how knowledge is created and accessed by and for whom, when and where and how it is smoothed into evidence for decision-makers (Stevens 2011). It is important to acknowledge the considerable constraints on policy actors and analysts working within government, as well as the considerable difficulties inherent in the project of measuring wellbeing for public policy, but a range of different views exist in society not only about what matters for wellbeing, what it constitutes, but also what sort of entity it is.

Such issues remain central to real-world debates on how to address wellbeing in public policy. On the one hand, there is the search for legitimacy and effective ways of promoting wellbeing through policy; on the other are intractable controversies about the selection of indicators and the efficacy and cost-effectiveness of different policy options. Added to this are ontological disputes about the appropriate role of the state. Thus, wellbeing is an agenda that can excite, frustrate and antagonise in equal measure. Yet the scale and pace of activity suggests this is an issue that is likely to be on the political agenda for some time, and—because contestation is at its heart—one in which politics will be central to its destiny.

THE CONTRIBUTIONS TO THIS VOLUME

The first part of this book offers original perspectives on wellbeing from political theorists on the ethical and philosophical grounds upon which wellbeing can be defined and policies justified in a democratic state. There is a need to reassess our traditional canons of political philosophy to judge their relationship to this new contemporary agenda and their relevance in a rapidly changing context of political economy, increasing inequalities, climate change, shifts in state–citizen relationships and multiculturalism. The recent rise of interest in wellbeing has arisen partly in response to these issues, yet political theory has generally not yet grappled with contemporary wellbeing developments in depth. A central issue of concern is whether wellbeing presents an opportunity for greater democratic engagement in reconfiguring social and political systems or a legitimising discourse that promotes particular interests. This part of the book seeks to inform some of these issues. It includes insights on how neo-Aristotelianism has shaped contemporary developments in wellbeing and how this movement has influenced policy (Evans); provides a defence of the Capabilities Approach, which combines wellbeing and social justice (Austin); and how we might use a 'theory-neutral' approach to help policy-makers seeking to bring wellbeing into policy (Taylor).

The second part of this book provides analysis in a range of contexts to understand how the rise of wellbeing may (or may not) promote political change. Some advocates of wellbeing see it as having transformative potential in politics and policy, while others have a less expansive vision that sees wellbeing contributing to more effective policies in a limited range of areas. These contrasting agendas are still relatively new and the conceptual spaces between these different perspectives offer creative insights. In addition, wellbeing agendas have largely arisen out of a complex web of concern regarding global economic, social and environmental security. Social norms and political agendas are shifting in response and this has led to increasing international activity and some consensus on issues of definition and measurement. However, national and sub-national/substate initiatives reflect the nuances of particular contexts, placing different emphasis on different drivers of wellbeing. It is for this reason that part two of this book provides analysis on the potential of wellbeing to inform or create a range of new political and policy agendas in different contexts. Specifically, the chapters examine whether wellbeing provides a useful concept for progressive political forces in the UK (Seaford); analyse the emergence of *Buen Vivir* (living well) as a political project in Ecuador (Bressa Florentin); consider the role of alternative wellbeing indicators in challenging the dominant economic narrative in Canada (Hayden and Wilson); and reflect on societal wellbeing as a catalyst for systems and social change in Northern Ireland (Doran and Hodgett).

The third and final part of the book offers a range of detailed critical analyses on the challenge of bringing wellbeing into policy and ensuring this reflects and is relevant to the lived experiences of a range of people. These chapters deal with ethical, methodological and scalar issues associated with transferring strategic ideas on wellbeing to the everyday lives of end users of policy. Specifically, they address the central tensions in the relationship between universal and local measurement frameworks (McGregor); critically evaluate the evidence base for wellbeing interventions in educational settings (Ecclestone); examine the wellbeing agendas and welfare changes being implemented under the New Zealand and UK national governments (Scott and Masselot); and highlight the normative nature of apparently neutral wellbeing statistics and the 'technocratic idealism' they underpin (Jenkins).

CONCLUSION

The discipline of politics can provide important contributions to theoretical debates on how to define wellbeing, what constitutes it and who has responsibility for it, alongside policy debates on the role and legitimacy of indicators used to determine wellbeing for public policy purposes. Considering how central notions of the good life, power, the policy process and democracy are to any investigation into measuring wellbeing, the lack of input from a discipline that has these concepts at its core is a substantial gap: this volume contributes to closing this gap.

NOTES

1. We are extremely grateful to Sarah Atkinson and Louise Reardon for their valuable comments on a draft of this chapter.
2. In some contexts this is more accurately described as happiness or quality of life. However, we employ wellbeing here as shorthand to describe a multidimensional phenomenon that incorporates ideas of happiness and quality of life. More nuanced discussions of these concepts and how they inter-relate will be explored in the book and different authors may prefer different terms.
3. Subjective wellbeing refers to people's own assessment of their lives.
4. Helped by popularised academic works like Robert Putnam's *Bowling Alone* (2000).
5. The report's authors state clearly that they were not trying to reach consensus on what quality of life means but to identify where 'credible measures' could be established and they also explicitly recognise that their 'attention is limited to areas where members of the commission had specific competencies' and where 'available indicators allow... assessment' (CMEPSP 2009, p. 143). For a discussion of national responses to the CMEPSP see Bache and Reardon (2016).
6. Such a list would typically include comparative politics, governance and public policy (or public administration), international relations, (international) political economy and political theory.
7. Mill was Bentham's godson. For an introduction to Mill's key works see *Mill* (Eds. Mark Philp and Frederick Rosen) (2015).
8. Sen's term is Capability Approach, while Nussbaum's, developed later and slightly differing in emphasis, is Capabilities Approach. The latter term is

employed in this and subsequent chapters when authors seek to encompass the work of both Sen and Nussbaum.

9. However, countries such as Ecuador and New Zealand have made attempts, prompted by the political demands and protests of indigenous people, to reflect plurinationalism and biculturalism respectively in their accounts of national wellbeing.

10. For example, on the UK see: http://webarchive.nationalarchives.gov. uk/20160105160709. https://www.ons.gov.uk/ons/about-ons/get-involved/ consultations/archived-consultations/2012/measuring-national-wellbe- ing-domains/consultation-on-proposed-domains-and-measures-of-nation- al-wellbeing--responses-received.pdf. On Canada, see: https://uwaterloo.ca/ canadian-index-wellbeing/.

References

Ahmed, S. (2010). *The Promise of Happiness*. Durham, NC and London: Duke University Press.

Allin, P., & Hand, J. (2014). *The Wellbeing of Nations: Meaning, Motive and Measurement*. New York: Wiley.

Anand, P., Hunter, G., Carter, I., Dowding, K., Guala, F., & van Hees, M. (2009). The Development of Capability Indicators. *Journal of Human Development and Capabilities, 10*(1), 125–152.

Annas, J. (1993). *The Morality of Happiness*. Oxford: Oxford University Press.

Annas, J. (1998). Virtue and Eudaimonism. *Social Philosophy and Policy, 15*(1), 37–55.

Annas, J. (2002). Should Virtue Make You Happy? In O. Rabbås, E. K. Eyjólfur, H. Fossheim, & M. Tuominen (Eds.), *The Quest for the Good Life: Ancient Philosophers on Happiness*. Oxford: Oxford University Press.

Atkinson, S. (2013). Beyond Components of Wellbeing: The Effects of Relational and Situated Assemblage. *Topoi, 32*, 137–144.

Bache, I., & Reardon, L. (2013). An Idea Whose Time Has Come? Explaining the Rise of Well-Being in British Politics. *Political Studies, 61*(4), 898–914.

Bache, I., & Reardon, L. (2016). *The Politics and Policy of Wellbeing: Understanding the Rise and Significance of a New Agenda*. Cheltenham: Edward Elgar.

Bentham, J., Burns, J. H., Hart, H. L. A. (Eds.). (1996). *An Introduction to the Principles of Morals and Legislation*. Oxford: Clarendon.

Brown, W. (2015). *Undoing the Demos: Neoliberalism's Stealth Revolution*. New York: Zone Books.

CMEPSP. (2009). Report by the Commission on the Measurement of Economic Performance and Social Progress. Available at: http://www.stiglitz-senfi- toussi.fr/en/index.htm. Accessed December 17, 2016.

Crick, B. (1982). *In Defence of Politics* (2nd ed.). Harmondsworth: Penguin.

Dolan, P., Peasgood, T., & White, M. (2006). *Review of Research on Personal Well-Being and Application to Policy Making*. London: Defra.

Dorn, D., Fischer, J., Kirchgässner, G., & Sousa-Poza, A. (2007). Is It Culture or Democracy? The Impact of Democracy and Culture on Happiness. *Social Indicators Research, 82,* 505–526.

Dorn, D., Fischer, J., Kirchgässner, G., & Sousa-Poza, A. (2008). Direct Democracy and Life Satisfaction Revisited: New Evidence for Switzerland. *Journal of Happiness Studies, 9*(2), 227–251.

Edwards, C., & Imrie, R. (2008). Disability and the Implications of the Wellbeing Agenda: Some Reflections from the United Kingdom. *Journal of Social Policy, 37*(3), 337–355.

Elster, J. (1983). *Sour Grapes: Studies in the Subversion of Rationality.* Cambridge: Cambridge University Press.

Flavin, P., Pacek, A. C., & Radcliff, B. (2011). State Intervention and Subjective Well-Being in Advanced Industrial Democracies. *Politics and Policy, 39*(2), 251–269.

Flinders, M. (2013). The Tyranny of Relevance and the Art of Translation. *Political Studies Review, 11*(2), 149–167.

Harvey, D. (2005). *A Brief History of Neoliberalism.* Oxford: Oxford University Press.

Irvine, W. B. (2009). *A Guide to the Good Life.* Oxford: Oxford University Press.

Jackson, T. (2011). *Prosperity Without Growth.* London: Earthscan.

Kroll, C. (2011). *Measuring Progress and Well-Being: Achievements and Challenges of a New Global Movement.* Berlin: International Policy Analysis.

Lasswell, H. D. (1936). *Politics: Who Gets What, When, How.* Cleveland/New York: McGraw-Hill.

Layard, R. (2005). *Happiness: Lessons from a New Science.* London: Allen Lane.

Michalos, A. C. (2011). What Did Stiglitz, Sen and Fitoussi Get Right and What Did They Get Wrong? *Social Indicators Research, 102*(1), 117–129.

Nussbaum, M. C. (1993). Non-Relative Virtues: An Aristotelian Approach. In M. C. Nussbaum & A. Sen (Eds.), *The Quality of Life.* Oxford: Clarendon Press.

Nussbaum, M. C. (2004). Mill between Aristotle and Bentham. *Daedalus, 133*(2), 60–68.

O'Donnell, G., Deaton, A., Durand, D., Halpern, D., & Layard, R. (2014). *Wellbeing and Policy.* Report commissioned by the Legatum Institute.

Offer, A. (2000). Economic Welfare Measurements and Human Well-Being, *Discussion Papers in Social and Economic History,* number 34, University of Oxford.

Okin, S. M. (1979). *Women in Western Political Thought.* Princeton, NJ: Princeton University Press.

Oman, S. (2015). Measuring National Wellbeing: What Matters to You? What Matters to Whom? In S. White & C. Blackmore (Eds.), *Cultures of Wellbeing: Method, Place, Policy.* UK: Palgrave.

Piketty, T. (tr. Goldhammer, A.). (2013). *Capital in the Twenty-First Century.* Cambridge, MA: Harvard University Press.

Rabbås, O., Eyjólfur, E. K., Fossheim, H., & Tuominen, M. (2015). Introduction. In O. Rabbås, E. K. Eyjólfur, H. Fossheim, & M. Tuominen

(Eds.), *The Quest for the Good Life: Ancient Philosophers on Happiness*. Oxford: Oxford University Press.

Rawls, J. (1971). *A Theory of Justice*. Cambridge, MA: Harvard University Press.

Rhodes, R. A. W. (2011). *Everyday Life in British Government*. Oxford: Oxford University Press.

Robyens, I. (2005). The Capability Approach: A Theoretical Survey. *Journal of Human Development, 6*(1), 4–13.

Rosendorff, P. (2005). Ideas, Interests, Institutions and Information: Jagdish Bhagwati and the Political Economy of Trade Policy. Paper Prepared for Presentation at the Conference in Honor of Jagdish Bhagwati on the Occasion of his 70th Birthday at Columbia University, New York, August 5–6, 2005.

Scott, K. (2012). *Measuring Wellbeing: Towards Sustainability?* Abingdon: Routledge.

Scott, K. (2015). Happiness on Your Doorstep: Disputing the Boundaries of Wellbeing and Localism. *Geographical Journal, 181*(2), 129–137.

Sen, A. (1980). Equality of What? In S. McMurrin (Ed.), *Tanner Lectures on Human Values*. Cambridge: Cambridge University Press.

Sen, A. (1999). *Development as Freedom*. Oxford: Oxford University Press.

Stevens, A. (2007). Survival of the Ideas That Fit: An Evolutionary Analogy for the Use of Evidence in Policy. *Social Policy and Society, 6*, 25–35.

Stevens, A. (2011). Telling Policy Stories: An Ethnographic Study of the Use of Evidence in Policy-Making in the UK. *Journal of Social Policy, 40*, 237–255.

Stiglitz, J. (2012). *The Price of Inequality*. New York: Norton.

Stuurman, S. (2000). The Canon of the History of Political Thought: Its Critique and a Proposed Alternative. *History and Theory, 39*, 147–166.

Tomlinson, M., & Kelly, G. (2013). Is Everybody Happy? The Politics and Measurement of National Wellbeing. *Policy & Politics, 41*(2), 139–157.

Weiss, C. (1999). The Interface Between Evaluation and Public Policy. *Evaluation, 5*(4), 468–486.

Weiss, C. (2001). What Kind of Evidence in Evidence-Based Policy? Third International Interdisciplinary Evidence-Based Policies and Indicator Systems Conference, July 2001. CEM Centre, University of Durham.

White, S., & Blackmore, C. (Eds.) (2015). *Cultures of Wellbeing: Method, Place, Policy*. London: Palgrave.

Wilkinson, K. (2011). Organised Chaos: An Interpretive Approach to Evidence-Based Policy in Defra. *Political Studies, 59*, 959–977.

Wilkinson, R., & Pickett, K. (2009). *The Spirit Level: Why Equality Is Better for Everyone*. London: Penguin.

PART I

Political Theory and Wellbeing

CHAPTER 2

The End of History and the Invention of Happiness

Jules Evans

INTRODUCTION

A new politics has appeared in the last two decades: the politics of well-being. At its heart is the idea that governments can increase their citizens' flourishing using the science of wellbeing. Nothing better indicates some policymakers' evangelical faith in this politics than the Christmas gift sent out by the former president of the European Council, Herman Van Rompuy, in 2012. As the Eurozone crumbled, Van Rompuy sent out *The World Book of Happiness* (Bormans 2011) to 200 world leaders, urging them to 'make wellbeing our priority'. He declared that: 'Positive thinking is no longer something for drifters, dreamers and the perpetually naive. Positive Psychology concerns itself in a scientific way with the quality of life. It is time to make this knowledge available to the man and woman in the street' (Casert 2011).

I have been writing about the politics of wellbeing since 2007, initially as a journalist and now as a research fellow at the Centre for the History of the Emotions, at Queen Mary University of London. What excited me about the movement was that it revived classical Greek ideas and techniques

J. Evans (✉)
Queen Mary University of London, London, UK
e-mail: jules.evans@mac.com

© The Author(s) 2018
I. Bache and K. Scott (eds.), *The Politics of Wellbeing*, Wellbeing
in Politics and Policy, https://doi.org/10.1007/978-3-319-58394-5_2

25

for flourishing and brought them to millions of people through public policy. I am particularly excited by government funding for Cognitive Behavioural Therapy, a type of therapy inspired by Stoicism, which helped me recover from social anxiety in my early 20s. Yet I also worried about the potentially illiberal aspects of the movement: are technocrats imposing their own definition of the good life onto 'the man and woman in the street'? In this chapter, I sketch a brief history of the politics of wellbeing in the UK over the last two decades. I explore how the movement has influenced policies in two areas—mental health and education. I also point out how the movement can be potentially illiberal and scientistic, before suggesting how wellbeing education could be made more pluralist and democratic.

Beyond Liberalism

In 1992, the philosopher Francis Fukuyama declared 'the end of history' (Fukuyama 1992). The Soviet Union had collapsed, and history had apparently arrived at the end-point of liberal, capitalist democracy. Ends are exciting to aim for, but boring once you reach them. Policy-makers grew restless. What to aim for next? There were various possible new avenues for activity—Western governments could try and export free market democracy abroad, as the EU, US, IMF and NATO attempted to do in the Nineties and Noughties. Or perhaps liberalism at home was still an unfinished project. Although Western citizens have become materially better off since the 1960s, our levels of happiness have apparently not gone up. In the next phase of liberalism, governments would discover the science of happiness and use it to liberate us from our misery (Christie and Nash 1998, pp. 3–15). Just as Nietzsche predicted in *Thus Spake Zarathustra,* at the end of history, the last men discovered happiness (Nietzsche 2008, p. 16).

This grand ambition took policy-makers beyond the limits of classical liberalism, which is based on the idea that a citizen's religious, spiritual or ethical beliefs are their own private business. This central liberal idea goes back to John Locke's *Letter Concerning Toleration* of 1689, where Locke insisted 'the care of souls cannot belong to the civil magistrate' (Locke 2016, p. 129). John Stuart Mill likewise insisted that individuals should be free to follow their own 'experiments in living' rather than being forced to conform to government-approved schemes for happiness. Mill had initially been attracted to the Positivist project of Auguste Comte, in which a country would be ruled by a scientific elite, who would create a secular, evidence-based 'Positive Philosophy' for the masses to follow. But Mill ultimately decided that a Positivist state would be 'a despotism of society over the individual, surpassing anything contemplated in the political ideal of the most rigid disciplinarian among the ancient philosophers' (Mill 2015, p. 8).

In the post-war era, after the horrors of fascism and totalitarianism, liberal philosophers were even more wary of state-imposed schemes for general happiness. In his famous essay of 1958, 'Two Concepts of Liberty', Sir Isaiah Berlin declared that governments should confine themselves to protecting citizens' 'negative liberty', by protecting rights and ensuring access to basic public services. Berlin warned that governments should never seek to go beyond the boundaries of negative liberty and be tempted to cultivate 'positive liberty', by which he meant a positive conception of freedom involving flourishing, moral freedom or spiritual fulfilment (Berlin 2002, pp. 166–217). Humans, Berlin insisted, will never agree on what constitutes the good life, so attempts by governments to impose one conception could easily degenerate into the sort of illiberal totalitarianism that plagued Germany, China and Russia in the twentieth century. We must resist, Berlin said, the 'metaphysical chimera' of believing we can discover a single formula for happiness, and instead content ourselves with a pluralist society in which government tries to maintain some sort of neutrality about how its citizens pursue happiness. The liberal philosopher Robert Nozick, in *Anarchy, State, and Utopia,* also argued that the utopian attempt to impose one philosophy of the good life onto the messy diversity of human temperaments would inevitably be oppressive. Liberal governments should restrict themselves to the 'nightwatchman' role of protecting our negative liberties, leaving us free to pursue our various personal utopias (Nozick 2001, pp. 310–312). Berlin's and Nozick's warnings held good for as long as the phantoms of Stalin and Mao still loomed in politicians' memories. But by the end of the century, policy-makers began to look beyond classical liberalism, and back to ancient Greek philosophy for inspiration, particularly the ethical and political philosophy of Aristotle.

THE NEO-ARISTOTELIANS

Unlike classical liberals, Aristotle argued that the proper goal of government is the flourishing or *eudaimonia* of its citizens. He declared in his *Politics:* 'we call that state best ordered in which the possibilities of happiness are greatest' (Aristotle, Book VII, Chaps. 13 and 14; see also Bache and Scott, this volume, Chap. 1). According to Aristotle, humans share a universal biological nature, and flourishing is the ful-filment of that nature: human nature is rational, social, political and spiritual, although we also have a strong dose of the irrational in our psy-ches. We become fulfilled or flourishing when we develop the rational part of our psyche and use it to cultivate virtuous habits in our character. Philosophical education has an important role to play in this self-culti-vation. It takes human nature in its raw form—irrational, suffering, and morally untrained—and cultivates it into an optimum state—rational, vir-tuous, happy and free. Politics and civic society also have central roles in this process: we are political animals and become fulfilled through civic engagement with our fellow citizens. Governments should provide an education and a form of society that enable citizens to develop *eudaimo-nia* (Aristotle, Book VII, chapter 15; see also Book VIII, Chaps. 2 and 3). While his teacher, Plato, expressed a pessimistic view of democracies' capacity to foster the good life, Aristotle was more optimistic, arguing in *Politics* that a democratic constitution was the best framework for mass *eudaimonia*. However, he thought this was only possible in small states (Aristotle, Book VII, Chap. 4) where the male elite's leisure to seek the good life is supported by a large slave population. Aristotle's virtue eth-ics, then, marries the 'is' of science with the 'ought' of ethics and pol-itics—the good life is the life that fulfils our biological nature, and the good society is one that enables our natures to reach flourishing.

The post-war Aristotelian revival began in the 1950s and made its way into political philosophy through Alasdair MacIntyre, the Scottish Aristotelian philosopher, who claimed in his 1981 book, *After Virtue,* that liberalism had become morally incoherent (MacIntyre 1981). MacIntyre argued that Western society had, since the Enlightenment, lost any sense of a common goal or a common moral framework. Moral discourse, including political discourse, had been reduced to an inter-minable shouting-match of competing slogans: 'justice', 'equality' and 'progress'. People fell back on emotivism—there is no right or wrong, it is just whatever feels right. Western governments had embraced a Weberian bureaucratic managerialism that aimed for technocratic goals like low inflation or high GDP, without any sense of whether these goals improved people's actual flourishing. The solution to this moral confu-sion, MacIntyre argued, was a return to Aristotle's idea that the com-mon *telos* (or purpose) of man and society is *eudaimonia*. Not all paths to *eudaimonia* are equal: some are better than others, and it is the task of the philosopher and the state to find these paths and guide the masses along them. He was pessimistic, however, about the possibility of introducing Aristotelian politics into the modern multicultural state. Later Neo-Aristotelians—such as Michael Sandel (2010), Martha Nussbaum (1997) and Robert and Edward Skidelsky (2012)—followed MacIntyre in suggesting the state should move to a more positive or Aristotelian conception of its role in encouraging human flourishing. However, unlike Aristotle, modern Neo-Aristotelians believed *all* citizens should be educated in the good life and enabled to participate in democracy, not just the rich, male elite.

THE NEW POLITICS OF WELLBEING

In the late 1990s, under Tony Blair's Labour government, Neo-Aristotelian political philosophy started to impact British policy-making. In 1998, a collection of essays published by the British think-tank Demos called *The Good Life* (Christie and Nash 1998) called for a new politics of virtue and flourishing. The collection referred to Aristotle in its opening essay, writing: 'A fulfilled life is one that has, in modern parlance, some 'project' or, as the ancient Greeks put it, a goal or end. But not [just] anything counts as a life project of a kind whose achievement brings real fulfilment' (Christie and Nash 1998, p. 10). Perhaps the most interesting contribution was by Geoff Mulgan, the founder and director of Demos and later Director of Tony Blair's strategy unit. Mulgan wrote that governments should not be afraid of moving beyond the traditional moral neutrality of the liberal state in order to actively promote a communitarian idea of the good life. He stated:

> A famous philosopher [Robert Nozick] once asked how the same good life could ever be right for a human race composed of people as different as Marilyn Monroe, Albert Einstein, Ludwig Wittgenstein and Louis Armstrong. Any single view of the good life, he argued, must inevitably be oppressive. The best that we can hope for is a society in which everyone is given as much freedom as possible to define the good life for themselves. This view is undeniably attractive. It accords with the 'non-judgemental' common sense of most Western societies today. Yet it is as profoundly wrong as any belief could be...because human beings have much in common. We share our biology, and many of the same drives and needs, however different we may appear on the surface. Moreover, it is wrong because it ignores the evidence that there have been remarkably constant features

of the good life across very different times and very different places – some things are timeless and universal. (Christie and Nash 1998, p. 127)

Mulgan signalled a move beyond neoliberalism and back to the Aristotelian idea that man has a core biological nature—rational, social, political and spiritual—and the good life is the fulfilment of this nature. Politics should promote the good life, because it is right, it fits our nature, and leads to the flowering of that nature. The 'evidence' proves it.

In the early Noughties, Neo-Aristotelianism seemed to be becoming a cross-party policy consensus. Richard Reeves, advisor to then-Deputy Prime Minister Nick Clegg, wrote in 2009: 'In political and policy circles, the Aristotelian idea of a good life informs contemporary concerns ... [and policy-makers are pursuing] the goal of creating a society in which individuals reach their potential – in a Neo-Aristotelian sense' (Reeves and Lexmond 2009). A network of figures across the British political spectrum embraced the Neo-Aristotelian politics of the good life. Supporters of Neo-Aristotelianism on the left included Lord Maurice Glasman, Lord Robert Skidelsky, Jon Cruddas, Geoff Mulgan and Tristram Hunt; Neo-Aristotelians on the right included James O'Shaughnessy, Steve Hilton, David Willetts, Nicky Morgan, David Cameron and Oliver Letwin—the latter actually did his Ph.D. on Aristotle (Letwin 2010). Key civil service support came from Sir Gus O'Donnell and David Halpern of the Behavioural Insights Team (Halpern 2015). Think-tank support came from Demos, Respublica and the New Economics Foundation, which published *A Well-Being Manifesto for a Flourishing Society* in 2004, confidently declaring: 'one of the key aims of a democratic government is to promote the good life: a flourishing society where citizens are happy, healthy, capable and engaged – in other words with high levels of wellbeing'. Neo-Aristotelianism seemed, briefly, to be the UK's ruling political philosophy: 'all our leaders are Aristotelian now', declared *Telegraph* columnist Mary Riddell in (2011).

How did British policy-makers become so confident that they had suddenly discovered the meaning of life and could guide the masses towards it? One answer is that they were emboldened by a new cognitive science of wellbeing that arose in the 1960s and came to prominence in the 1990s and Noughties. This science gave technocrats faith that they were not imposing their moral philosophy onto the masses: they were merely disseminating the objective evidence.

CBT: Stoicism for the Masses

In the late Noughties, as Bache and Scott discuss in this volume (Chap. 1), governments embraced the work of behavioural economists and psychologists like Daniel Kahneman and Ed Diener, who claimed it was possible to measure what makes people happy and satisfied with their life. France, the UK, the Organisation for Economic Co-operation and Development (OECD), the World Health Organization (WHO) and other bodies have since introduced measurements of happiness and life-satisfaction into their indicators. But what policies does this data suggest governments should pursue? Lord Richard Layard, a left-leaning economist who specialises in employment economics and is perhaps the central figure in the UK politics of wellbeing, says: 'The most obvious policy implication was for mental health services' (Evans 2013a). People with mental illness have levels of life satisfaction far below the national average. Yet mental health services attract a fraction of the funding that physical health services attract, despite the obvious suffering they cause. So a government that takes wellbeing seriously should increase funding to mental health services (Layard and Clark 2014). Lord Layard helped to drive a huge expansion of National Health Service (NHS) funding for Cognitive Behavioural Therapy (CBT), a form of therapy inspired by ancient Greek philosophy.

In the early Noughties, Layard became interested in the implications of wellbeing economics for mental health policy. In 2003, he met Dr David M. Clark, a psychologist, at a British Academy tea party (Evans 2013a). Layard asked Clark if he happened to know anything about mental health. Clark replied that he did. He was, in fact, the leading British practitioner of CBT. Clark explained to Layard that trials of CBT showed recovery rates of around 50 per cent for depression, anxiety and other emotional disorders and that the National Institute for Health and Care Excellence (NICE) had recently approved CBT as a treatment for these disorders. The problem, he said, was that there were very few CBT therapists available in the NHS. Layard decided he wanted to 'get something done about mental health' (Evans 2013a). So, at the age of 70, that is what he did. He and Clark drew up plans for a new mental health service, called Improving Access to Psychological Therapies (IAPT). They proposed doubling the NHS psychological therapy budget from £80 million a year to £160 million, in order to train an army of 6000 new CBT therapists. The new service would help millions of people to recover from depression and anxiety, and this would reduce the state's incapacity benefits budget—so the service would pay for itself. Layard and Clark presented their recommendations at a seminar at 10 Downing Street in January 2005. They managed to get IAPT into the Labour Party's manifesto for the 2005 election and were then faced with the task of turning it into a reality following Tony Blair's re-election. The service launched in 2008 across the country—after three years, over one million people had been treated through the service, with recovery rates at around 45 per cent. By 2016, it was treating around half a million people a year.

CBT has been brought into the heart of British health policy but few politicians or even cognitive therapists realise how much it owes to Greek philosophy. It was invented by two American psychologists—Albert Ellis and Aaron Beck—working separately in the 1950s but who came to the same conclusions about what kind of treatment was needed. In interviews, they both told me that they were inspired by Stoic philosophy, and the idea that 'men's suffering comes not from events, but from their opinion about events', as Epictetus put it (Evans 2012a). CBT, like Stoicism, tries to show people how their own beliefs and perspectives guide their emotions. We can change our emotions by using the 'Socratic method' to discover our underlying beliefs and values, and then changing those beliefs that are harmful, as well as changing our behaviour. Both CBT and Stoicism insist on our ability to take responsibility for our own thoughts, and they stress the importance of habits—we have to think or do something repeatedly, until the thought or behaviour is ingrained (an idea that also features heavily in Aristotelian and Buddhist virtue ethics). Stoicism was presented in the classical world as a form of therapy, a 'medicine for the soul' in Cicero's phrase. However, it was also a religious philosophy—we attain inner peace when we relinquish our attachment or aversion to externals and accept the will of the Logos, or pantheistic God.

CBT used the techniques and emotional theory of Stoicism, without accepting its austere ethics or pantheistic metaphysics. It reduced Stoicism to a secular technique for emotional therapy, much as mindfulness has done with Buddhism. Unlike the ancient Greeks, modern CBT psychologists then empirically tested if the therapy actually worked. Beck devised the Beck Depression Inventory, which evaluates how depressed or anxious a person is by asking them to what extent they agreed with questions like 'I feel my life is a failure' or 'I often consider suicide', on a ten-point scale. Using this measurement, Beck suggested psychologists could diagnose someone as suffering from depression or anxiety, and then see if they had recovered after a brief 8 to 16 week course of CBT. The depression and anxiety recovery rates achieved by this short-term therapy persuaded the British government to put more funding into the public provision of CBT (Layard and Clark 2014).

The development of IAPT is the most significant policy consequence of the politics of wellbeing in the UK. It is an interesting moment in the history of ideas—spiritual exercises developed two millennia ago by religious philosophers are now being provided by a government, on a mass scale, to try to cope with an apparent epidemic of mental illness. Some non-CBT psychologists have accused IAPT of Brave New World-style emotional totalitarianism—the government fixing smiles on its alienated workforce (Leader 2007). This is overblown, but certainly, the mass provision of psychotherapy—a word that comes from the ancient Greek for 'care of the soul'—does seem to move beyond Locke's classical liberalism, in which government leaves the 'care of the soul' to the individual. But many people *want* some guidance as to the care of the soul, as long as it is not intrusive, dogmatic or cultish, and in a country where only two per cent now go to church (Sherwood 2016), that pastoral role now seems to have fallen to the NHS.

IAPT is not a programme for mass spiritual reformation. CBT is a set of resolutely secular and instrumental techniques—there is no mention of ethics, God or the Logos. Unlike Stoicism, CBT does not tell people how to live; it simply gives them techniques to transform their emotions (although I would suggest there are, in fact, some ethics implicitly embedded in the techniques, such as the Socratic virtues of equanimity, self-discipline and wisdom). Crucially, IAPT is voluntary—people choose to sign up (via self or GP referral) because they want to suffer less. Some critics of the service worry about instances where job seekers have been told they will only receive benefits if they take a course in cognitive therapy (Friedli and Stearn 2015). Compulsory therapy is obviously both illiberal and a waste of money. But providing free talking therapy for people struggling with depression or anxiety seems a just and compassionate policy, and it may be surprising that IAPT is not more celebrated. Although, as Peter Fonagy, one of the founders of IAPT, remarks: 'Show me any aspect of mental health care that is celebrated' (Evans 2015).

Wellbeing Education in Schools

The second significant policy area that the politics of wellbeing has influenced is education. Schools, governments and corporations have, over the last two decades, increasingly attempted to teach children and adults how to be happy, how to be resilient, how to have character, 'grit', and so on. The idea that character can be taught goes back to the ancient Greek concept of *paideia* (Nussbaum 1997). Greek philosophers like Aristotle and the Stoics believed you could mould a person's character through philosophy, teaching them virtuous habits that would serve them well in later life. Renaissance humanists adopted the classical *paideia* programme as part of the education of the courtier (Weakland 1973), and a similar sort of character-building ethos was adopted by British public schools in the nineteenth and twentieth centuries (Arthur 2003).

In the 1990s, the psychologist Martin Seligman claimed to have developed the scientific equivalent of classical virtue ethics, which he called Positive Psychology (Seligman 2002). Seligman was a colleague of Aaron Beck's at the University of Pennsylvania. Observing the success of CBT in the 1970s, Seligman wondered if its techniques could be taught to people not just to help them recover from mental illness, but also to become more resilient and flourishing in life. Seligman aimed to move people not merely from ten to zero on the Beck Depression Inventory, but from zero to ten on the scale of flourishing (Seligman 2002). After all, Stoicism, Buddhism, Aristotelianism and other forms of virtue ethics were not intended merely as short-term interventions for the mentally ill. They were life-philosophies aimed at helping people to build good lives. Positive Psychology would discover the techniques and practices that genuinely helped people to flourish. Seligman launched Positive Psychology when he was president of the American Psychology Association in 1998. He proved an adept publicist, and the movement attracted a great deal of media interest and funding in the two decades that followed. Seligman and colleagues developed the Penn Resiliency Project, which aimed to teach young people basic techniques of emotional intelligence (in large part derived from CBT and Stoicism) in order to make them more resilient, more virtuous, and less likely to develop depression later in life (Seligman 2011). A handful of US schools made Positive Psychology part of their curriculum, notably the Knowledge is Power Program (KIPP) charter schools, which aimed to teach children 'grit' and even rate them through character score-cards (Snyder 2014).

In the UK, the first attempt to teach wellbeing within the national curriculum came in 2003 when a subject called Social and Emotional Aspects of Learning (SEAL) was introduced as a voluntary subject in state primary schools in 2003. It was then introduced into secondary schools in 2007 (see also Ecclestone, this volume, Chap. 10) where it became a core module in the compulsory primary and secondary subject

Personal, Social, Health, and Economic education (PSHE). SEAL was created in the late 1990s by the chief educational psychologist in Southampton local education authority, Peter Sharp, after he read a book of popular psychology, *Emotional Intelligence*, by the American journalist Daniel Goleman. Sharp was so enthused by Goleman's idea that emotional intelligence (EI) could be taught in schools, that he decided EI should be given priority alongside literacy and numeracy (Weare and Gray 2013). Unfortunately, Goleman's book, although a popular success, faced criticism in scientific circles (Epstein 1998, p. 3). It seemed to have thrown many different, and conflicting, psychological theories under one catch-all phrase. It also made unfounded claims, such as that EI classes led to better career prospects. Yet it took until October 2010 for the Department of Education to publish the first independent assessment of SEAL, by the University of Manchester (Humphrey et al. 2010). It found that SEAL had no quantifiable impact on children's emotional wellbeing or academic performance. The loose format of the subject enabled schools to teach more or less whatever they wanted. The Department of Education stopped promoting SEAL in 2011.

In 2007, Lord Layard spearheaded an attempt to make wellbeing education in schools more evidence-based. He helped to launch the UK Resilience Programme, a pilot-scheme in which three local education authorities adopted a resilience curriculum designed by the Penn Resiliency Project. The results were then evaluated in 2011 (Challen et al. 2011). The trial found a significant short-term impact on pupils' depression scores, school attendance rates and academic attainment in English, but no long-term impacts at two-year follow-up. While teachers could apparently teach whatever they wanted in SEAL classes, teachers in the UK Resilience Programme found the materials 'too didactic and thought they could be improved' (Challen et al. 2011). It was not a home run for the pilot.

Wellbeing and character education was not a priority for Michael Gove when he was Secretary of State for Education between 2010 and 2014 (Watson et al. 2012). It was more popular with his successor, Nicky Morgan, who declared in 2014 that she wanted the UK to become a 'global leader' in character education. But Morgan took few practical steps to make this happen during her brief stint at the ministry, besides launching a £5 million 'character fund' to finance small afterschool projects. The Minister of State for Children and Families at the time of writing, Edward Timpson, has said:

> We want schools to have a whole-school approach that makes talking
> about feelings, emotions and wellbeing as normal for pupils as talking
> about their physical bodies. That might include lessons taught as part of
> the PSHE curriculum, whole-school programmes such as mindfulness that
> become a normal part of the school day, role play in drama lessons, or
> offering meditation or yoga sessions (Dominiczak 2016).

However, Timpson had yet to come up with concrete proposals.
Lord James O'Shaughnessy, formerly head of David Cameron's Policy
Unit, suggests the Conservative Party prefers to encourage schools to
find their own best practice for teaching wellbeing rather than imposing a curriculum (Evans 2012b). Lord O'Shaughnessy subsequently left
government and set up a chain of state academy schools called Floreat,
in which Positive Psychology is a core part of the curriculum. He and
Lord Layard are now overseeing a four-year trial of a new curriculum for
Personal, Social and Health Education, called 'Healthy Minds'.[1]

Perhaps the biggest initiative in character education over the last few
years has been the introduction of the National Citizen Service, a volunteering scheme for 16–17-year-olds, which was launched by the government in 2010 and was set to receive £1.2 billion in funding in the 2016
Parliament. David Cameron became chair of its board of patrons after
leaving Number 10, declaring it was 'one of my proudest achievements'
(Cameron 2016). The scheme has the Aristotelian aim of teaching young
people the joy of volunteering and public service and participation in the
scheme was found to have a marked impact on young people's wellbeing
(Halpern 2015, pp. 250–252). It is also hoped the scheme will improve
social cohesion among people from different backgrounds by giving
them a sense of the common good (Wilson 2015).

Positive Education for Adults

There have also been some policy attempts to teach resilience, happiness, and other emotional aptitudes to adults. The NHS and some local
governments have used public health campaigns to promote the New
Economic Foundation's 'five ways to wellbeing'. In 2011, Lord Layard,
Geoff Mulgan and Wellington College former headmaster Anthony
Seldon launched a grassroots movement, Action for Happiness, which
aims to spread the insights of Positive Psychology to the masses through
events and courses (Seldon 2015a). David Cameron's government also
tried to encourage volunteering through the Big Society initiative, which

aimed to get community groups involved in providing local services. The army of volunteers who helped to run the London 2012 Olympics was probably its biggest success but the Big Society was promoted against a backdrop of cuts to local government funding, which seemed to undermine its ethos.

The most ambitious adult education programme is the US Army's resilience training course *Comprehensive Soldier Fitness*, designed by Martin Seligman's team at the University of Pennsylvania. At a cost of $125 million, the course was rolled out to all 1.1 million army personnel in 2010, in what has been described as 'the largest wellbeing intervention, military or civilian, ever undertaken' (Warner 2013, p. 47). It tries to improve resilience and reduce the incidence of Post-Traumatic Stress Disorder in soldiers by teaching basic Stoic self-management skills, like teaching people how their perspective or 'explanatory style' affects their emotional response to events (Cornum et al. 2011). Soldiers' social, emotional and spiritual fitness are then annually evaluated using an online questionnaire. The Australian Army started to pilot a similar programme in 2016 (Chen 2016). Some companies such as Zappos and Google have also introduced wellbeing or Positive Psychology courses for their employees, to try to boost employee engagement and reduce absenteeism (Hsieh 2010).

Problems with Mass Wellbeing Education

I suggested at the beginning of this chapter that, while I applaud many aspects of the politics of wellbeing—particularly government funding for talking therapies—there are other aspects of it that make me uneasy. The politics of wellbeing is potentially illiberal, scientistic, simplistic and patronising. It can lead to psychologists and technocrats declaring, 'we the experts have discovered the scientific formula for flourishing. Now you, the masses, should heed this proven formula, pull your socks up, and get happy' (or resilient, mindful, gritty, or whatever is this year's emotional goal). There are several problems with this attitude.

Firstly, can scientific experts really 'prove' a particular philosophy of the good life is true and valid for everyone? Can science replace religion and moral philosophy? The sociologist Max Weber scoffed at this idea. In his 1917 lecture 'Science as a Vocation', Weber insisted that science 'is not the gift of grace of seers and prophets dispensing sacred values and revelations, nor does it partake of the contemplation of sages and philosophers about the meaning of the universe'. Who, he asked, believes that science leads to happiness, 'aside from a few big children in university chairs or editorial offices', and insisted that:

> only a prophet or a saviour can give the answer [to the meaning of life]. If there is no such man, or if his message is no longer believed in, then you will certainly not compel him to appear on this earth by having thousands of professors, as privileged hirelings of the state, attempt as petty prophets in their lecture-rooms to take over his role. (Weber 1991, p. 143)

One might be able to measure how happy a person feels from moment to moment, though even here there are linguistic challenges regarding people's definitions. But what makes people happy is not necessarily good. As the Marquis de Sade pointed out, some people take the greatest happiness in cruelty and the suffering of others (De Sade 2016). Others take the greatest happiness in morphine. Should the government simply hand out the painkillers?

Martin Seligman appears to take a more Aristotelian and pluralist approach to happiness. He says he is more interested in *eudaimonia* or flourishing than happiness (Seligman 2011). He suggests that flourishing has different constituents, which he sums up in the acronym PERMA—Positive Emotion, Engagement, Relationships, Meaning and Achievement. Different individuals may focus on different aspects of the PERMA formula. Yet he still insists that empirical science can accurately quantify and measure all these aspects of flourishing. He ignores Aristotle's warning that the educated man should 'look for precision in things only so far as the nature of the subject admits' (*Nichomachean Ethics*, Book 1, Chap. 1). Can science quantify and measure the meaning of a person's life or their achievements? Can it quantify their virtue? You can ask for people's self-assessment of their moral value, but they might be wrong. As the Republican presidential nominee, Donald Trump declared in an interview with *60 Minutes* in 2016: 'I think I'm much more humble than you would understand'. Should we take him at his word?

The politics of wellbeing dispenses with God, but places huge faith in science, statistical measurements, and in the power of questionnaires to delve into a person's soul. For example, the US Army's resilience training programme claims to measure a person's emotional, social and even spiritual fitness with a set of simplistic questions, which is then quantified in a number. Likewise, Knowledge is Power Program (KIPP) charter schools measure children's character and grit to give them a 'character score card'. The Christian confessional has been replaced by the psychometric test. Who really believes you can scientifically measure a person's spiritual value and sum it up with a number, besides Scientologists?

Seligman himself has admitted that Osama bin Laden would probably have scored high on PERMA (Evans 2011): the former leader of Al-Qaeda would probably score high on positive emotion, high on engagement, have strong relationships, a deep sense of meaning, and a profound sense of personal achievement. What he did not have was a good ethical compass. This highlights the limits of an overly Positivist science of flourishing: you need practical moral reasoning, what Aristotle called *phronesis*, to guide your everyday decisions. That is why the good life can never be reduced to a science, or set of instrumental techniques, despite Seligman's claims. Practical moral reasoning shows us there is not a precise formula for flourishing that holds true for all people at all times—life is messy, tragic, circumstances change, priorities change. The risk of the attempt to mould character—whether in a school, an organisation, or an entire society—is that it degenerates into mindless conformism to a rigid and inflexible dogma. There is no room for discussion, rebellion, creativity and experiment. As John Stuart Mill wrote, 'the free development of individuality is one of the leading essentials of wellbeing' (Mill 1859, Chap. 3).

Action for Happiness, for example, has an 8-week wellbeing course called Exploring What Matters, in which small groups watch videos by Positive Psychology experts, and then have a discussion. It was inspired by Alpha, the ten-week charismatic Christianity course, which also features expert talks followed by small-group discussions (Evans 2013b). The Exploring What Matters website says: 'There are no single right answers to these questions and all constructive perspectives are welcome'. But I put it to Lord Layard that, in fact, the course *does* think there are 'right answers'—that is the whole premise of Positive Psychology. He agreed that the course is utilitarian, it suggests happiness is the goal of life, and science helps us to get there (Evans 2016). You can arrive at any philosophy you want, as long as it is utilitarian. This is just as dogmatic as the Alpha course, where the answer is always Jesus.

I am fairly sure that if I had attended Wellington College's wellbeing class and was force-fed its 'ten-point wellbeing programme', I would have done as much as I could to disrupt the class. And yet, perhaps para-doxically, I also wish I had been given more guidance in how to take care of my mind and emotions when I was at school and university. When I became mentally ill at the age of 18, I was terrified and ashamed of what was happening to me. My university was no help whatsoever; higher edu-cation was not designed to teach people any wisdom about their inner lives. When I finally found help through CBT and Stoicism in my twen-ties, I could not understand why this wisdom was not better known and why there was no mention of it in my 21 years of education.

Is there a way to teach the good life in schools, universities and organ-isations, without being illiberal, scientistic and patronising? I suggest we need to take a pluralist approach, recognising there are several different philosophies of the good life, with equally valid but competing ideas about the meaning and goal of life. What I have tried to do in the well-being workshops I have taught in schools, charities, companies, prisons and elsewhere is to embrace a two-step approach. Firstly, to teach some of the evidence-based techniques we can use to transform our emotions, techniques such as CBT or mindfulness. Secondly, to offer a space for people to discuss different models of flourishing (Platonic, Epicurean, Buddhist and so on), leaving them free to make up their own minds about the meaning of life. People do not want to just listen to the 'sage on the stage'; they want to share their own wisdom and hear from other people in the group. They want the freedom to disagree. The process of group discussion is itself cathartic and bonding.[2] But I do not know how significant such small-scale group discussions can be to national pol-icy. Ethical education works best in small groups, not in national pol-icy interventions. The bigger the intervention, the more likely it will be a crude, intrusive, automated and ultimately pointless exercise in box ticking.

THE LEGACY OF THE POLITICS OF WELLBEING

At the time of writing (October 2016), having followed the politics of wellbeing for a decade, I wonder if the movement has had its moment in the sun. The electorate seems to be less focused on national wellbeing measurements, and more focused on other statistics—particularly immi-gration figures. Aristotle warned that if a society becomes too unequal, too diverse or too socially divided, a politics of the common good would become impossible. Perhaps we are at such a moment; the centre-ground of politics seems to be splintering, to the benefit of the far-left and far-right. Nationalist movements such as the alt-right in the USA or UKIP in the UK show the extent to which populism can guide people's raw emotions, just as Plato warned in *The Republic*. The rhetoric and science of wellbeing have tended to be used to promote a progressive, liberal agenda, but it could be used for a more xenophobic agenda—some wellbeing studies show that the more ethnically diverse a community is, the lower the levels of trust in that community (Putnam 2007). The happiest country in Europe, Denmark, has one of the lowest levels of immigration. Bhutan seems to have maintained its high level of Gross National Happiness partly by exporting Nepali minorities into refugee camps (Dutt 2013). I wonder if historians will look back on the politics of wellbeing as two decades of technocratic optimism before a century of disruption through climate change and mass migration. Technocrats tried to introduce a more emotional, 'touchy-feely' type of politics. But we are now swamped in a politics of more violent emotions—fear, anger, disgust, utopian hope, fanaticism, ecstasy. Wellbeing policy-makers like Lord Layard insisted governments should take citizens' feelings seriously and use them as a guide to policy. But what if the electorate's feelings lead them to xenophobic and self-destructive voting decisions?

Still, it is likely that something will survive of the politics of wellbeing. The most obvious legacy, it seems to me, is the increased emphasis on mental health in public policy. Look at the period 2010–2016 in British politics. Nick Clegg, former leader of the Liberal Democrats and Deputy Prime Minister, made mental health policy a central focus of his leadership (Clegg 2014). One of the first speeches that Ed Miliband gave as leader of the Labour party in 2012 was on mental health (Miliband 2012). His successor, Jeremy Corbyn, even briefly created a new shadow Cabinet post in 2015—Minister for Mental Health (Stone 2015). When Prince William and Prince Harry looked for a public cause to champion, they turned to mental health (Brennan 2016). Two decades ago, mental health barely registered on the public policy radar, now it is right up at the top of the agenda. Likewise in media coverage, where 'there has been a seismic shift from mental illness being barely mentioned ... to being everywhere' (Sykes 2016). However, the rhetoric is still not backed up by funding—the campaign to get 'parity of esteem' between mental and physical health services still has a long way to go.

Another legacy of the politics of wellbeing might be in higher education. Ironically, considering the movement owes a lot to academic philosophers and psychologists, the politics of wellbeing has had little effect on what is taught at universities. Most wellbeing research centres at British universities do not offer practical courses in wellbeing to their own staff or students. Universities do have counselling services, but they are completely separate from academic teaching or research. They are a place students go when they are ill, rather than a place where all young adults can learn something about how to 'take care for the improvement of the soul' (as Socrates describes his mission in his Apology). Learning about the psyche and how to guide it to flourishing should be at the centre of student learning, not something you only consider if you break down. Likewise, academic and staff anxiety and stress levels are high, yet there is little sense that universities' own wellbeing research could help their staff. If university HR departments do anything at all for staff wellbeing (most do very little), it is outsourced to consultants. Why this disconnect between the search for academic excellence and the search for flourishing?

Anthony Seldon, co-founder of Action for Happiness and now vice-chancellor at Buckingham University, recently called for the development of 'positive universities', with proposed measures including free courses on mindfulness or resilience for first-year undergraduates (Seldon 2015b). I imagine many academics shuddered, but I heartily support this Neo-Aristotelian conception of the university's role, as long as courses in flourishing are pluralist, self-critical and nuanced, rather than banal, conformist, scientistic dogma. There are useful precedents for academic wellbeing centres that combine quality research with practical courses for students and the general public. One precedent is creation of mindfulness centres at universities including Oxford, Exeter, Brown and Virginia, which carry out research into contemplation, while also offering brief mindfulness courses to students, staff and the local population.[3] Another precedent is a research project I have been involved with, called Stoicism Today, working with therapists and classicists. We combine academic research on modern Stoicism with practical wellbeing courses for students and the general public. Several thousand people have taken our free online courses on modern Stoicism, and we have received exceptionally good feedback on how the course has improved people's lives.[4] However, both Stoic and mindfulness courses only teach one philosophy of the good life; they are not pluralist. A useful precedent for a more pluralist course is a freshman course in flourishing formerly taught at Virginia by social psychologist Jonathan Haidt. The course combined ancient wisdom with modern CBT and taught a variety of different moral philosophies. This is the type of wellbeing course I would like to see more of in British universities for undergraduates regardless of their degree, and for any post-docs, staff or members of the public who want to attend one. As the Stoic philosopher Seneca put it:

> There is no time for playing around. You have been retained as counsel for the unhappy. You have promised to bring help to the shipwrecked, the imprisoned, the sick, the needy, to those whose heads are under the poised axe. Where are you deflecting your attention? What are you doing?[5]

Notes

1. You can find out more about the project on the website of the Education Endowment Foundation, here: https://educationendow-mentfoundation.org.uk/public/files/Projects/EEF_Project_Protocol_DevelopingHealthyMindsInTeenagers.pdf.
2. You can read my report about an AHRC-funded trial of my Philosophies for Life course, which I ran in a prison, a mental health charity, and a rugby club, here: https://www.scribd.com/document/229504007/Philosophies-for-Life-Final-Report.
3. You can find out about Oxford's public mindfulness courses here: https://www.oxfordmindfulness.org/learn/.
4. You can read the feedback report for the 2015 Stoic Week here: https://blogs.exeter.ac.uk/stoicismtoday/2016/03/19/stoic-week-report-part-4-by-tim-lebon/.
5. The quote, from Seneca's Moral Letters to Lucilius, is quoted in Evans (2012a p. 22).

References

Arthur, J. (2003). *Education with Character: The Moral Economy of Schooling.* Hove: Psychology Press.

Berlin, I. (2002). *Liberty.* Oxford: Oxford University Press.

Bormans, L. (2011). *The World Book of Happiness.* Kuala Lumpur: Marshall Cavendish International Asia.

Brennan, S. (2016). Kate, William and Harry Support Mental Health Charity Campaign. *Mail* [online]. Available at: http://www.dailymail.co.uk/femail/article-3556081/Kate-William-Harry-supportmental-health-charity-campaign.html. Accessed August 6, 2017.

Cameron, D. (2016). I've Found My First Job After Politics, Building the Big Society. *Telegraph* [online]. Available at: http://www.telegraph.co.uk/news/2016/10/11/david-cameron-ive-found-my-first-job-after-politics-building-the/. Accessed September 6, 2016.

Casert, R. (2011). EU President Rompuy Spreads a Little Happiness. *Associated Press* [online]. Available at: http://www.sandiegouniontribune.com/sdut-eu-president-rompuy-spreads-a-little-happiness-2011dec22-story,amp.html. Accessed September 6, 2016.

Challen, A., Noden, P., West, A., & Machin, S. (2011). UK Resilience Programme Evaluation: Final Report. London: Department for Education. Available at: https://assets.publishing.service.gov.uk/government/uploads/system/uploads/attachment_data/file/182419/DFE-RR097.pdf

Chen, D. (2016). Australian Army Trial Tracks Soldiers' Health Via Smartphone App. *ABC News* [online]. Available at: http://www.abc.net.au/news/2016-08-30/army-trials-injury-prevention-program-to-create-safer-soldiers/7798272. Accessed September 6, 2016.

Christie, I., & Nash, L. (Eds.) (1998). *The Good Life*. London: Demos.

Clegg, N. (2014). Making Mental Health a Priority. Available at: https://www.gov.uk/government/speeches/nick-clegg-making-mental-health-a-priority. Accessed September 6, 2016.

Cornum, R., Matthews, M., & Seligman, M. (2011). Comprehensive Soldier Fitness: Building Resilience in a Challenging Institutional Context. *American Psychologist, 66*(1), 4–9.

De Sade, A. (2016). *Philosophy in the Boudoir: Or, the Immoral Mentors*. New York: Penguin Classics.

Dominiczak, P. (2016). Teach Yoga and Meditation to 'Unplug Children', Says Education Minister. *Telegraph* [online]. Available at: http://www.telegraph.co.uk/news/2016/09/07/teach-yoga-and-meditation-to-unplug-children-says-education-mini/. Accessed September 6, 2016.

Dutt, A. (2013). The Ethnic Cleansing Behind Bhutan's Happy Face. *First Post* [online]. Available at: http://www.firstpost.com/world/the-ethnic-cleansing-hidden-behind-bhutans-happy-face-918473.html. Accessed September 6, 2016.

Epstein, S. (1998). *Constructive Thinking: The Key to Emotional Intelligence*. Westport: Greenwood Publishing.

Evans, J. (2011). Is Osama Bin Laden the Model of a Flourishing Life? *Philosophy for Life Blog*. Available at: http://www.philosophyforlife.org/pow-is-osama-bin-laden-the-model-of-a-flourishing-life/. Accessed September 6, 2016.

Evans, J. (2012a). *Philosophy for Life: And Other Dangerous Situations*. London: Rider Books.

Evans, J. (2012b). How Tories Got the Well-Being Bug. *History of Emotions Blog*. Available at: https://emotionsblog.history.qmul.ac.uk/2012/05/james-oshaughnessy-on-how-the-tories-got-the-well-being-bug/. Accessed September 6, 2016.

Evans, J. (2013a). A Brief History of IAPT. *History of Emotions Blog.* Available at: https://emotionsblog.history.qmul.ac.uk/2013/05/a-brief-history-of-iapt-the-mass-provision-of-cbt-in-the-nhs/. Accessed September 6, 2016.

Evans, J. (2013b). Richard Layard on Happiness, CBT and Christianity. *History of Emotions Blog.* Available at: https://emotionsblog.history.qmul. ac.uk/2013/04/richard-layard-on-happiness-cbt-and-christianity/. Accessed September 6, 2016.

Evans, J. (2015). Peter Fonagy on Psychoanalysis and IAPT. *History of Emotions Blog.* Available at: https://emotionsblog.history.qmul.ac.uk/2015/05/peter-fonagy-on-psychoanalysis-and-iapt/. Accessed September 6, 2016.

Evans, J. (2016). The Politics of Wellbeing: Interview with Richard Layard and Will Davies. *Living with Feeling Podcast, Episode 2.* Available at: https://soundcloud.com/user-357683788/the-politics-of-wellbeing. Accessed July 4, 2017

Friedli, L., & Stearn, R. (2015). Positive Affect as Coercive Strategy: Conditionality, Activation and the Role of Psychology in UK Government Workfare Programmes. *Medical Humanities, 41,* 40–47.

Fukuyama, F. (1992). *The End of History and the Last Man.* New York: Free Press.

Halpern, D. (2015). *Inside the Nudge Unit: How Small Changes Can Make a Big Difference.* London: WH Allen.

Hsieh, T. (2010). *Delivering Happiness: A Path to Profit, Passion and Purpose.* New York: Grand Central Publishing.

Humphrey, N., Lendrum, A., & Wigelsworth, M. (2010). Social and Emotional Aspects of Learning (SEAL) in Secondary Schools: National Evaluation. Research Report RR049. Nottingham: DFE Publications. Available at: https://www.researchgate.net/publication/268179576_DFE-RB049_Social_and_emotional_aspects_of_learning_SEAL_programme_in_secondary_schools_national_evaluation

Layard, R., & Clark, D. M. (2014). *Thrive: The Power of Evidence-Based Psychological Therapy.* London: Penguin.

Leader, D. (2007). A Dark Age for Mental Health. *Guardian* [online]. Available at: https://www.theguardian.com/commentisfree/2007/oct/13/comment. publicservices. Accessed September 6, 2016.

Letwin, O. (2010). *Ethics, Emotion and the Unity of the Self.* London: Routledge.

Locke, J. (2016). *Second Treatise of Government and a Letter Concerning Toleration.* Oxford: Oxford World Classics.

MacIntyre, A. (1981). *After Virtue: A Study in Moral Theory.* Notre Dame: University of Notre Dame Press.

Miliband, E. (2012). Ed Miliband's Speech on Mental Health: Full Text. *New Statesman* [online]. Available at: http://www.newstatesman.com/politics/2012/10/ed-milibands-speech-mental-health-full-text. Accessed September 6, 2016.

Mill, J. S. (1859). *M. de Tocqueville on Democracy in America* (Vol. 2). John W. Parker and Son.

Mill, J.S. (2015). *On Liberty, Utilitarianism and Other Essays*. Oxford: Oxford University Press.

Nietzsche, F. (2008). *Twilight of the Idols*. Oxford: Oxford World Classics.

Nozick, R. (2001). *Anarchy, State and Utopia*. Oxford: Wiley Blackwell.

Nussbaum, M. C. (1997). *The Therapy of Desire: Theory and Practice in Hellenistic Ethics*. Princeton: Princeton University Press.

Putnam, R. (2007). *E Pluribus Unum*: Diversity and Community in the Twenty-first Century. *Scandinavian Political Studies, 30*(2), 137–174.

Reeves, R., & Lexmond, J. (2009). *Building Character*. London: Demos.

Riddell, M. (2011) Can Ed Miliband Find an Antidote for the Politics of Fear and Loathing? *Telegraph* [online]. Available at: http://www.telegraph.co.uk/comment/columnists/maryriddell/8251148/Can-Ed-Miliband-find-an-antidote-to-the-politics-of-fear-and-loathing.html. Accessed September 6, 2016.

Sandel, M. (2010). *Justice: What's the Right Thing to Do?* New York: Farrar, Straus and Giroux.

Seldon, A. (2015a). *Beyond Happiness: How to Find Lasting Meaning and Joy in all That You Have*. London: Yellow Kite.

Seldon, A. (2015b). Ten Steps to Address the Student Mental Health Crisis. *Times Higher Education* [online]. Available at: https://www.timeshighereducation.com/blog/sir-anthony-seldon-10-steps-address-student-mental-health-crisis. Accessed September 6, 2016.

Seligman, M. (2002). *Authentic Happiness: Using the New Positive Psychology to Realise Your Potential for Lasting Fulfilment*. New York: Simon & Schuster.

Seligman, M. (2011). *Flourish: A New Understanding of Happiness and Well-Being*. New York: Simon & Schuster.

Sherwood, H. (2016). Church of England Weekly Attendance Falls Below 1m for First Time. *The Guardian* [online]. Available at: https://www.theguardian.com/world/2016/jan/12/church-of-england-attendance-falls-below-million-first-time. Accessed September 6, 2016.

Skidelsky, R., & Skidelsky, E. (2012). *How Much Is Enough?: Money and the Good Life*. London: Penguin.

Snyder, J. (2014). Teaching Kids 'Grit' Is All the Rage. Here's What's Wrong with It. *New Republic* [online]. Available at: https://newrepublic.com/article/117615/problem-grit-kipp-and-character-based-education.   Accessed September 6, 2016.

Stone, J. (2015). Jeremy Corbyn Creates New Dedicated 'Minister for Mental Health' in His Shadow Cabinet. *Independent* [online]. Available at: http://www.independent.co.uk/news/uk/politics/jeremy-corbyn-creates-new-dedicated-minister-for-mental-health-in-his-shadow-cabinet-10500075.html. Accessed September 6, 2016.

Sykes, E. (2016). Media Coverage of Mental Illness Has Increased Significantly in Recent Years. *The Mental Elf blog*. Available at: http://www.

nationalelfservice.net/mental-health/media-coverage-of-mental-illness-has-increased-significantly-in-recent-years/. Accessed September 6, 2016.

Warner, R. (2013). *Solution-Focused Interviewing: Applying Positive Psychology.* Toronto: University of Toronto Press.

Watson, D., Emery, C., & Bayliss, P. (2012). *Children's Social and Emotional Well-Being in Schools: A Critical Perspective.* London: Policy Press.

Weakland, J. (1973). Renaissance Paideia: Some Ideals in Italian Humanism and Their Relevance Today. *The Social Studies, 64*(1973), 153–157.

Weare, K., & Gray, G. (2013). What Works in Developing Children's Social and Emotional Comptence and Well-Being? Department for Education and Skills. Available at: http://learning.gov.wales/docs/learningwales/publications/121129emotionalandsocialcompetenceen.pdf. Accessed September 6, 2016.

Weber, M. (1991). *Max Weber: Essays in Sociology.* London: Psychology Press.

Wilson, R. (2015). National Citizen Service Conference 2015 Speech. Available at: https://www.gov.uk/government/speeches/national-citizen-service-ncs-conference-2015-rob-wilson-speech. Accessed September 6, 2016.

CHAPTER 3

Well-Being and Social Justice: In Defence of the Capabilities Approach

Annie Austin

INTRODUCTION

The question 'Equality of what?' has been fiercely debated in both political theory and real world politics. What should be the focus of egalitarian social justice, and what should be measured to evaluate it? Political theorists have proposed several different answers to this question. Influential theories of the appropriate 'currency of justice' include resources (e.g. Rawls 1971), opportunity (e.g. Roemer 1998) and preference satisfaction (e.g. Arneson 1989). This chapter proposes that the most suitable answer to the question 'Equality of What?' is *well-being*.[1] In this chapter, I defend the Capabilities Approach (Sen 1985; Nussbaum 2000; see Chapter 1, footnote 8), an Aristotelian approach to well-being and social justice.

The first section discusses the arguments for and against resources, opportunities and subjective states as the currency of justice, and sets out a promising alternative—the Capabilities Approach. The second section considers how different accounts of well-being have different implications for policy. This section illustrates the objections against reliance

A. Austin (✉)
University of Manchester, Manchester, UK
e-mail: annie.austin@manchester.ac.uk

© The Author(s) 2018
I. Bache and K. Scott (eds.), *The Politics of Wellbeing*, Wellbeing in Politics and Policy, https://doi.org/10.1007/978-3-319-58394-5_3

on 'subjective well-being' alone, using empirical findings relating to the impacts of the economic crisis of 2007–2010 on quality of life in the UK. The final section concludes that, while resources, opportunities and subjective states are all important, each provides only a partial perspective. An account of well-being that is plural in both definition and measurement, such as the Capabilities Approach, is required as the foundation for a just society.

EQUALITY OF WHAT?

Theories of justice are theories of value. In the case of egalitarianism, different theories advocate equality of that which, in their view, is most valuable (resources, opportunities, preference satisfaction and so on). In the *Nicomachean Ethics*, Aristotle identified 'that which is most valuable' as *eudaimonia*. This translates from the ancient Greek as 'the living of a good, successful life' (Cooper 1975); that is, faring well, or *well-being*.

The meaning of well-being and how to achieve it was at the heart of ancient Greek ethics. Socrates set the agenda, asking how people should live in order to achieve *eudaimonia*—the good life. The Socratic Question is best understood as a question about the sort of life that could reasonably be evaluated as a life well or successfully lived. According to the Greeks, both people and objects have essential functions. Aristotle gave various illustrations of this principle—for example, the function of a harpist is to play the harp (EN1098a8), just as the function, or essence, of a hammer is to drive nails. The question of what constitutes a good human life is analogous to the question of what constitutes a good harpist or hammer: a good harpist plays the harp well, and a good hammer drives nails well. On this interpretation, human well-being is a matter of *being* human *well*.

The Greeks advocated different accounts of *eudaimonia*. For example, Epicurus defended a hedonic account of *eudaimonia* as a life of pleasure, while Aristotle dismissed the idea that well-being is constituted by something 'obvious and familiar like pleasure, money or fame' (EN1095a17), arguing instead that *eudaimonia* consists in living an active, flourishing life in the social and political world. This ancient debate is reflected in modern debates about the nature of well-being (see Bache and Scott, this volume, Chap. 1).

In the broadest sense, Aristotle defined well-being as 'that for the sake of which everything else is done' (EN1097a16)—the ultimate goal of human life. Theories of well-being are theories about what is most valuable in life. Egalitarian theories of social justice advocate equality of that which is most valuable in life; therefore, in this sense, different egalitarian theories of social justice are grounded in different theories of what it means to live a good life—that is, different theories of well-being. Hence the appropriate currency of social justice is well-being.

The next sections consider some of the major accounts of well-being and candidates for the most appropriate currency of justice: resources, opportunities, subjective well-being, and capabilities.

Equality of Resources

The simplest account of social justice defines and measures well-being as the possession of economic resources. At the individual and household level, this means income and wealth; at the national level, gross domestic product (GDP). On this account, social justice requires a fair distribution of income and wealth. However, it is widely recognised that GDP at the national level is not a sound indicator of national well-being (Stiglitz et al. 2009; Austin 2016a), nor is possession of economic resources at the individual level sufficient for a good and flourishing life.

In his landmark *Theory of Justice*, John Rawls (1971) developed the resourcist account of well-being and justice beyond material resources to include a wider set of *primary goods*. The primary goods are not only a set of basic rights, liberties and opportunities, including 'wealth and income', but also social goods such as 'the social bases of self-respect'. These goods provide individuals with the freedom and resources to pursue their personal conceptions of the good life. Rawls' theory exemplifies a classical politically liberal position: it does not specify the content of a good life, but assumes that, whatever goals and life plans a person chooses to pursue, all people would desire and require these all-purpose goods. On this account, a just society is structured to ensure that people start out with equal primary goods, and any deviations from strict equality are to the benefit of the least advantaged members of society.

However, resourcist accounts of well-being and justice pose problems for egalitarians. The first objection is that resources are not ends in themselves, but only means: it is not resources themselves that are valuable, but what they enable a person to be and to do in their lives (Sen 1985). Rawls recognises that the primary goods are not final ends in themselves, but nevertheless insists that they are the appropriate *equalisandum* (that is, the thing to be equalised). This falls short of a satisfactory conception of social justice, since it does not preclude inequalities in achieved well-being—that which really matters in a life.

The second objection is that different individuals have different resource requirements, as well as varying abilities to convert resources into valuable activities and outcomes (Sen 1985). Differential conversion of resources into well-being might be due to individual characteristics of a person, or structural features of a society, or the interaction of these. For example, a member of a group that is systematically discriminated against may have a lower ability to transform education into their occupation of choice, and a person with a physical impairment may require more resources than their able-bodied counterparts to achieve goods such as mobility. Therefore, equality of resources does not necessarily result in equality of the things that really matter.

These objections—the focus on means rather than ends, and differential conversion of resources into well-being—mean that the resourcist account provides only a partial perspective on well-being and social justice.

Equality of Opportunity

There are several varieties of Equality of Opportunity. Formal Equality of Opportunity (Rawls 1971) is the ideal that socially advantageous positions (e.g. career opportunities) are open to all, and applicants are assessed solely on their merits. In a society that upheld formal equality of opportunity, a person's socio-economic background (their class), or any other un-chosen characteristic, such as gender or race, would have no impact on their prospects for success in life; people of the same talent and ambition would be equally able to do well. However, there may be background inequalities in people's abilities to become qualified for such positions—for example, if qualifications depend on costly education and socialisation that are only available to the most advantaged. This leads to the need to go beyond formal equality of opportunity, since it is compatible with inequalities in achieved well-being. A focus on opportunity alone can also lead to a conception of social justice in which responsibility (and blame) for disadvantage is transferred to the individual, and structural inequalities are ignored.

Rawls' (1971) doctrine of Fair Equality of Opportunity acknowledges the existence of background inequalities and extends formal equality of opportunity to stipulate that, as well as opportunities being open to all, all should have 'a fair chance to attain them' (p. 73). The related 'level playing field' account (e.g. Roemer 1998) states that inequalities resulting from unchosen circumstances should be eliminated, but inequalities resulting from choices that a person makes are permissible. This version of equality of opportunity is held up as an ideal in liberal democracies, partly because it includes individual responsibility as a central consideration in how justice is evaluated. For example, in his address to the 2015 Conservative Party conference, the then UK prime minister cited equality of opportunity as a fundamental 'Conservative value' (Cameron 2015).

However, there are serious objections to equality of opportunity as the basis of an account of well-being and social justice. The first objection concerns the practicality of the concept of fair equality of opportunity. This ideal is designed to acknowledge that background socio-economic inequalities can damage people's ability to access opportunities that are, in some formal respect, open to them. However, specifying what counts as 'a fair chance' may prove impossible, especially in societies in which a person's values, social roles and aspirations are shaped by entrenched cultural norms around unchosen characteristics such as gender, class and race. There is often no neat division between what a person can be held responsible for and the influence of unchosen circumstances.

The second objection is that equality of opportunity is compatible with severe inequality of outcomes—the things in life that really matter. Final ends (outcomes) are, by definition, outside the scope of equality of *opportunity*. A theory of well-being and justice should recognise that opportunities are necessary but not sufficient; they are at best intermediate ends that are instrumental in the achievement of the ultimate end of living a good life. Additionally, even *within* the scope of equality of opportunity, some consideration of outcomes is desirable for two reasons. First, inequality of outcome can be a good indicator, at least at the group level, of underlying inequality of opportunity (Phillips 2004); second, every outcome is also an opportunity for future well-being, as advantages engender further accumulative advantages (Chambers 2009).

In summary, while resources and opportunities both seem important in some respects, individually and together they provide only a partial view of well-being as the currency of social justice, since final ends remain out of scope.

Equality of Subjective Welfare

An alternative position, and one that brings in a valuable end, is that the most suitable currency of egalitarian justice is 'welfare' (e.g. Arneson 1989). On the welfarist account, welfare is traditionally understood as either preference satisfaction or 'hedonic' welfare; the latter defined as 'a desirable or agreeable state of consciousness' (Cohen 1989, p. 909). The welfarist approach evolved from the classical utilitarianism associated with Jeremy Bentham, and it is this tradition that provides the theoretical foundations of 'the new science of happiness' (Layard 2005), which has found popularity in some policy circles (Bache and Reardon 2016).

In this most recent incarnation of welfarism, the term 'welfare' has been replaced with the more politically palatable 'well-being', defined as an agreeable subjective state. It is measured using indicators of happiness (a hedonic indicator), life satisfaction (a preference satisfaction indicator) and other positive states of consciousness, such as feelings of self-worth (e.g. ONS 2011a). The Subjective Well-being (SWB) approach goes beyond equality of resources and opportunities and places ultimate value on the final end of a positive state of consciousness consisting of pleasure and satisfaction. Advocates of SWB argue that it is anti-paternalistic and democratic, since it takes into account people's own evaluations of their own lives (Diener et al. 2009). Another crucial advantage of the SWB approach is that it is easily measured through social surveys and can be analysed using standard econometric techniques (e.g. Powdthavee 2010). The growing popularity of SWB as the default conception of well-being and therefore the favoured currency of justice was highlighted by a British economist who claimed on a prime-time television programme that 'In a decade's time we're going to be using happiness as the sole basis for judging the impact of public policy' (Dolan 2014).

There are, however, numerous objections to subjective well-being as the currency of justice, which apply to both the hedonic and preference-satisfaction versions. Taking first preference satisfaction (reflected in survey measures of 'Life Satisfaction'), the SWB approach does not distinguish between preferences that are normatively different. For example, sadists' and racists' preferences for harming or discriminating against others should not be counted as equally important for justice as other preferences. This has been called the problem of *offensive* tastes (Cohen 1989). The problem of *expensive* tastes is that, on a strong welfarist position (i.e. one where SWB is all that matters), the egalitarian must give more to a billionaire with a preference for expensive caviar and champagne than to a poor person who is satisfied with a diet of cheap food. Related to this is the problem of *adaptive preferences*, whereby the billionaire who is unable to satisfy his preference for champagne and caviar suffers a hedonic deficit, while a person living in multidimensional poverty remains cheerful in the face of disadvantage, having learned to accept their lot and 'take pleasure in small mercies' (Sen 1985). The strong welfarist or subjective well-being position again entails a counterintuitive conclusion, this time that policy should focus on rectifying the billionaire's hedonic shortfall, rather than on the poverty of the poor but cheerful person.

These objections lead to two conclusions. First, agreeable states of consciousness are not the only thing that matter in people's lives. Second, subjective well-being data is an unreliable source of information for socially just policy-making.

Beyond SWB: Equality of Capability

An approach to well-being that meets the criterion of value pluralism is the Capabilities Approach (Sen 1985; Nussbaum 2000). The Capabilities Approach (CA) was designed in response to the objections outlined above against resourcism and welfarism, and in recognition of the need to 'expand the informational basis' of evaluations of well-being and justice (Sen 1985). The foundational claim of the CA is that well-being is a question of the real freedoms (capabilities) people have to achieve valuable 'beings and doings' (known as 'functionings')—to live the kinds of lives they have reason to value. Proponents of the CA argue that the aim of public policy ought to be the expansion of capabilities—the space within which people can develop a conception of the good life, and have the opportunity and ability to live in accordance with that conception.

The CA conceives of well-being as determined by characteristics of individuals in interaction with features of their social, political and material environments. It deals with the question of differential conversion of resources into well-being through its theorisation of 'conversion factors' (Sen 1985). Conversion factors at the individual, social and environmental levels determine the rate of conversion of resources into capabilities (freedoms and opportunities) and functionings (outcomes). To illustrate, Sen (1985) gives the example of the resource of a bicycle. The capability of a woman who owns a bicycle to achieve the valuable functioning of independent mobility depends on various characteristics of her as an individual—such as whether she knows how to ride a bicycle and is physically fit enough to do so. It also depends on the external social and material environment—for instance, whether there are roads in good enough condition for bicycle riding, and whether local cultural norms allow or prohibit the riding of bicycles by women. The CA therefore entails multilevel measurement pluralism, since as well as measuring multiple outcomes, full capabilities assessments account for features of the individual *and* the external environment.

The next section illustrates how different accounts of well-being lead to different practical conclusions in relation to policy and social justice.

WELL-BEING, POLICY AND SOCIAL JUSTICE

The UK Measuring National Well-being programme is subtitled 'Measuring What Matters'. This entails two questions: (1) What matters? and (2) How should it be measured? The discussion above demonstrates that, while resources, opportunities and subjective well-being are each important, none is sufficient (on its own) as a conceptualisation of well-being and as a currency of social justice. Instead, justice should be grounded in a pluralist conception of well-being, whereby well-being is constituted by being well-off in multiple domains of life. This implies not only definitional pluralism, but also measurement pluralism, since the measurement of only resources, opportunities or subjective states is insufficient to reveal how well a person's life is actually going. More information is required. To illustrate this argument with respect to the welfarist SWB approach, this section draws upon empirical evidence about the impacts of economic crisis on people's lives in the UK and shows how measures of SWB failed to reflect the real impacts of the 'Great Recession' on people's lives and capabilities.

Economic Crisis, Well-Being and Social Justice

The global financial crisis that began in 2007 led to economic downturns in countries across the world. The economic crisis in the UK had many negative impacts on individuals and households in multiple domains. As would be expected, there were important impacts in the economic domain, but there were also wider impacts beyond direct economic effects. The following evidence is based on analysis of UK data from the European Social Survey (ESS 2014). Each of the figures below shows the impact of economic crisis in a particular domain of well-being. In each case, the period of economic crisis ('Hard Times'— 2008 to 2012) is compared with the time period immediately before it ('Times of Plenty'—2002 to 2006). Vertical inequalities (differences between income groups) are also shown. Table 3.1 contains all supporting data.

Direct Economic Effects

Figure 3.1 illustrates the impact of economic crisis in the domain of material security, showing the change in the proportion of people reporting that they were finding their household financial situation 'difficult' or 'very difficult'.

Figure 3.1 shows a statistically significant increase in material insecurity during the economic crisis among the UK population as a whole. The capability to live in material security is foundational: income and wealth are among Rawls' basic primary goods, and Aristotle argued that sufficient material resources are a necessary condition for a good life. Figure 3.1 therefore supports the idea that economic crisis was a constraint on well-being. This evidence corroborates findings from other studies of the economic crisis:

> [I'm] not able to clothe the kids in a certain manner… kids [add] another dimension. You can't take them anywhere. Even a bus to Heaton Park is too expensive.

> Manchester resident (Lupton et al. 2014)

The figure also shows that effects in this domain were not evenly distributed across the population, but concentrated among the less well-off. Material insecurity was higher among the less well-off group in both periods and increased more among the less well-off during the crisis. Economic crisis compounded inequality and social injustice in this domain.

Another direct economic effect of the crisis was the impact on employment. Employment is valuable in many ways, including its contribution to social connection, self-respect and material security.

Table 3.1 Economic crisis and well-being: descriptive statistics

Group	Period	Domains of well-being						SWB (average score)	
		Material Security (% finding things 'difficult' or 'very difficult')	Health (% 'Bad' or 'Very bad')	Social Isolation (% meet socially once a month or never)	Work and skills[a] (% 'Not true' or 'A little true' that you learn new skills at work)	Education (% currently enrolled in education)	Green Space[b] (% who access once a week or more)	Life satisfaction	Happiness
Population	Times of Plenty	14.70 (±0.06)	7.41 (±0.01)	8.71 (±0.00)	15.58 (±0.49)	8.20 (±0.13)	54.00 (±2.84)	7.06 (±0.01)	7.45 (±0.03)
	Hard Times	18.13 (±0.09)	8.23 (±0.02)	10.67 (±0.00)	20.99 (±0.70)	4.70 (±0.04)	48.00 (±1.85)	7.13 (±0.01)	7.45 (±0.01)
	Valid n	13,237	13,387	13,392	1755	13,403	3670	13,346	13,381
Below median income	Times of Plenty	22.33 (±0.33)	9.32 (±0.03)	10.50 (±0.00)				6.85 (±0.02)	7.31 (±0.03)
	Hard Times	29.89 (±0.64)	10.98 (±0.02)	12.88 (±0.00)				6.83 (±0.03)	7.19 (±0.03)
Above median income	Times of Plenty	7.39 (±0.04)	2.60 (±0.00)	6.36 (±0.00)				7.40 (±0.05)	7.68 (±0.05)
	Hard Times	8.52 (±0.04)	3.16 (±0.00)	9.18 (±0.00)				7.47 (±0.04)	7.77 (±0.04)

Notes

Unless otherwise stated, data are from the European Social Survey. Period 1 ('Times of Plenty') refers to rounds 1–3 (2002–2006), and Period 2 (Hard Times) refers to rounds 4–6 (2008–2012).

For ease of interpretation, the table shows confidence intervals at the 95% level (in parentheses). Standard errors are available on request.

[a]For this question, data for Period 1 are from 2004. Data for Period 2 are from 2010. This question appeared in a rotating module in these two survey years only

[b]For this question, data from DEFRA (2009) Public Attitudes and Behaviours towards the Environment tracker survey. Period 1 are from 2007. Period 2 are from 2009

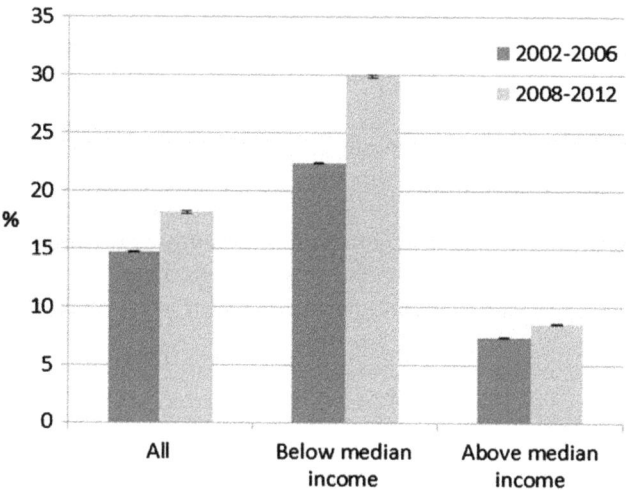

Fig. 3.1 Household income (finding things difficult or very difficult)

I was made redundant...I'm really rationing with the little funds that I have...I'm really stressed out you know...I've [dug] into savings and there's nothing left.

Birmingham resident (Slay and Penny 2013)

There were large increases in unemployment during the crisis, particularly among young people (Bell and Blanchflower 2011). The data also show that economic crisis had negative impacts in the domain of education and skills: during hard times, there were statistically significant decreases in the proportion of people enrolled in education; for those in work, fewer reported that they were learning new skills (Table 3.1). This suggests that economic crisis was a constraint on many people's capability to pursue self-development in the form of education and meaningful employment.

Non-economic Effects

As well as economic effects, the crisis also had wider, non-economic effects. A study of the UK population showed that as well as material security, people place priority value on their health and social relationships (ONS 2011b). Figure 3.2 shows the domain of health and the change in the proportion of people reporting that their health was 'bad' or 'very bad'.

The data show statistically significant declines in health during the economic crisis among the population as a whole, and across income groups. There are likely to be multiple causes of deteriorating health, and this analysis does not distinguish between physical and mental health issues. However, unemployment, financial stress and cuts in health spending and disability support payments (Lupton et al. 2015) are likely contributors. Also related to the health domain, the use of green space declined significantly during the economic crisis (Table 3.1). This could be due to individuals and families having lower capabilities for leisure, in terms of material resources and time, and funding cuts at local authority level for maintenance of parks and public green space (HLF 2014). Overall, the data show that economic crisis diminished people's capabilities to lead healthy lives.

Social relationships emerged as another highly valued domain in the UK (ONS 2011b). Figure 3.3 shows the effects of hard times on social isolation.

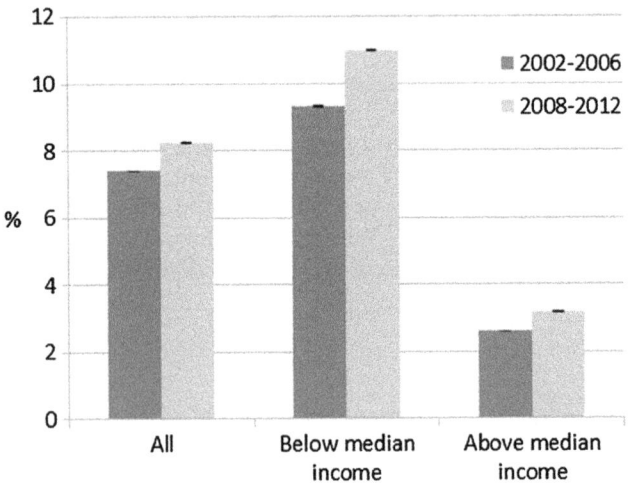

Fig. 3.2 General health (bad or very bad)

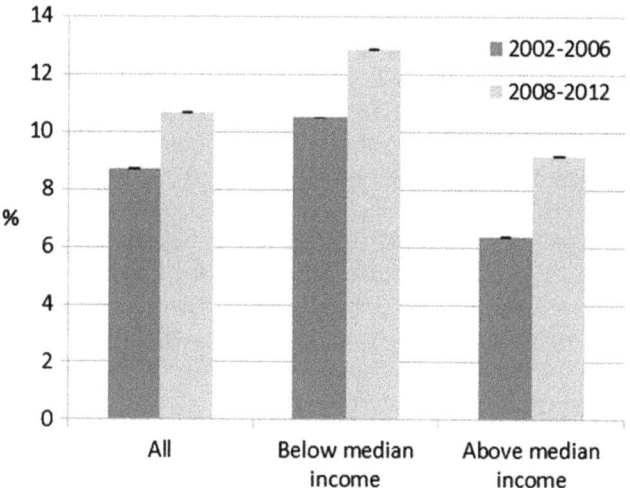

Fig. 3.3 Social isolation (meet socially once a month or never)

The data show statistically significant increases in social isolation during hard times. The quote below from a participant in a study about the effects of economic crisis summarises one of the ways in which hard times can have a direct effect on people's social relationships:

> People will be focusing on their basic needs…You become more inward looking rather than outward looking and concerned about the community. All your energy is taken up just surviving and holding it together.
>
> Birmingham resident (Slay and Penny 2013)

There are multiple other ways in which economic crisis might be expected to harm social relationships. For example, a reduction in disposable income may reduce people's ability to participate in social activities such as going out with friends, attending clubs or classes that cost money, or getting a bus or train for social visits and activities. Whatever the mechanisms, the data support the idea that economic crisis harmed social well-being.

Taken together, the evidence strongly supports the hypothesis that economic crisis posed external constraints on well-being in terms of people's capabilities to lead good, flourishing, meaningful lives. In addition, there is further evidence that economic crisis also created internal, subjective constraints on people's lives. Popular discourse and the interdisciplinary literature relating to the Great Recession suggest that economic crisis caused 'a downsizing of expectations' (Pew 2010) resulting in 'the crushed dreams of millions' (Treas 2010). In support of the idea of economic crisis posing subjective constraints on people's horizons of aspiration, research shows that during hard times there was widespread downgrading of goals and aspirations in the UK, away from ambitions involving creativity, self-development and adventure, towards basic security and survival goals such as safety and stability—a sort of 'hunkering down' in the face of economic crisis (Austin 2016b). Recall that the CA defines well-being in terms of people's freedom to achieve valuable outcomes, given their external environment and individual characteristics. This evidence shows that the Great Recession created not only external constraints on people's capabilities to flourish, but also internal constraints.

Subjective Well-Being

Overall then, there is strong evidence that economic crisis in the UK had negative effects in multiple domains of well-being, both in terms of people's opportunities for and achievement of valuable outcomes, and their internal lives, goals and aspirations. However, there was one domain that remained immune from the effects of hard times—the domain of subjective well-being. Figures 3.4 and 3.5 show the trends over time.

The data show that average happiness and life satisfaction scores were not affected during the period of hard times. The trends are flat, with no statistically significant variation at the population level or within income groups. These results are in line with other research using other data relating to the effects of the recent economic crisis on subjective well-being in the UK (e.g. Crabtree 2010; ONS 2012; OECD 2013), as well as past economic crises in other parts of the world (Veenhoven and Hagenaars 1989).

Although the SWB approach to well-being and justice goes beyond resources and opportunities to incorporate a final end, its focus is restricted to a single end only—an agreeable mind-state. This represents too narrow a conception of well-being, and, moreover, SWB suffers from distorted links to other important ends, as shown by the findings above

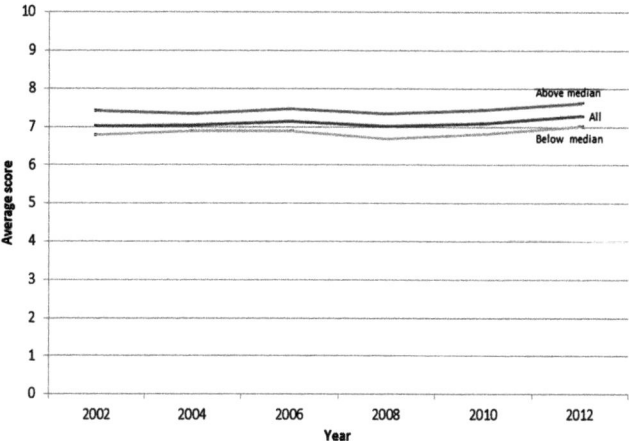

Fig. 3.4 Trends in life satisfaction

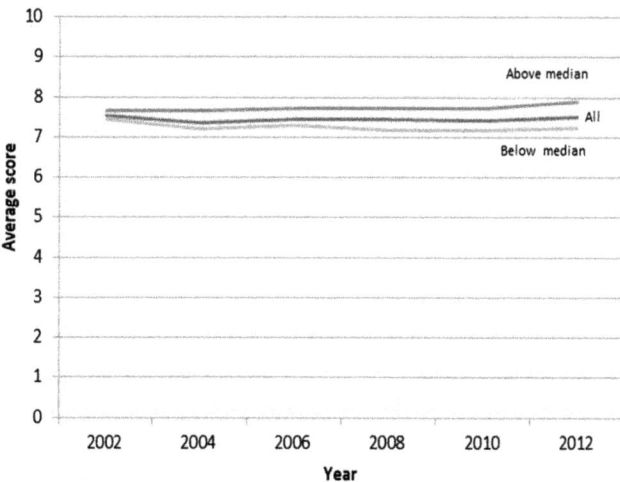

Fig. 3.5 Trends in happiness

that, in parallel with widespread negative impacts on people's capabilities in multiple domains, average SWB remained constant throughout the economic crisis in the UK.

DISCUSSION

As highlighted earlier, both the definition and metrics of well-being are important in specifying its role in public policy and social justice.

Defining Well-Being

With respect to the definition of well-being, an agreeable subjective state is only one among a plurality of important outcomes that people value. Similarly, resources and opportunities are necessary conditions for living a good life, but neither is sufficient. The CA clarifies and formalises the relationships between resources ('commodities'), opportunities ('capabilities') and outcomes ('functionings'). It conceptualises well-being as a function of features of the person and their environment, creating a framework for comprehensive evaluations of well-being and social justice that include both individual and structural factors.

The CA was designed as a broad theoretical framework, to be tailored to specific populations and contexts. Some theorists refrain from specifying which capabilities are most important, and say that this is an empirical question: it is context-specific and should be decided through the democratic participation of the relevant population (e.g. Sen 2002). Others argue for the existence of a core set of capabilities that are universally valuable. Nussbaum (2000) specifies a list of ten 'Central Human Functional Capabilities' which, she argues, are political entitlements that should be guaranteed to all people by state constitutions. The list consists of domains such as 'Bodily Health', 'Affiliation' and 'Control over one's Environment'. Nussbaum argues that the central capabilities are deliberately specified at a high, abstract level that can accommodate individual and cultural variation and are compatible with the principles of political liberalism. Nevertheless, her approach of stipulating specific core capabilities has been criticised as anti-democratic and paternalistic (e.g. Barclay 2003).

This question of outcomes—which are most important and who should decide—poses a dilemma for the CA. Sen's approach has been criticised for being too 'thin' and abstract to be of practical use (e.g. Rawls 1999), while Nussbaum's thicker approach is open to paternalism objections. The paternalism objection can be rebutted by conceiving of the central capabilities as an 'overlapping consensus', a broad consensus on a set of values that can form the basis of an agreement between different parties, while leaving room for individual and cultural diversity (Nussbaum 2000, p. 232). The inclusion of freedom, agency and practical reason as universal values further responds to the paternalism objection (Nussbaum 2000, p. 51). It can also be argued that a failure to set out an agreed set of universal values risks leaving a vacuum in which a much more damaging kind of paternalism can thrive (Nussbaum 2000, pp. 34–106).

The CA is sometimes criticised on similar grounds to equality of opportunity. For example, the emphasis on individual freedom leads some to conclude that the CA ignores the social-relational character of personhood and well-being (e.g. Dean 2009). It is also argued that, like equality of opportunity, the CA over-values hypothetical possibilities to the detriment of actual outcomes, and once again risks missing that which is most important in people's lives (Reader 2006).

The two objections of individualism and failure to focus on achieved outcomes are, however, misreadings of the CA. First, both Sen and Nussbaum defend relational definitions of well-being. Nussbaum's CA is explicitly grounded in an Aristotelian definition of the person as a social animal who depends on her social environment for her development of basic human capacities (Nussbaum 2000, p. 84) and derives her self-concept and well-being from her relationships of love, belonging and solidarity (Nussbaum 2007). Similarly, Sen argues that human beings are 'quintessentially social creatures', and that 'No individual can think, choose or act without being influenced in one way or another by the society around him or her' (Sen 2002, p. 80). Sociality and relationality are at the heart of the CA.

Second, the need to include achieved functionings (outcomes) in evaluations of well-being and justice is also recognised by both Sen and Nussbaum. For example, Sen (1992, p. 51) states that, to know how well a person's life is going, 'we do, of course, need to know what is chosen from each set, and not just what the set is from which the choice is being made'. He uses the term 'refined functionings' to refer to the combination of capabilities and functionings (e.g. 1985, p. 202). Refined functionings have been argued to represent 'the most complete informational basis' for evaluations of well-being and justice (Fleurbaey 2006). They represent a promising compromise between the thin and thick versions of the CA and are a strong candidate for a currency of justice.

Measuring Well-Being

The evidence also demonstrates the importance of how well-being is measured. As noted above, the 'new science of happiness' has gained momentum in recent years; however, empirical findings about the impacts of economic crisis demonstrate that subjective indicators do not always reliably reflect the actual quality of people's lives. While various sources show that hard times had no effects on national happiness and life satisfaction, analysis of separate spheres of well-being shows that there were real impacts on important aspects of people's lives. This demonstrates that the complexity of what it means to lead a good, flourishing life cannot be reduced to a subjective well-being metric. A reliance on SWB alone would entail different policy action to a pluralist measurement approach. A pluralist approach to the definition and measurement of individual and collective well-being provides domain-specific detail that can guide policy-makers to where action or intervention is most urgent.

As well as population-wide impacts, there were also vertical and horizontal inequalities[2] in the effects of hard times: impacts were concentrated among the least well-off and the young, and existing inequalities were compounded by the crisis. The finding that SWB indicators failed to reflect this crucial matter of justice supports the 'adaptive preferences' objection to a strong welfarist position.

The CA helps to make sense of what happened in people's lives during the Great Recession. In terms of 'combined capabilities' (the combination of personal and external factors that constitute capability), economic crisis can be seen as an external constraint that reduced people's ability to live well in multiple domains. Research also shows that, in addition to creating external constraints, economic crisis led to internal constraints on expectations and aspirations. Economic crisis therefore had a two-fold effect on well-being. This again reinforces the argument that the evaluation of social injustice requires a pluralist account of well-being that recognises both individual and contextual constraints on flourishing. The CA does not exclude resource-based or subjective indicators, but includes them as parts of a wider set of information that goes beyond a simplistic reliance on GDP or SWB.

The simplicity of an SWB metric is, however, one of its attractions as a definition of well-being and a currency of justice. The CA is richer and more informationally demanding than resourcist and welfarist approaches. Some doubt the very possibility of measuring 'freedom', which is constituted by unobservable hypothetical opportunities (e.g. Srinivasan 1994). However, there is much innovation in the measurement of capabilities and refined functionings on a large scale (e.g. Krishnakumar 2007; Anand et al. 2009), and there are successful examples of the approach in operation; for example, at the UK's Equality and Human Rights Commission (EHRC 2007). More challenging measurement requirements are not an adequate reason to discount the relevance of the CA to well-being and social justice (although they may explain why it is less popular than the SWB approach in some policy circles).

Conclusion

This chapter began with the question, 'Equality of What?' I have argued that *well-being* is the appropriate currency of social justice. Defining well-being in terms of resources, opportunities or subjective states all have merit, but each provides only a partial perspective. The Capabilities Approach brings together the most important aspects of these partial conceptions within a single approach. Definitional and measurement pluralism make the CA informationally demanding. However, the CA provides a sophisticated conceptualisation of the multilevel and multidimensional nature of well-being, and a sound currency of social justice.

Notes

1. In this chapter, the term 'well-being' (with a hyphen) is used in preference to the unhyphenated 'wellbeing'. This is to emphasise an Aristotelian conception of well-being as a dynamic process of living (*being*) well in the social world. 'Wellbeing' (unhyphenated) is used only in the context of 'subjective wellbeing' (SWB).
2. Vertical inequalities relate to differences between those with different incomes. Horizontal inequalities are inequalities among groups defined by different characteristics, such as age group, ethnicity or gender.

References

Anand, P., Hunter, G., Carter, I., Dowding, K., Guala, F., & Van Hees, M. (2009). The Development of Capability Indicators. *Journal of Human Development and Capabilities, 10*(1), 125–152.
Arneson, R. (1989). Equality and Equal Opportunity for Welfare. *Philosophical Studies, 56*, 77–93.

Austin, A. (2016a). On Well-Being and Public Policy: Are We Capable of Questioning the Hegemony of Happiness? *Social Indicators Research, 127*(1), 123–138.

Austin, A. (2016b). Practical Reason in Hard Times: The Effects of Economic Crisis on the Kinds of Lives People Have Reason to Value. *Journal of Human Development and Capabilities, 17*(2), 225–244.

Bache, I., & Reardon, L. (2016). *The Politics and Policy of Wellbeing: Understanding the Rise and Significance of a New Agenda.* Cheltenham: Edward Elgar.

Barclay, L. (2003). What Kind of Liberal is Martha Nussbaum? *Nordic Journal of Philosophy, 4*(2).

Bell, D., & Blanchflower, D. (2011). Young People and the Great Recession. *Oxford Review of Economic Policy, 27*(2), 241–267.

Cameron, D. (2015). Conference Speech 2015. Available at: http://press.conservatives.com/post/130746609060/prime-minister-conference-speech-2015. Accessed June 6, 2016.

Chambers, C. (2009). Each Outcome is Another Opportunity: Problems with the Moment of Equal Opportunity. *Politics, Philosophy & Economics, 8*(4), 374–400.

Cohen, G. A. (1989). On the Currency of Egalitarian Justice. *Ethics, 99,* 906–944.

Cooper, J. M. (1975). *Reason and Human Good in Aristotle.* Cambridge, MA: Hackett Publishing.

Crabtree, S. (2010). Britons' Well-Being Stable through Economic Crisis. London, Gallup 2010. Available at: http://www.gallup.com/poll/144938/britons-wellbeing-stable-economic-crisis.aspx. Accessed April 15, 2015.

Dean, H. (2009). Critiquing Capabilities: The Distractions of a Beguiling Concept. *Critical Social Policy, 29*(2), 261–273.

DEFRA. (2009). Public Attitudes and Behaviours towards the Environment, Department for Environment, Food and Rural Affairs, Environment Statistics Archive. Available at: http://archive.defra.gov.uk/evidence/statistics/environment/eiyp/index.htm. Accessed June 2, 2016.

Diener, E., Lucas, R., & Oishi, S. (2009). Subjective Well-Being: The Science of Happiness and Life satisfaction. In S. Lopez & C. Snyder (Eds.), *The Handbook of Positive Psychology* (2nd ed.). New York: Oxford University Press.

Dolan, P. (2014). Is Britain Happy? *Tonight, ITV* 23/10/14. Available at: http://www.itv.com/news/2014-10-23/tonight-is-britain-happy/. Accessed June 8, 2016.

EHRC. (2007). Fairness and Freedom: The Final Report of the Equalities Review. London: Equalities and Human Rights Commission. Available at: http://www.tedcantle.co.uk/publications/023%20Fairness%20and%20freedom%20%20report%20of%20the%20Equalities%20Review%20HM.pdf. Accessed June 8, 2016.

ESS. (2014). European Social Survey. Available at: http://www.europeansocial-survey.org/data/.

Fleurbaey, M. (2006). Capabilities, Functionings and Refined Functioning. *Journal of Human Development, 7*(3), 299–310.

HLF. (2014). State of UK Public Parks 2014. Heritage Lottery Fund. Available at: https://www.hlf.org.uk/state-uk-public-parks. Accessed June 15, 2016.

Krishnakumar, J. (2007). Going Beyond Functionings to Capabilities: An Econometric Model to Explain and Estimate Capabilities. *Journal of Human Development, 8*(1), 39–63.

Layard, R. (2005). *Happiness: Lessons from a New Science.* Penguin Press.

Lupton, R., Wong, C., Richardson, L., Webb, B., Kingston, R., & Shakeri, M. (2014). *Poverty In Greater Manchester: What Citizens Say.* University of Manchester, Greater Manchester Poverty Action Group and Church of England Diocese of Manchester.

Lupton, R., Burchardt, T., Fitzgerald, A., Hills, J., McKnight, A., Obolenskaya, P., et al. (2015). The Coalition's Social Policy Record: Policy, Spending and Outcomes 2010–2015. Social Policy in a Cold Climate Research Report 4. London School of Economics and University of Manchester, January 2015. Available at: http://www.nuffieldfoundation.org/news/coalition%E2%80% 99s-social-policy-record-policy-spending-and-outcomes-2010-2015.

Nussbaum, M. C. (2000). *Women and Human Development: The Capabilities Approach.* Cambridge: Cambridge University Press.

Nussbaum, M. C. (2007). *Frontiers of Justice: Disability, Nationality, Species Membership.* Cambridge MA: Harvard University Press.

OECD. (2013). How's Life? 2013. Paris: Organisation for Economic Co-operation and Development. Available at: http://www.oecd.org/std/3013071e.pdf. Accessed June 2, 2016.

ONS. (2011a). Measuring Subjective Well-Being for Public Policy: Recommendations on Measures. Newport: Office for National Statistics. Available at: http://eprints. lse.ac.uk/35420/1/measuring-subjective-wellbeing-for-public-policy.pdf.

ONS. (2011b). Measuring What Matters: National Statistician's Reflections on the National Debate on Measuring National Well-Being. Newport: Office for National Statistics.

ONS. (2012). Measuring National Well-Being: Life in the UK 2012. Newport: Office for National Statistics. http://www.ons.gov.uk/ons/rel/wellbeing/meas-uringnational-well-being/first-annual-report-on-measuringnational-well-being/ artmeasuring-national-well-being-annual-report.html. Accessed June 2, 2016.

Pew. (2010). *One Recession, two Americas.* Washington: Pew Research Centre 2010.

Phillips, A. (2004). Defending Equality of Outcome. *Journal of Political Philosophy, 12*(1), 1–19.

Powdthavee, N. (2010). *The Happiness Equation: The Surprising Economics of our Most Valuable Asset.* London: Icon Books.

Rawls, J. (1971). *A Theory of Justice* (Rev. ed. 1999). Oxford: Oxford University Press.

Rawls, J. (1999). *The Law of Peoples*. Cambridge, MA: Harvard University Press.

Reader, S. (2006). Does a Basic Needs Approach Need Capabilities? *Journal of Political Philosophy, 14*(3), 337–350.

Roemer, J. E. (1998). *Equality of Opportunity*. Cambridge: Harvard University Press.

Sen, A. (1985). *Commodities and Capabilities*. Amsterdam: North Holland.

Sen, A. (1992). *Inequality Reexamined*. Cambridge, MA: Harvard University Press.

Sen, A. (2002). Response to Commentaries. *Studies in Comparative International Development, 37*(2).

Slay, J., & Penny, J. (2013). *Surviving Austerity: Local Voices and Local Action in England's Poorest Neighbourhoods*. London: New Economics Foundation.

Srinivasan, T. (1994). Human Development: A New Paradigm or Reinvention of the Wheel? *American Economic Review, 84*(2), 238–243.

Stiglitz, J., Sen, A., & Fitoussi, J. (2009). Report by the Commission on the Measurement of Economic Performance and Social Progress. Available at: http://ec.europa.eu/eurostat/documents/118025/118123/Fitoussi+ Commission+report. Accessed September 20, 2015.

Treas, J. (2010). The Great American Recession: Sociological Insights on Blame and Pain. *Sociological Perspectives, 53*(1), 3–17.

Veenhoven, R., & Hagenaars, A. E. (1989). *Did the Crisis Really Hurt? Effects of the 1980–1982 Economic Recession on Satisfaction, Mental Health and Mortality*. Rotterdam: Rotterdam University Press.

CHAPTER 4

The Proper Role for Wellbeing in Public Policy: Towards a Pluralist, Pragmatic, Theory-Neutral Approach

Tim E. Taylor

INTRODUCTION

In recent years, the long-standing dominance of economic growth as the central policy goal of governments has increasingly been challenged. The reasons for this include concerns that GDP takes no account of the distribution of benefits and includes activity that is arguably detrimental rather than beneficial.[1] There is also a body of empirical research, beginning with the work of Richard Easterlin in the 1970s, which suggests that, at least in wealthy countries, levels of happiness over time do not correlate strongly with GDP. This called into question the assumption that GDP can be taken as a proxy for national wellbeing (Easterlin 1974).[2]

For a long time, it was commonly assumed by economists that there was no real alternative to GDP as a measure of national wellbeing. That assumption too is now widely rejected, both by practitioners of other disciplines and increasingly within economics itself, in the light of extensive

T. E. Taylor (✉)
Interdisciplinary Ethics Applied Centre, University of Leeds, Leeds, UK
e-mail: phltet@leeds.ac.uk

© The Author(s) 2018
I. Bache and K. Scott (eds.), *The Politics of Wellbeing*, Wellbeing in Politics and Policy, https://doi.org/10.1007/978-3-319-58394-5_4

empirical research on what has become known as subjective wellbeing (SWB), a field which has been hailed by economists such as Richard Layard as a 'new science' (Layard 2011). Layard and other economists who have embraced SWB as a measure of wellbeing now believe that the goal of public policy should be to maximise wellbeing within society as measured by indicators that include SWB.

However, a number of objections have been made to the idea that wellbeing should be maximised, or even promoted, by governments. This chapter will identify some of the most important objections, assess their force, and draw some conclusions concerning the appropriate role for wellbeing in public policy.

Terminology

It will be helpful at the outset to clarify the meanings of three distinct but closely related terms that appear in the literature. 'Wellbeing' in this context is roughly equivalent to 'quality of life'. It is a general term that reflects how well a person's life is going for them at a particular time: a person whose life is going well has high wellbeing.[3]

'Happiness' is a somewhat ambiguous term. It is sometimes used as a synonym for wellbeing. However, I would argue that in its primary sense it refers to a person's emotional and/or attitudinal[4] response to their life: a person is happy if their emotional state is positive and/or they have a high level of satisfaction with their life.[5] Happiness in this sense is *not* synonymous with wellbeing, though closely connected with it: one would, in general, expect a person whose life is going well to be happy, but it is possible to conceive of situations where this is not the case, or where a person is happy even though their life is going badly. These two senses of 'happiness' are not always clearly distinguished. In this chapter, I shall use it in what I consider its primary sense, to refer to a person's emotional/attitudinal response to their life. There is a further potential source of confusion in the fact that there are several competing theories of wellbeing, and some of these claim that it is wholly or partially consti-tuted by happiness (in this primary emotional/attitudinal sense).

SWB is a fairly recent term that emerged in psychology and has become the focus of a considerable body of empirical research. It has been defined as 'a person's cognitive and affective evaluations of his or her life' (Diener et al. 2009a). Research on SWB includes measures of both peoples' affective (emotional) state and their level of satisfaction with their lives (and sometimes particular aspects of their lives). SWB is thus quite close in meaning to 'happiness' in the primary sense discussed above, though there is room for argument about how close.[6]

Three Kinds of Objections

Objections to the idea that governments should promote wellbeing can be divided into three broad categories (these are discussed in more detail below). Firstly, there are ethical and ideological objections. Certain arguments target in particular the claim that wellbeing should be *maximised*—that it should be the ultimate aim of public policy, with other values having only derivative or, at best, secondary status. Others go deeper, claiming that governments should not attempt to promote wellbeing at all.

The second category of objections raises various political and practical issues that critics believe would attend any attempt to make wellbeing a policy goal for government. Some claim that governments cannot be trusted to promote (or measure) wellbeing, others that their attempts to do so would have little prospect of success, or would have undesirable consequences.

The third category of objections raises issues regarding what wellbeing is and how it should be measured. There are a number of competing theories of wellbeing and ways of measuring it, each of which is subject to criticism.

Do these objections undermine the case for the promotion of wellbeing by governments, or can they simply be refuted or ignored? Or is the reality somewhere in between these two extremes? In order to answer such questions, we need to look in more detail at the issues raised by these different kinds of objections.

ETHICAL AND IDEOLOGICAL OBJECTIONS

It seems sensible to look at the issues raised by the ethical and ideological objections first. If these objections were to prove justified, then the others would be irrelevant.

Objection (i) Wellbeing is primarily a concern of the individual and those close to her/him, rather than of government.

This view can be supported by the claim that the factors that influence wellbeing, such as social connectedness, rely more on individual choices rather than public policy (Duncan 2010, p. 173). Up to a point that claim is uncontroversial: it seems very plausible that people's personal aspirations and preferences, and the choices they make in pursuit of these, have a key influence upon their wellbeing. There are also limits on what governments can do to influence these factors: they cannot choose our friends or our personal projects for us, for example. But all this, and even the claim that wellbeing is *primarily* a concern of the individual, is compatible with the view that there is still *some* role for government here. Objection (i) as it stands thus suggests that there are limits on what governments can and should do to promote wellbeing. I will discuss this issue in more detail later on (under objection ix).

However, the objection could potentially be taken further. Perhaps it might be claimed that wellbeing is *exclusively* the concern of the individual. This would seem to imply a 'zero option': the idea that governments should not concern themselves with wellbeing *at all*. To assess this stronger claim we need to step back a little and consider what wellbeing is and why—contra this objection—people might regard it as something to which governments should pay attention.

The Value of Wellbeing

As discussed in the section on terminology above, the term 'wellbeing' denotes a state in which a person's life is going well. When we say that a person enjoys a high level of wellbeing at a particular time, we are saying that their life is going well, that it is in some sense[7] a good life (at that time). Thus, in saying that a person enjoys high wellbeing we are attributing a kind of positive value to their life. We are also, in effect, saying that wellbeing itself has a positive value. This does not necessarily imply that people care about their own wellbeing. We can conceive of individuals who are indifferent to it, and people do sometimes knowingly (or heedlessly) sacrifice it for the sake of other things they care about.

However, although not everyone is in the habit of reflecting consciously upon their wellbeing, I suggest that, if asked, an overwhelming majority of people would say that it *does* matter to them; that they do want their lives to go well. Even if people do not reflect consciously on whether they value their wellbeing as such, they are likely to value the constituents of their wellbeing. As noted above, there are different theories about what constitutes wellbeing. However, some of these (preference-satisfaction theories) define wellbeing in terms of what people value, whereas others will specify various constituents, such as pleasure, health or achievement, which in practice most of us do value, at least to some extent.

Thus, it is a reasonable generalisation that—for all or most people—their wellbeing is something that has value for them and matters to them (directly or indirectly). This does not imply that it is the only thing that matters, or that it trumps other values.

Respecting Wellbeing

We can now begin to address the stronger version of objection (i): that governments should not concern themselves with wellbeing *at all* (the 'zero option'). If wellbeing has value for people and matters to them, then an obvious thought is 'why would it *not* be a proper concern for government?' Surely governments ought to act for the benefit of their citizens. And what improves someone's wellbeing surely benefits that person, whereas what diminishes their wellbeing is a disbenefit to them.

We can back up that first thought with more detailed argument. The 'zero option' would imply not only that governments should not attempt to promote wellbeing, but that they should take no account of wellbeing whatsoever in determining public policy. This implies that, even if it could be predicted with a high degree of confidence that some course of action would have a *negative* impact on the wellbeing of a large number of people, governments should take no account of this in deciding what to do. This seems perverse: wellbeing matters to people. We do not need to claim that it is the only thing that matters or that it trumps other values to argue that it should be taken into account. We should therefore reject the 'zero option'. If wellbeing can be measured and reasonably predicted, it should at the very least be *respected* by governments in determining policy: that is, predictable negative effects on wellbeing should be taken into account.

Promoting Wellbeing

Is there a case in principle for going further and saying that governments should promote, rather than merely respect, wellbeing? 'Promoting' here means taking active steps intended to increase wellbeing. A government that seeks to promote wellbeing will want to implement policies likely to contribute to an upward trend in wellbeing, all else being equal. Promoting is not the same as maximising: promoting one value is consistent with also promoting another. Where they conflict some way would need to be found to strike a balance between them. But it is not possible to maximise two values—such as wellbeing and GDP—at the same time, if there is any conflict between them. Achieving the highest possible level of wellbeing may require accepting less than the highest possible level of GDP, and vice versa.

At this point, we need to consider a further objection. Sam Wren-Lewis (2013) has argued that the promotion of wellbeing by governments conflicts with political liberalism. He argues that:

Objection (ii) It is for individuals themselves to decide what a good life is for them; states should not 'promote a particular view of the good life'.

Wellbeing is not the only thing that people value, so promoting wellbeing is unfair to those who value other things more. The idea behind this objection is that governments should limit themselves to facilitating individuals' pursuit of their own goals. This thought is associated with Rawls' (1999) view that states should only concern themselves with providing the means ('primary goods') for people to pursue their own rational plans of life.

In arguing for this position, Wren-Lewis does not in fact oppose the promotion of wellbeing by governments *tout court*. Rather, he argues that the psychological aspects of wellbeing, as measured by SWB research, can be considered a Rawlsian primary good; he notes that positive affect has various advantages, such as making one more healthy and confident. These aspects of wellbeing can therefore legitimately be promoted by governments as a means to other ends, but they (and wellbeing in general) should not be promoted as ends in themselves. I wish to challenge this view: governments should promote wellbeing for its own sake, as an end in its own right, not merely as an enabler of other goals.

I have already argued that a person's wellbeing has value for that person; that people value their wellbeing and/or the constituents of their wellbeing. Why, then, would wellbeing not be something worth promoting in its own right? The promotion of wellbeing by government does not necessarily imply promoting a particular view of what constitutes wellbeing. It is compatible with an approach to wellbeing that is pluralist, flexible and respectful of individual sovereignty. Such an approach would, of course, have implications for how wellbeing could legitimately be promoted. Honouring the liberal concern to respect people's right to choose the kind of life they wish would suggest promoting wellbeing in ways that are not paternalistic: this leaves room for freedom of choice, and for a conception of wellbeing that respects individual sovereignty and allows for potential differences between people in what counts as a good life for them. It would rule out certain possible methods for promoting wellbeing, such as the compulsory medication of those prone to depression, but would leave many others open.

Wren-Lewis's response to this is that the freedom of choice that liberalism urges us to respect goes beyond the individual's right to decide what constitutes wellbeing for them, and includes the right to prioritise other things *over* wellbeing. He points out that not everybody values (their own) wellbeing to the same extent and that people value other things as well as—and perhaps sometimes more than—wellbeing. For example, people in collectivist cultures may value such things as group harmony and social cohesion (Wren-Lewis 2013, p. 3; Diener and Suh 2000). And people may sacrifice their wellbeing for others, or for an ideal. Wren-Lewis argues that the promotion of wellbeing by governments unfairly favours those people for whom wellbeing is their prime concern over others who may put other values first.

Wren-Lewis's factual claim is correct. People do often value other things beyond their own wellbeing, and the relative importance that people give to their own wellbeing in comparison with their other values will vary between individuals. However, this claim does not support the conclusion that governments should not promote wellbeing. The claim is not only true of wellbeing but also applies to all other values. It is true of *anything* that governments might seek to promote—economic prosperity, public health, the arts, environmental sustainability, for example—that not all citizens will value it to the same extent (if at all). A requirement that governments should only promote things that are valued by all citizens equally would be impossible to meet and would leave them unable to act for the benefit of their citizens at all. We should therefore reject objection (ii) on the grounds that it demands the impossible.

Maximising Wellbeing

The worry that promoting wellbeing is unfair to those who value other things speaks more strongly against the view that governments should seek to *maximise* wellbeing. A maximising strategy would treat wellbeing as a 'master value' and make the level of wellbeing within a society its dominant concern. Other values could be respected only insofar as they contribute to, or at least do not conflict with this objective. We can see how *this* would be objectionable to liberals who would want to respect the wishes of those who place other values over wellbeing.

At this point, we should consider some other possible objections that bear specifically on the idea that wellbeing should be maximised. First, let us consider:

Objection (iii) Maximising wellbeing as a single master value is wrong because it allows no independent role for considerations such as justice, the environment or human rights.

These things could have a bearing on policy only insofar as they contributed towards maximising wellbeing. To the extent that they conflict with this—suppose, for example, that we could maximise aggregate wellbeing by ignoring the human rights of a small number of people—they would be overridden, under a maximising strategy.

Defenders of objection (ii) would reject this dominant role for wellbeing on the grounds that it is unfair to people who care about things like the environment and human rights and might want them to take precedence over maximising wellbeing. Objection (iii) goes further—it invites us to consider that things like the environment and human rights may matter *in their own right*, not just because people happen to care about them.

One of the arguments that have been made against the dominant role of GDP in public policy is also applicable to the idea that happiness or wellbeing should simply replace GDP in the same monolithic role, leading to:

Objection (iv) The principle that we should maximise wellbeing tells us nothing about how it should be distributed. Maximising wellbeing is in principle compatible with great inequalities (Burchardt 2006).

This objection highlights another value that has a strong intuitive appeal—the idea of fairness in the distribution of wellbeing (and of the goods that enable us to enjoy wellbeing)—but which, again, can have no independent role in a maximising strategy. Maximisers would argue that the principle of diminishing marginal utility—the idea that someone who is worse off will gain more benefit from a given good than someone who is better off—would in practice work in favour of equality in the distribution of goods; and that large inequalities tend to cause resentments and tensions that are likely to militate against the maximisation of wellbeing. Their opponents would argue that there is no guarantee that maximisation would always be consistent with fair distribution, and that even if this were to be the case, it misses the point: they claim that fairness is important in its own right, not merely because it happens to be more efficient (in terms of maximisation) than unfairness (Burchardt 2006, p. 158).

Objection (v) Maximising implies that trade-offs can be made between the wellbeing of one person and that of another—a sacrifice of one person's wellbeing is justifiable by a larger gain in someone else's.

Contractarians object to the very idea of trade-offs, arguing that outcomes should be justifiable to each individual (Sugden 1989).[8] It is a structural feature of a maximising approach that it allows trade-offs between different people. Contractarians like Robert Sugden reject trade-offs entirely. Not everyone would accept a thoroughgoing contractarian position—many would accept some trade-off of the wellbeing of those who are well off in order to benefit those who are worse off, for example. However, a maximising strategy also implies that the reverse is acceptable, at least in principle: a sacrifice of the wellbeing of the worst off could be justified by greater gains to those who are better off. It is not only thoroughgoing contractarians who would regard this kind of trade-off as unacceptable. Trade-offs that benefit those who are already better off offend against our intuitive sense of fairness and the widely respected liberal principle put forward by Rawls as part of his second principle of justice, that social and economic inequalities are just if and only if they work as part of a scheme that improves the expectations of the least-advantaged members of society (Rawls 1999: 65–70, 266).[9]

It seems to me that the objections to maximising wellbeing (as opposed to merely promoting and/or respecting wellbeing) are collectively quite powerful. Considerations other than the total amount of wellbeing in a society, such as fairness in its distribution, human rights and the environment do have a strong intuitive appeal that constitutes a significant challenge to the maximising approach (though respecting such considerations is consistent with promoting wellbeing as one value among others). Broadly speaking, these objections reflect the wider criticisms that have been made of consequentialism and utilitarianism in ethics and political theory.[10]

With that in mind, we should consider a response made by some consequentialists to these criticisms (e.g. Hooker 2000). They accept that considerations such as fairness do have some force and might need to be respected in practical decision-making within a society, but argue that it is ultimately consequentialist considerations that underlie this force. Thus, for example, unfairness might be regarded as a bad thing because of its negative consequences such as resentment and conflict; that is because unfair distributions are inefficient, due to diminishing marginal utility (as already discussed). Thus, it is argued, in the long run, respecting considerations such as fairness is consistent with consequentialism. This view has been a factor in the development of various forms of indirect or 'rule' utilitarianism (Johnson 1991, pp. 17–19, 64–66; Hooker 2000).

A similar counter-argument might be made by defenders of a maximising approach to wellbeing. For example, they might use the argument given above about what gives fairness its force; and claim that our reasons for taking account of environmental considerations have to do with the negative effect of such things as climate change and pollution on the wellbeing of future (and to some extent present) generations, and possibly that of non-human animals.

This defence is itself open to challenge. Critics would continue to insist that the force of considerations such as fairness cannot be entirely accounted for in a consequentialist way and continues to hold when it parts company from consequentialist reasoning. However, the defence does make it difficult simply to dismiss the consequentialist position out of hand. The debate between consequentialists and non-consequentialists in ethics has been raging for many years and shows no sign of being resolved.[11]

However, in the present context, the power of the consequentialist defence is less than may appear at first sight. In its most plausible form, it is a philosophical claim about the origins of the normative force of non-consequentialist considerations, combined with an empirical (but not easily testable) claim about the long-term consequences of respecting or failing to respect such considerations.

Maximising wellbeing as a strategy in the context of public policy surely implies a more directly consequentialist approach, whereby increasing the overall level of wellbeing in a society, as indicated by wellbeing measures, would be the dominant goal of policy and those measures the single standard against which it would be measured.

Wellbeing measures capture only the wellbeing of present members of society. The wellbeing of future generations—and of non-human animals—is excluded. Thus, only the relatively short-term effects on the wellbeing of humans of considerations such as distributive justice, human rights and the environment could be taken into account by a strategy that sought to maximise measured wellbeing within a society. As a result, it is not only those who believe such considerations have value independently of their consequences for wellbeing who would object to such a strategy. Consequentialists should reject it too, since it does not enable long-term consequences to be taken into account. If these considerations are to be given a due role in public policy, they need in practice to be treated as separate values that have to be balanced against (or to constrain, perhaps) the promotion of wellbeing (even if the normative force of these values is to be explained ultimately in consequentialist terms).

I conclude, therefore, that even if one remains open to the possibility that the normative force of considerations such as distributive justice, human rights and the environment derives ultimately from consequentialist reasoning (and of course, many would deny this), such considerations do have a strong claim that cannot be fully accommodated within a maximising approach to wellbeing. As far as ethical considerations are concerned, there is every reason for governments to respect wellbeing and to promote it, but they should do so in a way that also respects other values that have a strong intuitive force. This militates against a maximising strategy and supports a more pluralist approach to public policy.

POLITICAL AND PRACTICAL ISSUES

We can now move on to the second category of objections. Even if wellbeing is in principle something that governments should promote, some doubt whether governments can be relied upon to do so.

Objection (vi) Making wellbeing a goal of public policy would give governments an incentive to manipulate wellbeing statistics to their own advantage, and also give individuals an incentive to misreport their own wellbeing in order to attract government support.

This point is made by Bruno Frey and Alois Stutzer (2010): they are talking specifically about measurement of happiness, but their points could also be applied to the measurement of wellbeing (see discussion above for the distinction between these two terms). Frey and Stutzer point out that governments have a history of changing the way in which indices such as unemployment statistics are compiled in order to suit their own purposes, typically to obscure data that might reflect badly upon them. They argue that if happiness was made an aim of public policy, governments would similarly manipulate the gathering of statistics in order to show themselves in a positive light.

The temptation for governments to show themselves in the best possible light is undeniable, and it is true that there have been many instances where statistics have been adjusted as a result. However, whilst this is clearly a potential problem, once it is recognised, attempts can be made to address it and therefore it does not constitute a valid objection to the view that wellbeing should be a consideration bearing on public policy.

The obvious way of addressing this risk is to make it more difficult for governments to manipulate wellbeing statistics, by placing responsibility for the gathering of those statistics outside the government chain of command. This has been done in the UK, for example, where in 2007, the Office for National Statistics, which is responsible for the gathering of data on wellbeing as in other areas, was made independent of government, reporting instead to a national Statistics Authority that is accountable directly to Parliament. Other safeguards that can help to reduce the risk of manipulation of wellbeing statistics are openness, consultation and public debate about the gathering of statistics and on their significance.

Similarly, though Frey and Stutzer's point that individuals might misrepresent their own happiness to attract government intervention identifies a potential difficulty, it is surely one that governments ought to be able to address, once aware of it. One means of doing so would be to measure wellbeing rather than happiness, and not to rely entirely on subjective as opposed to objective measures.

Over and above their worries about measurement, Frey and Stutzer also maintain a wider scepticism, believing that:

Objection (vii) Governments cannot be relied upon to promote happiness/wellbeing, particularly in democracies, where they are likely to respond instead to identifiable specific preferences of the electorate (Frey and Stutzer 2010).[12]

Again, there is some truth in this, but Frey and Stutzer's analysis seems overly pessimistic. If the public (and hence the electorate) shows no interest in wellbeing, then no doubt the motivation of government to promote it will be correspondingly weak. However, as we have already seen, wellbeing is something that citizens have reason to care about and in practice usually do care about. The extent to which this fact is likely to translate into an explicit concern for wellbeing that might affect voting behaviour and thus the motivation of governments will depend on the extent to which the notion of wellbeing and dialogue about its importance and role in public policy becomes established in the national consciousness. In the UK, there are encouraging signs that talk of wellbeing is becoming more widespread in society and government, though it remains to be seen whether this will be sustained in the long-term.

Others worry that:

Objection (viii) The adoption of wellbeing by governments as a policy goal might have undesirable impacts elsewhere—for example, the happiness of the many might conflict with the rights of the few.

Willem Van der Rijt (2014) is concerned that if people come to see their happiness as a right, they may be less willing to respect the rights of others, where these conflict with it. This seems to me to be a legitimate concern about a maximising strategy, under which the greater overall happiness/wellbeing will override minority rights. But we have already rejected a maximising approach to wellbeing. Under a more pluralist approach that seeks only to respect and promote wellbeing, other values such as the rights of minorities can be respected and promoted too.

This point goes a long way towards addressing Van der Rijt's concern but does not completely eliminate it. If wellbeing were seen as a 'right', then perhaps other rights that might otherwise constrain its promotion would be regarded as having no special status to justify their taking precedence over the promotion of wellbeing. In that case, there would be a greater danger of majoritarianism, as Van der Rijt fears. But there is no reason why endorsement of the promotion of wellbeing as a goal for public policy should be expressed in the language of rights. It is one thing to say that the improvement of general wellbeing is a desirable end that should bear upon the direction of policy, another to say that each individual has a *right* to the higher level of wellbeing that government intervention might potentially deliver. The case for promoting wellbeing is best expressed in consequentialist terms—though considerations such as minority rights may act as a constraint on how far governments should go in promoting it. Thus, Van der Rijt's point seems to bear more strongly on the language that governments should use in adopting wellbeing as a policy goal than on whether they should do so.

A final objection within this category is:

Objection (ix) It is not clear whether government intervention, however well intentioned, would actually succeed in raising overall levels of wellbeing within society.

We have already noted that there may be limits on what governments can do to influence wellbeing. Duncan (2010) has pointed out that there is, as yet, a lack of clear evidence of improvements in wellbeing as a result of government action (though there is certainly evidence of reductions in wellbeing due to bad government). He argues for caution regarding our expectations of even well-intentioned government programmes: just as the correlation between happiness and GDP growth in wealthy societies is weak, so might be the correlation between happiness and improvements in public services.

Others are more sanguine about the prospects of improving wellbeing over time. For example, Ed Diener and others examine the impact of processes such as adaptation and social comparison, which have been seen as militating against the possibility that intervention might succeed in changing wellbeing, concluding that the effects of these factors are not so large as to rule out the utility of wellbeing-based policy (Diener et al. 2009b, Chap. 6).

Perhaps it is right to be wary of over-optimistic expectations about what government intervention might achieve. However, I suggest that even if it were to prove true that attempts to raise the general level of wellbeing across the board have poor prospects of success, that does not imply that wellbeing should not have a role in public policy. Rather, it suggests that certain types of intervention are likely to be more productive than others. There will always be groups within society who, for one reason or another, experience wellbeing that is significantly lower than the general norm. If the prospects of improving general wellbeing are low (and this is not yet clear), this suggests that policies specifically aimed at improving wellbeing should be targeted at these disadvantaged groups, mitigating the factors that have adversely affected their wellbeing.

Objection (ix) does not diminish the importance of wellbeing as a consideration to be *respected* in pursuing other priorities. Where there are known associations between foreseeable consequences of possible government actions (such as unemployment) and reductions in wellbeing, that would be a *prima facie* reason not to pursue the course of action concerned, or to combine it with a plan to mitigate those adverse effects. It might not be conclusive, of course, depending upon the strength of the countervailing reasons, but once wellbeing is measured and recognised as a consideration relevant to public policy, it will be more difficult for governments to argue that it can legitimately be ignored.

Nor does the objection invalidate the role that wellbeing measures can play, in combination with other forms of information, in identifying priority areas for intervention (including, of course, identifying groups who experience wellbeing lower than the general norm) and in evaluating the success not only of interventions explicitly targeted at improving wellbeing but also of other initiatives.

The objections in this second category highlight a number of potential problems that may arise for the promotion of wellbeing by governments. These problems seem soluble at least to some extent; though they may affect how wellbeing can most effectively be promoted and how much can realistically be achieved. They call for the injection of a healthy dose of pragmatism into the promotion of wellbeing, but they do not provide any compelling reason to abandon the project.

DEFINING AND MEASURING WELLBEING

We come now to our third category of objections to the promotion of wellbeing. There are issues surrounding what wellbeing actually is, with implications for how (and whether) it should be measured. In particular:

Objection (x) There are a number of rival theories that make competing claims about what constitutes wellbeing. The question therefore immediately arises of what it is, exactly, that is to be maximised or promoted (Duncan 2010).

There has been a debate about what makes for a good life since the time of the Greek philosophers (see Bache and Scott, this volume, Chap. 1). Aristotle's account of *eudaimonia* (generally translated as 'happiness' or 'wellbeing') in terms of activity in accordance with virtue/excellence is still influential.[13] Other prominent contenders include hedonist theories, which define wellbeing in terms of pleasure or happiness (Feldman 2004); theories which define it in terms of the satisfaction of desires or preferences (Brandt 1979); and 'objective list' theories, which specify a heterogeneous set of goods that are held to contribute to wellbeing (Finnis 2011). An influential recent contender is the Capabilities Approach, which resembles an objective-list account, albeit with Aristotelian influences (Nussbaum 2000).

The debate between rival theories of wellbeing has been going on for centuries and shows no sign of being resolved. These theories make competing and incompatible claims about what constitutes wellbeing. If governments wish to promote wellbeing they must surely form a view about what wellbeing *is* in order to know what to promote. But how can they choose one of the competing theories without begging the intractable question of which theory is correct? Certainly, it seems question-begging to assume—as some advocates of SWB measures appear to—that SWB can be treated as equivalent to wellbeing. Furthermore, the controversy between the rival theories also gives rise to another objection regarding measures of wellbeing:

Objection (xi) All current measures of happiness and wellbeing either have known limitations or their validity is subject to challenge, typically from those who do not accept that the thing being measured is constitutive of wellbeing.

Thus, for example, those who favour more objective theories of wellbeing may believe that the value of happiness or life-satisfaction as a measure of wellbeing is vitiated by the fact that people adapt to their circumstances (Sen 1985, p. 22). Conversely, those who reject objective accounts of wellbeing ask what can justify the inclusion of some purported objective good upon a list (and thus the use of that good as a measure of wellbeing), if it is not ultimately people's subjective attitudes and concerns (Sumner 1996, pp. 45–60).

A Theory-Neutral Approach

The existence of rival theories of wellbeing, each widely supported in itself but disagreeing with the others on what constitutes wellbeing, threatens to create a serious obstacle to the measurement and promotion of wellbeing by governments. The worry is that even if—as I have argued above—wellbeing is in principle something that governments should indeed try to promote, it is not clear what promoting wellbeing would imply in practice, or how we would assess the success of wellbeing policy if all measures of wellbeing are also controversial.

However, there is a way out of this difficulty. Rather than being deterred by the differences between the competing theories of wellbeing, we can look for areas of common ground. The prospects of finding it are better than they might seem at first; once we recognise that, for the purposes of promoting wellbeing, we are not only interested in what is *constitutive* of wellbeing but also in what tends to be *productive* of wellbeing. Governments could promote wellbeing by targeting the latter as well as the former. And when it comes to measurement, we are also interested in things that are *indicative* of wellbeing. Whatever stands in one of these three relationships to wellbeing is relevant for the purposes of measuring it. I call such things 'markers' of wellbeing (Taylor 2015).

The important point for present purposes is that although the ongoing dispute about what constitutes wellbeing may be intractable, there is a much better prospect of consensus on the markers of wellbeing. This is because what is constitutive of wellbeing according to one theory may well be productive or indicative of wellbeing according to another. For example, health is a constituent of wellbeing for many objective theories of wellbeing. Subjective theories, such as hedonism or desire-satisfactionism will not regard it as a constituent in its own right—what counts as constitutive of wellbeing for those theories is, respectively, pleasure and the absence of pain, or the satisfaction of desires. Nevertheless, proponents of those theories would be likely to acknowledge health as something that is productive of wellbeing. Good health may be a source of pleasure, and bad health is certainly a source of pain. Similarly, good health is likely to be the object of some of our desires, and an enabler of the achievement of others. Thus, although the different theories will disagree on whether health is a constituent of wellbeing, they can nevertheless agree that it is a marker of wellbeing.

In earlier work (Taylor 2014, 2015), I have argued that it should be possible to identify markers of wellbeing that are shared, if not by all theories of wellbeing, then at least by the mainstream ones: those that are well-established—i.e. they have been around long enough to be tested through academic debate—and widely held. The four rival theories mentioned above—hedonism, desire/preference-satisfactionism, Aristotelian and objective-list theories—can all be seen as mainstream by this definition. If we regard the Capabilities Approach as, in effect, an objective-list approach with Aristotelian elements, and interpret hedonism broadly, to include views that define wellbeing in terms of how happy we are or how satisfied we are with our lives, these four categories can reasonably be regarded as encompassing *all* the mainstream theories.

To identify markers of wellbeing that can form the basis of a theory-neutral approach, we need to look for things that, from the standpoints of all of the mainstream theories, can be regarded as either: (a) at least partly constitutive of wellbeing; (b) reliably[14] productive of wellbeing; or (c) reliably indicative of wellbeing. I have already argued above that health could be accepted as a marker of wellbeing from a wide range of theoretical perspectives. For this purpose, I define it broadly to include all aspects of physical health: not only freedom from disease and injury, but also adequate nutrition and mental health.

Another marker that seems particularly secure is happiness, in the sense of having a positive emotional state and/or a high level of satisfaction with one's life. It is constitutive (wholly or partly) of wellbeing for hedonism, and also for certain objective-list and Aristotelian theories that include it alongside other goods. Some of our desires and preferences are for happiness, and for the positive emotional states that contribute towards it. To that extent, therefore, by satisfying those desires, happiness is productive of wellbeing, from the perspective of a desire-satisfaction theory. It also seems likely that people who do well in terms of Aristotelian and objective-list theories (those that do not already include happiness)—who have developed their physical and mental capacities or possess the objective goods specified by the theory—will tend to be happier than people who do not. Happiness is thus a likely indicator of wellbeing for objective theories.

Once health and happiness are accepted as markers of wellbeing consistent with the mainstream theories, we can make a case for other markers that have been shown to correlate well with these in the extensive empirical literature on wellbeing. On this basis, I have argued (Taylor 2015: pp. 81–87) that a number of further markers can be regarded as consistent with the mainstream theories: success in realising one's central life goals/values, supportive personal relationships, personal development, leisure, adequate income/resources and rewarding employment.

There is, of course, room for argument about which markers would be likely to be widely accepted, and *how* widely. Nevertheless, I think that there is a good prospect of finding an area of common ground broad enough to provide a shared basis for the measurement of wellbeing for the purposes of public policy. This would be a theory-neutral approach in that it would not require taking a stand on the debate between the rival theories of wellbeing, but would identify common ground between them regarding the markers of wellbeing.

Given the intractable debate between competing theories of wellbeing and the fact that no single measure of wellbeing is immune to challenge, there are good practical reasons for adopting a broad suite of measures including both objective and subjective components.[15] A theory-neutral approach based upon the identification of common ground between rival theories on the markers, as opposed to the constituents, of wellbeing provides a principled rationale for this strategy.

CONCLUSIONS

Having examined the three categories of objections to the promotion of wellbeing, I conclude that:

a. People's wellbeing is something that has value for them and matters to them (directly or indirectly). Thus, if the role of government is to serve its citizens, wellbeing is a proper concern of government policy.

b. Wellbeing should be *respected* by governments—they should take into account predictable adverse consequences for wellbeing in determining policy.

c. Governments should also *promote* wellbeing, at least in principle: the prospect of improving wellbeing is a consideration that should be taken into account in determining policy.

d. Governments should not seek to *maximise* wellbeing at the expense of all other values. Other considerations, such as human rights, the environment and fairness in distribution, have a claim to be taken into account in determining policy.

e. Liberal concerns about individual sovereignty and freedom of choice bear on *how* wellbeing should be promoted (avoiding paternalism).

f. Though it is prudent to examine the motives and practice of governments closely, there are no compelling reasons to assume *ab initio* that they can never be trusted to promote wellbeing, or that doing so will have unacceptable consequences elsewhere.

g. The prospects of improving levels of wellbeing in the general population through government intervention are subject to debate. If this were to prove difficult, intervention to promote wellbeing would be most effectively targeted at those whose wellbeing falls below the general norm.

h. Controversy concerning the definition and measurement of wellbeing can be addressed by identifying common ground between different theories, adopting a broadly based, theory-neutral approach to measurement, and by ensuring the political independence of data-gathering organisations.

In short, I conclude that there is good reason for governments to seek to promote wellbeing and no insuperable technical, political or practical obstacles that might prevent them from doing so. However, they should not seek to maximise wellbeing at the expense of other important values. Moreover, it remains to be seen how far, and in what ways, governments will succeed in promoting wellbeing.

This conclusion, and in particular the rejection of maximisation, implies that the adoption of wellbeing as a goal of public policy is less simple and straightforward than some of its advocates suggest. The wellbeing of current citizens must compete with other values such as the environment, and its pursuit will be constrained by considerations such as human rights. There will be room for argument about how the benefits of wellbeing policy should be distributed. That is all as it should be, but there is no simple formula for resolving the tensions between different values. There is no substitute for political debate as the means by which the strength of their competing claims can be tested. This has been recognised by Ian Bache, Louise Reardon and Paul Anand in a recent article in which they characterise wellbeing as a 'wicked problem'—one that is difficult to define and for which there are no definitive and objective answers. As they put it:

> Understanding wellbeing as a wicked problem … steers us towards deliberation and scrutiny as central to the agenda … cautions us against expecting to find a panacea, but can take us beyond irresolvable disputes by pointing to the need for pragmatic and legitimate government action. (Bache et al. 2016, p. 910).

NOTES

1. 'Gross National Product counts air pollution and cigarette advertising, and ambulances to clear our highways of carnage' (Kennedy 1968).
2. Though Easterlin's claims have been disputed (Veenhoven and Vergunst 2013).
3. In other contexts 'wellbeing' can mean other things—for example, a feeling of euphoria. It may also be used of things other than individual persons—e.g. communities.
4. The SWB literature tends to refer to life-satisfaction as a 'cognitive' evaluation of one's life (Diener et al. 2009a). I prefer the term 'attitudinal' (satisfaction is a positive attitude to one's life). However, I do not believe that anything hangs on the choice of terminology here.

Scheffler, S. (1988). *Consequentialism and Its Critics.* New York: Oxford University Press.

Sinnott-Armstrong, W. (2015). Consequentialism. In E. Zalta (Ed.), *The Stanford Encyclopedia of Philosophy* (Winter 2015 Edition). Available at: http://plato.stanford.edu/archives/win2015/entries/consequentialism/. Accessed October 24, 2016.

Smart, J., & Williams, B. (1973). *Utilitarianism: For and Against.* Cambridge: Cambridge University Press.

Sugden, R. (1989). Maximizing Social Welfare: Is it the Government's Business? In A. Hamlin & P. Pettit (Eds.), *The Good Polity: Normative Analysis of the State.* Oxford: Blackwell.

Sumner, W. (1996). *Welfare, Happiness, and Ethics.* New York: Oxford University Press.

Taylor, T. (2014). Towards Consensus on Well-Being. In J. H. Soraker, J.-W. van der Rijt, J. de Boer & P. H. Wong (Eds.), *Well-being in Contemporary Society.* Cham: Springer.

Taylor, T. (2015). The Markers of Wellbeing: A Basis for a Theory-Neutral Approach. *International Journal of Wellbeing, 5*(2), 75–90.

Van der Rijt, J.-W. (2014). The Political Turn Towards Happiness. In J. H. Soraker, J.-W. van der Rijt, J. de Boer & P. H. Wong (Eds.), *Well-Being in Contemporary Society.* Cham: Springer.

Veenhoven, R., & Vergunst, F. (2013). The Easterlin Illusion: Economic Growth Does Go With Greater Happiness. MPRA Paper No 43983, Munich Personal RepEc Archive. Available at: http://mpra.ub.uni-muenchen.de/43983/1/MPRA_paper_43983.pdf. Accessed June 26, 2016.

Wren-Lewis, S. (2013). Wellbeing as a Primary Good: Toward Legitimate Wellbeing Policy. *Philosophy and Public Policy Quarterly, 31*(2), 2–9.

PART II

Wellbeing: A Force for Political Change?

CHAPTER 5

Is Wellbeing a Useful Concept for Progressives?

Charles Seaford

INTRODUCTION

The crisis in politics—in the UK and much of the rest of the developed world—represents a breakdown of the deal between the political and economic elite and the mass of the population. 'Vote for us' (said the politicians), 'believe us' (said the experts) and 'accept our wealth' (said the business leaders)—'and we will deliver steadily improving lives for you and your children'. But the elite has not delivered on its part of the deal. As a result, the mass of the population has decided the deal is off— although many of the elite seem surprised and offended by this. In this chapter, I argue that progressives can use wellbeing concepts and evidence to help shape a new, and better, deal.

As everyone knows, an alternative and not very progressive deal is also on offer. In the USA, Donald Trump has been elected President. Across Europe, extreme right-wing politicians have been fostering fear and stoking up prejudices against minority groups, while proposing fewer immigrants and an assertion of old-fashioned national identity. In the UK, during the Brexit referendum campaign in 2016, one part of the Leave campaign's message was 'vote for us and at least you can belong

C. Seaford (✉)
An Economy that Works, London, UK

© The Author(s) 2018
I. Bache and K. Scott (eds.), *The Politics of Wellbeing*, Wellbeing in Politics and Policy, https://doi.org/10.1007/978-3-319-58394-5_5

to something you can call your own'. The political establishment has failed to respond in a convincing way to this threat, largely because it has continued to rely on the neoliberal theories that have guided economic policy over the last thirty years. Hillary Clinton really does believe that free trade is a good thing and many economic pundits still argue that the best way to improve lives is to reduce job security and cut pay (politicians themselves tend to avoid actually *saying* this).[1]

Of course, free trade generally is a good thing, and there is evidence that reduced job security and lower pay can reduce unemployment. That is not the point. The point, rather, is that free trade is sometimes a very bad thing, at least for some people, and job insecurity is a major cause of low wellbeing. The gains from trade have not been shared widely. These are realities that economic theory cannot overturn, so it is hardly surprising that elite wisdom based on that theory is being rejected. When the resulting populism turns the powerless into scapegoats, it is vile, but there is a progressive version that is quite different (although the elite like to elide the two). This progressive version would be strengthened if it were informed by wellbeing evidence.

This evidence is about what contributes to a good life and, assuming most people want a good life, it is therefore about how to deliver what most people want.[2] It helps answer the three big questions that are going to underpin any successful new deal between the elite and the mass of the population: how do people live? What will make their lives better? What does this require in practice? In doing so, it casts doubt on the easy assumptions of economists that growth and maximising employment, for example, is always a good thing. This means it can help open up the terms of the political debate from how best to manage an economic system—the main features of which are not called into question—to how best to deliver good lives. This then makes it easier to challenge the political and economic elites that run that system. Wellbeing concepts and evidence do not provide a complete solution, of course; they are only one set of tools amongst many. Moreover, as we shall see, the economic theory of wellbeing (that is the theory designed to help maximise wellbeing as opposed to welfare or utility) is still nascent. However, when the alternatives are the discredited neoliberalism of the traditional elite and the nationalism of the new right, then they are certainly worth looking at.

This chapter does that and is structured as follows. After a short account of wellbeing's rise to prominence, it sets out two different conceptions of wellbeing, how they are reconciled in the concept of flourishing, and how this can be measured. It then describes how well-being can be used in policy in general and its implications for economic policy in particular. It also describes how it can help those developing plans for sustainability. It then touches on its role as a unifying narrative before describing the way it can represent a break with standard welfare economics, and thus a break with the economic ideology that currently predominates. Finally, there are some very brief suggestions on next steps.

The Rise of Wellbeing

Over the thirty years to 2008, perhaps longer, the critics of capitalism were marginalised and government's role was seen as correcting a few market failures while maximising output and, depending on your political position, redistributing it to some extent. This was the process that was to deliver (and indeed often did deliver) improved chances of a good life. Not everyone has abandoned this *grow, tax and spend* model, but since 2008 it has become clear to a steadily widening group, even within the elite, that it cannot deliver better lives (that is improved wellbeing) for the mass of the population, and certainly not in a sustainable and socially just way.[3] The argument is no longer just about how much to tax and spend, although of course austerity politics have sharpened that disagreement, but also about the extent to which governments can and should influence the shape of the economy as well as its size.

So progressives who believe that the old deal offered by the elite has failed are starting to think about new structures to channel capitalist energies effectively. Designing these involves going back to fundamentals and asking how efficiently different forms of economic activity deliver what we really want, that is wellbeing or a good life. For while wellbeing may be partly a function of the *quantity* of economic activity (measured by GDP), it is not a simple one: the *quality* of the activity is also important. In addition, if we also ask what impact these different forms of activity have on the environment, we can start to manage the trade-off between wellbeing now and wellbeing in the future, making it easier to deliver wellbeing in a sustainable way.

These questions remain difficult, but are easier than they were because we can now draw on survey data about the quality of people's experience—what is normally referred to as 'subjective wellbeing' (see Bache and Scott, this volume, Chap. 1). We can then assess how much of this subjective wellbeing different forms of economic activity produce—their 'wellbeing efficiency'. And we can then use this to guide policy.

This possibility lay behind some of the recommendations of the Commission on the Measurement of Economic Performance and Social Progress (CMEPSP) (Stiglitz, Sen and Fitoussi 2009) as well as measurement initiatives in the EU, the OECD, and at national, regional and local levels; the UK's Office for National Statistics Measuring National Well-being programme is one of the leading examples. These initiatives typically measure subjective wellbeing alongside traditional measurement of its various drivers and components (income, a pleasant environment, relationships, job security and so on). In principle, regression analysis then allows us to assess the relative importance of these drivers to subjective wellbeing, and thus—to the extent that we know the impact of policies on the drivers and to the extent that subjective measurement is a reliable guide to life quality—the impact of different policies on our ultimate objective: the creation of good lives. This knowledge base is continuing to grow. The two qualifications—about our knowledge of policy impact and the reliability of subjective measurement—are important and the result remains an assessment, not perfect knowledge. Nonetheless, this is a potential improvement on existing practice. As yet, though, it remains mainly potential.

In existing policy making, wellbeing remains primarily a tool for improving certain kinds of public service delivery and one input amongst many into cost–benefit analysis (Bache and Reardon 2016). It is not used as part of a big-picture assessment of major policies. But the latter is more than a dream: the kind of measurement and associated analysis just described allows progressives to translate idealism into the language of bureaucracy and economics. It is much easier to argue that something is efficient than that it is right. They also point to a potentially larger prize: the incorporation of a richer and more expansive concept of wellbeing into government economic ideology, to replace the rather narrow, consumerist one that currently prevails.

In short, wellbeing is potentially useful for progressives because it allows them to outflank conservatives. They no longer have to fight on the ground preferred by their opponents—what it takes to deliver economic efficiency traditionally defined—but can engage in a broader argument about what it takes to deliver wellbeing, using measures of subjective wellbeing as the standard. This opens up new possibilities for change. And progressives can support the resulting arguments with analysis and evidence.

Two Concepts of Wellbeing:
Experience Versus Relationship

If we are to measure wellbeing, we have to know what it is. I am defining it as the state produced by the good life, but this begs the question 'what constitutes the good life?' Ultimately, this is a value judgement, but like any value judgement it can be informed by facts.

While many different accounts of the good life have been developed over the centuries (see Austin, this volume, Chap. 3), the most important disagreement in the modern debate is over whether wellbeing characterises a person's *experience* or her *relationship* to the world around her. Of course, we have experiences of relationships, but we can still distinguish between the value we attribute to the experience and the value we attribute to the relationship itself. Our concept of wellbeing will depend on where we attribute value.

Bentham is the best-known advocate of *experience;* for the pleasure and pain that form the foundation of his ethics are varieties of experience. In the nineteenth century, his utilitarianism became the ethical basis of economics and recently this doctrine has been enthusiastically propagated by Richard Layard and Paul Dolan of the London School of Economics, both progressive advocates of happiness as a policy objective and the so-called hedonic account of wellbeing (see Bache and Scott, this volume, Chap. 1). Dolan (2014) has developed a subtle variation, in which a sense of purpose is valued alongside happiness. This remains a version of utilitarianism, however, since it is still *a sense of* purpose that is valued rather than the purpose itself. Utilitarianism, incidentally, appears so obvious to its exponents that they sometimes simply cannot grasp that there is an alternative point of view: for example, if you say you value friendship or work for their own sakes, they are inclined to tell you that what you really value is the happiness they bring.

Advocates of the *relationship* view sometimes write within religious traditions, in which an individual's relationship with God and creation is paramount. However, secular writers will often refer to Aristotle's ethics, sometimes as re-stated by Alasdair Macintyre in the 1980s. Aristotle defined wellbeing as *eudaimonia*: an elusive concept, sometimes over-simplified by modern writers to mean the state achieved when living a life that is worthwhile (this 'eudaimonic wellbeing' is then contrasted with the hedonic version). Macintyre amplified this idea by emphasising the role of narrative in the good life:

> I can only answer the question 'what am I to do?' if I can answer the prior question 'of what story or stories do I find myself a part?'... What is better or worse for X depends on the character of that intelligible narrative which provides X's life with its unity (Macintyre 1981, pp. 216–225)

Two features of such narratives as conceived by Macintyre are relevant for our purposes. First, they are essentially social and rooted in the live traditions and 'practices' (activities with internal standards of excellence to be achieved through exercise of the virtues) that make up society. Second, they involve a *telos* or purpose just as individual practices do: a 'quest'. This is not for some predefined good. Instead, 'The good life for man is the life spent seeking the good life for man' (Macintyre 1981, p. 219) and involves ordering and balancing the fulfilments available from individual practices. The result should be a coherent, intelligible narrative both for the individual life and for the collective life of which it is part. Amartya Sen's and Martha Nussbaum's accounts of 'capabilities' can be interpreted as a focus on the conditions for achieving such narratives (Sen 1985; Nussbaum 2000).

The resulting conception of wellbeing is fundamentally social, in contrast to the utilitarian conception, which is fundamentally individualistic (although in both cases wellbeing is a property of *individual* lives). This reflects the fact that social entities can be and are described in terms of relationships, whereas they cannot be described in terms of experience (except metaphorically).

Of course, it is open to utilitarians to argue that what gives a life story coherence and purpose is the pursuit of pleasure and the avoidance of pain and that all the rest is simply a means to these overarching ends. It is difficult to *prove* this position is wrong. But arguably it reveals the failure of Benthamite utilitarianism to capture many of our intuitions—as Nussbaum says it cannot capture 'belief, desire, perception, appetite, emotion, impulse, inclination, intention'(quoted in Scott 2012, p. 17)— and many will shy away from its solipsistic conclusion. Above all, perhaps, relationships, being part of something bigger than oneself, the sense of meaning that is derived from narrative and engagement with the world (through participation in traditions and practices), make mortality less catastrophic: what matters in this conception of a life is not ourselves and our experience, but the universe of which we are part.

Furthermore, this preference for a view of the good life in which relationships rather than experience are primary has a sound philosophical basis. Man may not always be a political animal, as Aristotle claimed, but he is by his nature a social animal, and in a quite fundamental way: human consciousness is the result of language (allowing that there may be other varieties of consciousness experienced by dumb animals) and language is by its nature social.[4] In other words, so the argument goes, relationships are prior to human experience, are in some sense more fundamental than experience.

A MODERN PROGRESSIVE CONCEPTION OF WELLBEING

In the last decade or two, accounts of wellbeing have converged somewhat around the concept of 'flourishing'. This concept is underpinned by psychological research and to some extent draws together the two ethical traditions just described, with their emphasis on experience and relationship, respectively (it does not reconcile them).

Flourishing as a psychological concept has been elaborated by Corey Keyes and other members of the positive psychology school. Flourishing individuals, in Keyes's words, have positive feelings, an absence of negative feelings, and 'function' well, by which he means they

> like most parts of themselves, have warm and trusting relationships, see themselves developing into better people, have a direction in life, are able to shape their environments to satisfy their needs, and have a degree of self-determination (Keyes 2002, p. 208).

They also have a positive relationship with society: they

> see society as meaningful and understandable... as possessing potential for growth... they feel they belong to and are accepted by their communities... they accept most parts of society... they see themselves as contributing to society (Keyes 2002, p. 209).

The focus and unit of analysis remains the individual: this is, after all, part of Western psychology. However, the description is rather clearly a matter of *both* experience—positive feelings and an absence of negative feelings—*and* relationship, most obviously in the account of the relationship with society, but also in the more personal aspects of functioning. One might expect—though as far as I am aware it has not been demonstrated quantitatively—that someone living a good life as prescribed by Macintyre is relatively likely to flourish in the way described by Keyes.

Other psychologists, notably Richard Ryan and Edward Deci, have shown that good functioning—broadly as just described—is associated with good feelings, both being grounded in satisfaction of psychological needs (Ryan and Deci 2000). However, the functioning and the feeling remain conceptually distinct, and it has been pointed out that there are positive feelings that are not associated with good functioning (for example see Ryff and Singer 1998). As far Ryff and Singer are concerned, it is the functioning that matters, not the feeling. Yet, as we have seen, others such as Paul Dolan disagree. In short, the philosophical disagreement about what is important continues, even if for practical purposes both sides can converge on the concept of flourishing because as a matter of empirical fact it is a good way of delivering good feelings.

Importantly though, it is possible to question whether someone spending her life watching television game shows in solitude is flourishing, even if this is the activity she freely chooses, and even if she reports that as a result she feels pleasure and is highly satisfied with her life (the variable often picked up in wellbeing surveys). Similarly, it is possible to ask if someone taking a happy drug and spending all day content but in bed is flourishing. For we can examine whether these people demonstrate the characteristics identified by Keyes as signs of flourishing, or whether their psychological needs as identified by Ryan and Deci have been fulfilled: and we might well expect they are not.

What *do* people value? I am not aware of any Bentham versus Aristotle poll, but if the features of flourishing can be grouped into successful human relationships and successful human agency (the ability people have 'to shape their environments… and have a degree of self-determination'), then it appears that while relationships are valued everywhere, agency tends to be valued more highly in societies where more basic concerns of security and subsistence have been achieved (World Values Survey 2016). In line with this, it is arguable that the construct 'fits' better those societies demonstrating what have been called 'secular rational' and 'self-expression' values; that is, mainly the English speaking and Protestant European countries (Welzel 2013).

Finally, and crucially as far as policy is concerned, the extent to which a population is flourishing can be measured, at least approximately. For example, the Warwick Edinburgh Mental Well-being Scale (WEMWBS) is a survey instrument designed to measure 'positive mental health': a closely related construct including both hedonic aspects ('the subjective experience of happiness') and eudaimonic aspects ('psychological functioning, good relationships with others and self-realisation' and 'the capacity for self-development, positive relations with others, autonomy, self-acceptance and competence') (Stewart-Brown and Janmohamed 2008, revised 2016). The UK Office for National Statistics now publishes the results as one of 41 indicators of 'national wellbeing', alongside four other subjective measures of wellbeing (Office for National Statistics 2016). The surveys containing these questions also measure objective conditions that are more directly influenced by policy, such as housing, education, employment patterns, benefit entitlements and so on. It is thus possible to establish statistical relationships between these and flourishing and thus identify potential policy priorities, as I explore in greater detail below.

In fact, most studies around the world establish associations between objective conditions and life satisfaction rather than flourishing; this may be an adequate pro tem proxy at aggregate level, for even if the psychological state referred to is quite different, there is an association between the two states. Some economists, incidentally, have suggested that measuring life satisfaction is preferable because it is more value-neutral than measuring flourishing, but this is a confusion. A survey question about life satisfaction is indeed neutral as to the specific activities that produce satisfaction, but the choice of satisfaction as a variable is not itself value-free. It reflects either the value placed on life satisfaction, or the value placed on whatever life satisfaction is being used as a proxy for. Similarly, a question about flourishing can be neutral as to the specific activities that produce flourishing, while the decision to ask the question reflects the value placed on flourishing.

In short, flourishing looks like a pretty promising concept. Because it is now possible to measure flourishing and the conditions that encourage it, progressives can use it to judge current social institutions. When they find them wanting, they have some of the evidence needed to lobby for and design necessary reforms. Furthermore, given that many people want to flourish and that it makes them feel better, flourishing's advocates feel there must be a way of phasing, packaging and communicating the reforms so that they become electorally feasible: an alternative to the less attractive forms of populism now emerging. However, since life satisfaction is the variable used in most surveys, much of the rest of this chapter discusses the use of *wellbeing* concepts and evidence.

Wellbeing in Policy Making

There are two potential uses of the resulting evidence in policy. One is to help design or justify specific programmes that are likely to improve wellbeing, or where improving wellbeing can contribute to the programme's other objectives. For example, wellbeing evidence was used to justify the 'Improved Access to Psychological Therapies' programme in 2007 (see Evans, this volume, Chap. 2). More recently it has been used to help design and assess public health campaigns and in public procurement (to improve employee wellbeing and thus performance). Similarly, wellbeing surveys have been used to assess particular programmes, for example, the National Citizenship Service and the Troubled Families Programme (Cabinet Office 2013; Bache and Reardon 2016).

There is scope for increasing this kind of use and a What Works Centre for Wellbeing (WWCW) has been established in London, designed to pull together and disseminate relevant evidence amongst national and local government policy makers (see whatworkswellbeing.org). For example, employers, schools and voluntary sector organisations can be encouraged to use what we know about wellbeing in their work—to improve wellbeing at work, to improve educational performance and to reduce depression amongst young people. Government can design interventions to 'nudge' people into decisions that will improve their wellbeing—for example to spend more time exercising, or volunteering, and less time commuting. Of course, not all volunteering is good and not all commuting is bad. But this is simply to say that wellbeing evidence complements rather than replaces judgement and other forms of evidence.

This potential use of the wellbeing evidence is limited, however. As Matthew Taylor has argued in a New Economics Foundation essay collection, 'the capacity of the state to wield wellbeing measurements for good [probably] comes to a halt' once we move 'beyond the vulnerable and genuinely needy'; after all, for the most part 'it is up to individuals themselves to pursue their own wellbeing and happiness' (Taylor 2011, p. 32).

The other potential use of wellbeing evidence, which Taylor does not discuss in his essay, has broader applications. It is to modify and improve the trade-offs between potentially competing objectives when designing policy and public services. Wellbeing may be for individuals to pursue, but the state can create conditions that increase their chances of success. Given that wellbeing is 'what we really want', it is reasonable to see doing this as the ultimate objective of policy, with more specific policy outcomes as intermediate objectives. Wellbeing evidence—the statistical relationships between these outcomes and levels of wellbeing—can then be used to assess intermediate objectives and the trade-offs between them. In other words, wellbeing measurements help provide a common standard of success for diverse policies aiming at diverse intermediate objectives, whether economic or social. If a formal approach is adopted, the result will be a new kind of cost–benefit analysis, as advocated by former Head of the Civil Service Gus O'Donnell and others in a 2014 report (O'Donnell et al. 2014). This will not replace political judgement and bargaining, but it can inform them. It could also inform more deliberative forms of democracy, such as citizens' juries.

For example, consider the decision taken in 2016 about an additional runway for London's airports. How should the economic gains (assuming these are real) have been weighed against the loss of amenity now and the potential impacts on future generations? In fact, the Airports Commission did consider wellbeing impacts in its 2015 report, but as one of many factors and did not quantify the impact on wellbeing of all the different intermediate outcomes (Airports Commission 2015; Bache and Reardon 2016). Perhaps if it had, the subsequent discussion of the trade-offs would have been more rational, although any analysis would have left uncertainties and room for judgment.

A common wellbeing standard would also make it easier to consider interactions between policies in different areas in an integrated way. For example, consider public health policies to reduce sugar consumption and economic policies designed to increase employment: if there is currently a trade-off between these (in reality there may or may not be), how should both sets of policies be modified so as to maximise wellbeing over the long term? Arguably, this kind of integrated approach is essential if we are to achieve sustainable development.

This kind of analysis will also help policy makers—and citizens—ask questions about local policy. For example, what have been the relative impacts on wellbeing of steps to reduce unemployment in an area, and steps to preserve the environment? Have interventions to increase community cohesion and increase economic activity improved wellbeing? Are hospital closures still justified when the wellbeing of patients and visitors is considered alongside clinical and cost factors? Should there be greater investment in pedestrianisation schemes, which have been shown to increase social interactions and other drivers of wellbeing? Have the public health interventions in one city been more effective at increasing wellbeing than in another? Can reasons for any differences be identified?

In reality, this use of wellbeing evidence only happens at the margins, certainly within a UK context.[5] The objective of health policy remains better health, the objective of education policy remains better education and so on—in each case, 'better' is as traditionally defined, typically by professionals in the field. Wellbeing analysis has little purchase when traditional standards of policy success—lower death rates, better exam results, shorter journey times and so on—are taken as givens. Interactions between policies may arise, but are generally either relatively unimportant or are felt to be best dealt with through political negotiation or special projects. To the extent that wellbeing is admitted as an overarching objective, it is taken as read that it depends on achieving these intermediate objectives and that the challenge is to advance them, in general independently.

This is not inevitable, however. Objectives and standards can be called into question, either because of issues within the field (what are the objectives of education?) or because of interactions between fields (might this regulation improve health but damage employment?). And it is in economic policy that these questions are arising most urgently.

WELLBEING AND PROGRESSIVE ECONOMIC POLICY

The examples given so far of the potential of wellbeing evidence are, for the most part, cases of improving decisions where markets are not available, rather than a challenge to the market paradigm. The reader may well feel this is hardly an alternative to the *grow, tax and spend* model referred to earlier. However, there is much more to play for precisely because the traditional intermediate objectives of economic policy *have* been called into question and are no longer givens, at least amongst some progressive commentators and politicians. This is partly a matter of issues within the field (for example, is growth producing rising incomes and rising employment as traditionally assumed? Are there trade-offs between stability and growth?) and partly a matter of interactions between economic and other policy fields (what are the interactions between economic and environmental objectives? Or between economic and health objectives?). In other words, the conditions under which wellbeing analysis becomes relevant are satisfied.

What is more, we can draw some conclusions from this analysis. There is a wealth of evidence on the economy and wellbeing, and this suggests, amongst other things, that:

- Income is normally important to wellbeing, but only up to a certain level, which varies from society to society.
- Equality is positively associated with wellbeing, although the relationship is complex.
- Unemployment is often very damaging to wellbeing.
- Insecure employment and economic instability are both often damaging to wellbeing.
- The various components of a 'good job' (in addition to income and security) are strongly associated with wellbeing; this includes the right amount of work—not too much, but not too little either.
- Long commutes and having to move home to find work are often damaging to wellbeing; children's wellbeing in particular can be damaged by geographical mobility (Seaford 2014a).

These impacts can be quantified—not of course perfectly, but in a way that can inform and so improve judgments about priorities. For example, the average impact on life satisfaction when measured on a scale of 1–10 of moving from secure to insecure employment is reported in one study to be approximately one half of the impact of moving from secure employment to unemployment (Abdallah et al. 2013). It follows, as noted at the outset of this chapter, that policy that reduces job security but increases employment may well reduce rather than increase net levels of wellbeing: only if more new jobs are created than existing jobs are made insecure will net wellbeing increase.[6] These ideas are potentially politically attractive. Thus, for example, the All-Party Parliamentary Group on Wellbeing Economics recommended in 2014 that 'stable and secure employment for all should be the primary objective of economic policy' (Berry 2014, p. 5).

Now, everyone will agree that stable and secure employment for all is desirable—and indeed programmes such as the Regional Growth Fund, introduced in 2010, were specifically designed to increase employment where it was most needed. But this goal does not form the broad framework for policy. Instead, the latter follows neoclassical prescriptions to deliver growth and efficient markets, which are in turn meant to deliver employment for all. The problem is that growth and efficient markets have failed to deliver employment for all, certainly stable and secure employment. Initiatives such as the Regional Growth Fund are like putting a sticking plaster on a major wound.

The value that 'wellbeing economics' places on *good* jobs (in ways that go beyond income and security) reflects a more fundamental difference between it and conventional economics. The wellbeing evidence draws attention to the importance of *quality* work in a person's life—its role in flourishing. Thus in the wellbeing account of the economy, work itself is valuable and its value is dependent not simply on what someone will pay for it, but also on the extent to which it helps the worker flourish. This is hardly new. Karl Marx (1844) emphasised the centrality of work to human identity, writing that 'In creating a *world of objects* by his personal activity, in his *work upon* inorganic nature, man proves himself a conscious species-being'. However, he wrote, existing economic institutions prevent this from happening:

> In tearing away from man the object of his production, therefore, estranged labour tears from him his *species-life*, his real objectivity as a member of the species and transforms his advantage over animals into the disadvantage that his inorganic body, nature, is taken from him. (Marx 1844)

More recently, Pope John Paul II wrote in his encyclical *Laborem Exercens*:

> ...as the 'image of God' [a human] is a person, that is to say, a subjective being capable of acting in a planned and rational way, capable of deciding about himself, and with a tendency to self-realization. As *a person, man is therefore the subject of work*....[Work] actions must all serve to realize his humanity, to fulfil the calling to be a person that is his by reason of his very humanity....[Thus] in the final analysis it is always man who is *the purpose of the work*. (John Paul II 1981)

However, in neoclassical accounts of the economy what matters is output, and work is a cost to be minimised. This is reflected in a bias towards consumer rather than producer interests. As Sir Nick Macpherson, former Permanent Secretary to the Treasury has put it quite explicitly, 'From the repeal of the corn laws to the present day, [The Treasury] has tended to favour consumers over producers' (Macpherson 2014). In other words, if wellbeing were to be taken seriously on this score, it would require a fundamental rethinking of economic policy.

WELLBEING AND SUSTAINABILITY

Then there is sustainability—that is, ensuring that delivering wellbeing now does not compromise wellbeing in the future. In principle, this could be achieved through cost-free technological innovation, but this seems unlikely. In reality, it will probably require either a reduction in aggregate consumption in the developed world, or at least a change in what is consumed, driven by much higher prices for some natural resource-intensive goods.

To the extent that this is achievable in democracies, it will probably be because consumption is not a particularly important driver of wellbeing *once a certain living standard is achieved*. Other things then matter more, for example security, job satisfaction and relationships. This means it may be possible to change patterns of consumption or restrict growth in consumption without too much damage to wellbeing. Indeed, it may even be possible to increase wellbeing (Jeffreys and Seaford 2014).[7]

In other words, the wellbeing evidence suggests there could be a politically feasible pathway to lower or changed consumption; this need not involve a change to human nature (not possible) but rather to the particular conditions—the particular socio-economic structures and culture—that translate universal needs and aspirations into particular consumption patterns.

This may involve quite radical change, for example, to social institutions and relative wages so as to make a shorter working week feasible and attractive for more people. More generally, the economy can be managed explicitly to achieve the various drivers of wellbeing: economic security, social contacts, improvements to the physical environment, improved health and so on (Seaford 2014b). Wellbeing evidence does not on its own tell you what to do, what will or will not be feasible; analyses of the economy and of power structures are also needed.

Nonetheless, progressives can draw on it to *help* map out what to do, to turn aspirations into a plan.

THE WELLBEING NARRATIVE

Now it might still be asked, apart from the bit about sustainability, what is new? The need for stability and security of employment, the relative importance of raising low rather than high or middle-level incomes, the dignity of labour—these are all quite traditional social democratic themes. As Michael Jacobs has put it:

> Much of wellbeing science... has confirmed only what common sense – if not economic theory or free market ideology – has long told us. And so for Labour much of it is less a revelation than a reminder' (Jacobs 2011 p. 9).

But, he goes on to say:

> ...it's no less important for that. Wellbeing provides new justification and new language for goals which Labour already has. Where once Labour tended to make a collectivist argument for full employment, public goods and a fairer distribution of income – that these made for a better *society* – now it can make a more direct appeal to personal happiness or life satisfaction. It can argue that such social goods directly increase people's individual wellbeing, even where they may involve a loss or slower growth of private income. In an individualistic age, this may prove a helpful narrative to connect with the concerns of voters (Jacobs 2011, pp. 9–10).

At the same time, because wellbeing can be measured, it allows us to use the language of evidence and efficiency as opposed to justice and idealism, and sometimes it is useful to couch arguments in these terms. It becomes possible to quantify a critique of capitalism, to quantify the size of its failure to deliver good lives as understood by many people. Progressives can translate a subversive critique, all too often ineffective because vague and apparently elitist, into the language of bureaucracy, evidence-based policy, quantified analysis. In this, they are following in the footsteps of nineteenth-century social reformers who used health statistics as tools of advocacy.[8]

Jacobs's individualistic narrative and the evidence base are both important, and not just to persuade voters. They may also give progressive politicians the confidence that their interventions are legitimate and founded on a scientific analysis. And that, as anyone familiar with British politics knows, is crucial in the war of nerves between progressives and conservatives. Indeed, it is arguable that the only way the state can deliver 'stable and secure employment for all' (to say nothing of sustainability) is by creating a consensus, shared by progressive politicians and progressive business leaders alike—a consensus that supports a package of significant state interventions. Achieving this will be complex, but the attractions of the wellbeing narrative and evidence base mean they are likely to contribute to the process, particularly, as we will see in the next section, if the economics of wellbeing is further developed.

Towards a New Economics—And Next Steps for Progressive Politicians

The current debate between progressives and conservatives about wellbeing is primarily about the role of the market. The conservative view is rooted in a liberal version of neoclassical economics, and in particular welfare economics. Liberal welfare economists argue that wellbeing (welfare) cannot be measured directly, and that we are forced to fall back on *that which is chosen* as evidence of where wellbeing exists, with the quantity measured in money: ('utility' is the construct used, which is simply defined as that which individuals maximise when they make choices; it is then equated with welfare). Wellbeing thus becomes associated with market choices and serves to justify the market as a social institution. Indeed, given this assumption, it can be shown with elegance and rigour that if our original income distribution is optimal and if we take steps to preserve it, then a perfect market will produce optimal outcomes. It can then be argued (with strikingly less rigour) that politicians should focus on the distribution and economists on the markets.

Neoclassical economists remain correct, of course, that the market remains the best mechanism for allocating much (not all) productive effort. No one is proposing the creation of a wellbeing-based version of Gosplan[9], even if some sectors such as health care do require central planning. However, there are two important qualifications to the traditional view. One is that it was never in fact the case that neutral questions about how to maximise the value of output (the province of economists) could be separated from value-based questions about how to distribute that output (the province of politicians). This is partly because how you produce output affects the final distribution, given political constraints on redistribution (the argument put forward by advocates of 'pre-distribution'),[10] but also because it is always inefficient to redistribute after the event to the extent that markets generate production structures geared to particular patterns of demand, which are in turn a function of the distribution.[11] However, more important from our point of view is that the arrival of subjective wellbeing evidence means we are no longer forced to fall back on *that which is chosen* as evidence of where wellbeing exists. We now have statistical data to supplement or even replace this. Thus, even if we believe that the primary moral imperative is to maximise wellbeing (the normal assumption of economists) and even if we accept a little lamely that numbers trump moral conviction (another normal assumption of economists), the judgement that we should rely on markets has become empirical not axiomatic; in other words a judgement on the inevitably limited competence of central planners.

In practice, this means we can introduce elements into the economic calculus that are systematically excluded from neoclassical theory. Recognising that choices are functions of structures, we can use wellbeing evidence to critique structures, rather than simply using the choices they produce to validate them. In particular, we can address how to optimise two sources of wellbeing—work and community—where individual choices are circumscribed by existing structures. For example, in neoclassical economics free trade is always a good thing, except when tariffs are needed to protect an infant industry, since the extra output it results in can be redistributed to compensate losers. In reality, even if that redistribution takes place (a very big *if* indeed), the impacts of free trade on quality of work or on communities can be negative, and there is no reason to suppose that the additional output can, let alone will, be used to buy better quality work or better communities. So the net impact on many people's wellbeing will be negative.

This, it needs hardly be said, is a very different account of the world from that adopted by the UK Treasury and indeed most economists.

So what is to be done? The difficulty, to return to the free trade example, is that while at the moment we can be clear that free trade may not always be a good thing, it very often *is* a good thing. The Treasury has an advantage, as things stand, because it can use neoclassical analysis to argue that free trade is (almost) always a good thing—indeed, it has an easy answer to most things. What is needed is the construction of an empirical wellbeing economics, in which outcomes expressed in terms of wellbeing can be predicted given different policies and assumptions.

This is a long-term project. But significant progress can be made in the short to medium term. The first step is for progressive politicians and their advisors to use the wellbeing evidence to engage with citizens, and in doing so develop a view of the society the citizens wish to construct. Then they can consider the impact of alternative policies in advancing us towards that society (a matter at least in part of a form of economic analysis that incorporates wellbeing outcomes), together with the barriers to the effective introduction of those policies, and the actions needed to overcome those barriers. This work can begin now.

Is Wellbeing Useful for Conservatives as Well as Progressives?

Wellbeing is not the exclusive property of progressives. For while wellbeing, or the good life, *can* be a standard for judging social institutions—are they delivering it?—it can equally be defined in terms of those institutions. It then becomes the property of conservatives. In extreme cases, such as the Hindu caste system, these institutions define who is capable of living a truly good life: traditional justifications of caste refer to innate differences between the capacities and desires of members of different castes, differences that make them fit for higher or lower forms of life. Pre-modern attitudes in Europe were less rigid, but often justified inequality on what were in the end the same grounds.

However, even if it is agreed that the good life is and should be available to all, conservatives can still argue that it has to be understood in the context of existing institutions, rather than in the abstract. Indeed, they may argue that abstractions arise from institutions and tradition and not the other way round. In this spirit, Michael Oakeshott celebrated the conservative 'propensity to use and to enjoy what is available' (Oakeshott 1962, p. 408) and Edmund Burke emphasised that what is of value exists within a tradition, 'an inheritance from our forefathers', a matter of 'ancient laws and liberties' (Burke 1790). To talk of some better life that might exist under some alternative arrangements is at best utopian and at worst the first steps to tyranny.

The modern version of this 'inheritance' is the 'free market', an institution that in the neoliberal interpretation of welfare economics is the most efficient way of delivering wellbeing, and which is the contemporary embodiment of 'ancient laws and liberties'.[12] When progressive wellbeing advocates challenge its outcomes, neoliberals are even now inclined to see the shadow of Robespierre, the threat to liberties posed by state tyranny.

Conclusion

In this chapter, I have suggested that progressives can use wellbeing evidence and concepts to help shape a new deal between the political and economic elite and the mass of the population: a deal to replace the old, now failing one that was based on delivering steadily improving material conditions. This new deal will not be 'we will deliver flourishing'—a frighteningly top–down proposition—but 'we will work with you to create conditions that will help you to flourish, and that will help your children and their children flourish'. Whether this will happen, and what progressives have to do to make it happen, is beyond the scope of this chapter, but I have outlined some reasons why progressives should take the possibility seriously. First, flourishing, which I have argued is the core wellbeing concept, is a well-defined state, attractive to many people and consistent with our ethical traditions; second, we know some of the things that encourage flourishing and are likely to learn more; third, this knowledge can be quantified and turned into practical policy analysis tools; fourth, this knowledge has significant implications for major questions of economic policy, of the kind that progressives and much of the public are concerned with; fifth, this knowledge may assist the development of politically viable solutions to the environmental crisis; and sixth, the resulting narrative—individualistic and scientific—may be a good way of winning both popular and elite support. More work is needed to develop an empirically based wellbeing economics, but even in its absence progress can be made. If the main alternative to a defunct neoliberalism is a revival of aggressive nationalism, then wellbeing is indeed useful to progressives.

Notes

1. Typically this is presented as an insider–outsider problem, and the response is to reduce the advantages of the insiders by encouraging labour market flexibility and reducing benefits. For moderate and

apparently reasonable examples of this approach, see OECD (2014) and Cheptea et al. (2014).

2. I define 'wellbeing' as the state produced by the good life. There is nothing new in striving for this—what is new and advocated here is using wellbeing concepts and evidence as part of this endeavour. Note that it is not true that the only thing anyone wants is a good life for themselves and those they care about, but that is not the assumption I am making.

3. See for example OECD (2015).

4. As Daniel Dennett has put it, 'Perhaps... the kind of mind you get when you add language to it is so different from the kind of mind you can have without language that calling them both minds is a mistake' (Dennett 1996, p. 17). This has a neuroscientific basis in so far as split-brain research has shown that information is only fully conscious if it reaches the language-dominant left-hand brain (Dennett 1996; Dietrich 2007).

5. For example, wellbeing impacts are included in some transport cost–benefit assessments, and in assessing bids for Nature Improvement Areas. The Department for Culture, Media and Sport (renamed the Department for Digital, Culture, Media and Sport in July 2017) has commissioned analysis to guide priorities (Cabinet Office 2013; Bache and Reardon 2016).

6. Note that this is to ignore the distribution of that wellbeing and the long term structural impacts, both of which require separate analysis.

7. The evidence for this was drawn from Jackson (2009); Easterlin et al. (2010); and Sachs et al. (2012).

8. For example Edwin Chadwick (Chadwick 1842).

9. Gosplan was the planning agency of the former Soviet Union.

10. The term was coined by Jacob Hacker (Hacker 2011).

11. This point is made in a blog by Steve Waldman at www.interfluidity.com/v2/5537.html (Waldman 2014).

12. Indeed, Jonty Oliff-Cooper has made a similar point (Oliff-Cooper 2011).

References

Abdallah, S., Stoll, L., & Eiffe, F. (2013). Quality of Life in Europe: Subjective Well-Being. Dublin: Eurofound. Available at: https://www.eurofound.europa.eu/publications/report/2013/quality-of-life-social-policies/quality-of-life-in-europe-subjective-well-being.

Airports Commission. (2015). Final Report. Available at: https://www.gov.uk/government/publications/airports-commission-final-report.

Bache, I., & Reardon, L. (2016). The Politics and Policy of Wellbeing: Understanding the Rise and Significance of a New Agenda. Cheltenham: Edward Elgar.

Berry, C. (2014). Wellbeing in Four Policy Areas: Report by the All Party Parliamentary Group on Wellbeing Economics. London: New Economics Foundation. Available at: http://b.3cdn.net/nefoundation/ccd-f9782b6d8700f7c_lcm6i2ed7.pdf.

Burke, E. (1790). *Reflections on the Revolution in France.* London: J. Dodsley. Available at: http://www.constitution.org/eb/rev_fran.htm.

Cabinet Office. (2013). Wellbeing Policy and Analysis: An Update of Wellbeing Work across Whitehall. London: Cabinet Office. Available at: https://www.gov.uk/government/uploads/system/uploads/attachment_data/file/224910/Wellbeing_Policy_and_Analysis_FINAL.PDF.

Chadwick, E. (1842). Report into the Sanitary Conditions of the Labouring Population of Great Britain. London: HMSO. Available at: http://www.deltaomega.org/documents/ChadwickClassic.pdf.

Cheptea, C., Guajardo, J., Halikias, I., Jurzyk, E., Lin, H., Lusinyan, L., et al. (2014). What Do Past Reforms Tell Us about Fostering Job Creation in Western Europe? In *Jobs and Growth: Supporting the European Recovery.* Washington: IMF.

Dennett, D. (1996). *Kinds of Minds: Towards an Understanding of Consciousness.* New York: Basic Books.

Dietrich, A. (2007). *Introduction to Consciousness.* Basingstoke: Palgrave.

Dolan, P. (2014). *Happiness by Design.* London: Penguin.

Easterlin, R., McVey, L., Switek, M., Sawangfa, O., & Zweig, J. (2010). The Happiness–Income Paradox Revisited. *Proceedings of the National Academy of Sciences, 107*(52), 22463–22468.

Hacker, J. (2011). *The Institutional Foundations of Middle Class Democracy.* London: Policy Network.

Jackson, T. (2009). *Prosperity without Growth: Economics for a Finite Planet.* Abingdon: Routledge.

Jacobs, M. (2011). Wellbeing: The Challenge for Labour. In C. Seaford (Ed.), *The Practical Politics of Wellbeing.* London: New Economics Foundation.

Jeffreys, K., & Seaford, C. (2014). Report on Definitions of the Green Economy and Progress towards it. NETGREEN project deliverable 2.1. Available at: http://netgreen-project.eu/deliverables. Accessed September 22, 2016.

John Paul II. (1981). *Laborem Exercens.* Vatican City: Libreria Editrice Vaticana. Available at: http://w2.vatican.va/content/john-paul-ii/en/encyclicals/documents/hf_jp-ii_enc_14091981_laborem-exercens.html. Accessed September 22, 2016.

Keyes, C. (2002). The Mental Health Continuum: From Languishing to Flourishing in Life. *Journal of Health and Social Research, 43,* 207–222.

Macintyre, A. (1981). *After Virtue.* London: Duckworth.

Macpherson, N. (2014). Speech by the Permanent Secretary to the Treasury, The Treasury View: A Testament of Experience. Available at: https://www.

gov.uk/government/speeches/speech-by-the-permanent-secretary-to-the-treasury-the-treasury-view-a-testament-of-experience. Accessed February 21, 2017.

Marx, K. (1844). *Economic and Philosophic Manuscripts of 1844*. Available at: https://www.marxists.org/archive/marx/works/1844/manuscripts/labour.htm. Accessed September 22, 2016.

Nussbaum, M. (2000). *Women and Human Development: The Capabilities Approach*. Cambridge: Cambridge University Press.

Oakeshott, M. (1962). On Being Conservative. In M. Oakeshott (Ed.), *Rationalism in Politics and Other Essays*. Carmel: Liberty Fund.

O'Donnell, G., Deaton, A., Durand, M., Halpern, D., & Layard, R. (2014). *Wellbeing and Policy*. London: Legatum.

OECD. (2014). Economic Policy Reforms 2014: Going for Growth Interim Report. Paris: Organisation for Economic Co-operation and Development. Available at: http://media.rspp.ru/document/1/5/c/5c05f7ac8f8ce26fe4e-4ae3d446c5d5f.pdf.

OECD. (2015). All on Board: Making Inclusive Growth Happen. Paris: Organisation for Economic Co-operation and Development. Available at: https://www.oecd.org/inclusive-growth/All-on-Board-Making-Inclusive-Growth-Happen.pdf.

Office for National Statistics. (2016). *Measures of National Wellbeing*. Available at: https://www.neighbourhood.statistics.gov.uk/HTMLDocs/dvc146/wrapper.html. Accessed September 22, 2016.

Oliff-Cooper, J. (2011). Wellbeing: A Conservative Issue. In C. Seaford (Ed.), *The Practical Politics of Wellbeing*. London: New Economics Foundation.

Ryan, R., & Deci, E. (2000). Self-Determination Theory and the Facilitation of Intrinsic Motivation, Social Development, and Well-Being. *American Psychology, 55*, 68–78.

Ryff, C., & Singer, B. (1998). The Contours of Positive Human Health. *Psychological Inquiry, 9*, 1–2.

Sachs, J., Layard, R., & Helliwell, J. (2012). World Happiness Report. New York: The Earth Institute-Columbia University. Available at: https://world-happiness.report/.

Scott, K. (2012). *Measuring Wellbeing: Towards Sustainability?* Abingdon: Routledge.

Seaford, C. (2014a). What Implications Does Wellbeing Science have for Economic Policy? In T. Hamalainen & J. Michaelson (Eds.), *Wellbeing and Beyond*. Cheltenham: Edward Elgar.

Seaford, C. (2014b). Happy Planet, Happy Economy, Happy Consumers? In M. Tatzel (Ed.), *Consumption and Well-Being in the Material World*. Dordrecht: Springer.

Sen, A. (1985). *Commodities and Capabilities*. Amsterdam: North-Holland.

Stewart-Brown, S., & Janmohamed, K., updated by Taggart, S., Stewart-Brown, S. and Parkinson, J. (2016). Warwick-Edinburgh Mental Well-being Scale: User Guide Version 2. Edinburgh: NHS Scotland. Available at: http://www. healthscotland.com/uploads/documents/26787-WEMWBS%20User%20 Guide%20Version%202%20May%202015.pdf.

Stiglitz, J., Sen, A., & Fitoussi, J-P. (2009). Report by the Commission on the Measurement of Economic Performance and Social Progress. Available at: http://ec.europa.eu/eurostat/documents/118025/118123/Fitoussi+ Commission+report.

Taylor, M. (2011). In Favour of Life and Wholeness. In C. Seaford (Ed.), *The Practical Politics of Wellbeing*. London: New Economics Foundation.

Waldman, S. (2014). *Welfare Economics*. Available at: http://www.interfluidity. com/v2/5537.html. Accessed September 22, 2016.

Welzel, C. (2013). *Freedom Rising: Human Empowerment and the Quest for Emancipation*. Cambridge: Cambridge University Press.

World Values Survey. (2016). Findings and Insights. Available at: http://www. worldvaluessurvey.org/WVSContents.jsp. Accessed September 22, 2016.

CHAPTER 6

Between Policies and Life: The Political Process of *Buen Vivir* in Ecuador

Daniela Bressa Florentin

INTRODUCTION

The Spanish concept of *Buen Vivir* (usually translated as 'living well' or 'collective well living') is a hallmark of Andean culture. It is generally viewed as being a formative part of the Andean indigenous cosmology entailing a radical questioning of colonialism and the dominant model of development built upon economic growth and the capitalist order (Acosta 2008; Medina 2008; Gudynas 2009; Walsh 2010; Misoczky 2011; Radcliffe 2012). In brief, *Buen Vivir* expresses a harmonious relation between humans, on the one hand, and humans and nature, on the other. *Sumak Kawsay* (from the Kichwa native language in Ecuador, Colombia and Peru) is the indigenous name for *Buen Vivir*. *Sumak* means 'beautiful', 'good', 'tenderness' and 'perfect'. The meaning of *Kawsay* is 'to dwell' and 'to live with others' (Albó 2009; Salgado 2010); its antonym is *Waqcha* (Kichwa), meaning 'orphan' or 'abandoned'. These terms denote a strong relational component. Authors such as Gudynas (2011) and Thomson (2011) argue that the idea of *Buen Vivir*

D. Bressa Florentin (✉)
University of Bath, Bath, England
e-mail: d.f.bressa.florentin@bath.ac.uk

© The Author(s) 2018
I. Bache and K. Scott (eds.), *The Politics of Wellbeing*, Wellbeing
in Politics and Policy, https://doi.org/10.1007/978-3-319-58394-5_6

121

exists, with slight differences in meaning, in several indigenous groups in Latin America (Kichwa, Aymara, Mapuche, and Guaraní groups[1]). Nonetheless, it is in countries such as Ecuador and Bolivia where *Buen Vivir* has obtained a distinct symbolic, political and also legal status. *Buen Vivir* was incorporated as the guiding principle of the new national constitutions of Ecuador in 2008 and Bolivia in 2009, and translated into categories of policies, goals and rights. This inclusion has been widely regarded as an historical moment and an unprecedented opportunity for change (Escobar 2010; Walsh 2010). For the first time, an idea rooted in indigenous knowledge facilitated the convergence of multiple debates in the production of an alternative discourse challenging the dominant capitalist model of wealth creation and neoliberal political governance.

I argue that in order to understand the emergence of *Buen Vivir* in the political realm, as well as the power struggle over its definition and implementation, it is necessary to understand the dynamics of politics in contemporary Ecuador involving contentions between the state and organised collective actors. This chapter is principally focused on the relations between the state and the indigenous movement; more specifically, the main indigenous organisation in Ecuador, CONAIE (Confederation of Indigenous Nationalities of Ecuador). This organisation was able to articulate the Ecuadorian indigenous movement at the national level, presenting a coherent vision of a plurinational state, and it achieved important political goals establishing itself as a major social movement organisation in the Latin American region (Yashar 1999; Van Cott 2005; Andolina et al. 2009). For these reasons, CONAIE has been able to establish itself as a national and regional political actor.

This chapter investigates the political nature of the struggle over the meaning and implementation of *Buen Vivir*. I trace the political process since the emergence of *Buen Vivir* from the first moment of political articulation to a second moment of differentiation, fragmentation and concentration of power that redefines political boundaries in a renewal of political settlements. This renewal is primarily characterised by greater control and regulation by the state over market forces, while at the same time increasing state decision-making power over public policy. In relation to the first moment of articulation, the emergence of *Buen Vivir* as a political project representing a radical alternative model of development can only be thought of in Ecuador as the result of the confluence of two interrelated processes: (i) the cumulative struggles of highly organised indigenous social movements, particularly since the 1990s, against the implementation of neoliberal policies and towards the construction of a plurinational state; (ii) the emergence of new political leaders on the left and a popular centre-left government implementing public policies through state institutions. In other words, the emergence and rise of *Buen Vivir* as political discourse has been the result, on the one hand, of the impact of social demands, including those enacted by indigenous social movements, and on the other, of the contingent opening up of the political structure. Both the indigenous movement and the government of Rafael Correa have been fundamental to the rise and consolidation of *Buen Vivir* as the proxy for the way different sociopolitical agents in Ecuador define their position within the post-neoliberal turn in the country and the region.

In relation to the second moment of differentiation and fragmentation, this can be thought of as a power struggle over the meaning of *Buen Vivir* and the imposition of a dominant discourse. This moment is marked primarily by a process of strategic rationalisation of *Buen Vivir*, in which each actor claimed a certain type of *Buen Vivir* associated with their interest in access to power. By process of rationalisation, I refer to actions that make definitions of *Buen Vivir* consistent with the political objectives of the groups supporting them. This process reflected the expansion of instrumental and strategic rationality at the expense of normative and moral considerations (Habermas 1986; Gane 2002). This in turn led to the antagonism between different notions of *Buen Vivir*, mainly between the government, on the one hand, and the indigenous organisation, CONAIE, on the other. Each of them defined the concept in different ways according to their own interests, goals and political positions, defending the legitimacy of the discourse they mobilised while discrediting those held by political opponents. In this way, the definition and mobilisation of the discourses of *Buen Vivir* became powerful tools to create and openly redefine subjective positions in the political and social arena in Ecuador. This chapter proposes an original conceptualisation of competing discourses of *Buen Vivir* through the study of the constitutive dynamic of the different framings in dispute. It is argued that the tensions between the different stakeholders involved have opened a new phase of the political process, which is identified here as *the political process of Buen Vivir*.

The aim of this chapter is to trace and identify which elements are highlighted and placed at the centre of these discourses in order to draw political boundaries between competing forces. In the struggle over meaning, actors claim ownership of this idea, the truthfulness of their definition, and discredit the definition given by opponents. This makes *Buen Vivir* a porous and malleable concept, a symbol of the struggles at stake in contemporary Ecuador, which redefine areas of inclusion and exclusion within the political sphere.

This chapter is organised in two main parts. The first part explores the historical context that explains the emergence of *Buen Vivir* in institutional politics (the state being the locus and target of action of agents[2]). The second part deals with the strategic rationalisation of *Buen Vivir* by different agents. I argue that the struggle at stake in Ecuador is between three competing understandings of *Buen Vivir*: (1) the pluralist *Sumak Kawsay* (mobilised by the indigenous movement opposing Correa's government); (2) *Buen Vivir* as rational social transformation—the construction of the state (mobilised by the government); and (3) Deep *Buen Vivir*—ecology and post-development in action (mobilised by environmental activists). This analysis on the diverse discourses of *Buen Vivir* and their associated political uses was mainly drawn from 40 in-depth, semi-structured interviews with representatives of indigenous movement organisations, environmental organisations and political movements, and with governmental officials and academics. These interviews were carried out by the author in Quito between June and December 2014.

Historical Context: CONAIE and Rafael Correa

Ecuador is divided into three main geographical regions: the Andean highlands, the Amazon and the coast (lowlands). Indigenous groups are divided following the same geographical distribution and out of the total indigenous population, 78 per cent live in rural areas. The geographical place in which each indigenous community is located has functioned as a powerful factor, not only in the construction of their identity as peoples from the highlands, the Amazon and the coast, but also in their political organisation. Indigenous groups identify themselves and are legally recognised according to two interrelated categories: *nacionalidades* (nationalities) and *pueblos* (peoples).[3] There are 14 *nacionalidades* and 18 *pueblos* in Ecuador.[4]

Nacionalidad refers to the legal recognition of a territory (nation) with distinctive institutional, social, economic, legal and political forms of organisation. *Pueblo* refers to subgroups of collectives or communities sharing the same language and/or cultural costumes. One nationality usually encompasses several *pueblos*. The largest *nacionalidad* in Ecuador is Kichwa (or Quichua) which is located in the highlands. As will be explained later, indigenous peoples' demands to be recognised as both *pueblos* and *nacionalidades* correspond, on the one hand, to their political strategy to be closely connected with local spaces (*pueblos*), and on the other hand, being recognised as *nacionalidades*, which is intrinsically related to the indigenous political project *Plurinacionalidad*, the acknowledgement of Ecuador as a plurinational country (Lucero 2003; Zamosc 2004; Radcliffe 2012).

In 1986, the Confederación de Nacionalidades Indígenas del Ecuador (CONAIE—Confederation of Indigenous Nationalities of Ecuador) was founded, bringing together indigenous organisations from the Andean highlands, the Amazon and the coast. CONAIE was formed as a distinctive indigenous organisation trying explicitly to differentiate itself from political parties (Andolina 2003). Ethnic identity was placed at the core of its discourse, and its primary goal was to unify a fragmented indigenous population into one sole movement. In order to achieve such cohesion, CONAIE constructed a framework around the notion of *nacionalidades* (Jameson 2011). Lucero (2003) and Becker (2008) point out that while indigenous groups could have organised under different concepts (*pueblos*, cooperatives, *comunas*, and so forth), it was *nacionalidades* that became the discursive vehicle for their political project; in other words, the acknowledgement of Ecuador as a plurinational state. This is characterised as the distribution of power and control over territories among fully recognised nationalities in a unified state.

With CONAIE, the indigenous movement became the main protagonist and representative of the 'anti-neoliberal' struggle (Yashar 1999; Van Cott 2005; Becker 2008). In 1990, the organisation led a nine-day nationwide uprising, blocking roads and cutting food supplies to the main cities. The main demands were for land, a new agrarian reform, and the recognition of nationalities and their cultural and political rights. Becker (2010: 292) explains that '... it represented the emergence of indigenous peoples as one of the most powerful social-movement actors in the Americas'. The massive 1990 roadblock was the first demonstration of power by indigenous organisations, which was followed by roadblocks and mobilisations in 1992[5], 1994, 1997, 1999, 2000 and 2001 (Van Cott 2005).

Polling data showed that by 1999 Ecuadorians had more faith in CONAIE than in most of the traditional and dominant institutions (except for the church and the military) (Lucero 2003). The framing of the struggle was constructed around the idea of a plurinational state. CONAIE articulated a discourse in which local, regional and national dimensions were intertwined and shaped by the idea of 'indigenous nationalities', which resulted in a discourse defending Ecuador as a plurinational country (Lucero 2003).

Ecuador has been characterised by a profound volatility. Like many Latin American countries, Ecuador has a long tradition of unstable (civil and military) governments. Traditional political parties[6] have controlled the political scene since the return of democracy in 1979. Based on individual personalities, the political party system is highly fragmented, constructing its power mainly on clientelist practices (Machado Puertas 2007; Prevost et al. 2012). Traditional political parties, together with the National Congress and the judicial system, have been discredited after various corruption scandals. The last coup of the twentieth century in Ecuador was against President Jamil Mahuad [7] (1998–2000) in the early days of 2000, in a period of intense crisis:

...GNP shrank 7.3 percent, foreign investment fell by 34.7 percent, imports declined by 38.4 percent, and the value of the dollar against the sucre [national currency until 2000] rose by 362 percent ... almost 10 percent of the country's 12 million inhabitants emigrated ... In 1998 there were 42 banks in Ecuador; by 2000 there were only 26 (Lucero 2001: 60).

During Gustavo Noboa's presidency (2000–2003), unpopular measures (rises in gas and transport prices, privatisation and land concessions to private companies that deepened the extraction of natural resources) led to violent public demonstrations. As in the past, conflicts were solved by agreements signed between the national government and representatives of indigenous movements. With President Lucio Gutiérrez (2003–2005) in power, CONAIE's leaders (Luis Macas and Nina Pacari) were assigned posts in the ministries of agriculture and foreign affairs (Becker 2008). In 2005, Ecuador started negotiations with the USA to sign a Free Trade Agreement. This triggered popular uprisings across the country. Due to the support it offered to Gutiérrez and its participation in socially discredited state institutions, CONAIE faced widespread social discredit and internal fragmentation. For the first time, the indigenous movement was unable to articulate and represent popular demands.

In 2005, the third coup in ten years overthrew President Gutiérrez. While CONAIE was involved in the mobilisations against the president, this time the main protagonist was not the indigenous movement, but middle class urban citizens (self-identified as the *forajidos*, i.e. the outlaws) who did not ally themselves with any organisational or political structure (Acosta 2005; Philip and Panizza 2011). As in Argentina in 2001, the people's motto was *¡Que se vayan todos!* [all of them out!]. By this time, an unknown politician, Rafael Correa, was gaining popularity by representing popular unrest against traditional political parties.

In 2007, Correa was elected president of Ecuador. Throughout Latin America in the new millennium, widespread disillusionment with the perceived failings of neoliberal policies to solve issues of poverty and inequality (and in some cases economic instability) contributed to political changes. A new generation of centre-left leaders (such as Chávez in Venezuela, Morales in Bolivia and Correa) won power by suggesting the possibility of a new dynamic in the region (Arditi 2008; Grugel and Riggirozzi 2012). They put forward a provocative anti-neoliberal discourse: *Socialismo del Siglo XXI* (Socialism of the 21st Century).

Coined by the German Marxist scholar Heinz Dieterich, Socialism of the 21st Century aims to go beyond the limitations and mistakes of both neoliberalism and the Soviet model (i.e. socialism of the 20th century) (Kennemore and Weeks 2011). While neither rejecting capitalism nor promoting a collectivist system, its goal is the re-foundation of the state as a central institution responsible for the regulation of the economy and distribution of resources in a democratic and egalitarian way (Harnecker 2010; Pomar 2010). In addition, new schemes of regional integration were formed: ALBA, MERCOSUR, UNASUR[8] (Gardini 2010). These were intergovernmental organisations comprising South American countries which promoted social, economic and political integration. The new leaders led unprecedented transformations: nationalisation of natural resources—in the case of Ecuador the nationalisation of Petroecuador—redistribution of wealth and land, and the rewriting of national constitutions in their respective countries. Nevertheless, increasing sociopolitical conflicts have raised doubts about the viability and future of such transformations. In this respect, Kennemore and Weeks (2011: 267) argue that: '... a volatile economic climate, poorly implemented reforms, increased opposition and low political tolerance all indicate limitations to the viability of twenty-first-century socialism as a post-neoliberal development model.'

Davidov (2012) argues that Correa's strategy to differentiate his government from previous neoliberal ones is based on the articulation of the idea of a 'new moral economy', an economy that contrasts with the predominant market logic. This new moral economy emphasises the environment, collective action and intergenerational cooperation (Davidov 2012: 13). Natural resources are not regarded as commodities to be extracted but as a patrimony to be safeguarded (Rival 2010). Based on indigenous ancestral knowledge, the idea of *Buen Vivir* fits well with Correa's intention. It has been raised by Correa's government as an anti-neoliberal discourse, the alternative to previous economic and development models.

In 2007, a national referendum (approved by 80 per cent of Ecuadorian voters) finally led to the organisation of the Constituent Assembly. The writing of a new constitution was seen by both Correa's government and civil society actors as a historic moment marking the possibility of re-founding the state (Acosta 2008; Gudynas 2009). The Constituent Assembly was established in the city of Montecristi (Manabí province). A plurality of socially and politically organised agents participated in the debate; indigenous and Afro-American organisations, leftist political parties, environmental and feminist organisations were among the most noted (Cortez 2010). Each of these agents presented documents that directly or indirectly alluded to *Buen Vivir* or *Sumak Kawsay*.

The Constituent Assembly represents a space of deliberation with the participation of a heterogeneous group of agents seeking to incorporate their demands in the constitution. In doing so, they defined their visions of the state and society. This process of articulation between different sectors forced them to negotiate in order to reach a common definition of state institutions, decentralisation, environmental issues, popular participation, rights and so on. It was in the Constituent Assembly where the consolidation of *Buen Vivir* as the proxy for the way in which different sociopolitical agents defined their position within the post-neoliberal turn dominating the country and the region took place.

Finally, in 2008, Ecuador's national constitution was approved. It presented *Buen Vivir* as the guiding principle and the main goal of development. Ecuador gained regional and international recognition for this (Escobar 2010; Walsh 2010; Santos 2010). For the first time ever, nature was considered to be the subject of rights in a national constitution. And for the first time in Ecuador, a concept based on indigenous cosmology was taken as the guiding principle.

In 2010, the *Plan Nacional para el Buen Vivir: Construyendo un Estado Plurinacional e Intercultural 2009–2013* (National Plan for Living Well: Building a Plurinational and Intercultural State 2009–2013) was approved (SENPLADES[9] 2010). *Buen Vivir* was represented in the National Plan as a conceptual rupture; a new paradigm of development 'post-petroleum'; a radical change; a new social contract; and as the basis of social, economic and democratic justice. *Buen Vivir* is transformed into a set of policies, e.g. '[t]o promote a sustainable and territorially balanced endogenous economy for Good Living to guarantee rights. This economic system must seek productive transformation, diversification and specialisation, based on the promotion of diverse forms of production' (SENPLADES 2010: 86). It also incorporated a set of goals, which included reducing chronic malnutrition by 45% by 2013 (SENPLADES 2010: 78). Radcliffe (2012) argues that with the inclusion of *Buen Vivir* as the guiding principle of the national development plan, the intention is to establish a welfare regime system in Ecuador.

Many contradictions and disagreements on the definition and implementation of *Buen Vivir* emerged in relation to these policies. The most intense controversies related to the extractive activities, on which the Ecuadorian economy is still heavily dependent. Critics of the economic policies of the government have labelled this as progressive neo-extractivism (Gudynas 2010), pointing to the important reforms made in terms of the new role of the state in the economy and greater fiscal pressure on the wealthy, while maintaining at the same time the traditional model of development based mainly on extractive activities. The strongest critiques of these policies, put forward mainly by social and environmental movements, are concerned with the lack of diversification of the economy, the negative social and environmental impacts of natural resource extraction, and the resultant high dependency on the global fluctuations of commodity prices. In addition, the controversies over the limited popular participation in decision-making processes and the tense relationship between the government of Rafael Correa and some historical actors (such as parts of the indigenous movement) have also been a source of new conflicts.

The indigenous movement, along with environmentalists and the government of Rafael Correa, has been central in influencing the rise and consolidation of *Buen Vivir*. The increasing conflicts that have unfolded in the attempts to implement *Buen Vivir* have led to a greater distance between the indigenous and environmental movements on the one hand and the government on the other. Each group defines the concept in different ways according to their interests, goals and political battles, defending the legitimacy of the discourse they mobilise while discrediting those held by political opponents. In this way, the definition and mobilisation of the frameworks of *Buen Vivir* have become powerful tools to create and openly redefine subjective positions in the political and social arena in Ecuador. In what follows, I discuss the three main discourses on *Buen Vivir*. The construction of these three discourses is the result of my own qualitative thematic analysis.

PLURALIST *SUMAK KAWSAY*—THE INDIGENOUS MOVEMENT

The first discourse identified is the pluralist *Sumak Kawsay*. CONAIE identifies the plurinational state as the only mechanism for the operationalisation of *Sumak Kawsay*. It has long been a demand of the indigenous movement and forms the backbone of their political project (CONAIE 2012). To define these ideas, current leaders of the main indigenous organisations talk about power, redistribution, food sovereignty[10], the means of production, full participation in decision-making processes and governance.

> ...the participation in decision-making processes on equal ground, in decisive matters for the country as national security, the financial issue, justice, strategic resources like water, oil; making joint decisions would make clear the possibility of a plurinational state (Severino Sharupi, indigenous leader, Territories and Land, CONAIE. Interviewed August 2014).

I argue that the centrality given to the construction of a plurinational state in the *Sumak Kawsay* idea puts power at the heart of the discourse mobilised by this sector of the indigenous movement: political power, economic power, sociocultural power. According to this discourse, the construction of a plurinational state implies: firstly, the inclusion of peoples and nationalities in political and administrative spaces from which they have been largely and historically excluded; secondly, the restructuring of state institutions to recognise the authority of, and transfer of power and resources to, existing communal governments; thirdly, the support of languages, identities, practices, traditions, knowledge and education of distinctive cultures within the territory. A fourth aspect includes a different perspective on indigenous collective rights. The granting of collective rights (that is to say, the subject of these rights is a collective ethnic or cultural entity) has been a key aspect of indigenous struggles. Most of the rights demanded by indigenous peoples have been nationally and internationally recognised, ratified by national governments, and included in official documents (Yashar 1999; Van Cott 2005). But this is interpreted by many as 'dead words' if they are not implemented or fulfilled. The struggle now turns from the recognition of collective rights to their actual implementation. Also, according to the interpretation of the indigenous movement, what is needed to fulfil them, following Gramsci's definition as correlation of forces, is power:

> There is self-criticism. We fight for the legal, which is included in the constitution. But we now know that it does not depend much on the constitution or on what is written to be fulfilled. It depends on who has power in the country. We have forgotten to build power in the country. We have the best constitution but today we see that that is breaking apart, modified, violated. As we focused on the legal we forgot to build power at every level where you can negotiate on equal ground (Edwin Mina, indigenous leader, youth section ECUARUNARI[11]. Interviewed September 2014)

In this discourse, the *Pachamama*, the spiritual and transcendental phenomenon underpinning the relationship between human beings and the natural world, is used as a symbol representing the moral roots of *Sumak Kawsay*, the new civilising contract envisaged by the promoters of this definition. Indigenous leaders and intellectuals talk about solidarity, reciprocity, harmony and collective cooperation. In order to differentiate themselves from the discourse employed by the state, they do not talk about *Buen Vivir* but about *Sumak Kawsay*. *Buen Vivir* represents for them the co-optation of a radical idea in order to legitimise the implementation of policies dependent on extractive activities, which are perceived as particularly detrimental to the interests and lifeworlds of indigenous communities. *Buen Vivir* is mainly referred to as rhetoric aimed at deception. This differentiation between *Sumak Kawsay* and *Buen Vivir* is used to draw political frontiers between governmental and indigenous forces. It emphasises the epistemological and ontological bases of *Sumak Kawsay*, which give it distinctiveness and power of rupture with mainstream definitions of development, democracy, the state and so on. The indigenous elite deems the mainstream understandings of *Buen Vivir* as colonial and Eurocentric forms of oppression, exclusion and exploitation. The *Sumak Kawsay* proposal aims to break with this:

> In the Andean worldview, every being has a spirit, and all beings deserve respect in order to live in harmony and generate life. *Sumak Kawsay* seeks that, a coexistence to generate life. *Sumak Kawsay* is an attitude of respect towards the *Pachamama* and the understanding that I live because there are others who live in me, the forest lives in me, I live because that mountain lives in me, in my spirit, in my being. Politically, it is a big utopia to construct a new stage of civilization. It is not the wellbeing born out of the wealth of capital but is born out of the harmonic coexistence with the environment, is born fundamentally out of respect and of the understanding that we exist because there are others that make us (Carmen Lozano, indigenous leader ECUARUNARI. Interviewed July 2014).

However, indigenous leaders made clear in the interviews their concerns over the political use, effectiveness and representativeness of a discourse that puts *Pachamama* and communitarian life at the centre. Some of the interviewees even made ironic comments on the use of nature to define *Sumak Kawsay*. At the same time, some of them raised the issue of indigenous people living in the city and the latter's impact on their communitarian practices. They questioned the representativeness of a definition centred in communitarian life for those who, whether under duress or by choice, now live in the city, have an urban lifestyle, and are no longer peasants but workers. It was palpable during the interviews that the crucial question *What does it mean to be indigenous in the twenty-first century?* is under discussion and revision among the indigenous elite:

> On the one hand, there is an interpretation of *Sumak Kawsay* within the capitalist state. An example is when you see the sign 'Oil is life' in the Amazonia, that kind of *Sumak Kawsay*. Or you see big roads, motorways, the Panamericana, we can say that we are travelling in a better bus but at the end, who benefits from that? That is the expression of *Sumak Kawsay* from the government. But on the other, there is not a *Sumak Kawsay* from indigenous communities adapted to the current situation; there is one which is a sort of cultural interpretation, an antiquated one that can only be the product of an isolated, forest environment. But we need to debate about a *Sumak Kawsay* adapted to the current situation, one which proposes a real transformation of the Ecuadorian society as a whole. This

is something to be debated and constructed (Leonidas Iza, president of indigenous organisation UNOCAN[12]. Interviewed November 2014).

I argue that the emphasis placed on ancestral philosophy and communitarian practices risks essentialising indigenous cultural identity and neglects to some extent the pluralist contributions to the debate on *Sumak Kawsay* from feminists, ecologists, socialists and so on. The essentialising of *Sumak Kawsay* and indigenous identity can be taken as a strategy to differentiate the indigenous movement from other sectors associated with controversial government policies (Stefanoni 2010). However, an emphasis on the *Sumak Kawsay* philosophy with little connection to most people's everyday reality isolates a struggle that until recent years was able to represent the common interest and work as an inspiration. The retraction of this indigenous sector of an identity related to *Sumak Kawsay* and their rejection of *Buen Vivir* is proving risky in terms of their political strength at a time when those in power have been able to articulate a representative (and general) alternative project.

BUEN VIVIR AS RATIONAL SOCIAL TRANSFORMATION: THE CONSTRUCTION OF THE STATE—RAFAEL CORREA AND ALIANZA PAIS

The second discourse identified in this research I call the Rational *Buen Vivir*. The construction of this discourse is connected to the revitalisation of state institutions responsible for planning and development. It is mainly mobilised by the government and its allies with a strong technocratic and expert influence. While the revitalisation of state institutions is linked to progressive processes of decentralisation, consolidation of local self-government and citizen participation[13], the emphasis is mainly placed on reclaiming the central state as an institution of control, planning and management (SENPLADES 2013). Here, the state is presented as the privileged arena in which to deliberate the common good and national interests, recovering control over the public agenda. The supremacy of partial interests (indigenous, ecologist) over a general (universal) one is interpreted as going against the national project (Ramirez 2014).

At the heart of this project lies, firstly, the construction of a sovereign nation (*la patria es de todos* [the motherland belongs to everyone]; *volver a tener patria* [regain our motherland]), which in many ways opposes the project of a plurinational state and the predominance of the local above the national; secondly, the elimination of poverty via the redistribution of wealth; and thirdly, the guarantee of universal social security (which for some analysts can be thought of as an attempt to establish a welfare state in Ecuador). The project has one political horizon: the consolidation of the *Socialismo del Buen Vivir* or *bio-socialismo republicano* (Ramirez 2010) informed by neo-Marxist thought such as Dieterich's (2002) Socialism of the 21st Century and approaches to development such as Human Development (Deneulin and Shahani 2009).

The use of *Buen Vivir* to represent a 'national project of the left' by the promoters of this discourse is fundamental to their positioning as representatives of a radical change to neoliberalism, away from fiscal austerity, deregulation and the primacy of financial interests over the economy. *Buen Vivir* represents here an alternative to counteract the effects triggered by the crisis of the capitalist order. However, government officials are cautious in framing this project as a post-capitalist or post-neoliberal alternative per se. The need for foreign capital investment as well as the maintenance of old and new commercial agreements with global powers condition the scope of economic transformation in the country. Furthermore, some of the measures taken by the government of Rafael Correa (for example, restructuring and elimination of subsidies; the increase in oil and mining exploitation; a new loan from Goldman Sachs for 400 million dollars that brings the IMF back to examine the current state of the Ecuadorian economy) show that the economic project in the Ecuadorian case can be qualified more as a pragmatic one than a radical or post-capitalist alternative.[14]

The economic dimension of this discourse is centred on the state playing an important role in investment, control and regulation. A strong fiscal discipline together with public investment is the pillar of the economic dimension of the Rational *Buen Vivir*. The main financial source for state investment as well as for social spending is still oil revenues. Government officials argue that it is only through natural resources exploitation that the economy can be diversified, as high revenues would allow a higher investment in other areas of the economy. For the government, this reason is strong enough to dismiss many of the contradictions between its rhetoric and policies and what is included in official documents and laws in relation to environmental protection, agrarian policies and popular participation. These points constitute the main conflict with indigenous groups, among others.

Some of those who mobilise this discourse also point out critiques and shortcomings of this particular understanding of *Buen Vivir*. For example, in relation to popular participation, a government official working in SENPLADES (Secretaría Nacional de Planificación y Desarrollo) says that among the 12 objectives outlined by the *Plan del Buen Vivir* (2013–2017) popular participation is there as a 'purely decorative element. There is no political will from above to accept real and critical participation. Participation is only allowed to those who say everything is fine' (interview, August 2014). These critical voices coming from inside the government question how receptive the current government is to critiques coming from those who do not completely agree (or openly disagree) with the fundamental pillars defended by Correa's government.

The delimitation of political boundaries in this case is drawn between the government of the Revolución Ciudadana (Citizens' Revolution) and those who are strongly identified with the neoliberal past in Ecuador. The government of Rafael Correa questions the credibility and legitimacy of politicians of the *partidocracia* (party-bureaucracy), bankers and corporatist groups (mainly trade unions and indigenous organisations), remembering their involvement in governmental decisions during the 1980s and 1990s. *Prohibido olvidar* (forbidden to forget) is the main phrase used by Rafael Correa to refer to those who question current decisions of the government (belonging either to the political right or left) and who participated in controversial and unpopular actions during neoliberal times (cases of corruption, association with coups, privatisation and financial deregulation are used to exemplify this). In line with this view, the government has recently initiated a campaign against Restauración Conservadora (Conservative Restoration), accusing the movement of setting out to destabilise it.

The second political boundary is drawn between the government and those who strongly question the decisions of the government on environmental and economic matters. Young people involved with the *Yasunidos*[15] and other ecologist groups are denigrated as childish, traitors and enemies of the national project due to their opposition to extractive activities and their defence of the Yasuní-ITT proposal (Bebbington and Humphreys Bebbington 2011). The use of these political frontiers questions the government's openness to plural and antagonistic positions as well as its willingness to allow a plurality of actors to engage in public debates and participate in decision-making processes.

Deep *Buen Vivir*: Ecology and Post-Development in Action—the Environmentalists

A third discourse identified is that of Deep *Buen Vivir*. The promoters of this discourse are mainly academics, environmental activists and ecological organisations. The rights of nature granted by the national constitution are at the centre of this discourse, which are closely linked to the rights of a diversity of social groups such as indigenous, peasant, feminist, ecologist and socialist groups. Recognition of the rights of nature is used here to represent the path to a post-development era, a post-oil economy and a post-capitalist society. Capitalism is defined as the most extreme version of alienation, economic exploitation, inequality, coloniality of power and environmental degradation. The way to subvert this order is to focus on the local, communitarian and small-scale projects which can guarantee: first, the use of natural resources respecting the natural environment; and second, real participation of the people in both the definition and implementation of *Buen Vivir* as an alternative to development and neoliberal policies. Promoters of this discourse argue for an economy that promotes social solidarity, including agrarian reform that can guarantee food sovereignty, democratic access to land respecting collective ownership of territories, and the creation of incentives and financial credits given by the state to support small-scale projects. In addition, tourism is seen as a key economic sector which could replace extractive activities in the future.

The government of Rafael Correa is considered by these groups to be a betrayer of the process of change initiated in 2006. The 'pink tide' governments of the region are ironically depicted as complicit with international powers, which together aim to control natural resources and promote the intensification of the extractive economic model and with it, a new model of colonisation:

> The government of Rafael Correa (…) has changed direction, has betrayed the historical moment forged by popular and social forces that chose him as President. His mode of exercising power is more authoritarian, personalized and *caudillesco*[16] than ever; he encourages the modernization of capitalism, especially now that it is in a deep crisis, and the people's desire to

overcome it. A technocratic modernization of capitalism in Ecuador will not in itself save the country from the crisis of capitalism. This short-sightedness can only be understood as the result of the complicity of this government with transnational capital and with big national powers (Alberto Acosta, interviewed September 2014).

Those who mobilise this discourse point out the innovative effect of *Buen Vivir* in relation to hegemonic, dominant and monolithic understandings of sociopolitical and economic development. They conceive *Buen Vivir* as an idea that has to be constructed and reconstructed by the participation of a plurality of actors, although already showing its provocative power to deconstruct hegemonic truths. For this reason, and like the discourse mobilised by the indigenous sector, *Buen Vivir* and *Sumak Kawsay* are distinguished in order to highlight the different implications of each phrase according to the actors who mobilise it, and the co-option of the former by the forces in power in order to redefine and subsume it within conventional development.

The advances made by the government of Rafael Correa in relation to the role of the state in public investment and infrastructure are also recognised here. It can be argued that for those who question the actions of the *Revolución Ciudadana* that it is not only *what* the state does but *how* it does it, that matters. And in this 'how' lie the aspirations of many groups who conceive a different logic underpinning political, economic, social and cultural questions. In other words, what is important is not only the return of the state as a public arena of debate but equally, what state is built and who participates in it.

CONCLUSIONS

The analysis of these discourses shows no single that there is no single homogeneous, monolithic and essentialising notion of *Buen Vivir*, but that it is constructed and reconstructed in the process of power struggles between different forces. It has become apparent that new and provocative ideas are challenging a homogeneous and hegemonic understanding of economic, social, cultural and political issues. In this sense, this chapter shows that *Buen Vivir* has already affected the politics of Ecuador. Political groupings have strategically reframed *Buen Vivir* in terms of their interests, goals and political philosophies and continue to do so. This shows that *Buen Vivir* has been subjected to a process of rationalisation that allows the positioning of different forces in the political realm. This rationalisation has helped to create political boundaries (us and them) between stakeholders who are in competition for positions of power in a process of renewal of political settlements in Ecuador. In this way, I argue, the struggle over the meaning of *Buen Vivir* is of a deeply political nature, giving place to new demands and forms of insubordination.

NOTES

1. Kichwa people are mainly based in Ecuador; Aymaras in Bolivia; Mapuche groups in Chile and Argentina; and Guaraní groups are in Paraguay.
2. Offe (1985) makes a distinction between, on the one hand, 'institutional politics' in which actors' concerns are principally directed to the State; and on the other, 'non-institutional politics', where civil society becomes both the locus and target of action of social movements in order to defend their values (identity, autonomy and the creation of democratic spaces). Cohen and Arato (1992) term this as 'self-limiting radicalism' in order to emphasise the rejection by new social movements of the need or purpose to seize power. The focus of this chapter is placed on institutional politics, and therefore in the interaction between social movements and the state.
3. Even though Ecuador was not declared a plurinational country as demanded by indigenous organisations, the constitutional reform of 1998 recognised for the first time the existence of indigenous *nacionalidades* and *pueblos*.
4. Fourteen *nacionalidades*: Andoa, Awa, Siona, Espera, Chachi, Secoya, Shiwiar, Achuar, Huaorani, Zápara, Tsachila, Shuar, Kichwa Amazonia, Cofán. Eighteen *pueblos*: Huancavilca, Manta, Palta, Saraguro, Kañari, Pastos, Puruwa, Waranka, Kitu Kara, Salasaka, Panzaleo, Kisapincha, Chibuleo, Kayambi, Otavalo, Natabuela, Karanki, Tomabela (https://www.codenpe.gob.ec/) [Accessed August 2012).
5. The 1992 march was linked to '500 years of Resistance'; a campaign against official celebrations of the 500th anniversary of the 'discovery' of the Americas (Andolina 2003).
6. Ecuadorian traditional political parties: Partido Social Cristiano (PSC); Izquierda Democrática (ID); Democracia Popular—Unión Demócrata Cristiana (DP-UDC); Partido Roldosista Ecuatoriano (PRE).
7. Under Mahuad's presidency the Consejo para el Desarrollo de las Nacionalidades y Pueblos del Ecuador—CODENPE (Council for the Development of Ecuadorian Nationalities and Peoples) was created

6 BUEN VIVIR IN ECUADOR 139

by decree, and CONAIE was given a central role in its structure and administration.

8. ALBA: Alternativa Bolivariana para las Americas (2004). MERCOSUR: Mercado Común del Sur (1991). UNASUR: Union de Naciones Suramericanas (2008).

9. SENPLADES: Secretaría Nacional de Planificación y Desarrollo (Secretariat of National Planning and Development).

10. Food sovereignty is an international demand articulated and promoted by Via Campesina (international peasant movement) that has been recently endorsed by the United Nations Food and Agriculture Organization. Food sovereignty is related to land democratisation and communitarian distribution, small and community-led agricultural projects, and democratic access to water sources (Altieri Toledo 2011).

11. Indigenous organisation ECUARUNARI (Awakening of Ecuadorian Indigenous People).

12. Unión de Organizaciones Campesinas del Norte de Cotopaxi (Union of Peasant Organisations of Northern Cotopaxi).

13. The legal foundations of this process of state transformation are included in official documents such as the Código Orgánico de Ordenamiento Territorial, Autonomías y Descentralización (COOTAD, Organic Code of Territorial Organization, Autonomy and Decentralization [Accessed online: https://www.planificacion.gob.ec/sistema-de-informacion-para-los-gobiernos-autonomos-descentralizados/]; the *Plan Nacional de Descentralización* (National Plan for Decentralisation [Accessed online: https://www.planificacion.gob.ec/plan-nacional-de-descentralizacion/].

14. https://www.bbc.com/mundo/noticias/2014/07/140708_economia_ecuador_viraje_economico_correa_vp.shtml?ocid=socialflow_facebook.

15. The Yasuní is a national park located in the Ecuadorian Amazon and home to various indigenous peoples who consider it a sacred place. In 1999 part of the park was declared an 'untouchable zone', prohibiting its exploration and exploitation. The Ishpingo-Tambococha-Tiputini (ITT) is an oil field within the park. It is estimated that the oil reserves in this area are between 846 million to 950 million barrels, which represents 20% of the country's oil reserves (Rival 2010; Bebbington and Humphreys Bebbington 2011). The Yasuní-ITT initiative proposed to keep the oil in the soil in exchange for international monetary compensation. If that agreement was not reached, Ecuador planned to start the extraction of oil from the ITT field, which finally happened in August 2013. *Yasunidos* is a group of young ecologists formed after Correa's government decision to exploit the oil field. They were responsible for the collection of signatures to call a referendum to allow popular participation in the decision over the exploitation of the Yasuní. After collecting

more than the number of signatures required by law (a total of 756,623), the Consejo Nacional Electoral rejected most of these forms.

16. *Caudillesco* is difficult to translate. It describes a charismatic leader who, according to his (or her) adversaries, exercises political power in an authoritarian way.

REFERENCES

Acosta, A. (2005). La rebelión de los forajidos. *Iberoamérica, La Insignia.* Available at: http://www.lainsignia.org/2005/abril/ibe_071.htm.

Acosta, A. (2008). El 'Buen Vivir' para la construcción de alternativas. In A. Acosta (Ed.), *Entre el quiebre y la realidad: Constitución 2008* (pp. 27–37). Quito: Abya-Yala.

Albó, X. (2009). Suma Qamaña = el buen convivir. Centro de Investigación y Promoción del Campesinado (CIPCA). Available at: http://www.cipca.org.bo/.

Altieri, M. A., & Toledo, V. M. (2011). The Agroecological Revolution in Latin America: Rescuing Nature, Ensuring Food Sovereignty and Empowering Peasants. *Journal of Peasant Studies, 38*(3), 587–612.

Andolina, R. (2003). The Sovereign and Its Shadow: Constituent Assembly and Indigenous Movement in Ecuador. *Journal of Latin American Studies, 35*(4), 721–750.

Andolina, R., Laurie, N., & Radcliffe, S. (2009). *Indigenous Development in the Andes: Culture, Power, and Transnationalism.* Durham and London: Duke University Press.

Arditi, B. (2008). Arguments About the Left Turns in Latin America: A Post-Liberal Politics? *Latin American Research Review, 43*(3), 59–81.

Bebbington, A., & Humphreys Bebbington, D. (2011). An Andean Avatar: Post-Neoliberal and Neoliberal Strategies for Securing the Unobtainable. *New Political Economy, 16*(1), 131–145.

Becker, M. (2008). *Indians and Leftists in the Making of Ecuador's Modern Indigenous Movements.* London: Duke University Press.

Becker, M. (2010). The Children of 1990. *Alternatives, 35,* 291–316.

Cohen, J., & Arato, A. (1992). *Civil Society and Political Theory.* Cambridge, MA: MIT Press.

CONAIE. (2012). *Proyecto político para la construcción del Estado Plurinacional e Intercultural.* Quito: CONAIE.

Cortez, D. (2010). La construcción social del 'Buen Vivir' (Sumak Kawsay) en Ecuador. Genealogía del diseño y gestión política de la vida. In *Aportes Andinos* (28). Quito: Universidad Andina Simón Bolívar.

Davidov, V. (2012). Saving Nature or Performing Sovereignty? Ecuador's Initiative to 'Keep Oil in the Ground'. *Anthropology Today, 28*(3), 12–15.

Deneulin, S., & Shahani, L. (2009). *An Introduction to the Human Development and Capability Approach: Freedom and Agency.* London: Earthscan.

Dieterich, H. (2002). *El socialismo del siglo XXI*. Bogotá: Fundación para la Investigación y la Cultura.

Escobar, A. (2010). Latin America at a Crossroads: Alternative Modernizations, Post-Liberalism or Post-Development? *Cultural Studies, 24*(1), 1–65.

Gane, N. (2002). *Max Weber and Postmodern Theory: Rationalisation Versus Re-enchantment*. New York: Palgrave.

Gardini, G. (2010). Proyectos de integración regional sudamericana: hacia una teoría de convergencia regional. *Relaciones Internacionales, 15*, 11–31.

Grugel, J., & Riggirozzi, P. (2012). Post-neoliberalism in Latin America: Rebuilding and Reclaiming the State after Crisis. *Development and Change, 43*(1), 1–21.

Gudynas, E. (2009). La Dimensión Ecológica del Buen Vivir: entre el fantasma de la modernidad y el desafío biocéntrico. *OBETS: Revista de Ciencias Sociales, 4*, 49–53.

Gudynas, E. (2010). Más allá del nuevo extractivismo: Transiciones sostenibles y alternativas al desarrollo. In F. Wanderley (Ed.), *El desarrollo en cuestión. Reflexiones desde América Latina*. La Paz: Oxfam y CIDES UMSA.

Gudynas, E. (2011). Buen Vivir: Today's Tomorrow. *Development, 54*(4), 441–447.

Habermas, J. (1986). The Theory of Communicative Action. *Reason and the Rationalisation of Society*, Volume I. Cambridge: Polity Press.

Harnecker, M. (2010). El nuevo modelo económico del socialismo del siglo XXI. Algunos elementos para la discusión. In SENPLADES (Ed.), *Los Nuevos Retos de América Latina: Socialismo y Sumak Kawsay* (pp. 77–90). Quito: SENPLADES.

Jameson, K. P. (2011). The Indigenous Movement in Ecuador. *Latin American Perspectives, 38*(1), 63–73.

Kennemore, A., & Weeks, G. (2011). Twenty-First Century Socialism? The Elusive Search for a Post-Neoliberal Development Model in Bolivia and Ecuador. *Bulletin of Latin American Research, 30*(3), 267–281.

Lucero, J. A. (2001). Crisis and Contention in Ecuador. *Journal of Democracy, 12*(2), 59–73.

Lucero, J. A. (2003). Locating the 'Indian Problem'. Community, Nationality, and Contradiction in Ecuadorian Indigenous Politics. *Latin American Perspectives, 128*(30), 23–48.

Machado Puertas, J. C. (2007). Ecuador: el derrumbe de los partidos tradicionales. *Revista de Ciencia Política, 27*, 129–147.

Medina, J. (Ed.). (2008). *Suma Qamaña. La Comprensión Indígena de la Vida Buena*. La Paz: Componente Equidad Social.

Misoczky, M. C. (2011). World Visions in Dispute in Contemporary Latin America: Development x Harmonic Life. *Organization, 18*(3), 345–363.

Offe, C. (1985). New Social Movements: Challenging the Boundaries of Institutional Politics. *Social Research, 52*(4), 817.

Philip, G., & Panizza, F. (2011). *The Triumph of Politics: The Return of the Left in Venezuela, Bolivia and Ecuador*. Cambridge: Polity Press.

Pomar, V. (2010). Algunas ideas sobre la lucha por el socialismo en el siglo XXI. In SENPLADES (Ed.), *Los Nuevos Retos de América Latina: Socialismo y Sumak Kawsay* (pp. 141–148). Quito: SENPLADES.

Prevost, G., Oliva Campos, C., & Vanden, H. (Eds.). (2012). *Social Movements and Leftist Governments in Latin America: Confrontation or Co-optation?* London: Zed Books.

Radcliffe, S. (2012). Development for a Postneoliberal Era? *Sumak kawsay, Living Well* and the Limits to Decolonisation in Ecuador. *Geoforum, 43,* 240–249.

Ramírez, F. (2014). Autonomía estatal, cambio político y post-neoliberalismo. In E. Recalde (Ed.), *Construcción de un Estado Democrático para el Buen Vivir: análisis de las principales transformaciones del Estado Ecuatoriano 2007–2012.* Quito: SENPLADES.

Ramirez, R. (2010). *Socialismo del Sumak Kawsay o biosocialismo republicano.* Quito: SENPLADES.

Rival, L. (2010). Ecuador's Yasuní-ITT Initiative: The Old and New Values of Petroleum. *Ecological Economics, 70*(2), 358–365.

Salgado, F. (2010). *Sumaq Kawsay:* The Birth of a Notion? *Cuadernos EBAPEBR, 8*(2), 198–208.

Santos, B. (2010). *Refundación del Estado en América Latina.* Lima: Instituto Internacional de Derecho y Sociedad.

SENPLADES. (2010). *Plan Nacional de Buen Vivir, 2009–2013.* Quito: SENPLADES.

SENPLADES. (2013). *Plan Nacional de Desarrollo/Plan Nacional de Buen Vivir 2013–2017.* Quito: SENPLADES.

Stefanoni, P. (2010). *¿Una nueva izquierda?* Available at: http://www.rebelion.org/noticia.php?id=78813.

Thomson, B. (2011). Pachakuti: Indigenous Perspectives, *Buen Vivir, Sumaq Kawsay* and Degrowth. *Development, 54*(4), 448–454.

Van Cott, D. L. (2005). *From Movements to Parties in Latin America: The Evolution of Ethnic Politics.* Cambridge: Cambridge University Press.

Walsh, C. (2010). Development as *Buen Vivir:* Institutional Arrangements and (De)Colonial Entanglements. *Development, 53*(1), 15–21.

Yashar, D. (1999). Democracy, Indigenous Movements, and the Postliberal Challenge in Latin America. *World Politics, 52*(1), 76–104.

Zamosc, L. (2004). The Indian Movement in Ecuador: From Politics of Influence to Politics of Power. In N. G. Postero & L. Zamosc (Eds.), *The Struggle for Indigenous Rights in Latin America.* Brighton: Sussex Academic Press.

CHAPTER 7

Challenging the Dominant Economic Narrative Through Alternative Wellbeing Indicators: The Canadian Experience

Anders Hayden and Jeffrey Wilson

Introduction[1]

Questioning of Gross Domestic Product (GDP) as a proxy measure of prosperity and wellbeing has intensified in recent years, with important contributions to the debate from Canadian sources. Canadian researchers have played key roles in the study of wellbeing (e.g., Helliwell 2002; Michalos 2014) and in the new *World Happiness Report* (Helliwell et al. 2016). Canadian economists developed an Index of Economic Wellbeing in the late 1990s based on principles similar to those that the Stiglitz-Sen-Fitoussi (2009) Commission later highlighted, such as the need to consider multiple dimensions of wellbeing and give greater emphasis to income distribution (Osberg and Sharpe 2010). Canadians have made significant contributions to Bhutan's efforts to pursue and measure

A. Hayden (✉) · J. Wilson
Dalhousie University, Halifax, NS, Canada
e-mail: anders.hayden@dal.ca

J. Wilson
e-mail: jeffrey.wilson@dal.ca

© The Author(s) 2018
I. Bache and K. Scott (eds.), *The Politics of Wellbeing*, Wellbeing in Politics and Policy, https://doi.org/10.1007/978-3-319-58394-5_7

Gross National Happiness (GNH).[2] Innovative work on the calculation of a Genuine Progress Indicator (GPI) has taken place in two Canadian provinces, as discussed below. In 2011, with the release of the Canadian Index of Wellbeing (CIW), Canada became one of the first countries with its own composite wellbeing index.

In Canada and elsewhere, the green movement and academics sympathetic to it have been among the main voices calling for alternatives to GDP as a prosperity indicator, part of a broader challenge to the dominant narrative of progress that prioritizes economic growth (Daly and Cobb 1989; Anderson 1991; Jackson 2009; O'Neill 2012). More recently, interest in beyond-GDP indicators has spread to the academic and political mainstream (Bache and Scott, this volume, Chap. 1). Indeed, some critics of conventional economic measures and priorities argue that a 'chance to dethrone GDP is now in sight' (Costanza et al. 2014, p. 283).

Many of those calling for new indicators around the world have argued that they will contribute significantly to sustainability, equity, and greater wellbeing. Jonathon Porritt (2007, p. 255), then chair of Britain's Sustainable Development Commission, wrote that new indicators would be a 'short, sharp statistical shock to the system.' Meanwhile, *Limits to Growth* report co-author Donella Meadows (1998, p. 5) wrote that: 'changing indicators can be one of the most powerful and at the same time one of the easiest ways of making system changes—it does not require firing people, ripping up physical structures, inventing new technologies, or enforcing new regulations. It only requires delivering new information to new places.' However, not all voices in the debate seek radical change. A distinction is evident—in Canada and internationally, in both academic and policy debates—between a transformative vision of alternative indicators as a way to shift societal priorities away from GDP growth and a less expansive, reformist vision of alternative indicators as a tool for better policymaking without challenging the growth paradigm or seeking broad social transformation.

Development of beyond-GDP indicators has reached the point that an opportunity now exists to ask: What effect are they having in practice? Is there any evidence to date that they have shaped policy and public priorities in ways that live up to their supporters' hopes and expectations? What are the obstacles to fulfilling those expectations? What conditions and further changes are needed to achieve progress toward the respective visions for alternative indicators? Some work addressing similar questions has been conducted on recent beyond-GDP initiatives in Europe (e.g., Wallace and Schmuecker 2012; Whitby et al. 2014; Bleys and Whitby 2015), while there is also a more extensive literature on the impacts of other indicator sets, such as sustainable-development indicators (e.g., Rydin et al. 2003; Boulanger 2007; Scott 2012, Chap. 5; Rinne et al. 2013; Lehtonen et al. 2016). We examine these issues by looking at Canada's experience with alternative wellbeing measurement.

To answer these questions, 16 semi-structured interviews were conducted in 2014 and 2015 with elite respondents—Canadian politicians, senior public servants, academics, NGO researchers, and activists—involved in developing, applying, or advocating use of new wellbeing indicators (see Appendix for interviewee list). We sought out individuals involved with measurements that could potentially replace or complement GDP at national or provincial levels, notably the CIW, the GPI, and 'green GDP'; some interviewees also had related experience with local measurement initiatives. Interviewees were identified based on existing contacts with individuals working in this field, review of websites and documents produced by organizations involved in these issues, and snowball techniques as initial interviewees provided new contacts. After the research findings were written up, respondents were contacted again to review and, if necessary, revise and update points taken from their interviews. (New points or substantive revisions that interviewees made at this time are cited as personal communication, 2016.) The study also draws on analysis of relevant documents from organizations involved in producing, using, and advocating the use of alternative indicators.

ALTERNATIVE INDICATORS AND THE ENVIRONMENTAL/GREEN STATE

The beyond-GDP agenda includes more than environmental issues, but given the prominence of ecological concerns among many of the initial Canadian proponents of new wellbeing measurements, and our own interest in the possible links between new measurements and ecological transitions, we consider these issues in the context of the emergence of an environmental or green state (Dryzek et al. 2003; Eckersley 2004; Barry and Eckersley 2005; Meadowcroft 2012; Kronsell and Bäckstrand 2015; Duit et al. 2016). Like others, we distinguish between an 'environmental state,' which is a widespread, existing phenomenon, and a 'green state,' a normative ideal yet to be attained (Duit et al. 2016).

An environmental state is one that includes environmental management among its key functions (Meadowcroft 2012; Duit et al. 2016). Environmental state theorists argue that, in developed democracies, the environment has joined security, the economy, and the welfare state as a core domain of state activity. The state's environmental role, from regulating pollution to negotiating global environmental accords, has greatly expanded in recent decades and will likely continue evolving (Meadowcroft 2012; Duit et al. 2016). Beyond-GDP indicators, which incorporate environmental costs and benefits or include sustainability measures as a main component, can be seen as another step in the environmental state's evolution. Alternative indicators are closely linked to a key task of the environmental state: addressing problems caused by the negative environmental externalities of economic activity, i.e., environmental costs not reflected in market prices (Duit 2016; Sommerer and Lim 2016). As states increasingly take on that task, GDP becomes more limited as a measure of success since it does not account for those external costs. That said, measurement reforms, like other steps that expand the state's environmental role, need not lead to any downplaying of the pursuit of economic growth. Many environmental states have tried to pursue environmental goals and GDP growth through (weak) ecological modernization, or 'green growth,' that relies on improved technology and efficiency to decouple growth from negative environmental impacts (Christoff 2005; Mol et al. 2009; Tobin 2015). Such efforts are consistent with the reformist vision of alternative indicators, discussed above, as new indicators that complement GDP could guide the pursuit of 'green growth' (GCEC 2014, pp. 19–20; OECD 2014).

Emergence of a green state would involve a more radical transformation than in actually existing environmental states (Eckersley 2004; Tobin 2015; Duit et al. 2016). Christoff (2005, p. 41) writes that a green state's features would include commitment to 'strong ecological modernization' based on 'a driving and predominant moral purpose in directing social and economic activity toward ecologically sustainable (and socially just) outcomes.' Duit adds that a green/ecological state is one that has reversed the priority between economic growth and environment and consistently favours the latter when they conflict (Duit 2016). A green state thus has an affinity with a transformative vision for alternative indicators. Beyond-GDP measures could be part of a green state's prioritization of ecological sustainability and less consumption-oriented ways of achieving wellbeing (Barry 2015; Frugoli et al. 2015).

A green state would also need new sustainable wellbeing measures to show that alternative choices, such as work-time reduction over income growth (Coote and Franklin 2013), have social benefits that GDP's monetary focus fails to capture.

A transformative vision for beyond-GDP measures, like the wider transition to a green state, faces daunting obstacles as it clashes with what is widely considered a core political imperative of contemporary states. Economic growth is perceived to be essential to raise revenue to carry out other core functions, such as ensuring security and legitimizing the social order through social spending, in addition to its role in creating jobs and enabling profit-making and capital accumulation (Dryzek 1996; Dryzek et al. 2003; Hayden 2014). A transformative vision of beyond-GDP measures, which seeks to shift priorities away from growth, thus faces far greater obstacles than more limited formulations of new indicators as a tool for better policy and greener growth. At the same time, the indicators issue has opened up space for discussion about society's end goals and how to achieve them, creating opportunities for those who question the focus on economic growth. The beyond-GDP debate thus represents intriguing terrain as it is constrained by contemporary political imperatives and yet offers a platform upon which some political actors are trying to re-define those imperatives.

BEYOND-GDP MEASUREMENT INITIATIVES IN CANADA

As noted above, Canada has been a leader in academic and nongovernmental organization (NGO) work on alternative indicators (e.g., Osberg and Sharpe 2010). In the 1990s and into the 2000s, much work in this area, involving researchers and activists with a green critique of the conventional economic growth model, focused on the Genuine Progress Indicator (GPI). The GPI, which grew out of Daly and Cobb's (1989) Index of Sustainable Economic Welfare, adjusts GDP by including a wider range of costs and benefits. GPI Atlantic, an NGO based in the province of Nova Scotia, has played an important role in refining and promoting 'genuine progress' measurement (Pannozzo et al. 2008). Meanwhile, innovations in GPI calculations were applied in the province of Alberta by the Pembina Institute (an environmental NGO) and ecological economist Mark Anielski (Anielski et al. 2001, p. 1). Their work showed that while Alberta's GDP increased 483 per cent between 1961 and 2003, its GPI decreased 20 per cent (Taylor 2005). Follow-up work included a GPI for the province's capital city Edmonton (Anielski and Johannessen 2009).

In 2001, work began on the CIW, drawing on the expertise of leading thinkers in this area, including GPI researchers. The Atkinson Charitable Foundation, a backer of progressive social causes, supported the CIW during its development, while former Saskatchewan Premier Roy Romanow (New Democratic Party—NDP) and former federal health minister Monique Bégin (Liberal) acted as political champions. The CIW is based on 64 indicators in eight domains: community vitality, democratic engagement, education, environment, healthy populations, leisure and culture, living standards, and time use. Although there has been a public-sector contribution to alternative wellbeing measurement (discussed below), the CIW is not produced by any government agency. Researchers at the University of Waterloo have taken charge of its production, releasing national figures in 2011, 2012, and 2016, and provincial results for Ontario in 2014 (CIW 2012, 2014, 2016).

The CIW's (2016) figures showed that from 1994 to 2014, Canada's GDP grew 38.0 per cent, but the CIW rose just 9.9 per cent. The 'wellbeing gap' between economic output and the CIW grew after the 2008 recession as the CIW took much longer than GDP to return to pre-recession levels. These numbers—like the Alberta GPI figures above—were consistent with growth critics' argument that greater economic output was not strongly associated with increased wellbeing; however, they also showed that recessions and unemployment were highly destructive of wellbeing (see also CIW 2012). While Canada did well in some areas—e.g., education, health, and community vitality (notably falling crime)—the 'leisure and culture' and environment domains deteriorated after 1994. Pointing to Canada's increasing greenhouse gas (GHG) emissions and very large per capita ecological footprint, the CIW (2012, p. 5) highlighted 'the tension between the relentless pursuit of economic growth and the finite reality of a planet experiencing massive climate change and dwindling natural resources.' Many Canadians also faced a 'time crunch,' as almost one in five working-age adults felt high levels of time pressure, prompting the authors to write: 'Certainly economic growth is laudable. But what does it mean to a society if it comes at the expense of less free time, fewer social connections, lower personal satisfaction, and a more stressful life?' (CIW 2012, p. 9; see also CIW 2016, pp. 49–51).

The CIW has a number of strengths as a beyond-GDP alternative, illustrating the considerable intellectual work that went into its design.

There has been much debate over the merits of a single, attention-grabbing headline indicator that can rival GDP compared to a dashboard of indicators (e.g., Stiglitz et al. 2009; Fleurbaey and Blanchet 2013, Chap. 1). The CIW provides both, as one can compare change in the overall index to GDP and also see trends within different domains. A challenge with some alternative measures has been the difficulty of communicating the meaning of the results; for example, Bhutan's GNH Index is constructed in a very elaborate and complicated way. The CIW, in contrast, provides easy-to-understand percentage changes in the overall index and its domains. Indeed, significant resources were devoted to develop the Index in a way that it could be communicated effectively. 'We ensured that measurement experts had to work with communications people,' said the former Director of the Atkinson Foundation (Pascal interview 2014). By including environmental indicators, the CIW highlights the need to pursue wellbeing in sustainable ways—an issue that World Happiness Report rankings of countries, for example, do not address. Although criticisms have been raised, including objections to subjective choices about variables included in the Index and their weightings, the CIW offers a possible model that has attracted attention abroad (e.g., Wallace and Schmuecker 2012).[3]

Some interest in beyond-GDP measurement was evident under the Liberal federal governments led by Jean Chrétien and Paul Martin. In 2000, as finance minister, Martin provided $9 million to the National Round Table on the Environment and Economy to develop new environmental and sustainable development indicators. Martin (2000, p. 15) optimistically proclaimed: 'In the years ahead, these environmental indicators could well have a greater impact on public policy than any other single measure we might introduce.' Martin himself favored a 'Green GDP' adjusted for environmental depletion costs, although introducing the new measure did not become a top priority while he was finance minister or prime minister. Also in 2000, Liberal MP Joe Jordan introduced a private member's bill, the Canada Wellbeing Measurement Act, to require the federal government to produce new economic, social, and environmental wellbeing indicators.

Although Statistics Canada, the national statistics agency, did not take charge of producing a beyond-GDP alternative, some of its officials did contribute to developing the CIW and it is the main data source for the indicators used to calculate the Index. Statistics Canada has also collected data on life satisfaction for over a decade on large numbers of respondents through the General Social Survey and the Canadian Community Health Survey—indeed, it has collected survey data on subjective wellbeing in various forms for over 25 years (Bonikowska et al. 2013)—and has produced analysis of variables associated with life satisfaction (e.g., Lu et al. 2015).

Numerous local initiatives have calculated and used new social and environmental indicators. Much of this work has occurred through the Vital Signs programme of the Community Foundations of Canada (2015), with 49 communities measuring key quality-of-life indicators (see also Wallace and Schmuecker 2012). In recent years, the CIW's community wellbeing survey has played a greater role in such local-level measurements, noted CIW Director Bryan Smale (interview, 2014).

Hopes and Motivations

Interviewees involved in developing and promoting alternative economic and wellbeing indicators expressed a mix of radical and (mostly) reformist hopes and motivations.[4] Some saw their efforts as a challenge to the wider growth paradigm. Recognition that 'growth ever-lasting is not compatible with long-term wellbeing on planet earth' was the motivation for Green Party politician Peter Bevan-Baker to initiate, with fellow growth critic Mike Nickerson, work on the Canada Wellbeing Measurement Act in the late 1990s (interview, 2015)[5] Bevan-Baker also emphasized the 'disconnect between wealth and wellbeing,' arguing that 'having more stuff' is 'not the route to human satisfaction.' The Green Party of Canada (2015, p. 11) similarly linked its call for 'new measurements of our societal health and prosperity' to the idea that 'unending economic growth is a dangerous illusion.' Meanwhile, Dan O'Neill (2012), a UK-based, Canadian ecological economist, has worked on new indicator systems to assess 'de-growth' toward a sustainable, steady-state economy. However, most interviewees did not frame the issue as a direct challenge to a growth-based system.

On the related issue of whether the goal was to replace or complement GDP, the latter view dominated among interviewees, as in the wider debate. 'GDP is a useful measure, but it becomes less than useful is when it is your only measure,' former MP Joe Jordan stated (interview, 2015; see also Romanow 2009). 'I would not have gotten rid of the GDP as it is too historically rooted and the comparisons flowing from it are important to too many people,' said former Prime Minister Paul Martin (personal communication, 2016). His preferred alternative measure was, as mentioned, a 'green GDP' or 'GDP-plus' that accounted for environmental costs and resource depletion. Others expressed hopes that alternatives, such as the CIW, 'would be as prominent as GDP reports' (Messinger interview, 2014) or, similarly, that 'every time that GDP is reported, we'd get reported as well' (Smale interview, 2014).

A key goal of the CIW was to 'create an alternative measure that would change the conversation around the water coolers of the nation' (Pascal interview, 2014). Another explicit goal was that 'eventually governments would assume responsibility for this index and adopt it at the provincial, national, and municipal level to measure their progress' and use it to 'create policy' (Anielski interview, 2014). A respondent noted that official government adoption of alternative measures was important to give them legitimacy and to signal a shift in 'the objectives of society as a whole' (Nickerson interview, 2015).

Overriding goals included enabling governments to 'design better public policy' and 'make evidence-based decisions that respond to the values and needs of Canadians' (Romanow 2009; Romanow, quoted in Grant 2012). A related hope, expressed by Katherine Scott of the Canadian Council on Social Development, was for 'a more balanced perspective' between economic goals and other policy objectives (interview, 2015). Romanow (interview, 2014) referred to wellbeing indices as 'a counter-balance on a teeter-totter with GDP at the other end,' while Liberal MP Joe Jordan sought to counter the 'extreme bias toward economic indicators' that 'do not give the total picture' (Hansard 2003a). Reality Check (2001), a publication promoting 'new measures of progress' in Canada, proclaimed 'Such measures will prod our leaders to put the same energy into promoting social progress and preventing environmental decline as they currently put into promoting economic growth and preventing recession.'

New wellbeing measures have generated hopes, in Canada and abroad, of better decision-making by overcoming policy silos (e.g. APPGWE 2014, pp. 15–16). One interviewee seeking a more integrated approach to policy spoke of his appreciation for frameworks such as Bhutan's Gross National Happiness, which elevates wellbeing to 'the ultimate outcome that we are all striving for,' and allows cross-sector planning 'because no silo owns wellbeing' (Pennock interview, 2014).

Former MP Joe Jordan (interview, 2015) expressed an additional motivation that a wider set of wellbeing indicators would provide objective information akin to a 'report card' that enhances voters' capacities to 'decide whether governments are worth supporting.'

IMPACTS

Canadian work in this area has generated occasional blips of media attention. For example, the 2001 Alberta GPI report garnered a front-page headline in *The Globe and Mail,* a prominent national newspaper, proclaiming that 'Fat-Cat Albertans struggle with happiness' (Mittelstaedt 2001). Meanwhile, the CIW's 2012 release produced headlines such as 'Canadian economy grows, but quality of life on the decline' and 'Happiness lags prosperity, study finds' (CTV 2012; Scoffield 2012). In principle, such evidence and the media coverage it generated provided a political opportunity to those seeking to challenge existing societal and policy priorities. However, there is no sign that the conversation at the nation's water coolers has changed in any fundamental way, while there are only a few small-scale signs of impact on public policy, discussed below.

Despite advanced Canadian work on these issues, no government in Canada, federal or provincial, had by mid-2017 begun to calculate or use the CIW, or any other beyond-GDP alternative. Prior to taking power in 2009, Nova Scotia's center-left New Democratic Party (NDP) did pledge 'to incorporate Genuine Progress accounting into provincial policy analysis' (GPI Atlantic 2009); however, the NDP government did not act on this promise. The Canada Wellbeing Measurement Act of 2000—which, as noted above, would have required the federal government to produce new economic, social, and environmental wellbeing indicators—never made its way through Parliament, although the House of Commons did approve a related, nonbinding motion in 2003. In 2012, a similar private member's bill, the Canada Genuine Progress Measurement Act, was introduced by the country's small Green Party, which had become the main backer of new wellbeing measures among federal parties.

Many interviewees expressed disappointment at the limited impact to date. When asked if the CIW had been effective at changing or influencing policy, Smale replied, 'At this point, I have to say no. Our efforts to raise awareness through the release of our national and provincial indicators have gotten a lot of traction, attention. Has that transferred to policy change? Probably not. Not that I'm aware of, at the provincial or national level' (interview, 2014). 'We made the pitch for [the CIW], but couldn't get much reaction from political leaders or the bureaucracy,' explained Romanow (interview, 2015). Bevan-Baker noted that the political impact of work on the Canada Wellbeing Measurement Act, GPI, and CIW has been 'somewhere between minimal and non-existent, sadly' (interview, 2015).

Some interviewees saw greater awareness of alternative possibilities as one positive impact. While he could not trace any direct impacts from his work on the Canada Wellbeing Measurement Act, Nickerson said, 'We were able to reach a lot of people' and open a conversation about 'what we are trying to accomplish as a society' (personal communication, 2016.) Another respondent said that alternative indicators are 'a direction not yet taken, but on the positive side, at least people know the direction exists. ... it opens up a possibility for the future' (Charles personal communication, 2016). Similarly, Scott acknowledged a loss of momentum on the issue, but saw it as a 'long-term process' and was optimistic that the idea that 'wellbeing is not exclusively about the scale or scope of the Canadian economy has taken root' (interview, 2015).

Some interviewees were more optimistic about local use of alternative wellbeing measures. 'I think the action is at the community level,' said Scott (interview, 2015). She pointed, among other examples, to municipal dashboards with a comprehensive range of wellbeing measures and the 'exemplary community tracking' through Websites such as wellbeing Toronto and MyPeg in Winnipeg. Anielski, who similarly saw 'greater traction at the local level,' pointed to the city of Edmonton's use of the GPI in its strategic planning and a 30-year vision (interview, 2014). Smale noted that municipal and regional governments have used the CIW's community wellbeing survey in sustainability planning, adding that the 'community wellbeing survey probably has the greatest momentum right now' (interview, 2014). One example has been the Guelph Wellbeing Initiative, which used the CIW framework to measure wellbeing among the Ontario city's residents and identify priorities for programs and projects (Guelph 2015). The Association of Ontario Health Centres has also adopted the CIW framework to guide its work with local communities (Pascal personal communication, 2016; Smale interview, 2014).

Another below-the-radar example of impact was the 2014 decision by the Ontario Trillium Foundation, a provincial agency that distributes some $110 million annually in community grants, to use the CIW framework and a selection of its indicators to guide grant-making in six priority areas (Smale interview, 2014).

Obstacles to Greater Impact

Numerous obstacles to greater impact are evident, including some that are typical with pursuit of any reform: 'inertia' that kept the focus on the GDP as the key economic variable in policymaking (Charles interview, 2014); resistance from those who did not understand the idea and its potential, which highlights the importance of strong communications (Pascal interview, 2014); and the need for a 'reorientation of our thinking' to see wellbeing in wider terms (Pennock interview, 2014). Beyond such common difficulties, some more specific challenges are evident.

Challenges of Constructing and Agreeing on Alternative Measures

Accessing high-quality and conceptually valid data in a timely manner and finding the resources to produce alternative measures have been among the difficulties faced. 'At the end of the day, you're held hostage to the data that are available, and the methods and periodicity with which it is produced,' said Scott (interview, 2015). Ron Colman of GPI Atlantic noted that GDP is measured monthly, but Canada has only studied wealth distribution three times, and time-use studies of unpaid work only happen every seven years (personal communication, 2016). With cutbacks to Statistics Canada, data-availability challenges have grown (Duffy 2014). While government has not taken on responsibility for a beyond-GDP alternative, those producing the CIW do so without secure funding, spending significant time fundraising and taking on small projects, while still trying to maintain focus on regular production of the Index (Smale personal communication, 2016).

Another key challenge has been a lack of consensus on the best alternative measures and how to construct them. Although much work has come to focus on the CIW, there has not been universal agreement on its merits. One anonymous interviewee (2015) recalled disagreements over the way the various measures that make up the CIW were aggregated. Former Prime Minister Martin favored including environmental depletion costs in a 'green GDP' or 'GDP-plus,' but he disagreed with others over inclusion of wider wellbeing indicators in a single measure: 'I believe so strongly in the environmental indicators that I want to win that battle first. I'm worried that if we are fighting on too many fronts at once that we are not going to win it.' He stated that 'GDP-plus' could be 'measured objectively and serve as the fundamental indicator,' but he was concerned that wellbeing and happiness indicators were more subjective and could lack credibility (personal communication, 2016). In contrast, another interviewee maintained that 'we need to be triple bottom line' and measure progress in economic, environmental, and social terms (Pascal interview, 2014).

What Are Alternative Indicators for? Who Leads the Way?

Closely related to the lack of full agreement on the best alternative is the pursuit by proponents of alternative indicators of many different agendas. Some individuals are strongly motivated by the need for better environmental indicators, although they are divided between those seeking reforms to a growth-based system and others seeking to challenge the growth paradigm. Distinctions also exist between those motivated primarily by environmental and various social concerns, such as former Saskatchewan Premier Romanow, who saw the issue primarily in health and wellbeing terms, emphasizing the need to look beyond the treatment of illness to address the full range of social determinants of health (interview, 2014). In principle, ways exist to integrate many of these different perspectives—to take the 'triple bottom line' approach mentioned above—but the challenges are significant in bridging the different priorities, agendas, and messages.[6] Multiple agendas and conflicting values behind different approaches to wellbeing measurement have also been evident beyond Canada (Cassiers and Thiry 2015; McGregor 2015).

While beyond-GDP measurement could potentially serve a variety of political agendas, Scott noted that in Canada it has yet to be 'attached to an action agenda.' She contrasted the situation with poverty measurement, which, in some provinces, has been closely linked to poverty-reduction plans. 'Why does this matter? That has to be the first question .... I don't think we've made that particularly clear,' she added, identifying a limitation that has also arisen in other countries and with other types of indicators (interview, 2015).[7]

There are also unresolved questions about who can drive the change in measurement and raise the issue's profile. Although important support has come from former political leaders, as well as backbench MPs and the Green Party, no leader while in power federally or provincially has prioritized introducing a beyond-GDP alternative. The need for a 'bold leader' was voiced by Bevan-Baker (interview, 2015), while an anonymous interviewee expressed hope that the issue would be taken up by a 'Tommy Douglas' reformer in government or a 'David Suzuki' civil-society leader capable of building public support.[8] Former MP Joe Jordan saw a need for grass-roots pressure to overcome the hesitancy of politicians unsure that the issue is a 'political winner,' adding that 'this is going to have be something that Canadians demand' (interview, 2015). However, Canadian governments to date have faced little public pressure to calculate and use new wellbeing indicators—research in Europe has similarly identified a 'lack of a clear political imperative' to use beyond-GDP indicators (Whitby et al. 2014, pp. 6, 29). Although new indicators have elicited interest among various groups within Canadian society, no constituency with significant political force has made it a priority demand. An anonymous interviewee (2015) noted that many civil-society groups wanted more social and economic data, and issues such as restoring Canada's long-form census were 'on their agenda,' but alternatives to GDP such as the CIW were far lower on the priority list.

Anti-reflexive Conservatism

Although Smale noted that the CIW has been accused of being on the political left, one need not be left-leaning to support beyond-GDP measurements (personal communication, 2016). That was evident, for example, in support for the Canada Wellbeing Measurement Act from a Canadian Alliance (right-wing) MP, who was interested in ways to 'measure the cost of crime and the value of work in the home,' according to Nickerson (interview, 2015). Indeed, many Canadian Alliance MPs, including then leader Stephen Harper, voted for Motion 385 in 2003 calling for a new set of social, environmental, and economic indicators (Hansard 2003b). High-level conservative interest in alternative wellbeing measures has been evident in other countries, including France under President Sarkozy (2010) and Britain during David Cameron's time as Prime Minister (Cameron 2006; Bache and Reardon 2016, pp. 73–76).

That said, there were particular challenges during Stephen Harper's Conservative government (2006–2015). New wellbeing indicators are premised on the idea that they can provide a valuable evidence base, whether for improved policymaking or to support more transformative change. However, the Harper government's disregard for evidence, particularly that which could challenge its priorities, was apparent in actions such as cancelling the mandatory long-form census, silencing federal environmental scientists, and closing the National Round Table on Environment and Economy. Critics spoke of the 'death of evidence' (DoE 2012) and a 'war on science' (Turner 2013). Several interviewees, speaking before the October 2015 election of a centre-left Liberal government, commented on this theme. One stated that Statistics Canada is 'being decimated as we speak. ... Harper has declared Ottawa as an evidence free zone' (Pascal interview, 2014). Former Prime Minister Martin saw obstacles from 'those who battle not from an evidential basis, but from an ideological basis and do not want to have real numbers' (interview, 2014). Alternatives to GDP have been 'one of many victims' of the 'larger attack on evidence making,' said Scott. 'It's like 10 years of being in a dark room' (interview, 2015).

In their analysis of US conservative climate-science denial, McCright and Dunlap (2010) characterized the American right as a force of anti-reflexivity. That is, the conservative movement sought to undermine the social and environmental 'impact science'—as well as the associated social movements—that could serve as the basis for a reflexive, ecological modernization in which society gained the capacity to critically evaluate and choose alternative paths beyond 'business-as-usual' industrial capitalism. The Harper government's resistance to evidence-based policymaking, with regard to wellbeing measurement and other issues, can be seen in this light.

Shortly after coming to power in 2015, Justin Trudeau's Liberal government restored the mandatory long-form census, generating hopes of a renewed commitment to evidence-based policymaking.

The Economic Growth Imperative Vs. the Radical Vision for Alternative Indicators

While the impact of the reformist vision of alternative indicators as a basis for better policymaking has been very limited, the more radical vision of redirecting society toward priorities other than economic growth has faced even greater obstacles. The existence of a measurement such as the CIW showing that wellbeing has not increased in line with economic growth, that the environment has seen the greatest deterioration among any measured domain, and that material affluence coincides with significant 'time poverty' does offer some opportunity to make the case for alternatives to the growth paradigm (Hayden 2014, pp. 151–152). It has, however, been a very limited opportunity to date. Although some voices in the public debate express the radical green critique of a growth-based economy, that growth critique has been downplayed in the way the CIW has been presented; the effort to take the demand for alternative indicators into the mainstream has involved engagement with and advocacy by political actors with a moderate reformist agenda. In addition, the critique of a growth-based economy was not a prominent theme highlighted by most interviewees. As Wilson and Tyedmers (2013, p. 196) wrote, 'The focus has changed from using alternative metrics to question failings of GDP and economic growth toward promoting a growth platform with fewer associated environmental and social costs.'

The perceived political imperative of economic growth creates a playing field heavily tilted against ideas that seek to turn away from growth. Peter Bevan-Baker suspected that the radical implications of a new measurement system framed as a challenge to 'the prevailing economic and business mentality of growth being good' had provoked resistance: 'You are challenging some very sacred cows when you are talking about alternative measurements' (interview, 2015; see also Whitby et al. 2014, p. 31). He pointed to the 'extraordinary power of the vested interests' who are doing well under the current system and resist change, as did Nickerson (interview, 2015). Although Bevan-Baker continued to challenge the idea of 'growth ever-lasting,' he acknowledged that, as he has gone from a fringe political candidate over the years to someone with a seat in a legislature, 'I'm more measured in how I bring it up now.'

Conclusion

While efforts continue to promote alternative economic and wellbeing indicators, the hopes of Canadian proponents of new measurement frameworks have been largely disappointed to date. Although Canadians have played leading roles in developing alternative approaches to wellbeing measurement and Canada has a homegrown wellbeing index in the CIW, as well as other available options such as the GPI and a 'green GDP,' federal and provincial governments have not adopted beyond-GDP measures. In this respect, Canada has fallen behind other jurisdictions—including Bhutan, Britain, Belgium, Italy, and Vermont and Maryland (USA), among others—where official statistical agencies have begun to calculate alternative wellbeing measures alongside GDP. Despite a few small-scale and local examples, no significant impact on public policy at provincial or federal levels is evident. Alternative wellbeing measurement certainly has not become equal to GDP in media reporting and public discussion, nor has it noticeably changed the public conversation as some had hoped, let alone replaced GDP as in more radical formulations.

Progress has been very limited regardless of the degree of transformation sought. The more radical vision of using alternative indicators to challenge economic growth's status as the dominant societal priority, and to achieve wellbeing in less consumption-oriented ways, would be in line with the emergence of a green state with an overriding purpose to ensure ecological sustainability. Such a radical transformation remains elusive, while even the less expansive, reformist vision of using beyond-GDP alternatives to achieve more balanced and effective policymaking has made only very small steps forward. Canadian policymakers and the public do now have more indicators available than in the past, such as a low-public-profile set of environment and sustainability indicators; these represent a minor expansion to the role of an environmental state that has added environmental management to its core functions alongside pursuit of economic growth, security, and provision of social welfare. However, the idea of incorporating environmental—as well as social—externalities into a new headline indicator, or small set of headline indicators, that can respond to the limits of GDP and help guide policymaking has not yet been adopted by federal and provincial governments. That said, the election in 2015 of a Liberal federal government and possible shifts in provincial and territorial interest created some optimism that those in power could become more open to new wellbeing and sustainability indicators.

The idea that 'changing indicators can be one of the most powerful and at the same time one of the easiest ways of making system changes' (Meadows 1998, p. 5) is certainly not borne out by the Canadian experience with beyond-GDP measurement to date. Similarities are evident in the literature on sustainable-development indicators, which has expressed disappointment with limited impacts (e.g., Rydin et al. 2003; Rinne et al. 2013). Some of that research has found limited 'instrumental' use in which indicators directly influence policymaking, but instead emphasizes indirect pathways of influence over a longer term through 'conceptual' use—i.e., by introducing new ideas and reshaping frameworks of thought and mental models (Rinne et al. 2013; Lehtonen et al. 2016). Indeed, some Canadian interviewees remained optimistic that the seeds of new ideas had been planted, potentially leading to greater impacts over time.

Whatever the long-term outcomes, present-day obstacles in Canada have included: accessing the necessary data and resources to produce new measures; lack of consensus on the best alternative measure; multiple agendas behind calls for new indicators; and unresolved questions about how to link new measures to an action agenda and who can drive the political action needed for governments to adopt new measures and use them in policymaking. European studies have found similar obstacles to the uptake and influence of such indicators. However, one particular Canadian obstacle that has not featured strongly in recent European research on beyond-GDP measurement (Whitby et al. 2014; Bache 2015; Bleys and Whitby 2015) is the existence of an anti-reflexive conservativism; when governments, such as that of Stephen Harper, show no interest in the evidence that such indicators and other social statistics provide, there is little prospect that new indicators will generate policy change, let alone system change. Recent concern over the rise of a 'post-fact politics' (e.g., Pomerantsev 2016) suggests that similar obstacles may be emerging elsewhere. Meanwhile, transformative efforts to challenge the growth paradigm face more fundamental obstacles. The prioritization of growth and the capital accumulation it enables is a product of much more than the information contained in the GDP indicator; it is rooted in the way a capitalist economy is structured, the structural power of capital vis-à-vis the state and other political actors, the current dependence on growth to solve key problems such as unemployment, and frameworks of thought that celebrate expansion, profit, and consumerism above social and ecological concerns.

Although some have hoped that alternative indicators would in themselves be a transformative force that drives a change in societal priorities, they are better seen as a small piece of a much bigger puzzle—one element of much broader political efforts to transform society in a more ecologically sound and equitable direction, and at least as much a product of such efforts as a driver of change in themselves. For a transformative green vision of alternative indicators to come to fruition, considerable work remains in areas such as developing and building support for a new social narrative emphasizing objectives such as equity, sustainability, and less consumption-intensive sources of wellbeing; getting governments not only to adopt new measurements but also the values behind them; and—over a longer term—building up the institutions of an economy that does not require infinite expansion. One interviewee in Britain, where we conducted similar research into that country's wellbeing measurement program, likened alternative indicators to the 'flag on the castle.' Canadian advocates of alternative indicators have an impressive flag in the CIW, and other viable options such as the GPI, but as yet no castle to fly them on.

NOTES

1. This chapter is a revised account of the Canadian experience in Hayden and Wilson (2016).
2. Ron Colman, founder of the non-governmental organisation GPI Atlantic, has played a key advisory role in Bhutan, while Michael Pennock, who later became the Senior Epidemiologist at the Office of the Provincial Health Officer in British Columbia, played a central role in developing Bhutan's GNH policy screening tool and the survey used to calculate the GNH Index.
3. One way the CIW, at least in its first two iterations, has differed from some beyond-GDP measures is that it does not include subjective wellbeing data, which limits its appeal among those who see subjective wellbeing as the key measurement innovation.
4. This conclusion reflects the views of those who ended up in our sample of major players involved in the CIW and related initiatives. We are not trying to generalize from the sample to any larger population. That said, our own impression of the wider debate is in line with what we heard in interviews, namely that reformist perspectives have come to be more prominent than a transformative vision.
5. The Act was later introduced in Parliament by Joe Jordan, as noted above.
6. Meanwhile, those who favour a pro-market, minimal state agenda can point to their own beyond-GDP alternatives. The Fraser Institute (2015), a right-wing Canadian think tank, claims that its Economic Freedom Index, which reflects a particular neoliberal conception of freedom, has a stronger relationship with average life satisfaction in a country than does per-capita income or whether a country has a democratic political system. For counter-evidence, see Helliwell et al. (2016, pp. 61–63).
7. With regard to the UK, Bache and Reardon (2013, p. 909) wrote: 'What the "problem" is that demands the measurement of wellbeing is not particularly well articulated ....' Meanwhile, research on sustainable-development indicators identified the need for greater emphasis on linking such indicators to policy action and the governance process (Rydin et al. 2003).
8. Douglas was the Saskatchewan premier who introduced Canada's first universal health coverage at the provincial level. Suzuki is Canada's most well-known environmentalist.

Appendix: Interviewees

Anielski, Mark. Director and Co-founder, Genuine Wealth Inc., 11 June 2014

Bevan-Baker, Peter. Member of Legislative Assembly, Green Party leader, Prince Edward Island, 22 July 2015

Charles, Anthony. Saint Mary's University, 23 June 2014

Jordan, Joe. Former Member of Parliament, 8 July 2015

Martin, Paul. Former Prime Minister and Finance Minister, 18 June 2014

Messinger, Hans. Former Director, Statistics Canada, 19 August 2014

Nickerson, Mike. Director, 7th Generation Initiative, 9 June 2015

O'Neill, Dan. Ecological economist, University of Leeds, 4 July 2014

Pascal, Charles. University of Toronto; former Executive Director, Atkinson Charitable Foundation, 15 August 2014

Pennock, Mike. Senior Epidemiologist, Office of the Provincial Health Officer, BC Ministry of Health, 27 June 2014

Romanow, Roy. Former Saskatchewan Premier and Advisory Board Chair, Canadian Index of Wellbeing, 27 November 2014

Scott, Katherine. VP Research & Policy, Canadian Council on Social Development, 5 August 2015

Smale, Bryan. Director, Canadian Index of Wellbeing, 15 August 2014

Taylor, Amy. Chief Operating Officer, Green Analytics, 19 June 2014

Two interviewees who requested anonymity: a federal public servant, 19 June 2014, and an NGO researcher, 19 & 20 June 2014

References

Anderson, V. (1991). *Alternative Economic Indicators.* London: Routledge.

Anielski, M., Griffiths, M., Pollock, D., Taylor, A., Wilson G., & Wilson, S. (2001). Alberta Sustainability Trends 2000: The Genuine Progress Indicators Report 1961 to 1999. Drayton Valley, AB: Pembina Institute. Available at: http://www.pembina.org/pub/alberta-sustainability-trends-2000.

Anielski, M., & Johannessen, H. (2009). The Edmonton 2008 Genuine Progress Indicator Report. Edmonton: Anielski Management Inc. Available at: http://www.anielski.com/wp-content/docuploads/Edmonton%20GPI%202009%20Report.pdf.

APPGWE. (2014). Wellbeing in Four Policy Areas. London: All-Party Parliamentary Group on Wellbeing Economics. Available at: http://b.3cdn.net/nefoundation/ccdf9782b6d8700f7c_lcm6i2ed7.pdf.

Bache, I. (2015). Measuring Quality of Life—An Idea Whose Time Has Come? Agenda setting Dynamics in Britain and the European Union. In J. H. Søraker et al. (Ed.), *Well-being in Contemporary Society* (pp. 197–214). Cham, Switzerland: Springer International.

Bache, I., & Reardon, L. (2013). An Idea Whose Time Has Come? Explaining the Rise of Well-being in British Politics. *Political Studies, 61*(4), 898–914.

Bache, I., & Reardon, L. (2016). *The Politics and Policy of Wellbeing: Understanding the Rise and Significance of a New Agenda*. Cheltenham: Edward Elgar.

Barry, J. (2015). Beyond Orthodox Undifferentiated Economic Growth as a Permanent Feature of the Economy. In T. Gabrielson, C. Hall, J. M. Meyer & D. Schlosberg (Eds.), *Oxford Handbook of Environmental Political Theory* (pp. 304–317). Oxford: Oxford University Press.

Barry, J., & Eckersley, R. (Eds.). (2005). *The State and the Global Ecological Crisis*. Cambridge, MA: MIT Press.

Bleys, B., & Whitby, A. (2015). Barriers and Opportunities for Alternative Measures of Economic Welfare. *Ecological Economics, 117,* 162–172.

Bonikowska, A., Helliwell, J., Hou, F., & Schellenberg, G. (2013). An Assessment of Life Satisfaction Responses on Recent Statistics Canada Surveys. Ottawa: Statistics Canada. Available at: http://www.statcan.gc.ca/pub/11f0019m/2013351/part-partie1-eng.htm.

Boulanger, P.-M. (2007). Political Uses of Social Indicators: Overview and Application to Sustainable Development Indicators. *International Journal of Sustainable Development, 10*(1–2), 14–32.

Cameron, D. (2006). David Cameron's Speech to Google Zeitgeist Europe 2006. *The Guardian,* 22 May. Available at: http://www.guardian.co.uk/politics/2006/may/22/conservatives.davidcameron. Accessed October 26, 2016.

Cassiers, I., & Thiry, G. (2015). A High-Stakes Shift: Turning the Tide From GDP to New Prosperity Indicators. In I. Cassiers (Ed.), *Redefining Prosperity* (pp. 22–40). London: Routledge.

Christoff, P. (2005). Out of Chaos, a Shining Star? Toward a Typology of Green States. In J. Barry & R. Eckersley (Eds.), *The State and the Global Ecological Crisis* (pp. 26–52). Cambridge, MA: MIT Press.

CIW. (2012). How are Canadians *Really* Doing? Waterloo, ON: Canadian Index of Wellbeing and University of Waterloo. Available at: http://www.unesco.org/fileadmin/MULTIMEDIA/HQ/CLT/pdf/howarecanadiansreallydoing.pdf.

CIW. (2014). How are Ontarians *Really* Doing? Waterloo, ON: Canadian Index of Wellbeing and University of Waterloo. Available at: https://uwaterloo.ca/canadian-index-wellbeing/sites/ca.canadian-index-wellbeing/files/uploads/files/ontarioreport-accessible_0.pdf.

CIW. (2016). How are Canadians *Really* Doing? Waterloo, ON: Canadian Index of Wellbeing and University of Waterloo. Available at: https://uwaterloo.ca/canadian-index-wellbeing/sites/ca.canadian-index-wellbeing/files/uploads/files/c011676-nationalreport-ciw_final-s_0.pdf

Community Foundations of Canada. (2015). *'Vital Signs'*, Ottawa: Community *Foundations of Canada*. Available at: http://www.vitalsignscanada.ca/en/home. Accessed May 30, 2015.

Coote, A., & Franklin, J. (Eds.). (2013). *Time on Our Side: Why We All Need a Shorter Working Week*. London: New Economics Foundation.

Costanza, R., Kubiszewski, I., Giovannini, E., Lovins, H., McGlade, J., Pickett, K., Vala Ragnarsdóttir, D., Roberts, R., De Vogli, R., & Wilkinson, R. (2014). Time to Leave GDP Behind. *Nature, 505*(7483), 283–285.

CTV. (2012). Canadian Economy Grows, But Quality of Life on the Decline. *CTV News,* 23 October. Available at: http://www.ctvnews.ca/canada/canadian-economy-grows-but-quality-of-life-on-the-decline-1.1006524. Accessed February 16, 2016.

Daly, H. E., & Cobb, J. B. (1989). *For the Common Good*. Boston: Beacon Press.

DoE. (2012). The Death of Evidence. No Science, No Evidence, No Truth, No Democracy. Available at: http://www.deathofevidence.ca/. Accessed May 31, 2015.

Dryzek, J. S. (1996). Political Inclusion and the Dynamics of Democratization. *The American Political Science Review, 90*(3), 475–487.

Dryzek, J. S., David Downes, D., Hunold, C., Schlosberg, D., & Hernes, H-K. (2003). *Green States and Social Movements: Environmentalism in the United States, United Kingdom, Germany, and Norway*. Oxford: Oxford University Press.

Duffy, A. (2014). The State of StatsCan Survey. *Ottawa Citizen*. 30 August, D1. Available at: https://ottawacitizen.com/news/local-news/the-state-of-statscan-survey.

Duit, A. (2016). The Four Faces of the Environmental State: Environmental Governance Regimes in 28 Countries. *Environmental Politics, 25*(1), 69–91.

Duit, A., Feindt, P. H., & Meadowcroft, J. (2016). Greening Leviathan: The Rise of the Environmental State? *Environmental Politics, 25*(1), 1–23.

Eckersley, R. (2004). *The Green State: Rethinking Democracy, and Sovereignty*. Cambridge, MA: MIT Press.

Fleurbaey, M., & Blanchet, D. (2013). *Beyond GDP: Measuring Welfare and Assessing Sustainability*. Oxford: Oxford University Press.

Fraser Institute (2015) Economic Freedom of the World, 2015 Annual Report, https://www.fraserinstitute.org/studies/economic-freedom-of-the-world-2015-annual-report.

Frugoli, P. A., Almeida, C., Agostinho, F., Giannetti, B. F., & Huisingh, D. (2015). Can Measures of Well-Being and Progress Help Societies to Achieve Sustainable Development? *Journal of Cleaner Production, 90,* 370–380.

GCEC. (2014). Better Growth, Better Climate: The New Climate Economy Report—Synthesis Report. Washington, DC: Global Commission on the Economy and Climate/World Resources Institute.

GPI Atlantic. (2009). 'New Policy Directions' Urged for Nova Scotia; NDP Will Bring 'Genuine Progress Accounting into Policy Analysis'. Glen Haven, NS: GPI Atlantic. Available at: https://www.gpiatlantic.org/releases/pr_manual.htm. Accessed May 31, 2015.

Grant, T. (2012). Study Finds Canadians Aren't Feeling Economic Growth in their Daily Lives. *The Globe and Mail*, October 23, p. A8.

Green Party of Canada. (2015). Vision Green 2015. Ottawa: Green Party of Canada. Available at: https://www.greenparty.ca/en/vision-green.

Guelph. (2015). Guelph Wellbeing Final Report. Guelph, ON: City of Guelph. Available at: http://guelph.ca/wp-content/uploads/GuelphWellbeingFinal-Report.pdf.

Hansard. (2003a). *37th Parliament, 2nd Session* (Edited Hansard, Number 109. June 2). Ottawa: Parliament of Canada.

Hansard. (2003b). *37th Parliament, 2nd Session* (Edited Hansard, Number 110. June 3). Ottawa: Parliament of Canada.

Hayden, A. (2014). *When Green Growth is not Enough: Climate Change, Ecological Modernization, and Sufficiency.* Montreal: McGill-Queen's University Press.

Hayden, A., & Wilson, J. (2016). Is It What You Measure That Really Matters? The Struggle to Move beyond GDP in Canada. *Sustainability, 8*(7), 623.

Helliwell, J. (2002). *Globalization and Well-being.* Vancouver: UBC Press.

Helliwell, J., Layard, R., & Sachs, J. (2016). World Happiness Report 2016. New York: Sustainable Development Solutions Network. Available at: http://worldhappiness.report/wp-content/uploads/sites/2/2016/03/HR-V1_web.pdf.

Jackson, T. (2009). *Prosperity Without Growth.* London: Earthscan.

Kronsell, A., & Bäckstrand, K. (Eds.). (2015). *Rethinking the Green State: Environmental Governance Towards Climate and Sustainability Transitions.* London: Routledge.

Lehtonen, M., Sébastien, L., & Bauler, T. (2016). The Multiple Roles of Sustainability Indicators in Informational Governance: Between Intended Use and Unanticipated Influence. *Current Opinion in Environmental Sustainability, 18*, 1–9.

Lu, C., Schellenberg. G., Hou, F., & Helliwell, J. (2015). How's Life in the City? Life Satisfaction across Census Metropolitan Areas and Economic Regions in Canada, Economic Insights, no. 46, Ottawa: Statistics Canada. Available at: http://www.statcan.gc.ca/pub/11-626-x/11-626-x2015046-eng.htm.

Martin, P. (2000). The Budget Speech 2000: Better Finances, Better Lives. Ottawa: Department of Finance. Available at: http://publications.gc.ca/collections/Collection/F1-23-2000-2E.pdf.

McCright, A. M., & Dunlap, R. E. (2010). Anti-Reflexivity: The American Conservative Movement's Success in Undermining Climate Science and Policy. *Theory, Culture, and Society, 27*(2–3), 100–133.

McGregor, A. (2015). Global Initiatives in Measuring Human Wellbeing: Convergence and Divergence. *CWiPP Working Paper Series No. 2.* Sheffield, UK: Centre for Wellbeing in Public Policy, University of Sheffield.

Meadowcroft, J. (2012). Greening the State? In P. Steinberg & S. VanDeveer (Eds.), *Comparative Environmental Politics* (pp. 63–88). Cambridge, MA: MIT Press.

Meadows, D. H. (1998). *Indicators and Information Systems for Sustainable Development.* Hartland Four Corners, VT: The Sustainability Institute.

Michalos, A. C. (Ed.). (2014). *Encyclopedia of Quality of Life and Well-Being Research.* New York: Springer.

Mittelstaedt, M. (2001). Fat-Cat Albertans Struggle with Happiness. *The Globe and Mail,* April 23, p. A1. https://www.theglobeandmail.com/news/national/fat-cat-albertans-struggle-with-happiness/article25438584/.

Mol, A. P. J., Sonnenfeld, D. A., & Spaargaren, G. (Eds.). (2009). *The Ecological Modernisation Reader: Environmental Reform in Theory and Practice.* London: Routledge.

OECD. (2014). *Green Growth Indicators 2014.* Paris: Organisation for Economic Co-operation and Development.

O'Neill, D. W. (2012). Measuring Progress in the Degrowth Transition to a Steady State Economy. *Ecological Economics, 84,* 221–231.

Osberg, L., & Sharpe, A. (2010). The Index of Economic Well-Being. *Challenge, 53*(4), 25–42.

Pannozzo, L., Colman, R., Ayer, N., Charles, T., Burbidge, C., Sawyer, D., Stiebert, S., Savelson, A., & Dodds, C. (2008). *The 2008 Nova Scotia GPI Accounts: Indicators of Genuine Progress.* Glen Haven, NS, Canada: GPI Atlantic.

Pomerantsev, P. (2016). Why We're Post-Fact. *Granta.* Available at: https://granta.com/why-were-post-fact/. Accessed October 28, 2016.

Porritt, J. (2007). *Capitalism As If the World Matters.* London: Earthscan.

Reality Check. (2001). Why We Need New Measures of Wellbeing. *Reality Check, 1*(1), 1.

Rinne, J., Lyytimäki, J., & Kautto, P. (2013). From Sustainability to Well-Being: Lessons Learned from the Use of Sustainable Development Indicators at National and EU Level. *Ecological Indicators, 35,* 35–42.

Romanow, R. (2009). There's More To Life Than GDP. *Toronto Star,* 10 June, p. A23. Available at: https://www.thestar.com/opinion/2009/06/10/theres_more_to_life_than_gdp.html.

Rydin, Y., Holman, N., & Wolff, E. (2003). Local Sustainability Indicators. *Local Environment, 8*(6), 581–589.

Sarkozy, N. (2010). Foreword. In J. Stiglitz, A. Sen, and J. P. Fitoussi (Eds.), *Mismeasuring Our Lives: Why GDP Doesn't Add Up* (pp. vii–xv). New York: The New Press.

Scoffield, H. (2012). Happiness Lags Prosperity, Study Finds. *Regina Leader-Post*, October 24, p. C4. Available at: https://www.pressreader.com/canada/regina-leader-post/20121024/281904475425100.

Scott, K. (2012). *Measuring Wellbeing: Towards Sustainability?* London: Routledge.

Sommerer, T., & Lim, S. (2016). The Environmental State as a Model for the World? An Analysis of Policy Repertoires in 37 Countries. *Environmental Politics, 25*(1), 92–115.

Stiglitz, J. E., Sen, A., & Fitoussi, J. P. (2009). Report by the Commission on the Measurement of Economic Performance and Social Progress. Paris: CMEPSP. Available at: http://ec.europa.eu/eurostat/documents/118025/118123/Fitoussi+Commission+report.

Taylor, A. (2005). The Alberta GPI Summary Report. Drayton Valley, AB: Pembina Institute. Available at: http://www.pembina.org/pub/alberta-gpi-summary-report.

Tobin, P. (2015). Blue and Yellow Makes Green? Ecological Modernization in Swedish Climate Policy. In A. Kronsell & K. Bäckstrand (Eds.), *Rethinking the Green State: Environmental Governance Towards Climate and Sustainability Transitions* (pp. 134–146). London: Routledge.

Turner, C. (2013). *The War on Science: Muzzled Scientists and Wilful Blindness in Stephen Harper's Canada*. Vancouver: Greystone.

Wallace, J., & Schmuecker, K. (2012). Shifting the Dial: From Wellbeing Measures to Policy Practice. Newcastle Upon Tyne, UK: IPPR North. Available at: https://www.carnegieuktrust.org.uk/carnegieuktrust/wp-content/uploads/sites/64/2016/02/pub1455011624.pdf.

Whitby, A., Seaford, C. Berry, C., & BRAINPOoL consortium partners (2014). BRAINPOoL Project Final Report: Beyond GDP—From Measurement to Politics and Policy. *BRAINPOoL deliverable 5.2*, No. 283024. Hamburg: World Future Council.

Wilson, J., & Tyedmers, P. (2013). Rethinking What Counts: Perspectives on Wellbeing and Genuine Progress Indicator Metrics from a Canadian View Point. *Sustainability, 5*(1), 187–202.

CHAPTER 8

Societal Wellbeing: Catalyst for Systems and Social Change in Northern Ireland?

Peter Doran and Susan Hodgett

Improving wellbeing for all …

(Draft Northern Ireland Programme for Government, 2016).

INTRODUCTION

After more than 40 years of low-intensity conflict over the constitutional future of Northern Ireland (NI), a complex legacy of suffering has impacted on individual and collective wellbeing. Even after the establishment of new democratic institutions in 1998[1] a series of recurring political crises has regularly destabilised the region and threatened political settlement. This instability culminated in a collapse of the NI Assembly[2] in January 2017 (Hughes 2017).

As part of its response to recurring crises in governance and overdue public sector reform, the executive arm of government, along with the senior civil service, looked to the global policy conversation on wellbeing

P. Doran
Queen's University Belfast, Belfast, Northern Ireland
e-mail: p.f.doran@qub.ac.uk

S. Hodgett
Ulster University, Jordanstown, Northern Ireland
e-mail: p.f.doran@qub.ac.uk

© The Author(s) 2018
I. Bache and K. Scott (eds.), *The Politics of Wellbeing*, Wellbeing
in Politics and Policy, https://doi.org/10.1007/978-3-319-58394-5_8

(Diener 2009; Deneulin and McGregor 2010) to inform a series of discussions across government, the public sector and civil society. These conversations contributed to the adoption of Northern Ireland's *Draft Programme for Government (PfG)* 2016–2021 (NI Executive 2016) and an outcomes-based framework based on the delivery of 'wellbeing for all' with the promise of a systems change in pursuit of 'whole-of-government' delivery. The achievement of a wellbeing focus was notable in a situation of increasing political instability and suspicion. However, critiques emerged that were centred on a decision by the NI Executive[3] to adopt an 'off-the-shelf' approach to outcomes-based accountability, as a substantive response to the wellbeing policy conversation in the region.

With the collapse of the Assembly and its Executive[4] and the calling of a new election on 2 March 2017, the development of a fresh programme for government was expected to follow intense negotiations on a wider political agreement between the Assembly parties and the governments in London and Dublin. This might afford an opportunity to revisit some of the complicated methodological issues identified below. During the Executive's interregnum the civil service proceeded apace, in collaboration with Northern Ireland's powerful third sector, to embed the Outcomes-Based Accountability (OBA) methodology with a series of trainings and briefings even as questions about the utility of the approach began to take hold.

This chapter outlines the development of the process leading up to the stalled *PfG* including an innovative Roundtable on Measuring Wellbeing in Northern Ireland (Carnegie UK 2014) inspired by the Report of the Commission on Measurement of Economic Performance and Social Progress (CMEPSP 2009). It describes the emergence, and critique, of a unique public policy experiment that supported the adoption of the outcomes-based performance framework in the *PfG* for Northern Ireland (2016–2021)[5] together with the incorporation of wellbeing as a core organising principle across the public sector. In the context of the collapse of the political institutions and of deteriorating relations between the two main governing parties, the policy conversation about wellbeing and governance comes at a critical time, with increasing public anxiety about the fate of the devolution experiment and effective policy delivery. The UK's decision to leave the European Union, following the 2016 referendum, with far-reaching implications for the border on the island of Ireland, has added a new layer of complexity and has come to dominate political discourse in the region. In a significant development in June 2017, the Conservative and Unionist Party of United Kingdom

(UK) Prime Minister Theresa May called on the NI Democratic Unionist Party to support her new minority administration after a calamitous decision to call an early general election that saw her party lose its majority in Parliament.

THE ORIGIN AND ROLE OF INVESTIGATING WELLBEING IN NORTHERN IRELAND

Dimensions of trauma in NI are inter-generational. Interest in wellbeing grew out of the suffering, both visible and hidden, endured during the 30 years of 'the Troubles' and since. 'The Troubles' is a euphemistic phrase used by the NI and UK media to refer to the low-level conflict that consumed the region, and impacted both the Republic of Ireland and England, between the late 1960s to the 1990s when a 'peace process' was initiated following a ceasefire by the Provisional Irish Republican Army in 1994 and renewed soon afterwards following a short breach. Throughout the emergent policy debate on wellbeing there has been a focus on the specifics of Northern Ireland's status as a society emerging from conflict, and on the implications of a legacy of conflict impacting people, directly or indirectly, physically and mentally.

The damage to people and place is evident in more than 3500 deaths during this time (Rogers 2010) and the impact continues today, as numbers of the population suffering from post-traumatic illnesses rise across generations. According to a major study undertaken at Ulster University (2011), Northern Ireland has the world's highest recorded rates of Post-Traumatic Stress Disorder (PTSD), at a yearly cost to the public purse of around £175 million. It cites a World Health Organization report stating that NI 'has the highest level of 12-month and lifetime PTSD among all comparable studies undertaken across the world including other areas of conflict'. It estimated too that nearly 40 per cent of the population had experienced a conflict-related traumatic experience. Worryingly, the report noted that those suffering these conditions would worsen without treatment as they aged. In addition to, and exceeding, the number of deaths from violence during the Troubles, 3600 people died by suicide between 1999–2016, with 318 deaths so attributed in 2015 (Hughes 2016). Statistics demonstrate NI's much higher suicide rates compared to England with figures of 16.5 versus 10.3 (per 100,000) in 2014 (ONS 2014).

As government has struggled to deal with the immediate imperative of keeping the political show on the road, there has been insufficient recognition and planning to address these complex and costly social problems, despite the growing unease amongst academics and the medical profession.[6] In grappling to understand the experience of the Troubles and the later difficult transitional path towards post-conflict, researchers have sought ways to reconceptualise these chronic political and social problems. Reviewing the quality of life in NI, Hodgett (2008, p. 165) commented on the importance of considering alternatives because 'it is a person's *overall freedom* that influences their opportunity to have *valuable outcomes to their lives*, prov[ing] important to the whole society's development' (emphasis added).

In considering what happens to the whole society, we need to begin by contemplating the individual's experience of their personal wellbeing and the quality of everyday lives in that place. Such is the foundation of the interest in wellbeing as a contribution to transition. Wellbeing has been viewed as a generative theme (Galtung 1967) because part of the legacy of the NI conflict that has not yet been addressed by institutions is the direct and indirect suffering experienced by communities. Legacy issues range from agreement on the definition and treatment of 'victims', approaches to the prosecution of historic cases, including murder, and truth recovery. Concerns about an apparent paucity of respect and equality feature at the core of current societal and political distrust, notably between the two largest parties, the Democratic Unionist Party (DUP) and Sinn Féin (SF). This less tangible dimension is driven, in part, by the continuing politicisation of the legacy agenda at the centre of the constitutional conflict wherein the parties continue to mobilize around deeply disputed versions or narratives of the past, including the circumstances that sowed the seeds of the most recent protracted period of political violence involving unionists, republicans and the British State. In many ways—in the absence of felt reconciliation – the wider geopolitical dispute addressed by the Belfast (or Good Friday) Agreement, 1998 is being repatriated to the territory of Northern Ireland and played out again within the domestic politics of the Northern Ireland Executive and Assembly, due in part to the incentives and rewards built into the consociational arrangements that lie at the core of Strand One of that Agreement.

The wellbeing policy conversation in NI takes place in particularly complex conditions due to the transitional nature of post-conflict governance institutions, wherein the over-arching objective is to secure continuing accommodation and the conditions necessary for parties to the conflict to adapt to democratic norms. Devolution in Northern Ireland, with its Assembly and Executive institutions, is part of a complex inter-governmental arrangement designed, in part, to transcend residual constitutional contestation over the future of its people and their divided loyalties to London and Dublin. There is a radical uncertainty or contingency at the heart of the institutions that feeds a recursive process of politicising the legacy agenda.

While the tipping point that led to the collapse of the Assembly was a financial scandal over the Renewable Heat Incentive (RHI) scheme, the underlying problem had been the diminishing trust between the two main parties making up the Executive and a growing concern about the impact on effective delivery.[7] All of this was compounded by the nature of consociational arrangements with the two main Executive parties, resulting in an incentivisation of negative behaviours ranging from wholesale clientelism to allegations of corruption.[8,9] Wellbeing and common purpose are increasingly viewed as potential keys to achieve a new and urgent shift in the political conversation or narrative(s) about the role of civil society in addressing legacy issues and identifying pathways to 'living well together'.[10] Public sector reform and the role of the political institutions are regarded as a necessary enabler of that aspiration.

THE WELLBEING POLICY CONVERSATION

Scholars have referred to at least two waves of activity that have carried forward the political interest in the wellbeing debate into politics and policy (see Bache and Scott, this volume, Chap. 1), while noting that conversations about the 'good life' have been a tacit dimension of political and philosophical discourse going back to the time of ancient Greeks. Hodgett (2008) reflected concerns about the good life in her earlier work on Northern Ireland over the period 1999–2004 when seeking to understand how progress towards peace might be theorised pursuant to apply ideas of human flourishing or *eudaimonia* to the region's public policy. This research supported the development of the Integrated Capabilities Framework (ICF) for investigating human wellbeing (Hodgett and Clark 2011), piloted in Canada and made operational through fieldwork with practical policy relevance. Based on the work of Amartya Sen (1999), the ICF brought together emphases on wellbeing, resources, quality of life and considered how people moved in and out of poverty over time.[11] This work was presented to the NI Roundtable on Measuring Wellbeing in 2014. The interest internationally in frameworks based on wellbeing was used to support the developing argument for policy in this field with government in Northern Ireland.

The Roundtable was initiated and supported by the School of Law[12] at Queen's University in partnership with the Carnegie United Kingdom Trust (CUKT). In an unusual expression of cross-community and cross-party consensus, a Minister and Assembly Committee Chair representing the two main parties in NI, the DUP and Sinn Féin, supported the initiative. In addition, Roundtable members were drawn from the highest ranks of the civil service and civil society, local government, academia and the private sector. The Roundtable's recommendations were expected to inform the design of outcomes drawn up for the 2016 *PfG* in Northern Ireland.

The recommendations made by the Roundtable encouraged the inclusion of a framework that placed wellbeing at the heart of governance. One of the key learning points was the observation[13] that shared aspirations exist across Northern Irish society for transformation in governance and citizen engagement. Co-production, and meaningful engagement of all sectors of society, at all stages in the policy cycle was identified as an essential approach (see Appendix for a brief chronology of the wellbeing conversation in Northern Ireland).

The Roundtable itself acted as a catalyst for a high-level conversation about the NI system of governance to 'speak to itself' at a moment characterised by desire for change across the public sector and of palpable loss of public confidence during an earlier period of political instability. It further developed a global policy debate on wellbeing as a departure point for far-reaching local systems change and provided a lynchpin for the integration of a number of other initiatives. These included an OECD Public Governance Review of the public sector in Northern Ireland (the first to be carried out at the sub-state level on local government reform: OECD 2016); a rationalisation of departments from twelve to nine; and reforms in the Fresh Start Agreement (FSA) of 2015 including political accommodations intended to bring the instability in inter-party relationships to a conclusion. The FSA encompassed plans for private high-level ministerial workshops on the proposed wellbeing framework.

Before the collapse of institutions in early 2017, the *PfG* was launched as part of an innovative consultation process, inviting citizens and organisations to respond to a series of draft outcomes, indicators and key measures, and to take on a new role in co-delivering the agreed outcomes. Meanwhile, Hodgett and Clark's (2011) ICF formed the basis of investigations in a successful national public dialogue on wellbeing carried out in Northern Ireland over a number of meetings in 2015 (What Works Wellbeing 2006) and later doctoral research amongst communities in NI. After a period of prolonged instability in the Northern Ireland government, the growing wellbeing initiative was welcomed by senior politicians, including the then First and deputy First Ministers, Arlene Foster (DUP) and Martin McGuinness (SF), as an opportunity to put government on a footing focused on the quality of its policy delivery.[14]

WELLBEING, GOVERNANCE AND AN OUTCOMES-BASED APPROACH: A GLOBAL AND LOCAL CONVERSATION

While the movement calling for a move beyond an exclusive focus on GDP as a society's key measure of economic progress[15] was beginning to incorporate the holistic concept of wellbeing, a parallel development in social policy had also been nudging governments. By the mid-2000s, the literature was shifting from support for new public management (with its focus on targets) towards increased public value. Public value consists of three distinct, interrelated processes (Benington and Moore 2011): clarifying and specifying strategic goals and public value outcomes; creating the environment necessary to achieve these outcomes; and utilising the required operational resources, staff, skills and technology. This trend received a boost from Public Governance Review conducted by the OECD in NI 2014–2015, building on earlier recommendations on measuring outcomes in public services (OECD 2005).

As outcomes-based performance management has developed, a plethora of guides has been published to help service providers understand and measure outcomes (Friedman 2015). Belfast City Council has been working to apply Results-Based Accountability (RBA) to their work while signature projects were sponsored by the Office of the First Minister and deputy First Minister (OFMdFM) (Friedman 2015).[16,17] These projects aimed to develop whole-systems approaches to public service interventions and outcomes. Moreover, their inclusion of a dashboard of wellbeing indicators met some of the recommendations set out by the Sarkozy Commission on measuring economic progress (CMEPSP 2009). This pattern of bringing together outcomes-led public sector reforms and a wellbeing policy narrative was influential in NI. The Roundtable was also informed by Scotland's National Performance Framework and its collaborative policy design and delivery with local government and the third sector. It also noted international research by the CUKT that wellbeing frameworks can inform policy in five key ways: creating a vision for society; building support and community buy-in; developing new policies; evaluation; and communication.

All of this indicated that wellbeing is about the experiences of citizens and communities and the outcomes that matter to people's quality of life and the distribution of this across society. Therefore, it can provide a useful complement to system-level measures of performance. Wellbeing also highlights *gaps and omissions* exposing outcomes that have not been systematically included. Outcomes such as social connections, quality of place, civic engagement and work–life balance raise issues about groups that are disadvantaged across the range. Third, concentrating on wellbeing helps *improve scrutiny* by requiring policymakers to state clearly what they understand wellbeing to be and how they intend to monitor improvements or declines over time. Finally, such approaches support *joined-up policy working*, bringing trade-offs between different outcomes into sharper focus. A clear range of outcomes needs to be considered when designing the likely impact of policy and evaluating results.

Still, some caution is merited. In their submission to the Roundtable, the OECD remarked that '[wellbeing] should not be understood as providing a technocratic solution to solve the prioritisation dilemmas that are at the heart of government—which concern values as much as numbers' (see Doran et al. 2015). This OECD observation signals a potential source of tension in the conflation of public value agendas and wellbeing agendas: a concern running through all the wellbeing work in NI has been the risk of appearing to short-circuit the legitimate role of political parties in setting out their mandated priorities. For this reason, the final report of the Roundtable underlined that 'The determination of high-level government commitments are, most fundamentally, the responsibility of the Executive parties' (Doran et al. 2015, p. 8). The publication of the Draft *PfG* triggered some scepticism from opposition parties who criticised the lack of detailed policy commitments, ignoring plans by the Executive to publish parallel high-level strategic economic and social policy papers aligned to the outcomes-based methodology.

In 2014, the Northern Ireland Executive's Department of Finance and Personnel invited the OECD to assess its public sector reform agenda. Its report, 'Northern Ireland (UK): Implementing Joined-up Governance for a Common Purpose' (OECD 2016), covers three dimensions of reform, including the adoption of a multi-year outcomes-based approach to future programmes for government. The report cited the findings of the NI Roundtable on measuring wellbeing.

ADOPTION AND IMPLEMENTATION OF AN OUTCOMES AND WELLBEING APPROACH

Towards the close of the Northern Ireland Executive's last mandate (2010–2016), the First and deputy First Ministers, Arlene Foster MLA (Member of the Legislative Assembly) and Martin McGuinness MLA, appeared before the Northern Ireland Assembly's Committee with responsibility for the scrutiny of the OFMdFM (9 March 2016). In her evidence to the Committee,[18] the First Minister announced that her aspiration for the Executive's forthcoming *PfG* was to try to establish a shared vision for the public sector in shared outcomes and to foster collaboration and support for greater efficiency and effective delivery. Speaking in the wake of the FSA,[19] which allowed the main parties to re-commit to cooperation, First Minister Foster announced that wellbeing would become central to the role of government and the new *PfG*:

> It will be important that the processes that lead to the development of the next Programme for Government take into account critical influencing factors, in particular the aspirations of our people and their priorities; the financial position of the Executive, of course, and the budgetary responses to that position; and the increasing recognition that the achievement of well-being is at the centre of government's role, and that a coordinated cross-sectoral outcome-focused model of governance is required to deliver on that.[20]

The significance of the First and Deputy First Ministers' commitment to an outcomes-focused approach, including a cross-departmental collaborative approach, cannot be underestimated in the NI context. The tradition of silo-bound policy and service delivery has been entrenched by the nature of Northern Ireland's political dispensation, wherein ministerial appointments lead to party ownership of departmental remits. The shift to a more collaborative approach, including co-design alongside local government, the third sector and the private sector, is more significant given this pattern in the past.

After the May 2016 elections, Foster and McGuinness headed up a new government. Shortly after the formation of the new Executive, a draft *PfG* was published. Responses to the consultation approached 1000 submissions. Town hall meetings organised by the Executive explained the structure of the new draft programme, with its 14 outcomes, 42 indicators and 42 key measures. During the consultation process, the two party leaders announced that they would be engaging outside government to develop plans with local government, the private sector, the voluntary and community sectors and beyond.

The key features of the programme are as follows:

- A focus on outcomes that people can identify (e.g. living longer and healthier lives), to be measured over time.
- Indicators to demonstrate the change the government wants to bring about.
- Key measures that will show whether government is hitting its goals.
- A focus on shifting what happens in people's lives in areas such as jobs, education and health.
- A focus on impact rather than the amount of money ('inputs') or the number of programmes introduced.
- An opportunity for the Executive to work with local government, the private sector and the voluntary and community sector on how to tackle the greatest challenges to society in Northern Ireland.
(Source: NI Draft Programme for Government Framework 2016)

Controversially, the Executive Office agreed that the measuring of outcomes would be based on an approach designed and promoted by Mark Friedman[21] of the US-based Fiscal Policy Studies Institute and the private company Clear Impact. Outcomes-based Accountability (OBA) (also known as Results-based Accountability or RBA) outlined in Friedman's book, *Trying Hard is Not Good Enough* (2015), is a do-it-yourself manual for public officials and community-based organisations seeking to improve the performance of programmes and track their impact, at the level of whole populations and of organisational performance. OBA is broadly described by Keevers et al. (2012) as a methodology underpinned by three ideas: justifying service provision on the basis of outcomes; demonstrating outcomes by data-based evidence; and assuming that setting targets ('results') and measuring progress will improve the social service system.

OBA (Keevers et al. 2012) guides individuals and organisations involved in service delivery through a step-by-step process, focusing on the following:

1. The identification of the 'results' they want to achieve.
2. The selection of quantitative measures or indicators for each 'result' and the construction of a baseline graph tracking an indicator with a history, and a projected forecast, and the desired 'turning of the curve'.
3. A discussion of the factors and 'causes' influencing baselines.
4. Identification of the partners with a stake in 'turning the curve'.
5. Identification of solutions, with a recommendation that initial consideration be given to low-cost approaches.
6. Agreement on a strategy.

A network of licensed consultants and partners linked to Clear Impact offer training.[22] Users of the methodology begin with a series of desired conditions of wellbeing ('Residents with good jobs', 'A safe neighbourhood') and work their way back to the means of improving those conditions, using baseline data. The chief selling point is simplicity. Friedman (2015, p. 12) explains '[t]he most basic version of RBA can be done in less than an hour and produces ideas that can be acted on immediately. RBA is an inclusive process where diversity is an asset and everyone in the community can contribute'.[23]

CRITIQUES OF OUTCOMES-BASED MEASURES IN NI

The OBA approach is controversial, however, and many challenge this perspective, arguing that it will over-simplify complex social problems and risk excluding valuable contributions made by locally based community organisations to the *PfG* outcomes. For example, Inspiring Impact is a UK-based network that has been working closely with the community and voluntary sector on evaluation methods and measuring impact. The Northern Ireland Director of Inspiring Impact, Aongus O'Keefe, underlined a shared concern over 'the singularity of approach through which these outcomes and their related indicators will be monitored and measured' while highlighting the dangers of relying on a model that prioritises quantities over qualities (Inspiring Impact 2016: 2). In the context of a Northern Ireland voluntary and community sector already in danger of losing its identity and independence due to complex relationships with Government and funders during and following the period of conflict (Ulster University 2015) the draft *PfG* methodology could risk further embedding a service delivery model working to a pre-written script and pulling back from critical and innovative intervention. Ulster University (2015, p. 10) research on the independence of the voluntary community and social enterprise sector in Northern Ireland found that:

- Pressure from some funders is making some organisations copy the practices of the public and private sectors or dominant organisations within the sector, with the result that the sector is losing some of its distinctiveness and becoming internally homogeneous.
- Many organisations feel that government funding is available only for activities that meet pre-defined objectives, making it difficult for organisations that wish to develop innovative ways to meet newly identified needs.
- Access to funding has become the new measure of success amongst many organisations, and competition for funding is having a negative effect on collaborative relationships and trust.

Perhaps most worrying within Northern Ireland's fragile governance arrangements is the reported moderation of actors' critique of government and policy directions, often out of fear of losing funding. Increasingly, Northern Ireland's voluntary and community sector has become a set of arms-length bodies delivering out-sourced public policy objectives and programmes. Such practice has been strongly criticised as a means to control devolution of services and government accountability procedures (Keevers et al. 2010). Indeed, a report prepared for the Roundtable (Doran et al. 2015) recommended caution in the adoption of an outcomes-based approach, noting that they should form part of a wider shift in governance that must go *beyond measurement*. Wider lessons have been learned on this front in broader human development internationally, as a plethora of literature has demonstrated the importance of *going beyond numbers* in understanding *what is well-being and quality of life* for citizens (Hodgett and Deneulin 2009).

In fact, Keevers et al. (2010, 2012) demonstrate that performance measurement and accountability frameworks such as OBA are 'not technologies that peer and measure innocently and disinterestedly from a distance' (2012: 1). Rather, they operate as a bundle of material-discursive practices that work to include some things and exclude others. They (Keevers et al. 2012, p. 37) conclude that the mandating of OBA in community organisations encourages their focus to shift from actual practice to the correspondence between 'results' and 'reality' and measurement. In addition, the implicit privilege granted to 'facts' and quantification renders practices, relationalities, values and context marginal or invisible, hampering inclusion of the local practice experience of both workers and service participants. Finally, the introduction of Friedman's methodology—when deployed using computerised case-management monitoring technology and entangled with funding to individualised outcome targets—can unravel some of the daily organising practices of social justice that create a sense of belonging, assist young people to have a sense of control over their lives and build hope for their futures.

Professor Derek Birrell (2016, p. 5–9), a long-standing observer of public policy in Northern Ireland, has highlighted the weaknesses and risks of OBA:

> An immediate problem with this approach is that OBA is an evaluation and performance methodology and as such cannot and does not prescribe any policies for a programme for government. Such models and methodologies have been subject to a range of criticisms … [I]n a response to the consultation on the [*PfG*] the BMA expressed concern that the Framework was based solely on OBA and questioned whether it constituted a robust evidence base and was fit for purpose.

He observes that OBA demonstrates conceptual flaws. First, it uses 'desired outcomes or imagined outcomes not actual outcomes' (Birrell 2016, p. 5). This places Northern Ireland's outcomes in the realm of a hypothetical exercise and 'significantly involves a rejection of other outcome based methodologies using actual outcomes' (ibid). Birrell is critical of Friedman's grasp of causation because achieving policy objectives is a much more complex and multi-faceted exercise. A third criticism is the re-introduction of indicators, 'which have largely fallen into disuse' due to difficulty in finding consensus on what should be measured, the potential for manipulating data and the problem of attribution. Fourth, Birrell (2016, p. 7) questions the OBA's evaluative criteria of 'is anyone better off?' He notes that this phrase can vary in meaning, interpretation and calculation. He points out that many current UK government policies are not intended to make people better off, but have other aims such as reducing expenditure, achieving fairness or making people less dependent.

At the very least, in conditions of complexity, an outcomes-focused approach needs to be taken up with an acceptance of uncertainty, abandoning the false assumption that real-world impacts of a given policy intervention can be accurately modelled in advance. This suggests a new approach to policymaking that values innovation and experimentation, focusing less on pre-implementation analysis and more on post-implementation evaluation. According to the New Economics Foundation (2015), the Roundtable's background report also made a number of cogent observations, noting that focusing on outcomes can create unwelcome paradoxes, distorting priorities and practices, including gaming and goal displacement. The report highlights an emergent consensus in opposition to 'command and control' target setting and promotes the value of a distinction between population and performance level accountability. It argues for the essential involvement of partners in discussions about desired 'end states', foregrounding conditions of trust and the desirability of an Asset-Based Community Development approach together with co-production. Lastly, it observes the essential role of evidence-informed narratives and stories behind baseline analyses, which has been noted as crucial in studies of policymaking internationally (Hodgett 2012; Acheson and Hodgett 2012) and in NI (Hodgett 2008).

The convergence of the wellbeing policy narrative and the political imperative to respond to 'austerity', with the subsequent need to demonstrate 'value for money' from public investment in resources, has opened opportunities and risks for the wellbeing narrative in NI. The Roundtable tracked public sector reform and the adoption of an outcomes-based approach in the National Performance Framework. Developments in NI have subsequently mirrored the hybrid approach in Scotland insofar as there is a coming together of an agenda to generate more 'public value' from decreasing resources (cuts to the block grant from the UK Treasury), the adoption of an OBA that will distribute responsibility for policy delivery and pick up on the wellbeing policy narrative. It remains to be seen how the convergence of these agendas delivers; for example, how the fiscal narrative might come to compete with and even undermine attempts to embed a shared governance narrative around an ill-defined understanding of wellbeing; one that is reduced to an aggregate of activities derived from a series of outcomes and indicators. It is this tension that lies behind the controversial decision by the Executive Office to base the working of the new framework on Friedman's OBA system, essentially a stripped-down value-for-money-driven evaluation methodology imported from the private sector.

Discussion: The Wellbeing Narrative in a Post-Conflict Society

The original recommendations by the Roundtable envisaged an approach, such as Sen's Capability Approach (Alkire 2002) or the OECD's wellbeing measures, that would establish internationally-agreed benchmarks against which outcomes and policies in Northern Ireland might be tested and measured. These were to focus on qualitative data and critical engagement by policy actors, notably think tanks and citizens, using the framework as a platform for a standing conversation facilitated by social media and real-time data visualisation. The Roundtable, in 2016, expressed some reservations about the adoption of an 'off-the-shelf' methodology for the facilitation of the outcomes approach. Compared to the wellbeing methodology that might have been constructed in the work of Sen and Nussbaum or other normative benchmarking approaches, the OBA approach risks falling short of fundamental infrastructure and capacity support. This includes opportunities for civil society actors to offer their own methods for evaluating their work (a pluralist approach to evaluation methodology), a capacity for longitudinal studies (at organisational performance level and population level) and demonstrating its value to government. Indeed, there is a serious hazard that the intrinsically emergent properties of outcomes in a post-conflict society, such as embedding reconciliation, democratisation and social justice practices, might be ill-served by the off-the-shelf approach. Such short cuts illustrate the insufficiency of current public administration in Northern Ireland and how investment is needed to improve local political and administrative capacity to assist the public imagination.

The authors have been deeply influenced by the work of Amartya Sen (1992, 1999, 2000, 2002, and 2011) and the contributions to develop the Capabilities Approach (CA, see page 11) made by Martha Nussbaum (2011) and others (Crocker 2008; Terzi 2014) when addressing well-being. We have seen the clear opportunity to link societal wellbeing as a shared policy narrative to strengthen the demos of the region; in a post-conflict society, there is a challenge that goes beyond agreeing a shared vision of the future. It is no less than the trial of *cultivating the societal conditions and capabilities*—'internal' and 'combined'—that go towards the construction of a non-violent political culture, a culture emergent as a function of reasoned argument and debate. This includes NI's critical investment in the cultivation of skills and conditions associated with a transition to a non-violent decision-making and institutions.

Northern Ireland's 'peace process' has a sophisticated geopolitical architecture (internal to NI together with institutions that embrace relations across Ireland, and between NI, the Republic of Ireland and Britain). These institutions have been operated by political elites; insofar as the internal dimensions lock parties into ancient antagonisms, they reproduce communal fractures, contested identities and deep disconnects between their institutional expressions (symbolisms, policy priorities) and the different constitutional aspirations of large numbers of citizens. The 'peace process' has yet to translate into a citizen-owned process of transformation, wherein the conditions for a peaceful and a truly non-threatening debate can take place on the evolution of NI's constitutional status. Public reasoning, insofar as it is accommodated at all, is translated into a repetitive series of disabling and debilitating stand-offs between the Nationalist and Unionist parties and within their own constituencies. This has recently been evidenced by the collapse of institutions and speculation that NI may not be able to resuscitate the Assembly, so necessitating a period of direct rule from Westminster (Belfast Telegraph 2017). A vast chasm continues to lie between the lives, aspirations and identities as they are *lived* by the people and the repetitive calculations from the party leaderships of the political institutions.

What we are coming to recognise in the most recent crisis of the devolved institutions in NI is that even the tripartite architecture of the Belfast (Good Friday) Agreement of 1998 is not sufficient for the cultivation of new political relationships and dispositions. Alongside the controversies over post-conflict legacy issues, policy differences and dysfunctions in governance, there is a quantum gap in the levels of trust between certain parties. This gap, in the case of SF and the DUP, sat at the heart of the mandatory coalition process and proved corrosive. This problem calls to mind Sen's (2011) insight into the nature of justice, wherein he argues that the principles of justice are not solely defined in terms of institutions, rather in terms of the lives and freedoms of the people involved (2011, xii). Such insights from the CA provide a compelling case for the continued consideration of its theory and practical application. While societal institutions may facilitate scrutiny of values and priorities and shape public discussion, successful democracy should be assessed in terms of public reasoning and the promotion of 'government by discussion' (Sen 2011, xiii). So, bringing a sense of reason into diagnosing justice and injustice while concentrating on the actual lives that people may lead. It is at this intersection between institutional approaches to post-conflict accommodation and the less tangible, dispositional, attitudinal, demands of transitional justice where the wellbeing policy debate has something original to offer.

It was often stated during the Roundtable discussions that wellbeing, in the context of an evolving post-conflict democratic settlement, is a means and an end. It is a means, insofar as wellbeing invites policymakers to address the felt circumstances of citizens, on the journey of transition out of conflict. Issues such as mental health and post-conflict trauma are not only symptoms of the conflict, but remain potential obstacles to progress. They may impede the emergence of new attitudes and capacities to embrace 'otherness', including otherness-as-emergent future; as opposed to the over-determination of the present by the weight of an imperative for historical justification. Wellbeing introduces a language that counters the colonisation of Northern Ireland's politics by the language of pure calculation; it introduces an alternative set of languages that begin to place value on liberating concepts such as 'care' and 'forgiveness' without diminishing the importance of justice understood as institutional guarantees of rights and protections. Wellbeing, in a post-conflict society, contributes to ends by inviting politicians and citizens to cast the management of their fragile—perhaps contingent—democratic institutions in a context that lies beyond the immediate need to fixate on political accommodation of constitutional differences. Instead, it allows them to begin to embrace an emergent style of politics, tolerant of uncertainty while focusing on the cultivation of those dimensions of freedom (Sen's articulation of wellbeing) that are valuable in their own right. An understated dilemma for NI remains the degree to which core political or constitutional antagonisms—that provide the raisons d'etre of the two main parties—implicitly render all policy prospects vulnerable to instrumentalization in the service of larger constitutional preferences, so virtually all policy considerations are seen as proxy battles over unresolved fractures rehearsed by political elites.

CONCLUSION

Peter Senge (2009) has commented on the ability of societies to comprehend change, noting that the limited social or learning field remains largely unchanged because the level of attention renders the scope of the need for change invisible. Societies do not see the subtle forces shaping what happens because they are too busy *reacting* to immediate forces and acting out of embedded—often redundant—assumptions or worldviews, thus limiting the scope of policy responses to incremental or short-term calculations. This applies, especially, to under-developed systems of governance where styles of administration, thought and practice, have been inhibited and insulated by the all-consuming agenda of societal conflict and managing of the politics of accommodation.

Such forces have shaped the NI public sector, where the immediate imperative of conflict management has led to levels of introversion and risk aversion in the policy process. For this to change, Senge notes: 'people [must] truly start to recognize their own taken-for-granted assumptions and [...] hear and see things that were not evident before' (Scharmer 2009: xiv). When the structure of attention moves deeper, so, too, does the ensuing change. The invitation to engage in a collective reflection on a narrative on wellbeing must include an inner regard ('seeing our seeing') so that collective learning is not limited to drawing lessons from the past, but is open to learning from an emergent future. This necessitates accommodating greater levels of ambiguity, uncertainty and willingness to experiment, while contemplating and permitting failure. Interrupting the collective and institutionalised narratives and practices of the past is a critical challenge in successful post-conflict societies. Wellbeing offers a germane and generative platform for this delicate and gradual process.

The current political hiatus may provide a breathing space for senior civil servants to begin to absorb emergent criticisms and reservations about the Executive's adoption of the OBA approach to the delivery of 'wellbeing'. Ironically, if we are to note the work of Keevers et al. (2010,

2012), the approach of the NI Executive not only risks falling short of the original ambition raised by the Roundtable but also risks embedding a methodology that may be antithetical to the transformative animus of societal wellbeing, running counter to the notion of wellbeing as a significant contribution to social justice and freedom, as articulated by Sen and Nussbaum.

The NI Executive (2016) has demonstrated receptivity to an initiative designed to explore recommendations on the relevance of wellbeing as an organising principle for policymaking in a highly complex, post-conflict society. As identified by the Roundtable in 2015 and the OECD's (2016) work on public governance in NI, there are pressing obstacles to effective governance that must be addressed in parallel with, and at the service of, the taking up of wellbeing as an organising principle for policy design. For the moment, the NI Executive and civil service governance capacity has demonstrated a deep fragility when it comes to policy design and accountability. This has been apparent in the collapse of the institutions over the botched Renewable Heat Incentive scheme and to an extent in the Executive's decision to conflate its response to the global wellbeing policy debate with the adoption of the OBA methodology for its draft *PfG*. This decision was driven by a desire on the part of senior civil servants for simplification in meeting the multiple challenges identified as part of the wellbeing agenda, including parallel needs to engage stakeholders more closely in the policy design cycle while also embedding universal performance measurement protocols to ensure value for money.

In some ways, the initial responses by the NI Executive to the wellbeing agenda have fallen victim to the very weaknesses identified in the governance arrangements and style by the Roundtable and the OECD. This has resulted, for now, in a significant shift away from the challenging and iterative wellbeing agenda that attempted to consider the specific circumstances of the conflict. The CA could make significant contributions on matters of trust and freedom both individually and collectively. Only where such an approach is taken up are we likely to encourage a politics of emergence that counters the risks of over-determination and the repetition of crises in NI.

Developing an emphasis on wellbeing governance in Northern Ireland could open further positive and exciting possible futures for the region. It has already offered a contribution to the increasing drive to blur genres in policy evolution internationally (AHRC 2016), alongside substantial intellectual developments in interpretive policy analysis worldwide (Yanow 2000). Such positive optimism should not be allowed to fall at the last staging post, just as others globally (Arndt and Volkert 2007) recognise the wisdom it can impart. In the circumstances following the collapse of the NI institutions, confidence building and moves to promote wider wellbeing have become more important than ever and deserve closer examination for how we might increase desperately needed societal trust.

APPENDIX: CHRONOLOGY OF THE WELLBEING CONVERSATION IN NORTHERN IRELAND

- 2008: Hodgett applies Sen's Capability Approach on wellbeing to ideas of quality of life in NI in the UN's *Journal of Human Development*.[24]
- 2011: Development of the Integrated Capabilities Framework (ICF) on wellbeing by Hodgett and Clark (Ulster and Cambridge Universities) piloted internationally.[25]
- 2012: QUB School of Law and New Economics Foundation conference on wellbeing.
- 2013: CUKT invited to collaborate in conference and formation of Roundtable on Measuring Wellbeing in NI.
- 2013–2017 Hodgett supervises doctoral research on wellbeing in NI, including modelling the ICF, investigating the experiences of the LGBT community, and the voluntary and community sector in NI (Ulster University).
- 2014: Publication of *Measuring Wellbeing in Northern Ireland: A New Conversation for New Times*.[26]
- 2014–2016: Four meetings of the CUKT-School of Law *Roundtable* on measuring wellbeing, which includes Hodgett's work.
- 2015: Conduct of, and publication a year later, of the What Works Well-being's National Public Dialogue on (Community) Wellbeing in NI informed by Hodgett and Clark's (2011) ICF framework.[27]
- 2015: Publication of *Towards a Well-being Framework: Findings from the Roundtable on Measuring Well-being in Northern Ireland*.[28]
- 2016: Publication of the *Draft Programme for Government Framework 2016–2021*.[29]

Notes

1. The Belfast (Good Friday) Agreement of 1998 brought to an end the 30 years of sectarian conflict in Northern Ireland known as 'the Troubles'. See http://www.bbc.co.uk/history/events/good_friday_agreement was ratified in a referendum in May 1998. The agreement set up a power-sharing assembly to govern Northern Ireland by cross-community consent.
2. The Northern Ireland Assembly is the devolved legislature for Northern Ireland. It is responsible for making laws on transferred matters from Westminster and for scrutinising the work of NI Ministers and Government Departments see http://www.niassembly.gov.uk/.
3. The NI Executive is made up of the First Minister and deputy First Minister, two junior Ministers and eight departmental Ministers. The Executive Committee exercises executive authority on behalf of the Northern Ireland Assembly and takes decisions on significant issues and matters that cut across the responsibility of two or more Ministers. It agrees proposals put forward by Ministers for new legislation in the form of 'Executive Bills' for consideration by the Assembly. It is responsible for drawing up a programme for government and an agreed budget for approval by the Assembly see https://www.northernireland.gov.uk/topics/your-executive.
4. For a detailed review of the collapse of both, see http://www.bbc.co.uk/news/live/uk-northern-ireland-politics-38635708.
5. Following the 2016 election to the devolved Northern Ireland Assembly, the main parties expected to form a new coalition government and launched a public consultation on a draft *Programme for Government (PfG) 2016–2021*. For the first time, the draft outcomes and indicators were presented as a framework for measuring wellbeing, and outcomes were presented as part of a new wellbeing narrative. The *PfG* sets the strategic context for the Budget, Investment Strategy and Economic Strategy for Northern Ireland.
6. Interview with consultant psychiatrist on NI high suicide rates over 10 years and rates of poverty http://www.bbc.co.uk/programmes/b07myr3f (Accessed 7/8/2016).
7. For an explanation of the RHI scandal see http://www.bbc.co.uk/news/uk-northern-ireland-38301428 (Accessed 7/11/2017).
8. For insight into the events see http://www.bbc.co.uk/news/uk-31489031.
9. See https://www.theguardian.com/uk-news/2017/jan/16/northern-ireland-power-sharing-government-expected-to-collapse-sinn-fein-cash-for-ash.

10. Our thanks to the Corrymeela Community of Reconciliation in North Antrim for this beautiful and evocative phrase.

11. This chapter develops an Integrated Capabilities Framework for investigating human wellbeing in multicultural settings, shows how it can be made operational through fieldwork and argues it has practical and policy relevance for studying immigration, multiculturalism and social cohesion in Canada. https://www.erudit.org/revue/ijcs/2011/v/n44/1010086ar.html.

12. The process leading to the establishment of the Roundtable was initiated by one of the authors, Dr Peter Doran, and his colleague at the School of Law, John Woods. The second author, Dr Susan Hodgett, contributed to the work of the Roundtable with a presentation on the Capabilities Approach and societal wellbeing.

13. 'That's why our proposed Framework is much more than an attempt to capture and share information. Our era is confronted less by the demand to measure and more to understand. The proposed Framework is a platform, a process, a way of engagement and much more. It is a communications process designed to support the emergence of a "learning society", much more agile and inclusive in the co-design and deliberation of policy options, insightful with regard to the difficult trade-offs that accompany policy choices, and creatively engaged with the world of ideas and deep social trends locally and globally. A Wellbeing Framework can provide a single point of reference to which all public services and partners are aligned. It can become part of a transformative shift in how policy is made, and a key enabler of public service reform. By aligning the whole public sector around a common set of goals—that have been the subject of public deliberation, even contestation—government can deliver lasting collaboration and partnership working. Organisations across the community, including local government and community planning partnerships, can begin to work towards shared goals defined in terms of benefits to citizens, tailored to local places, rather than simply efficient service delivery' (Doran et al. 2015).

14. See First and deputy First Ministers addressing the First Minister and deputy First Minister Committee of the Northern Ireland Assembly on 20 January 2016. The website: https://www.youtube.com/watch?v=6camyw24AeY.

15. The Beyond GDP initiative is about developing indicators that are as clear and appealing as GDP, but more inclusive of environmental and social aspects of progress. See http://ec.europa.eu/environment/beyond_gdp/index_en.html.

16. Friedman, M. Results-Based Accountability http://resultsaccountability.com/ 2015.

17. Now the Executive Office.
18. Northern Ireland Assembly, Committee for OFMDFM, Official Hansard Report, March 2016, 'Programme for Government', http://data.niassembly.gov.uk/HansardXml/committee-17722.pdf.
19. A Fresh Start—The Stormont Agreement and Implementation Plan involving the main political parties and the Irish and British governments was published on 17 November 2015. The agreement brought to an end an extended period of instability for the Northern Ireland Executive and Assembly, following disagreements among the parties over paramilitary activity and difficulties in reaching an agreed response to welfare reforms introduced by the British government. The Agreement is available at: http://data.niassembly.gov.uk/HansardXml/committee-17722.pdf.
20. Ibid., p. 2.
21. Friedman, Mark, 2015, *Trying Hard is Not Good Enough: How to produce measurable improvements for customers and communities.* Santa Fe: FPSI Publications.
22. One of the Clear Impact (US) partner organisations is the National Children's Bureau in Northern Ireland.
23. Friedman, p. 12.
24. Hodgett, Susan L. (2008) Sen, Culture and Expanding Participatory Capabilities in Northern Ireland. *Journal of Human Development,* 9(2). pp. 165–183.
25. Hodgett, Susan and Clark, David (2011) Capabilities, Wellbeing and Multiculturalism: A New Framework for Guiding Policy. *International Journal of Canadian Studies,* 44 (2). pp. 163–184.
26. http://pure.qub.ac.uk/portal/files/15384858/1095_Measuring_Wellbeing_in_NI_v3.1.pdf.
27. https://whatworkswellbeing.files.wordpress.com/2015/05/community-public-dialogue-final.pdf.
28. http://pure.qub.ac.uk/portal/files/15385327/carnegie_short_report_compressed.pdf.
29. https://www.northernireland.gov.uk/consultations/draft-programme-government-framework-2016-21-and-questionnaire.

References

Acheson, N., & Hodgett, S. (2012). Narratives of Citizenship: Welfare State Reform and Civil Society in Canada. *British Journal of Canadian Studies,* 25(2), 152–159.
AHRC (Arts and Humanities Research Council). (2016). Blurring Genres Network: Recovering the Humanities for Political Science and Area Studies. Available at: http://gtr.rcuk.ac.uk/projects?ref=AH/N006712/1.

Alkire, S. (2002). *Valuing Freedoms: Sen's Capability Approach and Poverty Reduction*. Oxford: Oxford University Press.

Arndt, C., & Volkert, J. (2007). A Capability Approach for Official German Poverty and Wealth Reports: Conceptual Background and First Empirical Results, January, Institut für Angewandte Wirtschaftsforschung. Available at: http://www.iaw.edu/RePEc/iaw/pdf/iaw_dp_27.pdf.

Belfast Telegraph. (2017). Northern Ireland Faces Brutal Election and Return to Direct Rule, Warns Arlene Foster. Available at: http://www.belfasttelegraph.co.uk/news/northern-ireland/northern-ireland-faces-brutal-election-and-return-to-direct-rule-warns-arlene-foster-35358295.html. Accessed January 31, 2017.

Benington, J., & Moore, M. (Eds.). (2011). *Public Value: Theory and Practice*. London: Macmillan.

Birrell, D. (2016). Assessing the Programme for Government. Agenda NI Online. Available at: http://www.agendani.com/assessing-programme-government/. Accessed January 12, 2017.

Carnegie UK. (2014). Roundtable on Measuring Wellbeing in Northern Ireland. Available at: https://whatworkswellbeing.org/case-study/48524/.

CMEPSP. (2009). Report by the Commission on the Measurement of Economic Performance and Social Progress. Available at: http://ec.europa.eu/eurostat/documents/118025/118123/Fitoussi+Commission+report. Accessed December 17, 2016.

Crocker, D. (2008). *Ethics of Global Development: Agency, Capability, and Deliberative Democracy*. Cambridge: Cambridge University Press.

Deneulin, S., & McGregor, J. A. (2010). The Capability Approach and the Politics of a Social Conception of Wellbeing. *European Journal of Social Theory, 13*(4), 501–519.

Diener, E. (Ed.). (2009). *Assessing Well-Being: The Collected Works of Ed Diener* (Social Indicators Research Series). Heidelberg: Springer.

Doran, P., Wallace, J., & Woods, J. (2015). Towards a Wellbeing Framework: Background Report Prepared for the Roundtable on Measuring Wellbeing in Northern Ireland. Scotland: CUKT.

Friedman, M. (2015). *Trying Hard is Not Good Enough: How to Produce Measurable Improvements for Customers and Communities*. Santa Fe: FPSI.

Galtung, J. (1967). Theories of Peace: A Synthetic Approach to Peace Thinking. Oslo: International Peace Research Institute. Available at: https://www.transcend.org/files/Galtung_Book_unpub_Theories_of_Peace_-_A_Synthetic_Approach_to_Peace_Thinking_1967.pdf.

Hodgett, S. (2008). Sen, Culture and Expanding Participatory Capabilities in Northern Ireland. *Journal of Human Development, 9*(2), 165–183.

Hodgett, S., & Deneulin, S. (2009). On the Use of Narratives for Assessing Development Policy. *Public Administration, 87*(1), 65–79.

Hodgett, S., & Clark, D. (2011). Capabilities, Well-being and Multiculturalism: A New Framework for Guiding Policy. *International Journal of Canadian Studies, 44*(2), 163–184.

Hodgett, S., & Cassin, M. (2012). Feelingful Development: Redefining Policy Through Interpretation. *British Journal of Canadian Studies, 25*(2), 267–286.

Hughes, B. (2016). More Have Died by Suicide Than Were Killed During Troubles. *Irish News.* Available at: http://www.irishnews.com/news/2016/01/11/news/more-have-died-by-suicide-that-were-killed-during-troubles-378739/. Accessed January 27, 2017.

Hughes, L. (2017). Snap Election Announced in Northern Ireland as Power-sharing Agreement Collapses. *Telegraph.* Available at: http://www.telegraph.co.uk/news/2017/01/16/snap-election-announced-northern-ireland-power-er-sharing-agreement/. Accessed January 28, 2017.

Inspiring Impact. (2016). *Submission to Consultation on Programme for Government.* Belfast: Inspiring Impact.

Keevers, L., Treleaven, L., Backhouse, H., & Darcy, M. (2010). *Practising Social Justice: Measuring What Matters, Locally-based Community Organisations and Social Inclusion.* Wollongong: Illawarra Forum Inc. Available at: http://www.academia.edu/565132/Practising_Social_Justice.

Keevers, L., Treleaven L., Sykes C., & Darcy M. (2012). Made to Measure: Taming Practices With Results-based Accountability. *Organizational Studies, 33*(1), 97–120. Available at: http://journals.sagepub.com/doi/abs/10.1177/0170840611430597?journalCode=ossa.

New Economics Foundation. (2015). *Note to Consultation on Measuring Wellbeing in Northern Ireland.* London: NEF.

NI Executive. (2016). *Northern Ireland Draft Programme for Government 2016–2021.* Available at: https://www.northernireland.gov.uk/sites/default/files/consultations/newnigov/draft-pfg-framework-2016-21.pdf.

Nussbaum, M. (2011). *Creating Capabilities: The Human Development Approach.* Cambridge, MA: Harvard University Press.

OECD. (2005). *Modernising Government: The Way Forward.* Paris: Organisation for Economic Co-operation and Development. Available at: http://www.oecd.org/gov/modernisinggovernmentthewayforward.htm. Accessed January 27, 2017.

OECD. (2016). *Northern Ireland (United Kingdom): Implementing Joined-Up Governance for a Common Purpose.* Paris: Organisation for Economic Co-operation and Development.

ONS (Office of National Statistics). (2013). Personal Wellbeing Across the UK, 2012/2013. Available at: http://webarchive.nationalarchives.gov.uk/20160106200641/ http://www.ons.gov.uk/ons/rel/wellbeing/measuring-national-well-being/personal-well-being-across-the-uk--2012-13/sb---personal-well-being-across-the-uk--2012-13.html.

ONS (Office of National Statistics). (2014). Suicides in the UK: 2014 Registrations. Available at: https://www.ons.gov.uk/peoplepopulationandcommunity/birthsdeathsandmarriages/deaths/bulletins/suicidesintheunitedkingdom/2014registrations. Accessed January 27, 2017.

Palmer Parker, J., & Zajonc, A. (2010). *The Heart of Higher Education: A Call to Renewal.* San Francisco: Jossey-Bass.

Rogers, S. (2010). Deaths in the Northern Ireland Conflict since 1969. *The Guardian.* Available at: https://www.theguardian.com/news/datablog/2010/jun/10/deaths-in-northern-ireland-conflict-data. Accessed January 27, 2017.

Scharmer, C. O. (2009). *Theory U: Leading from the Future as it Emerges.* San Francisco: Berrett-Koehler Publishers.

Sen, A. (1992). *Inequality Re-examined.* Cambridge, MA: Harvard University Press.

Sen, A. (1999). *Development as Freedom.* Oxford: Oxford University Press.

Sen, A. (2000). The Reach of Reason: East and West. *New York Review of Books, 47* (20 July).

Sen, A. (2002). *Rationality and Freedom.* Cambridge, MA: The Belknap Press.

Sen, A. (2011). *The Idea of Justice.* London: Allen Lane.

Senge, P. (2009). Foreword in Scharmer, O. *Theory U: Leading from the Future as it Emerges.* San Francisco: Berrett-Koehler Publishers.

Terzi, L. (2014). Capability Approach: Martha Nussbaum and Amartya Sen. In D. Phillips (Ed.), *SAGE Encyclopedia of Educational Theory and Philosophy.* London: Sage.

Ulster University. (2011). NI Has World's Highest Rate of Post-Traumatic Stress Disorder. Available at: https://www.ulster.ac.uk/news/2011/december/ni-has-worlds-highest-rate-of-post-traumatic-stress-disorder. Accessed January 28, 2017.

Ulster University. (2015). *Independence of the Community, Voluntary and Social Economy Sector in Northern Ireland: Finding a New Story to Tell.* Belfast: Institute for Research into Social Sciences.

What Works Wellbeing. (2016). What Works Wellbeing Public Dialogues Northern Ireland. Available at: https://whatworkswellbeing.files.wordpress.com/2015/05/community-public-dialogue-final.pdf and https://whatworkswellbeing.files.wordpress.com/2016/05/guide-toolkit_pdtoolkit.pdf p. 28. Accessed August 7, 2016.

Yanow, D. (2000). *Conducting Interpretive Policy Analysis.* Thousand Oaks, CA: Sage.

PART III

Between Wellbeing Policy and Everyday Lives: Critical Perspectives

Reconciling Universal Frameworks and Local Realities in Understanding and Measuring Wellbeing

J. Allister McGregor

INTRODUCTION

Amongst the burgeoning number of national and international initiatives to measure progress, there remains a profound tension between the imposition of 'universal' frameworks for measuring wellbeing and using wellbeing assessment to create the space for a greater recognition of 'local' realities and priorities. This tension is sometimes not recognised, and in some cases, it is simply overridden by 'the universalist imperative': that is, the drive on the part of high-level policymakers and many academic disciplines to impose frameworks for understanding and policy action that emphasise the commonality of the human condition in all parts of the world and that seek to avoid the problems of cultural or moral relativism (Doyal and Gough 1991). However, the problem of how the relationship between the 'universal' and the 'local' is dealt with in wellbeing measurement has significant political ramifications as this

J. A. McGregor (✉)
University of Sheffield, Sheffield, UK
e-mail: j.a.mcgregor@sheffield.ac.uk

© The Author(s) 2018
I. Bache and K. Scott (eds.), *The Politics of Wellbeing*, Wellbeing in Politics and Policy, https://doi.org/10.1007/978-3-319-58394-5_9

field develops and particularly where there is an ambition to apply the concept in public policy processes.

One of the appeals of the new wave of wellbeing initiatives is that it can be presented as an effort to offer an alternative to an orthodox economic growth paradigm that is perceived by many as having failed (viz. persistent poverty, increasing inequality and environmental degradation). Some consider the focus on wellbeing as representing a possible paradigm shift, while others see it more as providing a reformist correction to the existing growth agenda (O'Donnell et al. 2014; Levis 2015; Bache and Reardon 2016). When considered as a movement on a global scale, some observers view the imposition of new universal wellbeing frameworks as being just the next episode in the neocolonial project (Jaggar 2006; Bayo-Ogunrotifa 2015).

Recently, this tension between the universal and the local has been played out in the negotiations towards the newly adopted Sustainable Development Goals (SDGs). The UN General Assembly Resolution, titled 'Transforming Our World: The 2030 Agenda for Sustainable Development', is explicitly presented as a 'universal agenda' (UN General Assembly September 2015). The adopted SDG framework has a strong wellbeing underpinning and has drawn heavily on progress with the wellbeing agenda in the wake of the Stiglitz Commission (below: also, see Bache and Scott, this volume, Chap. 1). The call for the SDG Resolution to be 'universal' follows strong pressure from developing and transition countries that the SDGs should be applied not just to 'poor countries', as the Millennium Development Goals had been (Amin 2006), but to wealthy countries also. At the same time, however, the importance of the 'local' has also been asserted and it was also argued that 'difference' should be recognised. The idea of a set of goals that could be 'common but differentiated' was a prominent and sometimes contentious theme throughout the negotiations (Adams and Luchsinger 2015).

While in part this was a discussion about cause and responsibility (about a common problem that might be differentially caused: where countries have different resource capacities to cope with the problem and thus where responsibility for funding the solution might need to be differentially distributed), it was also just a fundamental recognition that difference matters when one is trying to achieve change. As the Resolution finally puts it, 'All of us will work to implement the Agenda within our own countries and at the regional and global levels, taking into account different national realities, capacities and levels of development and respecting national policies and priorities' (United Nations General Assembly 2015, Resolution 70/1, p. 6).

In order to explore the political implications of the tension between the universal and the local, this chapter will begin with a brief review of a number of the most prominent recent wellbeing initiatives at the national and international levels; it will consider their disciplinary roots and where they stand in a universalist-local continuum. This chapter then explores how more careful consideration of the issues of 'purpose' and 'scale' might provide us with a means of better understanding the need for a more sophisticated approach to universalist and local perspectives. One possible conceptual and methodological approach to resolve the universalist–local tension will be introduced. This approach requires the clarification of the distinction between dimensions, domains and indicators and then uses this to focus more carefully on the policy purpose that a multidimensional conception of wellbeing is being applied to. This chapter will conclude by discussing some of the political hazards of the particular universalizing direction of the emergent international discussion around the adoption of a conception of wellbeing for public policy.

The Diverse Range of Wellbeing Initiatives

Even before the Final Report of The Commission on the Measurement of Economic Performance and Social Progress in 2009 (hereafter referred to as the Stiglitz Commission, Stiglitz et al. 2009), which issued a global call for a shift from measuring progress in terms of production to measuring it in terms of human wellbeing, there had been a wide range of initiatives that were working on how to use a concept of human wellbeing as a means of better understanding the human condition and the social problems that surround it (Noll 2011; Michalos 2011). These have had a diverse range of different roots: some are disciplinary in character, while others have their roots in particular cultures and societal movements. The different disciplines that have contributed to the development of current thinking on human wellbeing have different predispositions towards either universalist or localist framings.

In disciplinary terms, psychology has had a long tradition in the study of wellbeing, but often under the nomenclature of *Quality of Life* or *Life Satisfaction*. This has sometimes drawn on connections to health sciences, where more enlightened members of the medical professions had understood the importance of taking into account what patients regarded as important for their own wellbeing (see, e.g. Ruta et al. 1994).

In social psychology in the USA, Ed Diener has been a long-standing champion of subjective wellbeing measurement. The specific instrument that has been developed from this work is the Satisfaction With Life Scale (SWLS), which is a short, five question research instrument that seeks to provide a measure of the respondent's overarching judgment of satisfaction with their life as a whole (Diener et al. 1985). From its foundational work in the USA, the SWLS has been developed into a popular universalist framing for wellbeing in terms of life satisfaction (Pavot et al. 1991). The SWLS has been applied in many countries and translated into 33 languages to date.

While this is what is referred to as a 'global' measure of life satisfaction (i.e. an overarching view of satisfaction with life as a whole), social psychologists have also developed a considerable number of more detailed satisfaction with life approaches (Schmidt and Bullinger 2007). These approaches consider life in terms of a number of domains that are considered important for wellbeing and assess levels of satisfaction in each domain. The Personal Well-being Index (PWI), based on the Australian Unity Index of Subjective Well-being, is one of the most prominent examples of this and has been constructed based on a long-standing body of work by social psychologist Robert Cummins (2000). The PWI currently considers wellbeing in terms of seven domains[1] (IWB 2013). From its original 'localist', Australia-specific purpose, this has been developed into a more 'universalist' framework that has been adopted subsequently in a range of countries across the world as a means of providing a basis for comparing the subjective wellbeing of citizens in different societal contexts (Lau et al. 2005).

Exemplifying a more country-specific model and cutting across the psychological and sociological traditions, the Canadian Index of Wellbeing (CIW), developed at the University of Waterloo seeks to provide Canadians with an independent view of their development by offering '… clear, valid and regular reporting on progress toward wellbeing goals and outcomes Canadians seek as a nation'. (Canadian Index of Well-being n.d., Mission and Vision; see also Hayden and Wilson, this volume, Chap. 7)

This type of effort to develop nation state-specific wellbeing measurement regimes is becoming increasingly common.[2] In some of these initiatives, pre-existing wellbeing type frameworks have been adapted, while in others the development of a national wellbeing framework has been preceded by a national consultation of one form or another (notably in the cases of the UK, Australia and Morocco). These consultations typically ask: 'what is important for the wellbeing of Australians, Britons, Moroccans?' and they are then intended to provide the rationale for the national data collection effort.[3]

The sociological and social policy traditions have been similarly focused at national or society levels. The idea of 'Quality of Life' has longstanding roots in sociology that can be traced back to Durkheim and more specific recent work that reaches back to the 1970s. Noll (2013) traces the work on subjective social indicators back to the work of Mark Abrams in 1973 and then to further initiatives during the 1970s and 1980s in the USA, UK and in continental Europe. Work on social quality and social cohesion that fits into similar and longstanding sociological and social policy traditions has enjoyed particular resurgence in Europe and in East Asia (Lin and Herrman 2015). These developments in sociology and social policy have tended to be grounded in specific societal contexts and driven by particular public policy concerns.

The re-emergence of the idea of wellbeing was spotted early by a small number of economists (Oswald 1997; Frey and Stutzer 2002a; Blanchflower and Oswald 2004), but has subsequently gathered momentum, moving from the fringes of the discipline to being a major topic of study. Most of the work in which wellbeing is addressed by orthodox economists has not sought to develop its own conception of wellbeing but has rather 'adopted' it from work in other disciplines (Frey and Stutzer 2002b). However, the historic connection between economics and the idea of wellbeing that runs back to Bentham's work establishing the utilitarian roots of neo-classical economics has ensured a strong convergence in economics around the idea of happiness.[4] The work of Daniel Kahneman et al. (1999) has been crucial in this respect and his work on hedonic happiness has been seized on and championed by economists such as Layard (2006). Contemporary economics is perhaps the most universalising of disciplines in the social sciences and the recent body of work in economics has gleefully adopted happiness measures as a substitute for a monetised notion of utility. The discipline can then use this measure to explore a whole range of phenomena through quantitative regression analysis and make authoritative policy-relevant pronouncements (Powdthavee 2010).

THE ANTHROPOLOGICAL TURN AND WELLBEING
IN DIVERSE CULTURES

In counterpoint to economics, social anthropology is firmly located at the localist end of the spectrum in the social sciences. It could be argued that anthropology has always been concerned with the wellbeing of the people it has studied, but recently it has explored its relationship to the newly emergent wellbeing agenda more explicitly (Corsín Jiménez 2008). Much of the new work on wellbeing in other disciplines discussed above has been conducted in relation to people in more wealthy, industrialised countries and it has tended to broadly and blandly assume a similar cultural context, but there are an increasing number of examples of expanding the study of human wellbeing to other cultural contexts and to less wealthy country contexts.

In social psychology, the work of Biswas-Diener and Diener (2001) provides one striking and early example of the 'local' application of a subjective wellbeing approach to the context of slums in Calcutta. This study may be somewhat deceptive since it is largely the application of a universalist framework in a different cultural and economic context, but since then, there have been an increasing number of more grounded applications of a range of subjective wellbeing approaches in other cultural contexts, exploring a range of different issues from poverty to urbanisation (Rojas 2008; Camfield and McGregor 2009).

In terms of a broader, multidimensional conception of wellbeing, the work of Amartya Sen has provided a leading light. Sen's work, and that of fellow travellers such as Martha Nussbaum, has, from the outset, been hinged around a notion of human wellbeing (Sen 1993). His work on capabilities and functionings has both expanded the discussion of what human wellbeing might mean in different societal contexts and contributed to changes in policy thinking by providing the underpinning for the 'human development' framework that was adopted by the United Nations Development Programme (UNDP).

The work of Sen provided one of the foundational strands of thinking for a body of more sustained conceptual, methodological and empirical work under the auspices of the Wellbeing in Developing Countries (WeD) Research Group funded by the UK Economic and Social Research Council (ESRC) between 2001 and 2008 (Gough and McGregor 2007).[5] Drawing on all of the disciplines discussed above, the approach developed by this group was used to 'develop a conceptual and methodological framework for understanding the social and cultural construction of well-being in specific societies'.[6]

In order to develop a framework for understanding and studying, wellbeing was understood as being '... a state of being with others, (that can arise) where human needs are met, where one can act meaningfully to pursue one's goals, and where one enjoys a satisfactory quality of life'. (McGregor 2008, p. 1). This framing was not developed as an effort to resolve the historical philosophical debates about what wellbeing is (van der Deijl 2016). Rather, and in somewhat post-modern fashion, it built on both empirical observation in different cultures and a review of the broad range of literature on wellbeing across disciplines. In non-philosophical language, the approach to wellbeing that was operationalized hinges around the observation that in all societies, in order to be well in a holistic sense, there are things that we need to *have*, there are things that we need to *do* and there are things we need to *feel* and *be*. These are universal categories, but in different societies, there are different things that we need to have, that we need to do and that we need to feel and be if we are to be well.

As noted, this framing of wellbeing was constructed to provide a basis for empirical study and particularly to understand the conditions and characteristics that produced chronic wellbeing failures (such as hunger, social exclusion and indignity) on a systematic basis, for some groups of people. The methodology that was built from this framing emphasises that the analysis for public policy application must take account of wellbeing as both outcome and process and that it can be understood in terms of the interplay of three basic dimensions (the material, the relational and the subjective). The interplay of the person's condition across all three of these dimensions (their wellbeing outcomes at any one point in time) produces different outcomes for different people in the context of particular social, cultural, economic and political structures (McGregor 2007). In a political economy analysis of progress, these different outcomes then become visible as structured patterns of success and failure for different groups.

When the WeD study started out, there was very little work explicitly bringing together these new conceptions of wellbeing in other cultures, but since then there has been a growth in the number of studies and during this same period another cluster of increasingly visible national wellbeing initiatives emerged from particular cultural or religious traditions. These bear some similarity to the wellbeing frameworks that have arisen from the challenge raised by the Stiglitz Commission and they have allied themselves in the global movement, but they have quite different sources of inspiration and different value bases.

Despite its small size, Bhutan has been prominent in the recent global discussions about alternatives to GNP and it has operationalized a concept of Gross National Happiness (GNH). This has become increasingly sophisticated and well developed in its application. While, on the surface, the GNH appears to be consistent with the Stiglitz Commission approach, it is important to note that the concept is infused by a particular set of spiritual values and that it thrives in Bhutan because it is fully embedded within a particular national culture and polity (Government of Bhutan 2016).

The notion of 'happiness' that is at the heart of the Bhutanese approach is a distinctively Buddhist conception, emphasising ideas such as spiritual wellness and mindfulness. Although the Bhutanese and Western secularist happiness movements colourfully embrace on global stages, it is important to note that the Buddhist notion of happiness is quite different from the hedonic 'happiness' that the neo-utilitarian Layard has heralded as the 'New Science' in the recent Western literature (Layard 2006). While there may be some short-term strategic gain to be made in terms of advancing some 'alternative' to orthodox GDP thinking, in the longer run the values underpinning these two conceptions are not consistent and commensurate with each other (Evans 2011; Davies 2016).

From a very different cultural, religious and political tradition, a number of countries in South America (particularly Bolivia and Ecuador) have been developing initiatives based on the notion of 'vivir bien' or 'buen vivir'—living well (Bressa Florentin, this volume, Chap. 6). These initiatives have been boosted by the rise to power of leaders from indigenous Andean cultural backgrounds and the 'buen vivir' approach seeks to establish a distance between itself and more Europeanised (and capitalist) notions of development (Salgado 2010).

The 'buen vivir' tradition places particular emphasis on the issue of 'living well with nature' and as such highlights the environmental sustainability concerns that cut across many of these initiatives. It is now increasingly understood that the 'buen vivir' idea is deeply contentious in the region, but one of its political claims was that it was seeking to establish a path to development that reflects indigenous societal-cultural values; this has had resonance across many Latin American countries, including, increasingly, in Brazil. With this impetus and other pathbreaking work on subjective wellbeing, Latin America has been one of the leading regions in pressing for the development and promotion of new thinking about how to measure development and progress (https://mfps.inegi.org.mx/en/Default.aspx).

Finally, and in distinct contrast to the 'buen vivir' tradition, there have been two major non-governmental approaches that deserve particular mention here. The Social Progress Index[7] (Porter et al. 2016) and the Legatum Prosperity Index (The Legatum Institute Foundation 2016) are both founded in more mainstream capitalist and liberal traditions. This emerging body of thinking takes an enlightened prosperity approach. They both emphasise the continued production of prosperity in conventional economic terms but with greater attention to the moral and political concerns that have been highlighted by critiques of selfish, money-focused wealth creation. They both emphasise the positive importance of freedoms and particularly the freedom to do business. Their selection of indicators focuses attention on the extent to which conditions within societies enable the ongoing production of wealth alongside the translation of that wealth into wellbeing and societal progress.

PUBLIC POLICY PURPOSES AND SCALE

In the broadest sense, there are grand ideological purposes at play in debates over new measures of progress. On the one hand, some initiatives frame it as a means of reforming and saving globalised capitalism and, on the other, some see it as a means of subverting it. These larger ideological purposes are seldom explicitly talked of and, in the meantime, much of the focus has been on how the introduction of wellbeing measures might improve public policy and governance. We will return to the broader ideological issues in the concluding discussion of this chapter, but this next section focuses on the possible purposes of wellbeing metrics in public policy processes.

Since the publication of the Stiglitz Commission Report, the Organisation for Economic Co-operation and Development (OECD) has taken a more prominent leading global role in promoting the development of new measures. The OECD Better Life Initiative was launched in 2011 under the auspices of a broader stated aim: to promote 'Better Policies for Better Lives'. As part of that initiative, the 'How's Life?' Report set out a framework for the assessment of progress in terms of human wellbeing and identified possible statistical indicators that could be employed in country-level assessments (OECD 2011).

A second 'How's Life?' Report was published in 2013, giving a detailed analysis of the performance of 28 countries in terms of the 'How's Life?' indicators (OECD 2013a).

The OECD has driven an initiative that encourages and supports national statistical offices around the world to take up the 'measuring progress' challenge. For the OECD and other globally focused organisations like it, one of the main purposes is to be able to compare the performance of countries around the world in generating 'genuine' progress as defined by improvements in human wellbeing.

Comparison is a significant policy purpose for wellbeing measures at the global, national and sub-national levels. Wellbeing performance can be compared between geographical areas, over time and between population groups. Many countries that have developed their own wellbeing measurement schemes are particularly wary of uneven or iniquitous development dynamics and are explicitly seeking to understand which regions within their country or which groups of people are doing better (or worse) than others. This concern for uneven development is very much to the fore in the UK's Measuring National Well-being Initiative, and the regular reports spend much of their time breaking down the data into regional performance and performance by population group (UK ONS 2016a, b).

It is a relatively small step from comparison to evaluation. *Evaluation* is a significant possible purpose for wellbeing data in the public policy sphere. Historically, much public policy evaluation has used some form of adapted economic metrics to proxy the impact of policies on society but advances in the availability of wellbeing data would allow a more direct assessment of the impact of policies on peoples' lives.

When considering the purpose of evaluation, it becomes more apparent that the scale at which wellbeing data is to be used matters. If the evaluation is intended to be at a high level of abstraction (e.g. at a national level, assessing a broad policy regime type) then generalist, universal wellbeing data are likely to be appropriate. However, if the evaluation is to be more detailed, assessing the impacts of a particular policy in particular regions or localities or on particular populations (e.g. women or young people), then more fine-grained wellbeing data will be required.

As of yet, the use of wellbeing metrics in policy evaluation is more promise than reality. A number of sets of guidelines are emerging in the UK (NEF 2008 and Public Health England 2016), but these are relatively thin and deal with limited conceptions of wellbeing. There are as of yet no prominent published examples of rigorous policy evaluation using wellbeing metrics. There are a number of possible reasons for this, not least that although wellbeing data is increasingly available, it is not necessarily available at the level of detail required for evaluation; it is not necessarily consistent across different locations; and there is not yet sufficient longitudinal wellbeing data to carry out evaluations from a baseline that would permit an assessment of whether policies have had an effect on wellbeing outcomes.

The concept of wellbeing could also have policy *formulation* purposes. Focusing policy formulation on the question as to whether and how a policy might protect or improve human wellbeing could involve a radical departure from the current orthodoxy of policy formulation. In rationalist policy formulation frameworks, techniques such as cost–benefit analysis continue to play a key role, and even though these may be modified by various social and equity considerations and be supported by other techniques, they still focus primarily on effectiveness and efficiency rather than on human wellbeing impacts.[8]

For wellbeing to be used in policy formulation, it would be necessary for policymakers to use a 'theory of change' that offered a plausible (and preferably evidence-supported) route from policy intervention to wellbeing outcomes. This would be demanding for wellbeing thinking at this time for two main reasons. First, it requires that we have a clear conception of what wellbeing is and what its determinants are and, second, that it is underpinned by a good analytical understanding of wellbeing processes. As has been indicated in this chapter, there is currently a range of different wellbeing concepts at play in the public policy arena and, in consequence, establishing a dominant theory of change would be difficult. When wellbeing is conceived as multidimensional and when one moves beyond the aggregated picture that high-level wellbeing data provides, then it becomes apparent that policy interventions may have differing impacts on different groups of people and may differ in different social and geographical contexts. This implies that for realistic policy purposes, the analysis of wellbeing processes will need to be based to a greater extent on complexity thinking than on rationalist linear models. In a complexity approach to wellbeing, it would be necessary to understand the interactions of agency and structure, across inter-connecting levels of scale, that constitute the processes, whereby wellbeing is generated or denied (Ramalingam et al. 2008; Dyson and Todd 2010; McGregor 2011).

As the broad statement of the SDGs Resolution illustrates, it is possible to develop some broad guidelines on how wellbeing could be used in policy formulation, but at the moment this application is sketchy and incomplete. While it may be possible to apply a new and multidimensional conception of wellbeing at the highest level of abstract agreement, as policy becomes more specific, both in terms of the particular issue being addressed and in terms of population and location, then more carefully specified models and more fine-grained wellbeing data will be required.

Wellbeing Data: From the Universal to the Local

We have briefly discussed only three possible policy purposes that the concept of wellbeing and wellbeing metrics could be applied to, but there could be a range of other purposes (e.g. monitoring, human resource strategies). These three examples, however, already illustrate that different policy purposes set different requirements for wellbeing data. They also show that the level of scale at which the concept and metrics are to be used will also determine the level of detail of wellbeing data required. At the highest level of scale and for the most general purposes, data that accords to universal and broad wellbeing dimensions and domains may be adequate, but for more specific policy purposes, then more detailed, more precisely defined and more locally relevant data will be required.

With different wellbeing data needs at different levels of scale and for different policy purposes, there is always the possibility of a muddle of unconnected and incoherent data being generated. There are already signs of this happening, with many initiatives proceeding apparently unaware of or indifferent to the developments made in parallel initiatives. If this fragmentation were to continue, then this would be a profound step backwards for the progressive hopes for a wellbeing paradigm. The paradigm will undermine itself with a proliferation of competing and contradictory data, founded in differing claims about wellbeing.

This chapter builds on the principle that if we are to measure wellbeing in a way that is to be significant for change in public policy thinking, then it is essential that all measures of wellbeing should be founded in the reality of peoples' lives and that what is measured at the top should reflect and be consistent with what is being measured at the bottom. In an effort to achieve this, this chapter now presents one possible way of thinking about a unified framework that could be used to ensure consistency of wellbeing data at all levels. The framework is set out in Fig. 9.1 below and can be seen as consisting of three levels: Dimensions, Domains and Indicators. In this case, the figure is illustrated using the eleven domains[9] that are set out in the OECD How's Life framework, but a different list of domains could equally be used.

Dimensions

As per the earlier discussion in this chapter, we argue here that for public policy purposes it is possible to conceive of wellbeing as involving three universal dimensions. This triumvirate is broadly acknowledged in one form of words or another across the range of current literature. The terms material, relational and subjective broadly correspond to the notion that wellbeing arises from what a person has, what they are able to do with what they have and how they feel about what they have, can do and can be.

The material dimension refers to the material conditions of the person; the relational dimension refers to the relationships that person has with others in society;[10] and the subjective dimension refers to the meaning that the person attaches to their life and how they evaluate it. A person may be doing well in any one of these dimensions but for wellbeing to be achieved in the round, then it is necessary for the person to be doing sufficiently well in all three. The acceptance of a three-dimensional approach explicitly rejects the proposition that all information can be sufficiently conveyed just through a measure of subjective wellbeing. This framework also suggests that there can be no meaningful, synthesised single number metric for the level of wellbeing being achieved by a person that could then be aggregated up to give the level of wellbeing in a society. Rather it implies a dashboard approach in which it is necessary to look for sufficiently good performance across all three dimensions. To illustrate, it is perfectly possible to identify people (and societies) that are achieving high levels of material wellbeing but where their achievement in relational terms and/or in terms of the subjective evaluation of wellbeing is surprisingly low (Graham 2010).

Domains

At the second level, these three dimensions can be broken down into sets of domains in which it is necessary to identify more specifically what

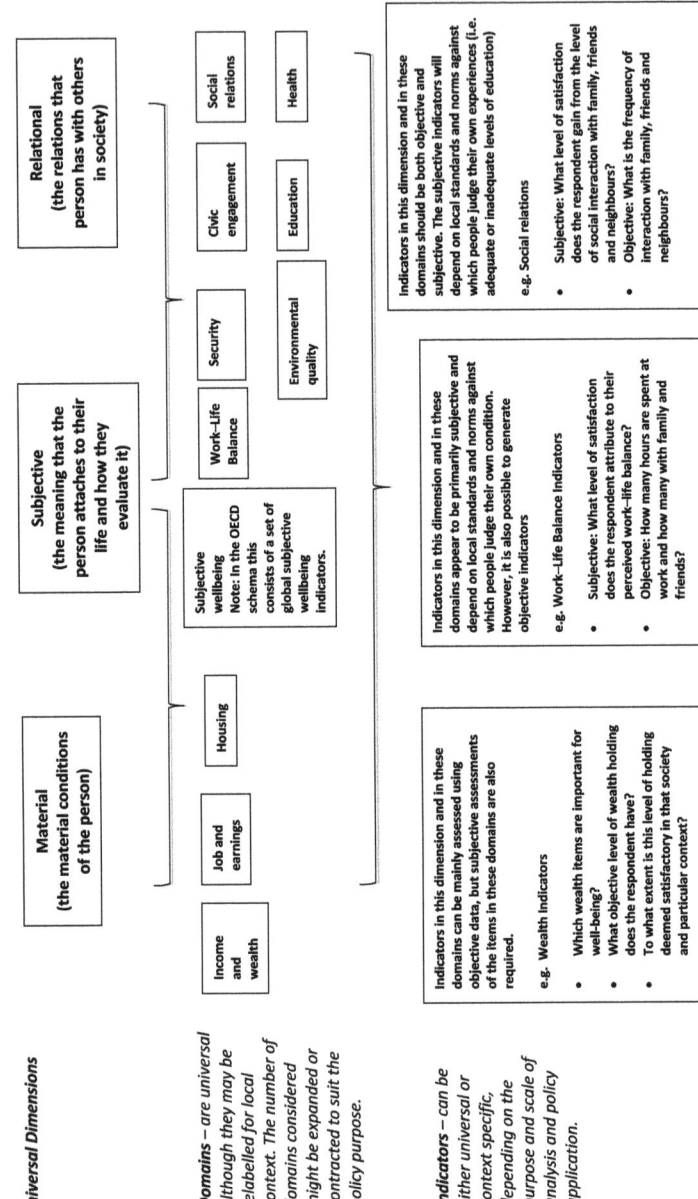

Fig. 9.1 Dimensions, domains and indicators (illustrated by the domains of the original OECD How's Life? framework, 2011)

kinds of thing we need to have, we need to be able to do, and need to be able to feel or be. There are many different lists of possible domains, some of which have been generated from empirical observation in particular disciplines and others that have been generated on the basis of particular theoretical or philosophical positions. The number of domains proposed varies across the contributions and this seems to be driven by the stated or implicit purpose of the proposition and/or by the disciplinary bias of the proposer.[11] Nevertheless, all of these lists tend to cover similar ground: there are no real surprises in the kinds of issue covered by any of these lists of domains although there may be dispute over whether some constitute domains that are essential for all human wellbeing, in all societies. In Fig. 9.1, the level of domains is illustrated using the eleven domains set out in the OECD framework.

Before we move on to explain the proposed approach, there are a number of caveats that must be made about using the OECD domains to illustrate this framework. The first is the somewhat awkward position of a distinct subjective wellbeing domain. In the OECD schema, this is used to house a range of global assessments of subjective wellbeing (happiness, life satisfaction, etc. see OECD 2013b). The inclusion of this as a distinct domain could be seen as providing a useful overview of the state of subjective wellbeing of the person, but it also could be regarded as somewhat anomalous since it might be interpreted to imply that no subjective assessment is either possible or required in other domains in the schema. This is not the case. In the OECD framework, this points to the more general problem that there is confusion over the role of objective and subjective data in the assessment of wellbeing for public policy purposes. This is discussed in more detail elsewhere (see McGregor et al. 2016), but it is enough here to note that in all domains, it is likely that both objective and subjective data can be generated and that both types of data can be of value in the application of wellbeing to political and policy purposes. For example, although the domains in the material dimension look as if they should be assessed primarily in objective terms, the information provided by subjective assessments in these domains cannot overlooked (after all, and if we follow a logic such as that suggested by the ILO's Decent Work agenda, it is not just a matter of whether one has a job but also whether that job is experienced as demeaning or harmful). Similarly, in both the relational and subjective dimensions, objective data can be collected and will be of value (e.g. the number and frequency of social contacts or the number of experiences of physical assault). Figure 9.1 also suggests that the domains generated by organisations like the OECD do not always fit neatly into just one of the three universal dimensions. In the How's Life? framework, some domains can be thought of as spanning across two or more of the dimensions. This can be illustrated with reference to the 'security' and 'work–life balance' domains. These could be interpreted as having mainly a subjective orientation (they are both primarily about how the person is experiencing their life),[12] but they can also both be seen to have significant relational content.[13] This implies that when we consider the third level of indicators, there may be some indicators of security that fall into the subjective dimension and others that fall into the relational dimension.

In this Figure (9.1), I have used the example of the OECD domains, but the argument that is advanced here is that, for policy purposes, a pragmatic view is required.[14] Given that, as noted, we are not seeking to resolve a philosophical debate using such a framework but rather seeking a practical application of indicators that convey meaning about a multi-dimensional notion of wellbeing, the absolute number of domains is not so important. Although all of the domains that are included should be universal,[15] the number of domains that are included might be expanded or contracted to suit the policy purpose. While there may be a need for a consistent body of data covering a similar set of domains, the number of domains included in any policy-oriented wellbeing framework could be decided as a matter of administrative agreement or convention. Similarly, although all domains must be universal, they may need to be re-labelled in particular contexts in order to better reflect the lived reality of people in those local contexts.

At the third level—the level of indicators—so long as the choice of indicators remains consistent with the domains and dimensions above, then specific indicators can be either universal or context specific. This will depend on the purpose and scale of analysis and policy application. Where broad comparisons are called for, then more directly comparable indicators will be required, but where the policy purpose is more specific to the issue, or is sensitive to the location, then more locally defined indicators will be required.

This can be illustrated with reference to a recent study of wellbeing and resilience in coastal communities in four developing countries (see Béné et al. 2016). It was agreed through a bottom–up process involving a series of focus groups that owning a motorised fishing boat was an important indicator of the wellbeing of fishermen, but the type of boat and engine size were different in all four countries. In order to contribute to the development of local and national fisheries policy that would be mindful of human wellbeing outcomes, then it was important that the type of boat and size of engine be taken into account. However, for cross-country comparison and analysis, what was important was to understand whether the person had or had not met the nationally determined threshold of motorised fishing boat ownership.

This type of approach follows the logic advanced by Len Doyal and Ian Gough in their *Theory of Human Need* (1991). There they argued that there are only two universal basic human needs (health and autonomy), but they proposed that these were met through a combination of intermediate needs satisfiers. In their schema, they reasoned that there are eleven universal need satisfiers (broadly similar to domains in this framework), but they argued that the specific form of the need satisfiers would depend on the local context. Thus while 'adequate protective housing' was one of the intermediate universal needs satisfiers, the type of housing that would satisfy the need would be different in different geographical contexts. This mechanism allows the necessary flexibility to recognise that in different societies, in different geographies and cultures, and at different levels of societal wealth, there may be different indicators that would tell you about the extent to which wellbeing was being achieved by the population in respect of each of the domains and dimensions.

CONCLUDING DISCUSSION

In the desire to advance the idea of new measures of progress and development, there has been considerable emphasis on the development of universal frameworks for understanding and measuring wellbeing. This is important for a number of reasons that we have discussed, but when we look in greater depth at possible public policy purposes and the scales of application of measures, then we can recognise that in many cases there is a need for more local content in what is deemed to constitute wellbeing and more locally specified data.

This chapter has presented one possible approach to maintain a coherent conceptual relationship between a universal framework and local realities. As has been noted, the challenge of having a universal framework that nevertheless can be differentiated in response to the needs and situation of different societies and cultures has been a key issue for the recent Sustainable Development Goals declaration.

The Statement of Vision in the UN SDG Resolution explicitly identifies with a multidimensional conception of human wellbeing and states:

> In these Goals and targets, we are setting out a supremely ambitious and transformational vision. We envisage a world free of poverty, hunger, disease and want, where all life can thrive. We envisage a world free of fear and violence. A world with universal literacy. A world with equitable and universal access to quality education at all levels, to health care and social protection, where physical, mental and social well-being are assured. (2015, p. 2/35).

The need for a fully functioning multidimensional framework for wellbeing for policy purposes looks obvious when one considers the multidimensional character of most of the problems that face policymakers (e.g. poverty, inequality and sustainability), but there is a danger of a reductionist move in the global wellbeing movement at this time. The ever greater emphasis that is being placed on subjective wellbeing interpretations of wellbeing, and particularly on a neo-utilitarian notion of happiness, begins to limit the space available for thinking about how a multidimensional framework might be applied. And, because the notion of happiness drives a new universalistic model, it also restricts thinking about how the problem of relating the universal and local might be constructively resolved for real and pressing policy purposes.

Illustrating this shift with reference to the case of the UK, Annie Austin has argued that we are seeing an emergent 'hegemony of happiness'. As she notes,

> … as in the economics and psychology literatures, the default definition of wellbeing among British policy actors has become a subjective definition: when the term 'wellbeing' is used, it implicitly refers to SWB, to the extent that alternative meanings of 'wellbeing' are not even considered. In sum, a hegemony of happiness has emerged. (2016, p. 128).

This shift is not just observable in the case of the UK, and its global manifestation is admirably demonstrated by the now annual *World Happiness Report* (Helliwell et al. 2016). This reduction to a focus on 'happiness' raises a bigger set of ideological issues for the measuring progress movement than is commonly acknowledged. The increasing dominance of the happiness approach reflects a post-financial crisis reassertion of the hegemony of economics, but in enlightened neo-utilitarian form (Frawley 2015; Davies 2016). This combines with the privilege given to 'parsimonious' and 'tractable' (simplistic) quantitative data and modelling to set boundaries to think in a number of ways. This has serious intellectual, ethical and political shortcomings, and in this concluding discussion, I argue that by increasingly setting the agenda for policy thinking, it is restricting debate about what values we want to see embedded in our notions of societal progress.

Homogenising Happiness

The vast array of data and many tables in reports such as the World Happiness Report appear to convey much about the different levels of happiness in different countries around the world, but they also conceal much. This is the application of a crude universalist framework that asserts that this particular notion and measure of happiness is globally applicable and can be used to provide insight into a wide range of policy issues in any societal or cultural context.

Leaving aside the fact that the meaning of the concept of happiness across different societies and cultures is ontologically problematic (Oishi et al. 2013), the imposition of a new, largely Western-driven metric will be interpreted by many as a further attempt to impose a new straightjacket on policymakers and peoples in other societies. Once again, rather than engaging in a process that gives priority to bottom–up processes that enable people to say what is important for them to be 'happy', or rather to 'be well', in their society and culture (and thus define their targets and routes to progress), we see these processes being driven out by a technocratically driven, top–down policy project.

The Political Economy of Wellbeing Dynamics

The happiness regression approach may be useful for some abstract analytical purposes, but it produces a limited picture of wellbeing dynamics both at the global scale and within particular countries. It tells us little about differences between peoples and groups and about the complex processes that relate wellbeing outcomes and processes in particular structural configurations of economy and society, across global and societal levels. As we know, persistent or growing inequality is a pressing problem both globally and within nation states (Wilkinson and Pickett 2009; Bourguignon 2015), but this approach tells us little about how the key and systemic differences in wellbeing outcomes for different groups of people come about and are reproduced.

The unifying framework that has been presented in this chapter is multidimensional, and it argues that for policy purposes, it is necessary to consider all of the dimensions of wellbeing and that their interplay must be understood if we are to engage wellbeing as a means of developing innovative policy approaches to real-world problems. The same type of multidimensional framework underpins the SDG resolution and goals. The upshot of adopting a multidimensional approach is that the issues of how to protect and promote human wellbeing are viewed as complex.

The 'happiness project' is developed through the exploration of statistically significant relations between happiness scores and other variables, and it uses standard linear modelling in a relatively limited way. In doing so, it maintains the principles of parsimony and simplicity but avoids the issues of complexity. In particular, by largely avoiding the issue of the role of power in wellbeing relationships and dynamics, the reductionist happiness approach can produce hand-wringing observations about poverty and inequality, but it yields only a neutered insight into the political economy of wellbeing. While this more simple approach may be appealing to a technocratic policy audience, it largely ducks the bigger political issues that lie behind many of the current major global challenges. In the three-dimensional model that is presented here, recognition of the importance of the interplay between individual agency and structure in multidimensional terms, at and between levels of scale, provides the beginnings of a more realistic and complex systems view of wellbeing.

Metrics and Governance

The shift towards a universalising happiness approach also ignores the important observation made by Hall and Rickard that, aside from the promise of better policymaking founded in more locally relevant metrics, a methodology that builds wellbeing indicators from the ground up can have significant governance benefits (McGregor et al. 2009; Hall and Rickard 2013). The governance downside of the global happiness hegemony in the new wellbeing movement is that it disempowers the people in villages, towns and cities all around the world, who understand their own wellbeing circumstances very well and who are desperate for politicians and policymakers to engage with their real-world aspirations and wellbeing failures. The approach also runs counter to the demand in the SDG framework for a universalist framework that recognises local values and realities. Once again, rather than being asked what is important for their wellbeing, there is the risk that people will be told from above what is important for their happiness. And, once again, they will become bystanders in their own development processes and political systems.

Happiness and Values

A key ideological issue that lies beneath this debate is whether our notion of wellbeing is to focus on people being well as individuals or people being well together in societies. The distinction between an individualising account of wellbeing and a social conception of wellbeing is crucial and is central to a broader political and policy debate. The neo-utilitarianism that underpins the happiness approach largely depends on the notion of 'living well as an individual'—it is a reassertion of *homo economicus*. In doing this, it systematically underplays the issue of what is required for people to 'live well together' (Deneulin and McGregor 2010).

This difference between an individualised and a social conception of wellbeing is founded in ontological and epistemological differences in the approach to wellbeing that go to the heart of our social sciences; each of the disciplines discussed in this chapter has ongoing debates around these issues (Beck and Beck-Gernsheim 2001; Frawley 2015; McKenzie 2016; McGregor and Pouw 2016). However, by ignoring or side-stepping this key debate, the 'happiness hegemony' reduces the possibility of explicitly considering and debating what values are important for wellbeing in political and policy debates. Not only does it use this individualised approach in its analysis, it implicitly promotes it in its engagement with policy processes. The policy ramifications of this have been pointed out in academia and in public commentary (Furedi 2004; Davies 2016; Uchida and Oishi 2016): from the individualising perspective, the responsibility for wellbeing becomes that of the person and we are encouraged to explore individualised ways of achieving personal wellbeing (e.g. the 'five ways to wellbeing' or taking up therapies). This neo-utilitarian approach systematically and conveniently allows policy attention to shy away from the structural conditions that are generating wellbeing inequalities and that are producing harmful and unsustainable wellbeing failures for many.

NOTES

1. With an option of adding an eighth domain on 'spiritual and religious belief'.
2. For a report of a number of the most developed of these see Boarini et al. (2014).
3. As the subsequent UK ONS Measuring Well-being framework illustrates, it is not always clear that the consultation process properly informs the choices of what measures are subsequently used (Oman 2015. See also Australian Bureau of Statistics 2013).
4. Bentham's work on 'the balance of pain and pleasure' being assessed in terms of happiness provides some of the foundations for contemporary neo-classical economics.
5. The other strands were the participatory development and livelihoods literatures.
6. This was the statement of objective in the original Wellbeing in Developing Countries (WeD) proposal to the UK ESRC in 2001.
7. Funded by the Skoll Foundation.
8. The 2011 update of the UK Government's Green Book on 'Appraisal and Evaluation in Central Government' introduced the possibility of using 'subjective wellbeing' in policy and project appraisal and evaluation (UK Treasury 2011). However, the addition refers only to the subjective dimension of wellbeing and even that remains something of a 'bolt-on' to the mainstay of CBA techniques. The overall approach does not embrace any particularly profound conception of wellbeing.
9. Domains are referred to in the OECD Framework as Dimensions.
10. And to other species and the natural environment.
11. The number of domains tends to range between 5 and 12. For example, from social psychology Cummins proposes 7–8 domains; Nussbaum proposes ten central universal capabilities; and the OECD list of 11 only varies marginally from the eight dimensions proposed in the Stiglitz Commission Report. For further information on a range of frameworks, see Boarini et al. (2014, pp 21–24).
12. Security is about being or feeling secure, and work–life balance depends fundamentally on the person feeling they have a work–life balance that is appropriate to them.
13. Security also could be measured in terms of the level of relationships with whom there is trust (e.g. high levels of relationship with friends and family or being surrounded by strangers with whom there is little trust),

whereas work–life balance will depend on the relationships to those one works with and where and whether there is a line is drawn between work and the rest of life.

14. This could be described as a 'phronetic' approach to the challenge of applying wellbeing to real policy challenges (Flyvberg et al. 2012).

15. I have found no empirical studies in any location or culture that reveal new items that are important for wellbeing that do not fit in some way into one of the possible universal domains that the literature provides.

References

Adams, B., & Luchsinger, G. (2015). (SDGs) Fit for Whose Purpose? Global Policy Watch Briefing Paper No. 8, Social Watch/Global Policy Forum. Available at: https://www.globalpolicy.org/home/270-general/52799-fit-for-whose-purpose.html.

Amin, S. (2006). The Millennium Development Goals: A Critique from the South. *Monthly Review, 57*(10). Available at: https://monthlyreview.org/2006/03/01/the-millennium-development-goals-a-critique-from-the-south/.

Austin, A. (2016). On Well-being and Public Policy: Are We Capable of Questioning the Hegemony of Happiness? *Social Indicators Research: An International and Interdisciplinary Journal for Quality-of-Life Measurement, 127*(1), 123–138.

Australian Bureau of Statistics. (2013). Measures of Australia's Progress. Aspirations for Our Nation: A conversation. ABS: Belconnen. Available at: http://base.socioeco.org/docs/measures_of_australia_s_progress_consultation_report.pdf

Bache, I., & Reardon, L. (2016). *The Politics and Policy of Wellbeing: Understanding the Rise and Significance of a New Agenda*. Cheltenham: Edward Elgar.

Beck, U., & Beck-Gernsheim, E. (2001). *Individualization: Institutionalized Individualism and Social and Political Consequences*. London: Sage.

Bayo-Ogunrotifa, A. (2015). Grand Developmentalism: MDGs and SDGs in Sub-Saharan Africa. *Pambazuka News*, May 2015. Available at: https://www.pambazuka.org/governance/grand-developmentalism-mdgs-and-sdgs-sub-saharan-africa.

Béné, C., Al-Hassan, R. M., Amarasinghe, O., Fong, P., Ocran, J., Onumah, E., et al. (2016). Is Resilience Socially Constructed? Empirical Evidence from Fiji, Ghana, Sri Lanka, and Vietnam. *Global Environmental Change, 38*, 153–170.

Biswas-Diener, R., & Diener, E. (2001). Making the Best of a Bad Situation: Satisfaction in the Slums of Calcutta. *Social Indicators Research, 55*, 329–352.

Blanchflower, D. G., & Oswald, A. J. (2004). Well-being Over Time in Britain and the USA. *Journal of Public Economics, 88*, 13549–13586.

Boarini, R., Kolev, A., & McGregor, J. A. (2014). Measuring Well-being and Progress in Countries at Different Stages of Development: Towards a More Universal Conceptual Framework. *OECD Working Paper 325*, Paris: OECD Publications. Available at: http://www.oecd-ilibrary.org/development/oecd-development-centre-working-papers_18151949.

Bourguignon, F. (2015). *The Globalization of Inequality*. Princeton: Princeton University Press.

Camfield, L., & McGregor, J. A. (2009). Editors' Introduction: Quality of Life and International Development Policy and Practice. *Applied Research in Quality of Life, 4*(2), 129–134.

Canadian Index of Wellbeing. (no date). Vision, Mission, Goals and Objectives. CIW website. Available at: https://uwaterloo.ca/canadian-index-wellbeing/about-canadian-index-wellbeing/vision-mission-goals-and-objectives.

Corsín Jiménez, A. (Ed.). (2008). *Culture and Well-being: Anthropological Approaches to Freedom and Political Ethics*. London: Pluto Press.

Cummins, R. A. (2000). Objective and Subjective Quality of Life: An Interactive Model. *Social Indicators Research, 52*, 55–72.

Davies, W. (2016). *The Happiness Industry: How Government and Big Business Sold us Happiness*. London: Verso.

Deneulin, S., & McGregor, J. A. (2010). The Capability Approach and the Politics of a Social Conception of Wellbeing. *European Journal of Social Theory, 13*(4), 501–519.

Diener, E., Emmons, R. A., Larsen, R. J., & Griffin, S. (1985). The Satisfaction with Life Scale. *Journal of Personality Assessment, 49*, 71–75.

Doyal, L., & Gough, I. (1991). *A Theory of Human Need*. Basingstoke: Palgrave Macmillan.

Dyson, A., & Todd, L. (2010). Dealing with Complexity: Theory of Change Evaluation and the Full Service Extended Schools Initiative. *International Journal of Research and Method in Education, 33*(2), 119–134.

Evans, J. (2011). Our Leaders Are All Aristotelians Now. *Public Policy Research*, December–February, 214–221.

Flyverg, B., Landman, T., & Schram, S. (Eds.). (2012). *Real Social Science: Applied Phronesis*. Cambridge: Cambridge University Press.

Frawley, A. (2015). Happiness Research: A Review of Critiques. *Sociology Compass, 9*(1), 62–77.

Frey, B., & Stutzer, A. (2002a). *Happiness and Economics: How the Economy and Institutions Affect Wellbeing*. Princeton: Princeton University Press.

Frey, B. S., & Stutzer, A. (2002b). What can Economists Learn from Happiness Research? *Journal of Economic Literature, 40*(2), 402–435.

Furedi, F. (2004). *Therapy Culture: Creating Vulnerability in an Uncertain Age*. London: Routledge.

Gough, I., & McGregor, J. A. (Eds.). (2007). *Wellbeing in Developing Countries: From Theory to Research*. Cambridge: Cambridge University Press.

Government of Bhutan. (2016). Gross National Happiness Report 2015: A Compass towards a Just and Harmonious Society. *GoB*. Available at: http://www.grossnationalhappiness.com.

Graham, C. (2010). *Happiness Around the World: The Paradox of Happy Peasants and Miserable Millionaires.* Oxford: Oxford University Press.

Hall, J., & Rickard, L. (2013). People, Progress and Participation: How Initiatives Measuring Social Progress Yield Benefits Beyond Better Metrics, Global Choices 1. Germany: Bertelsmann Stiftung. Available at: http://alleuropalux.org/fileserver/2013/78/xcms_bst_dms_37947_37948_2.pdf.

Helliwell, J., Layard, R., & Sachs, J. (2016). World Happiness Report 2016. New York: Sustainable Development Solutions Network. Available at: http://world-happiness.report/wp-content/uploads/sites/2/2016/03/HR-V1_web.pdf

International Well-being Group (IWB). (2013). *Personal Well-being Index (Adult): Manual.* Available at: http://www.acqol.com.au/iwbg/well-being-index/pwi-a-english.pdf. Accessed December 21, 2016.

Jaggar, A. M. (2006). Reasoning About Well-being: Nussbaum's Methods of Justifying the Capabilities. *The Journal of Political Philosophy, 14*(3), 301–322.

Kahneman, D., Diener, E., & Schwarz, N. (1999). *Wellbeing: The Foundations of Hedonic Psychology.* New York: Russell Sage.

Layard, R. (2006). *Happiness: Lessons from a New Science.* London: Penguin.

Lau, A. L. D., Cummins, R. A., & McPherson, W. (2005). An Investigation into the Cross-cultural Equivalence of the Personal Well-being Index. *Social Indicators Research, 72,* 403.

Legatum Institute Foundation. (2016). The Legatum Prosperity Index. London: The Legatum Institute. Available at: http://www.prosperity.com/application/files/1614/7809/7434/Legatum_Prosperity_Index_2016.pdf.

Levis, L. (2015). Putting Social Progress on a Par with Prosperity. *Harvard Magazine, 2015,* 15–16.

Lin, K., & Herrmann, P. (Eds.). (2015). *Social Quality Theory: A New Perspective on Social Development.* Oxford: Berghahn.

McGregor, J. A. (2007). Researching Human Wellbeing: From Concepts to Methodology. In I. Gough & J. A. McGregor (Eds.), *Wellbeing in Developing Countries: From Theory to Research* (pp. 316–350). Cambridge: Cambridge University Press.

McGregor, J. A. (2008). Wellbeing, Poverty and Conflict. Wellbeing in Developing Countries Research Group Briefing Paper 1. Bath: University of Bath. Available at: http://www.bath.ac.uk/soc-pol/welldev/research/bp/bp1-08.pdf.

McGregor, J. A., Camfield, L., & Woodcock, A. (2009). Needs, Wants and Goals: Wellbeing, Quality of Life and Public Policy. *Applied Research in Quality of Life, 4*(2), 135–154.

McGregor, J. A. (2011). Reimagining Development Through the Crisis Watch Initiative. *IDS Bulletin, 42*(5), 17–23.

McGregor, J. A., Camfield, L., & Coulthard, S. C. (2016). Competing Interpretations: Human Wellbeing and the Use of Quantitative and Qualitative Methods, Ch. 10. In Camfield & Roelen (Eds.), *Mixed Methods Research in Poverty and Vulnerability*. London: Palgrave Macmillan.

McGregor, J. A., & Pouw, N. (2016). Towards an Economics of Well-being. *Cambridge Journal of Economics, 41*, 1123–1142.

McKenzie, J. (2016). Happiness vs. Contentment? A Case for a Sociology of the Good Life. *Journal for the Theory of Social Behaviour, 46*(3), 252–267.

Michalos, A. C. (2011). What Did Stiglitz, Sen and Fitoussi Get Right and What Did They Get Wrong? *Social Indicators Research, 102*(1), 117–129.

NEF. (2008). Well-Being Evaluation Tools: A Research and Development Project for the Big Lottery Fund. London: New Economics Foundation.

Noll, H.-H. (2011). The Stiglitz-Sen-Fitoussi-report: Old Wine in New Skins? Views from a Social Indicators Perspective. *Social Indicators Research, 102*, 111–116.

Noll, H.-H. (2013). Subjective Social Indicators: Benefits and Limitations for Policy Making. *Social Indicators Research, 114*, 1–11.

O'Donnell, G., Deaton, A., Durand, M., Halpern, D., & Layard, R. (2014). Wellbeing and Policy: Report of the Commission on Wellbeing and Policy. London: The Legatum Institute. Available at: https://www.li.com/docs/default-source/commission-on-wellbeing-and-policy/commission-on-wellbeing-and-policy-report---march-2014-pdf.pdf?sfvrsn=2.

OECD. (2011). *How's Life? Measuring Well-being*. Paris: OECD Publishing. doi: 10.1787/9789264121164-en.

OECD. (2013a). *How's Life? 2013. Measuring Well-being*. Paris: OECD Publishing. doi: 10.1787/9789264201392-en.

OECD. (2013b). *Guidelines on Measuring Subjective Well-being*. Paris: OECD Publishing.

Oishi, S., Graham, J., Kesebir, S., & Costa Galinha, I. (2013). Concepts of Happiness Across Time and Cultures. *Personality and Social Psychology Bulletin, 39*(5), 559–577.

Oman, S. (2015). Measuring National Well-being: What Matters to You? What Matters to Whom? In Sarah C. White (Ed.), *Cultures of Well-being: Method, Place, Policy*. Basingstoke: Palgrave Macmillan.

Oswald, A. (1997). Happiness and Economic Performance. *Economic Journal, 107*, 1815–1831.

Pavot, W. G., Diener, E., Colvin, C. R., & Sandvik, E. (1991). Further Validation of the Satisfaction with Life Scale: Evidence for the Cross-method Convergence of Well-being Measures. *Journal of Personality Assessment, 57*, 149–161.

Porter, M., Stern, S., & Green, M. (2016). The Social Progress Index 2016. The Social Progress Imperative. Available at: http://www.socialprogressimperative.org/global-index/.

Powdthavee, N. (2010). *The Happiness Equation: The Surprising Economics of Our Most Valuable Asset*. London: Icon Books.

Public Health England. (2016). Arts for Health and Well-being: An Evaluation Framework. Available at: https://www.gov.uk/government/uploads/system/uploads/attachment_data/file/496230/PHE_Arts_and_Health_Evaluation_FINAL.pdf.

Ramalingam, B., Jones, H., Reba, T., & Young, J. (2008). Exploring The Science of Complexity: Ideas and Implications for Development and Humanitarian Efforts. ODI Working Paper 285, Overseas Development Institute, London. Available at: https://www.odi.org/sites/odi.org.uk/files/odi-assets/publications-opinion-files/833.pdf.

Rojas, M. (2008). Experienced Poverty and Income Poverty in Mexico: A Subjective Well-being Approach. *World Development, 36*(6), 1078–1109.

Ruta, D., Garratt, A. M., Leng, M., Russell, I. T., & MacDonald, L. M. (1994). A New Approach to the Measurement of Quality of Life: The Patient-generated Index. *Medical Care, 32*(11), 1109–1126.

Salgado, F. (2010). Sumaq Kawsay: The Birth of a Notion? *Cadernos EBAPE.br* 8(2): 198–208.

Schmidt, S., & Bullinger, M. (2007). Cross-cultural Quality of Life Assessment: Approaches and Experiences from the Health Care Field. In Ian Gough and J. Allister McGregor (Eds.), *Wellbeing in Developing Countries: From Theory to Research*. Cambridge: Cambridge University Press.

Sen, A. K. (1993). Capability and Well-Being. In M. Nussbaum & A. Sen (Eds.), *The Quality of Life*. Oxford: Clarendon Press.

Stiglitz, J. E., Sen, A., & Fitoussi, J-P. (2009). Report by the Commission on the Measurement of Economic Performance and Social Progress. Available at: http://ec.europa.eu/eurostat/documents/118025/118123/Fitoussi+Commission+report. Accessed December 17, 2016.

Uchida, Y., & Oishi, S. (2016). The Happiness of Individuals and the Collective. *Japanese Psychological Research, 58*(1), 125–141.

UK Office of National Statistics. (2011). Measuring What Matters: National Statistician's Reflections on the National Debate on Measuring National Well-Being. Newport: ONS.

UK Office of National Statistics. (2016a). Measuring National Well-Being in the UK, Domains and Measures. Newport: ONS.

UK Office of National Statistics UK. (2016b). Personal Well-Being in the UK 2015–2016. Newport: ONS.

UK Treasury. (2011). *Green Book: Appraisal and Evaluation in Central Government* (2011 update of 2003 document). Available at: https://www.gov.uk/government/uploads/system/uploads/attachment_data/file/220541/green_book_complete.pdf.

United Nations General Assembly. (2015). *Transforming Our World: The 2030 Agenda for Sustainable Development*, Resolution 70/1, September 2015. Available at: https://sustainabledevelopment.un.org/post2015/transformingourworld

van der Deijl, W. (2016). Are Measures of Well-being Philosophically Adequate? *Philosophy of the Social Sciences, 47*(3): 209–234.

Wilkinson, R., & Pickett, K. (2009). *The Spirit Level: Why More Equal Societies Almost Always Do Better*. London: Allen Lane.

CHAPTER 10

'Therapeutic Entrepreneurialism' and the Undermining of Expertise and Evidence in the Education Politics of Wellbeing

Kathyrn Ecclestone

INTRODUCTION

Encompassing very diverse interests and goals in areas such as economics, the environment, welfare and education, a view that citizens' social and economic wellbeing should be a prominent political aspiration has gained strong traction amongst policy makers, academics, the public and the media in Britain and other countries (Bache and Scott, this volume, Chap. 1). There have been corresponding studies of the relationship between contemporary policy applications of wellbeing and earlier philosophical traditions and the social, psychological and economic complexities that make wellbeing a 'wicked' problem (e.g. Ecclestone 2013; Bache et al. 2016). Of course, enthusiastic policy rhetoric and academic activity do not necessarily signify that wellbeing has actually become a major tenet in different political arenas (Bache and Reardon 2016). It is also important to recognise that wellbeing gains traction as a policy problem in a particular political and sociocultural context that

K. Ecclestone (✉)
University of Sheffield, Sheffield, UK
e-mail: k.ecclestone@sheffield.ac.uk

I. Bache and K. Scott (eds.), *The Politics of Wellbeing*, Wellbeing
in Politics and Policy, https://doi.org/10.1007/978-3-319-58394-5_10

simultaneously sidelines, marginalises and privileges certain interpretations, types of claims makers, evidence and expertise.

This chapter explores these dimensions in the rise of wellbeing as a policy problem in British educational settings between 1997 and 2015. Drawing on Stephen Ball's critical approach to analyse education policy as 'text', 'discourse' and 'trajectory' (Ball 1994), I explore the ways in which the trajectory of wellbeing from policy discourse to practice has become embedded in an intensification of popular crisis discourses about childhood and, more recently and specifically, about mental health. Recognising the danger of over-attributing influence to particular texts or to individual actors involved in their production and promotion, and acknowledging limits to analytical space in a single chapter, I focus on three policy texts: two produced during the 1997–2010 Labour governments and one produced during the 2010–2015 Conservative-led coalition, to make three arguments. First, the education policy trajectory of wellbeing has become embedded in a circular, self-referential consensus amongst influential claims-makers that elides wellbeing with mental health, mental capital and character, thereby narrowing wider understandings of wellbeing, and then asserts that an associated, lengthening list of psycho-emotional 'skills' can and must be taught in order to prevent lifelong problems. Second, this narrow understanding of wellbeing-as-mental health/character has created a policy and practice market of therapeutic entrepreneurs competing to promote their favoured universal or generic interventions. Third, these developments both generate and arise from dubious claims to expertise and evidence and the sidelining or marginalising of richer philosophical, sociological and historical understandings of wellbeing that might offer more educationally meaningful approaches to develop it. I conclude with some brief thoughts on what these more meaningful approaches might be.

APOCALYPTIC DISCOURSES OF CHILDHOOD CRISIS

Mental Health

A steady stream of policy reports since the late 1990s has responded to, and fuelled, political and public discourses of childhood and youth crisis, generating a strong consensus across the political spectrum that contemporary experience of childhood is qualitatively different from other historical eras, marked by the decline of wellbeing with myriad damaging social and individual effects (e.g. Sharples 2007; Layard and Dunn 2012; O'Donnell et al. 2014). Associated calls for preventative and ameliorative state action in schools have drawn in related calls for early psycho-emotional intervention in families (e.g. Field 2010; Allen 2011). Ideas about dysfunctional families and the increasingly 'toxic' nature of childhood (Palmer 2006) have been taken up extensively in the popular press, lifestyle magazines and internet groups such as Mumsnet over the past ten years or so. A striking feature of these developments is a series of 'relentlessly repetitive problematisations' about a growing array of children's and young people's experiences (Isin 2004, p. 228).

In historical terms, an alarmist 'youth in crisis' thesis is far from new (e.g. Myers 2012). For example, earlier periods have seen profound political and public concern about behaviour, parenting, disaffection and disengagement, and corresponding concerns about children and young people who do not fit into education, welfare and guidance systems (e.g. Thompson 2006; Stewart 2011; Myers 2011). A particular concern over the past 40 years or so has been the transition from school to the labour market, unemployment or further education (e.g. Valentine and Skelton 2003; Lumby 2012). Here, a 'youth in crisis' discourse is not confined to the UK: academic, public and political concerns about young people's wellbeing in the face of increasingly difficult life, education and work transitions have also become prominent in countries such as Finland and Australia (e.g. Wright and McLeod 2014; Brunila and Silvonen 2014). Education is seen as both a source of profound pressure and an essential remedy. According to Jacky Lumby:

> ... From Willis's (1977) seminal study of the educational roots of inequality to more recent explorations of the burgeoning mental health and behavioural issues among adolescents, or the effects of globalisation on at-risk youth... their fragility and degree of exposure has made many apprehensive. Education is depicted as a structural aspect of a risky environment, presenting perils which some young people fail to navigate successfully, with lasting detriment to their lives (Lumby 2012, 261).

These expanding contemporary concerns have gained particular traction amidst intensifying alarm about mental illness, seen as a worsening global epidemic by the World Health Organization, UNICEF and the OECD, pharmaceutical companies, professional bodies representing psychologists and global corporations (e.g. Mills 2014). For example, the WHO constructs mental illness (and depression in particular) as a global epidemic and a leading cause of disability worldwide, estimating more than 350 million sufferers (WHO 2012). A British National Health Service report in 2011 stated that the proportion of 16–64-year olds with at least one common mental disorder rose from 15.5 per cent in 1993 to 17.5 per cent in 2007 (NHS 2014). Ubiquitous statistics that '20 per cent of children have a mental health problem in any given year' and that, for 50 per cent, problems begin in childhood and increase in adolescence (Mental Health Foundation (MHF) 2015), parallel statements that anxiety and depression are two of the most common mental health problems that people face, with one in five people feeling anxious 'all of the time or a lot of the time' and people being 'more anxious now than they were 5 years ago' (MHF 2015). Other reports point to a sharp 30-year increase in young people's levels of anxiety, stress and depression (e.g. Collishaw et al. 2010). Concerns are also fuelled by a large expansion in formal diagnoses of mental health problems, psycho-emotional and behavioural disorders and a corresponding rise in targeted interventions (see Harwood and Allan 2014).

There are equally alarming claims about the far-reaching effects of such problems. For example, an All Party Parliamentary Group (APPG) on Mental Health states that 'Mental illnesses disable millions, disrupt and destroy lives, cause early deaths, lead to human rights abuses, [and] damage the economy…. Mental illnesses are killer diseases. They need to take their place among the other killer diseases for investment and priority' (Thornicroft cited in APPG 2014: 5). Other reports suggest that those 'suffering from a condition' are less likely to find paid employment or be homeowners (NHS 2014).

A common strand in these claims is a highly generalised construction of mental health, epitomised by one of the architects of the Labour government's Social and Emotional Aspects of Learning (SEAL) strategy, introduced in 2005 and discussed in more detail below:

> Mental health as it is now commonly defined includes the ability to grow and develop emotionally, intellectually and spiritually; to make relationships with others, including peers and adults; to participate fully in education and other social activities; to have positive self-esteem; and to cope, adjust and be resilient in the face of difficulties (Weare 2004, p. 7).

Such expansive interpretations of what comprises mental health have two interrelated effects: they generate growing numbers of those deemed not to meet their wide-ranging criteria and depict problems in alarming ways. For example, the Department for Education (2015) estimates that 1 in 10 pupils are eligible for a diagnosis of a mental disorder, leading the Conservative government, elected in 2015, to continue its coalition predecessors' characterisation of children's mental health as a social 'ticking time bomb' that educational institutions are uniquely placed to deal with and prevent (Morgan 2015a, b).

Wellbeing-as-Mental Health

These widely cited claims are rooted in both vague definitions and slippages between mental illness, issues, problems, conditions and disorders. For example, a 2008 Foresight Report aligned mental capital with wellbeing, and mental health with learning difficulties, to argue for significant government investment, not merely as a policy aspiration but to 'be considered at the heart of policy development in government' (Government Office for Science 2008 quoted by Bache and Reardon 2016, p. 101).

Such elisions became more prominent in educational policy after the election of a Conservative-led coalition government in 2010, leading to a further blurring of lines between education and health that began in 2003 with the national priorities laid out in the Labour government's landmark welfare legislation, Every Child Matters (ECM): be healthy; stay safe; enjoy and achieve; make a positive contribution; and achieve economic wellbeing. Notably, while emotional wellbeing and/or mental health were not specified, a widening of the remit for educational institutions from 2000 onwards has continued to be driven by influential claims that an expanding range of weaknesses or difficulties indicates children's actual or potential poor mental health and that there are social and economic benefits in prioritising this. Here, for example, an influential report *Future in Mind: Promoting, protecting and improving our children and young people's mental health and wellbeing* in March 2015 (NHS 2015) built upon the Children and Young People's Improving Access to Psychological Therapies programme (CYP-IAPT) to recommend psychological services for all young people across England and Wales, operating across education, health and social care and encompassing educationally based interventions (on IAPT see Evans, this volume, Chap. 2). These were seen as 'essential' for addressing inextricable links between mental health problems, lower educational attainment and behaviours that pose a risk to their health (NHS 2015). Another report, published in 2014, aligned 'character building' with mental health to call for an expansion of the IAPT programme and other services to address the 'unmet need' for therapy in childhood. The report called for the teaching of life skills, measuring children's wellbeing regularly and training teachers in mental health and child behaviour and endorsed growing cross-party political interest in more intensive and extensive psycho-emotional intervention in families (O'Donnell et al. 2014).

The Influence of Cultural Narratives

It is important to relate the increasingly blurred policy boundaries between health and education reflected in the reports and claims summarised above to what some sociologists call 'therapeutic culture', where eclectic, popularised vocabularies, assumptions and practices from branches of psychology, therapy, counselling and self-help permeate popular culture, politics, education, legal and welfare systems, institutional and everyday life (e.g. Nolan 1998; Furedi 2004; Ecclestone and Hayes 2009; Wright 2011; McLaughlin 2011). Crucially, as I argue below, therapeutic culture goes far beyond the expansion of 'psy-experts' across political, public and private life noted in earlier well-known studies (e.g. Rose 1999). Through popularised versions of therapeutic interventions in schools and workplaces, lifestyle and popular media, books, articles, self-assessment quizzes and software applications such as *Headspace*, therapeutic culture normalises everyday preoccupation with our own and others' emotional states, our effectiveness in relating to people and the psychological causes of difficulties, and encourages proficiency in using therapeutic ideas and vocabularies.

The concept of therapeutic culture illuminates a central characteristic of the policy trajectory of wellbeing-as-mental health/character, namely the strong populist resonance of its expanding terminologies, assumptions and claims. Amongst many media examples, a popular musician who uses music to 'break taboos of therapy and mental illness' states: 'I'm 26 and I don't know any of my friends who haven't suffered from some sort of mental illness' (Woodhall 2016). Writing in the *Sunday Express* to promote a new royal family campaign for children's mental health, Prince William asserted that 'A fifth of children will have a mental-health issue by their 11th birthday. And, left unresolved, those mental-health issues can alter the course of a child's life forever' (*Sunday Express* 2016). Citing the figure that one in four children have a mental health problem,

Natasha Devon, the government's children's mental health 'champion' between 2015 and 2016, argues that this crisis is 'spiralling out of control' (Devon 2016). A survey of 1093 students in 2015 carried out by the National Union of Students made similarly alarmist claims that 85 per cent of had a mental health problem in 2015 (Smith 2016).[1]

These ubiquitous and vague claims encourage policy makers to relay their personal experience as expert knowledge. For example, announcing funding for programmes to tackle the 'stigma of mental health problems', the government's Secretary of State for Education between 2014 and 2016 cited her own personal experience in a familiar apocalyptic tone:

> As a mum myself, I know growing up today is no easy task. Young people are under more pressure than ever before in ways that are unimaginable to my generation. This is driven home to me every week when I visit schools across the country and talk to pupils about the issues affecting them—and mental health comes up time and time again (Morgan 2015a).

This personalised example of a government response to a poorly defined problem hints at the types of knowledge and claims-makers that legitimise the education policy trajectory of wellbeing: I turn to explore these next.

THE POLICY TRAJECTORY OF WELLBEING IN EDUCATION

A Psycho-Emotional Skills-Based Approach to Wellbeing

There is not space here for a comprehensive review of the various types and respective legislative status of policy texts in the education politics of wellbeing since the late 1990s. It is important, though, to note here that non-statutory guidance and APPG reports have been highly influential as a lobbying space that, simultaneously, reflects and diffuses the popularised representations of crisis outlined above. In this section, I examine guidance for the Labour government's SEAL strategy, produced in 2005 by the then-Department for Education and Skills and reproduced by the Department of Children, Families and Schools between 2007 and 2010, and two APPG reports, *Wellbeing in the Classroom* (Sharples 2007) and *Character and Resilience* (Paterson et al. 2014). Outside a specific focus on education, two other APPG reports,

Mental Health and *Mindfulness*, both produced in 2015, have been influential.[2] I aim to show that the political and public resonance of these reports is rooted in the 'cannibalised' features that, according to Ball, characterise formal policies:

> The policies themselves, the texts, are not necessarily clear or closed or complete. The texts are the product of compromises at various stages (at points of initial influence, in the micro-politics of legislative formation, in the parliamentary process and in the politics and micro-politics of interest group articulation. They are typically the cannibalised products of multiple (but circumscribed) influences and agendas. There is ad hocery, negotiation and serendipity within... the policy formulation process (Ball 1994, p 16)

Seen in this light, I identify some of the cannibalised influences, key claims-makers and agendas permeating three policy texts.

(a) *Social and Emotional Aspects of Learning Strategy for Primary and Secondary Schools (SEAL)*

While a policy emphasis on targeted interventions for those with formal diagnoses of various behavioural and emotional disorders continued between 1997 and 2015, the Labour government's enthusiastic introduction of SEAL marked growing political interest in American school-based initiatives that privilege universal, generic and embedded approaches to build psychological, emotional and social attributes, behaviours and dispositions as both an ameliorative and preventative measure (see Humphrey 2013; Humphrey et al. 2016). Designed by educational psychologists from local authority initiatives in which they had worked, SEAL was sponsored by the Labour government between 2005 and 2010 as the 'operational arm' of ECM (Watson et al. 2012, p. 209).

Crucial to its political profile and wider dissemination inside and outside policy circles was the emotional literacy pressure group Antidote, founded by then-Secretary of State for Health, Patricia Hewitt, and Anthony Giddens, architect of the 1997 Labour government's third-way ideology and director of the London School of Economics. Antidote's advisory board included other high-profile supporters, such as MEP Glenys Kinnock, human rights lawyer Helena Kennedy, film producer David Puttnam, media guru Clive Hollick and Tom Bentley, Director of the left-of-centre DEMOS think tank between 1999 and 2006[3] (see Emery 2016).

According to official guidance at the time of its introduction in 2005, SEAL was a 'comprehensive, whole-school approach to promoting the social and emotional skills that underpin effective learning, positive behaviour, regular attendance, staff effectiveness and the emotional health and wellbeing of all who learn and work in schools' (DfES 2005). The initiative drew directly on Daniel Goleman's 1995 best-selling book on why emotional intelligence matters more than cognitive intelligence, translating Goleman's key tenets into the 'skills' of emotional literacy (including empathy and self-esteem), emotional management (including deferred gratification), relationship and decision-making. All are deemed essential for effective learning and life success (DfES 2005; Sharples 2007).

In his analysis of SEAL's competing interests, agendas and policy actors, Carl Emery shows that its cannibalised conceptual approach created equally cannibalised pedagogic strategies that combined selected bits of emotional intelligence, Maslow's needs-based humanist psychology, person-centred counselling, cognitive behavioural therapy (CBT) and positive psychology (see Emery 2016). Predictably, policy makers could highlight its ambitious and elastic social and educational goals selectively to demonstrate specific commitments, such as eradicating disruptive behaviour in schools (e.g. Balls 2007).

Given that SEAL had no statutory status, its legitimacy was tied closely to Antidote's lobbying and media coverage where, in addition to Antidote's Director James Park and well-known psychotherapist Susie Orbach, various celebrities and well-known figures endorsed the Labour government's commitment to emotional literacy. Some political supporters publicly endorsed SEAL's evangelical proselytising of its far-reaching effects as a uniquely progressive aspect of 'New Labour'. For example, making extensive claims in broadsheet newspapers such as the *Observer*, Tom Bentley claimed that 'emotional literacy is becoming the political issue of our time, but it's emerging quite gradually as something with a hard-edged political dimension' while Tony Colman, Labour MP and Antidote supporter claimed that: 'this new thinking is part of New Labour, although it's not overtly government policy. It's a thread of sanity and a holistic approach that defines New Labour' (quoted by Emery 2016, p. 118).

SEAL's alignment of behaviours and dispositions associated with emotional literacy and with left-liberal ideas about education appealed to large numbers of teachers who might not see themselves as experts in wellbeing interventions yet support traditions of child-centred learning and holistic education and related initiatives such as 'life and social skills', 'entrepreneurial education', 'employability', 'personal, social and health education', 'citizenship', 'personal development', 'reflective practice', 'learning to learn' and 'thinking skills'.

(b) *APPG Wellbeing in the Classroom Report 2007*

The APPG seminar that I attended in 2007 attracted an extremely varied audience of 60, including teachers, headteachers, educational and clinical psychologists, researchers and representatives from diverse government and non-government organisations, including ex-Labour government Secretary of State for Education between 2001 and 2002, Estelle Morris. Epitomising SEAL's eclectic, inclusive approach, the event aimed to respond to SEAL's architects, who asserted that better evidence for intervention was needed:

> It is clear from the research and from practice in the field that, in some cases, claims are made without clear evidence to support them. There is a responsibility to evaluate, to sift the evidence carefully, and distinguish hopes and values from sound demonstrated effect (Weare and Gray quoted by Emery, 2016, p. 116).

In this vein, the seminar's chair, Susan Greenfield, Professor of Neuroscience, stated: 'as wellbeing appears increasingly in public and political discourse, there has also been a growing focus to understand the social and neuroscientific basis of wellbeing through systematic scientific study'. A key aim was therefore to 'collectively ensure that policy and practice is informed by the best evidence from this emerging research' (Sharples 2007, p. 2).

The format comprised three keynote presentations and audience discussion. The most well-known speaker was Richard Layard, a Labour peer since 2000 and co-founder of the Action for Happiness (AfH) campaign.[4] Introduced at the seminar as 'Founder-Director of the Economic Performance Centre at the London School of Economics [who has written widely] on unemployment, inflation, education, inequality and post-Communist reform' (Greenfield in Sharples 2007, p. 4), he was followed by Felicia Huppert, Professor of Psychology and Director of the Centre for Wellbeing at the University of Cambridge, and Guy Claxton, then-Professor of Learning Sciences at the University of Bristol.

Despite its organisers' espoused aims, the seminar did not attempt to debate the merits of the evidence presented or propose that this should be done, but instead endorsed speakers' and audience's contributions enthusiastically and non-judgmentally. Notwithstanding the congenial tone of the event, examination of the transcript reveals strong disagreement about the effectiveness of discrete universal skills-based interventions versus embedding skills and dispositions in mainstream subject teaching and a whole school ethos. Unsurprisingly, this inclusive approach encouraged speakers to contribute their own conceptual elisions and 'essential skills' to SEAL's already extensive list. For example, Layard's 'little list [includes] understanding your own emotions and those of other people, developing empathy, love, sex (yourself as a future parent) and parenting, healthy living and community engagement'. He asserted that '....the search of what are the true sources of satisfaction in life in all these different areas...[is underpinned] by the central discipline [of] psychology' (Layard in Sharples, 2007, pp. 6–8). He concluded with a call for measurement: 'if we take the emotional side of life as seriously as the cognitive side [we need to consider if] there needs to be some form of national measurement of the emotional wellbeing of children at different stages' (Sharples 2007, p. 9).

(c) APPG on Social Mobility, Character and Resilience Manifesto 2014

While the key premises of the ECM agenda continued to exert an influence in English schools after the election of the Conservative-led coalition in 2010, the government removed official sponsorship of the SEAL programme in 2011 and resurrected the much older discourse of 'character'. As Humphrey et al. (2016) observe, some commentators have seen this as a rejection of 'soft skills' associated with wellbeing and the privileging of 'traditional' forms of teaching and curriculum knowledge. Yet I would argue that the language of lifelong character development, mental toughness, resilience and 'grit' that permeates this discourse merely embellishes SEAL's universal skills-based approach with new dispositions and attitudes deemed to be social and emotional competences, including 'hope', 'aspiration', 'community mindedness' and 'dealing with failure' (e.g. Paterson et al. 2014). A powerful political endorsement of the wellbeing-as-mental health/character elision came in 2010 from then-Prime Minister David Cameron's stated commitment to proposals for the Office for National Statistics to measure citizens' wellbeing. In the light of the strong psychological/mental health focus in education policy on wellbeing, it is important to note here the wider scope of the ONS approach to wellbeing.

Claims for the social and economic benefits of government intervention in wellbeing-as-mental health/character expanded when the APPG on social mobility followed its 2012 report with a 'Character and Resilience Manifesto' in 2014. Highlighting 'seven key truths about social mobility' and concluding that 'personal resilience and emotional wellbeing are the missing link in the chain', the report reinforced SEAL's earlier calls for policy makers 'to recognise that social and emotional skills underpin academic and other success – and can be taught' (Paterson et al. 2014, p. 11).

The manifesto was published with the CentreForum, a Liberal Democrat think tank set up by Richard Reeves, Director of DEMOS between 2006 and 2010, and Character Counts, an American not-for-profit company specialising in motivational work with young people and organisations, founded and directed by Jen Lexmond, who had previously been a researcher at DEMOS. Presaging the policy shift to a character discourse after the election of the coalition government, Lexmond had already co-authored two reports that moved DEMOS' earlier endorsement of SEAL's emotional literacy approach to a broader remit that linked character, social mobility, early intervention and psycho-emotional measurement (Reeves and Lexmond 2009; Lexmond and Grist 2011). The character manifesto aligned these interests with cross-party support for more extensive intervention in families by calling for psychometric assessments in early years (Paterson et al. 2014). Although the government's commitment to measure personal and subjective wellbeing was framed by a broader understanding of societal wellbeing, elisions between wellbeing, character and mental health seen in education reflected a wider emphasis on psycho-emotional measures in other policy areas such as family policy and welfare programmes for the unemployed (e.g. Pykett et al. 2016).

Since 2010, British research into character development has attracted significant funding, including a five-year (2012–2017) £25 million grant from the American John Templeton Foundation at the University of Birmingham. Drawing on positive psychology, this programme promotes a skills-based approach that augments all the notions listed in the APPG report with moral standpoints such as 'virtue', 'humility' and 'gratitude' that transmogrify as teachable skills (see Jubilee Centre 2015). In July 2015, the Conservative government's Secretary of State for Education earmarked resources to support her 'strong' view that schools and early years settings are essential sites for 'developing emotional wellbeing, mental health and character', presenting these as important as educational achievement (Morgan 2015a, b).

Cannibalised Texts and Claims Makers

The salient point of the brief and selective overview of policy texts above is that shifting but intertwining discourses enable successive governments to respond to rarely-challenged assumptions that children, young people and their parents lack a lengthening list of interpersonal and intrapersonal skills. Crucially, the espoused privileging of a return to 'traditional' curriculum knowledge by governments since 2010 has not hindered the prevalence or popularity of these ideas and their overwhelmingly psycho-emotional behavioural training focus.

In summary, the policy trajectory of wellbeing-as-mental health-and-character can be characterised as 'cannibalised' in three ways. First, a seemingly amoral skills-based approach and an eclectic array of activities and techniques encompass dispositions, attitudes, behavioural responses and 'appropriate' mindsets that are actually morally or spiritually rooted, such as empathy, hope, humility and gratitude. Underpinned by equally extensive and ad hoc psychological claims and practices, universal interventions introduced in schools, colleges and universities since 1998 have included positive psychology, person-centred and relationship counselling, mentoring based on life-coaching techniques, self-help, psycho-dynamic therapy, CBT, neuro-linguistic programming (NLP), emotional literacy/emotional intelligence and the increasingly popular trend for mindfulness. Second, international and national reports cited earlier in this chapter, as well as the three policy texts singled out for closer examination, reflect extensive circular referencing of each other and certain sources. Here, according to Ashley Frawley, the prevalence of second-hand circular citing turns claims and underpinning assumptions into self-evident truths (Frawley 2014). This promulgates alarming depictions of child and youth crisis and an accompanying consensus that educational settings must build psychological, social and emotional attributes and competences in the present whilst also preventing problems in the future. Third, the three reports examined above reflect the extent to which often incompatible psychological fashions can simultaneously run alongside each other and compete whilst absorbing or incorporating new ideas and practices as they appear in popular culture.

In this context, policy and research questions and associated evaluation studies are confined to the respective merits and effectiveness of discrete universal interventions or embedded curriculum-based approaches. As I aim to show next, the shifting and inclusive yet confined nature of these questions enable new types of claims-makers to navigate formal and informal networks and discourses to affirm perceived problems and promote their particular therapeutic products.

The Rise of Therapeutic Entrepreneurialism

Policy Entrepreneurs

One understanding of the ways in which particular policies gain traction and influence is that expert knowledge accumulates and then generates policy proposals. Sometimes this is a gradual process leading to the development of new policy proposals, at other times a more faddish and random process where ideas may sweep through policy communities without any obvious movement in the science of knowledge (Bache and Reardon 2016, pp. 20–21). From either perspective, certain 'policy entrepreneurs' play a key role in defining policy problems, shaping norms and then framing problems in particular ways according to their preferred approach (Bache and Reardon 2016). For example, as Bache and Reardon note, academics such as David Halpern (ex-Lecturer in Social Psychology and the head of the government's Behavioural Insight Team since 2010) and Professors Richard Layard (Economics), Andrew Oswald (Economics and Behavioural Sciences) and Paul Dolan (Behavioural Sciences) work at the interface of university-based research and policymaking to bring wellbeing onto government agendas, alongside individuals from left-of-centre think tanks such as DEMOS and the Young Foundation. As part of government agendas to shape citizens' behaviours and mindsets across diverse areas of public life, the same individuals and organisations have also been highly influential in behaviour change initiatives (e.g. Pykett et al. 2016).

A question therefore arises about why particular claims-makers and advocates gain influence at different moments in policy time and across policy agendas and, in the case of wellbeing, why psychological agendas are so appealing to policy makers. From a therapeutic culture perspective, a psycho-emotional understanding of wellbeing was already established by Conservative and Labour governments' increasing receptivity to a more explicitly therapeutic orientation for the state during the 1990s. This orientation had precedents in the late 1970s, when a Conservative government supported the idea that lack of psycho-emotional skills and dispositions both caused and was caused by unemployment and other socioeconomic problems and provided funding for access to counselling as part of employment preparation schemes (see Furedi 2004). Psycho-emotional roles for the state were integral to Anthony Giddens' design of the 1997–2010 Labour governments' 'third way' between social democracy and neo-liberalism (Giddens 1998). Drawing on ideas he developed in an earlier sociological study of the changing nature of personal relationships, Giddens advocated a much stronger 'psychic' role for the welfare state in developing reflexive, self-aware, emotionally literate citizens who can learn and use psychological techniques for individual and social benefits (Giddens 1991; see also Scott and Masselot, this volume, Chap. 11).

A psycho-emotional understanding of wellbeing was therefore a key strand in New Labour's approach, supported enthusiastically by then Prime Minister Tony Blair and promoted by numerous individuals moving between policy advisory and think tank roles. Some of these individuals have maintained their influence through successive psychological policy agendas, including Richard Reeves, Director of CentreForum, ex-strategic advisor to the Deputy Prime Minister in the 2010–2015 coalition government and, as Director of DEMOS, co-author of 'Building Character' in 2010; Matthew Taylor, ex-Director of the Institute for Public Policy Research, Director of Tony Blair's Policy Unit, then his strategic adviser, and Director of the RSA (Royal Society for the encouragement of Arts, Manufactures and Commerce) since 2006; and Geoff Mulgan, ex-Director of Tony Blair's Strategy Unit, co-founder of DEMOs, and ex-Director of the Young Foundation.

In the wider context of a therapeutic culture, all these claims-makers epitomise the extent to which the diffusing of a wellbeing-as-mental health/character discourse is derived from populist adaptations of academic psychology. Here, Martin Seligman, Professor of Positive Psychology, and former President of the American Psychological Association that created the Diagnostic and Statistical Manual, is a high-profile advocate of state-sponsored applications of positive psychology in, for example, the army and schools, in both the UK and other countries. An important characteristic of the policy popularising of psychological expertise is the prominence of non-psychologists. For example, alongside economist Richard Layard, Anthony Seldon is the author of numerous political biographies, including one on ex-Prime Minister David Cameron, and therefore has good insider access to policy makers. Currently Vice-Chancellor of Buckingham University, Seldon aims to make Buckingham Britain's first 'health positive university', campaigning 'passionately' for these goals through the media and inside policy circles (e.g. Seldon 2015; Parker 2016). With the exception of psychotherapist Susie Orbach, the high-profile New Labour luminaries who promoted SEAL, discussed above, also exemplify the crucial policy-lobbying role played by lay adapters of psychological expertise.

While particular policy insiders and fashionable interventions come and go, prominent international public figures and celebrities legitimise the broad trajectory of wellbeing-as-mental health/character. These include the Dalai Lama, patron of the AfH campaign, and American celebrities, actor Goldie Hawn and comedian Ruby Wax who have both promoted school-based universal mindfulness programmes with the British public and policy-maker audiences, including ex-Labour and Conservative Prime Ministers and Michael Gove, Secretary of State for Education between 2010 and 2014.

Alongside lobbyists and luminaries who sustain their influence across shifting discourses and subtle changes to policy agendas, there are more fleeting interfaces between policy sponsorship and intervention entrepreneurialism. For example, in 2012, American army general Rita Cornum promoted the 'resilience fitness training' programme she designed for preventing post-traumatic stress disorder amongst soldiers (based on collaboration with Martin Seligman) to an enthusiastic audience of practitioners and managers from British police youth engagement projects, community outreach programmes, schools and third sector organisations, think tank researchers and Michael Gove (Cornum 2012). Cornum also exemplifies another important characteristic of the cannibalised politics of wellbeing, namely the growing involvement of commercial interests. Sponsored by the

Macquarie Group Foundation, a global provider of financial, advisory, investment and fund management services and a key funder of the Young Foundation, her access to British policy makers was facilitated by one of Macquarie's directors, Gus O'Donnell, a leading civil servant whose roles included Permanent Secretary to the UK Treasury, co-author of the Legatum report on wellbeing and policy with Richard Layard and David Halpern, amongst others, and Chair of APPG Wellbeing and Economics meetings.

'Charismatic' Entrepreneurs

Legitimised by a therapeutic culture beset by fears about mental health problems, a therapeutic state can expand its legitimacy through a new type of charismatic, entrepreneurial expert. Reflected by popular, academic and political claims-makers identified above, this also exposes the state to new and competing claims to expertise and evidence of effectiveness. Here, Max Weber's account of different types of authority in periods of social change is useful (e.g. Spencer 1970). While it is not possible in this chapter to do justice to the nuances of Weber's analysis, his 'ideal types' of traditional, legal and charismatic expert illuminate the rise of therapeutic entrepreneurialism in the policy trajectory of wellbeing in education and the challenge this presents to older types of expertise.

The political rise and popular appeal of therapeutic entrepreneurs are linked inextricably to what Ball and Junnermann (2012) characterise as the patchwork combinations of third sector and private providers that comprise an education market. Bankrolled by the state, fragmented, outsourced and privatised public education services are fertile ground for a growing market of campaign groups, third sector organisations, charities and profit-making consultancies selling their favoured approach to local authorities, individual schools, colleges and universities. A huge increase in entrepreneurial individuals and organisations includes the relationship counselling service Relate; the charity Family Action (a philanthropic organisation founded in the nineteenth century to work with the poor), which leads some local authority-funded family welfare and school wellbeing initiatives; the Amy Winehouse Foundation, funded by the Lottery to work in schools and youth clubs to build resilience against risk-taking behaviours; and freelance consultants in the AfH campaign and myriad other consultancies and companies. Paralleling their policy counterparts, these therapeutic entrepreneurs offer reductionist, culturally familiar interpretations of psychological ideas and practices, often downplaying formal expertise in favour of empathy that comes from surviving difficult experiences or seeing the light from attending a course. In order to compete, traditional psychological specialists, such as educational and clinical psychologists, especially those outsourced to private companies or working in local authority traded services, offer programmes such as mindfulness, NLP and life coaching.

The growing prominence of these new types of expert in policy and practice raises difficult and contested questions about what counts as legitimate expertise and knowledge. It also highlights the erosion of boundaries between specialist-authoritative and non-specialist, or non-authoritative, claims-makers, and also between formal and personal knowledge. For example, Ruby Wax has a Masters in Mindfulness-based Cognitive Therapy and speaks openly about her personal experience of mental illness. Populist discourses are also integral to the political rationale for measuring subjective wellbeing promoted by academics such as Richard Layard, Andrew Oswald and Paul Dolan. This rationale is founded in economics as a discipline, increasingly intertwined with behavioural science, as a way of boosting citizens' economic performance, yet draws strongly on and contributes to populist depictions of psycho-emotional wellbeing. Other new claims to expertise might come from a Master's degree in any of the areas listed above, including one in the philosophy and science of happiness arising from the character and virtue research programme, cited earlier, or a short training programme in areas such as mental toughness, life coaching and mindfulness, accredited by some universities or bodies such as the British Association for Counsellors and Psychotherapists. Meanwhile, the Dalai Lama's deeply held Buddhist principles for mindfulness and a lifelong commitment to a spiritual and holistic approach to wellbeing are absorbed easily in a wide spectrum of reductionist, popularised skills-based approaches.

These developments are therefore a powerful challenge to traditional expertise in educational and clinical psychology, psychiatry and counselling. My point here is not to evaluate the respective merits of these claims to authority but to offer a critique of problems arising from therapeutic entrepreneurialism as a foundation for influential claims-making about wellbeing in education and, in turn, as a replacement for or equation with scientific evidence. As I argue next, these developments render espoused commitments for evidence to underpin interventions, and for those supported by dubious or inadequate evidence, as mere policy rhetoric. In the final section, I suggest some ways to counter or challenge these worrying trends.

ERODING EVIDENCE

There have been numerous meta-reviews of evidence for the effectiveness of diverse approaches that are presented as school-based wellbeing/mental health interventions, including peer mentoring, anti-bullying schemes and nurture groups, amongst others (e.g. Weare and Nind 2011; Bywater and Sharples 2012; Wigglesworth et al. 2016). It goes without saying that there is not space here to undertake my own comprehensive meta-evaluation of these studies. Nevertheless, it is important to note some serious drawbacks to the existing evidence base reflected in the reviews cited above. According to Wigglesworth et al. (2016), problems include inconclusive or contradictory evidence of effects from the intervention itself; not attributing effects to other changes in the school or classroom; design flaws including evaluations carried out by intervention developers, implementers or those already in favour of the intervention; difficulty in transferring or replicating interventions; and evaluations done too soon after implementation. The latter also means that positive effects can arise from the novelty of the intervention, perhaps as a distraction from normal routines, or the well-known 'Hawthorne' effect first noted in industrial psychology experiments, namely the effects of positive attention by observers or experimenters (e.g. Hseuh 2002).

As well as these important methodological difficulties, formal evaluations of SEAL have shown no conclusive evidence of positive effect and, at the same time, huge variation in practices and some of the methodological problems summarised above (Humphrey et al. 2016). Similarly, the government's own evaluation of the Penn Resiliency programme, based on CBT and positive psychology and trialled in three local authorities between 2007 and 2010, showed little long-term impact. This study also found negative effects for some children who tried to transfer the programme's prescriptive thinking strategies to a dangerous situation (Challen et al. 2011).

Analysis in this chapter also suggests other conceptual and practical drawbacks in the broader policy trajectory of wellbeing-as-mental health/character. First, the APPG wellbeing seminar's report, discussed earlier, shows how an inclusive, non-judgmental, elastic format for debate and the prominence given to Layard's lay adaptations of psychological ideas, and his general lack of educational expertise, reflects wider problems with incoherent or vague conceptual definition and measurement. For example, his reliance on the 2007 UNICEF report to claim extensive benefits from resilience-building programmes overlooks the report's sweeping self-report measures. These ranged from trust, availability of a good breakfast and having kind and helpful classmates, to experience of child abuse. Tellingly, in the light of the seminar's espoused commitment to evidence, he claimed dramatic benefits for the Penn Resiliency Programme before any evaluation had been done (see above and Challen et al. 2011).

Unsurprisingly, problems highlighted here parallel media oversight of weak measures and conceptual confusions, as well as distortions of both. For example, 10 years before the UNICEF report was published, newspaper articles by influential popular psychotherapist Oliver James slipped casually from noting a flat-lining in data about the public's reported happiness to claim not only widespread unhappiness but also that 'we are massively unhappy today compared with 1950' (Frawley 2014, p. 86). While such sweeping historical comparisons are commonplace in media headlines, they are largely spurious. For example, as historian Kevin Myers notes, claims of 'massive' changes in mental health should acknowledge not only different applications of measures, diagnoses and sample populations but, crucially, also changing cultural interpretations of these in different historical periods (Myers 2011, 2012).

In this vein, some critics argue that impositions of universal psychoemotional interventions in schools fail to discriminate between normal adolescent emotions and depression or question changing cultural understandings and constructions of mental health problems (e.g. Craig 2007). In the face of these drawbacks to data gathering and subsequent claims for intervention, the few public challenges that do appear, such as journalist David Aaronovitch's questioning of the categories in the UNICEF report and the conclusions being widely drawn at the time, tend to go unnoticed (see Frawley 2014).

In a shifting and fragmented organisational context, these conceptual and methodological difficulties inhibit independent evaluation of wellbeing initiatives. For example, a local authority-commissioned evaluation of 'emotional wellbeing and mental health' interventions in what remains of its schools in one of Britain's largest cities underpinned competitive tendering to run the programme with extremely wide-ranging definitions of emotional and mental health and wellbeing and correspondingly slippery estimates of the scale of the city's problems (Billington et al. 2016). As well as predictably diverse claims to expertise and equally diverse practical approaches used by different organisations, short-term funding streams, complex commissioning arrangements, reorganisation of mental health services and consequent changes to organisations running the interventions were further hindrances to proper evaluation of effectiveness and accountability (Billington et al. 2016).

CONCLUSIONS

Profound and widespread alarm about young people's mental health is the latest turn in therapeutic culture, encouraging advocates of cannibalised psychological ideas and practices to compete for influence in the policy trajectory of wellbeing in education since 1997. I have argued that the apocalyptic tone in which these developments are couched and justified elides wellbeing with mental health and psychologised, skills-based understandings of character. In its trajectory from cannibalised policy text to shifting and confusing practices in educational settings, wellbeing-as-mental-health/character is promoted through formal and informal networks of celebrities, policy-based advocates and practitioners. All diffuse popularised perceptions of problems through circular citing that creates unchallenged truths. Here, highly popularised psychological and therapeutic discourses stray into the area of expertise of economists and education professionals and challenge traditional psychological experts. These developments encourage therapeutic entrepreneurs to sell a contagious view that there are huge problems with people's wellbeing and a subsequent consensus that there is 'an absolutely overwhelming argument for the state taking a major responsibility for the character development of the children of each family' (Layard in Sharples 2007, p. 24).

It is not therefore surprising that important questions about what comprises wellbeing expertise and acceptable evidence for intervention and how proper evaluations of cannibalised discourses and practices can be carried out in a market of vested interests are marginalised. I am aware that my arguments suggest a dispiriting prognosis, not just for genuine evidence-based policy and practice for wellbeing, but also for possibilities of a more positive educational approach to wellbeing. It is easy for critical policy analysts to highlight tensions, difficulties and contested complexities in a cannibalised policy trajectory and which also arise from the ways in which wellbeing discourses, like all discourses, privilege some voices and ideas whilst silencing or marginalising others (Ball 1994). It is therefore important to suggest what practical responses might offer a more holistic, educationally meaningful approach to develop wellbeing. I highlight three areas here.

First, what should be the boundaries of education's legitimate role in developing wellbeing-as-mental-health/character? Although elisions of mental health and wellbeing happen, in part at least, because of conceptual incoherence, the lines between them are genuinely blurred. Nevertheless, I would argue that we need to rein in apocalyptic claims about mental health problems and careless erosions of crucial distinctions between emotional wellbeing, mental health, character and wellbeing. A more judicious deployment of terms would, as the Chief Medical Officer argued in her 2013 report on priorities for public health, help in making clearer assessments of the extent of problems with mental illness, establish better evidence for intervention and enable better allocations of scarce specialist resources for genuine need (Davies 2015). There is a related need to consider the legitimate and realistic role of educationalists in preventing mental health problems (Coleman 2009).

In addition, sociological, historical and philosophical understandings of wellbeing are, I would argue, almost entirely absent in the policy trajectory of wellbeing. Here, for example, and in addition to some of the historical challenges to measures and interpretations and criticisms of a circular referencing between economists, psychologists and policy advisers, cited earlier, philosophers of education promote the development of holistic understandings of wellbeing in education. In particular, they make two important arguments that are overlooked or marginalised in the current context. First, to reinstate emotions that, amidst apocalyptic crisis discourses about mental health, are seen routinely as unpleasant or even dangerous (such as anxiety, depression and anger), proposing instead that they are normal life expectations and can be a crucial stimulus for action and transformation (e.g. Suissa 2008; Cigman 2012; Clack 2012).

Second, they make a related proposal to elevate the role of subjects such as literature, history, philosophy and religious education in developing a broader, philosophical and moral sense of wellbeing, the idea of what it means to live a worthwhile life (Suissa 2008; Cigman 2012; Pett 2012). As philosopher Beverly Clack argues, the wellbeing agenda in schools and its alarmist, instrumental skills-based approach erodes an educational commitment to *'developing an enquiring mind, cultivating habits of thought and practice that* encourage the questioning of what lies outside the self' (Clack 2012, p. 507, my emphasis). In this vein, John Tomsett, a secondary school head teacher, proposes that schools should prioritise inspired and meaningful subject teaching and much more empathetic and authentic communication with young people—an approach that is more likely to detect problems with wellbeing rather than responding unthinkingly to a self-fulfilling prophecy of a mental health crisis (Tomsett 2016).

Third and finally, I have argued that tenuous claims to expertise, together with vested commercial interests, characterise claims-making in the education politics of wellbeing. This necessitates critical challenges to three intertwined trends: ubiquitous attributions of mental health problems or problems with character to a perceived absence of emotional and social skills; evangelical assertions that wellbeing as mental health and character comprises a definable, assessable list of attributes, dispositions and behaviours that can be taught and transferred across life experiences and contexts, and the commercial benefits that follow those claims.

Notes

1. Other media reports put the figure at 78 per cent. https://www.theguardian.com/education/2015/dec/14/majority-of-students-experience-mental-health-issues-says-nus-survey.
2. APPG reports have no formal legislative status; rather, they enable policy makers at various levels to identify a pressing topic or concern and listen to ideas and representations from various organisations and individuals.
3. Since the election of a Labour government in 1997, left-liberal think tanks—including DEMOS, the Young Foundation (e.g. Bacon et al. 2010) and the Royal Society of Arts (RSA)—have been very influential in promoting a more active government role in the psycho-emotional lives of citizens.
4. AfH is a not-for-profit organization founded in 2010 by Richard Layard, Geoff Mulgan and Anthony Seldon (the then headmaster of Wellington College), which has pioneered a happiness curriculum (see Morris 2009; Seldon 2015). It is part of the Young Foundation, a left-of-centre think tank (see footnote above).

Acknowledgements I am very grateful to Ian Bache, Aki Tsuchiya and Karen Scott for their helpful feedback and insights on an earlier draft of this chapter.

REFERENCES

APPG. (2014). Mental Health for Sustainable Development. London: Mental Health Innovation Network and All Party Parliamentary Group.

Allen, G. (2011). Early Intervention: The Next Steps. Independent Report, Department for Education, London. Available at: https://www.gov.uk/government/uploads/system/uploads/attachment_data/file/284086/early-intervention-next-steps2.pdf.

Bache, I., & Reardon, L. (2016). *The Politics and Policy of Wellbeing: Understanding the Rise and Significance of a New Agenda.* Cheltenham: Edward Elgar Publishing.

Bache, I., Reardon, L., & Anand, P. (2016). Wellbeing as a Wicked Problem: Negotiating the Arguments for the Role of Government. *Journal of Happiness Studies, 17*(3), 893–912.

Bacon, N., Brophy, M., Mguni, N., Mulgan, G., & Shandro, A. (2010). *Can Public Policy Shape People's Wellbeing and Resilience?* London: The Young Foundation.

Ball, S. J. (1994). *Education Reform: A Critical and Post-structural Approach.* Buckingham: Open University Press.

Ball, S. J., & Junnermann, C. (2012). *Networks, New Governance and Education.* London: Routledge.

Balls, E., (2007). Pupils to Get Lessons in Respect. BBC News. Available at: http://news.bbc.co.uk/1/hi/education/6274736.stm.

Billington, T., Williams, A., Abdi, M., & Lahmar, J. (2016). Evaluation of the Emotional Wellbeing and Mental Health Service for Schools. School of Education, University of Sheffield and Sheffield City Council.

Brunila, K., & Siivonen, P. (2014). Preoccupied with the Self. Towards Self-responsible, Enterprising, Flexible, and Self-centred Subjectivity in Education. *Discourse: Studies in the Cultural Politics of Education, 37*(1), 56–69.

Bywater, T., & Sharples, J. (2012). Effective Evidence-based Interventions for Emotional Well-being: Lessons for Policy and Practice. *Research Papers in Education, 27*(4), 389–408.

Challen, A., Noden, P., West, A., & Machin, S. (2011). UK Resilience Programme Evaluation: Final Report. Department of Education, DFE-RB097. Available at: https://www.gov.uk/government/uploads/system/uploads/attachment_data/file/182419/DFE-RR097.pdf.

Cigman, R. (2012). We Need to Talk About Wellbeing. *Research Papers in Education, 27*(4), 449–462.

Clack, B. (2012). What Difference Does it Make? Philosophical Perspectives on the Nature of Well-being and the Role of Educational Practice. *Research Papers in Education, 27*(4), 497–51.

Coleman, J. (2009). Wellbeing in Schools: Empirical Measure, or Politician's Dream? *Oxford Review of Education, 35*(3), 281–292.

Collishaw, S., Maughan, B., Natarajan, L., & Pickles, A. (2010). Trends in Adolescent Emotional Problems in England: A Comparison of Two National Cohorts Twenty Years Apart. *Journal of Child Psychology and Psychiatry, 51*(8), 885–894.

Cornum, R. (2012). *Can We Teach Resilience?* Keynote Presentation to Young Foundation/Macquarie Group Seminar, Teaching Resilience in Schools, Ropemaker, London, 7th February 2012.

Craig, C. (2007). The Potential Dangers of a Systematic, Explicit Approach to Teaching Social and Emotional Skills (SEAL). Glasgow: Centre for Confidence and Well-Being. Available at: http://www.centreforconfidence.co.uk/docs/EI-SEAL_September_2007.pdf.

Davies, W. (2015). *The Happiness Industry: How Government and Big Business Sold us Happiness and Well-being.* London: Verso.

Department for Education. (2015). New Action Plan to Tackle Mental Health Stigma in Schools [online]. Available at: https://www.gov.uk/government/news/new-action-plan-to-tackle-mental-health-stigma-in-schools. Accessed July 22, 2016.

Department for Education and Skills. (2005). Excellence and Enjoyment: Social and Emotional Aspects of Learning Guidance. London: DfES. Available at: https://www.foundationyears.org.uk/files/2011/10/SEAL_-getonfallout.pdf.

Devon, N. (2016). I'll Tell You What Isn't Helpful at All: Telling Children with Mental Health Problems that They're Namby-Pamby. *Times Educational Supplement.* Available at: https://www.tes.com/news/school-news/breaking-views/ill-tell-you-what-isnt-helpful-all-telling-children-mental-health.

Ecclestone, K. (2013). (Ed.), *Emotonal Well-being in Policy and Practice: Interdisciplinary Perspectives.* London: Routledge.

Ecclestone, K., & Hayes, D. (2009). *The Dangerous Rise of Therapeutic Education.* London: Routledge.

Emery, C. (2016). The New Labour Discourse of Social and Emotional Learning (SEL) Across Schools in England and Wales as a Universal Intervention: A Critical Discourse Analysis. Unpublished PhD thesis, University of Manchester.

Field, F. (2010). The Foundation Years: Preventing Poor Children Becoming Poor Adults. Independent Review on Poverty and Life Chances. Department for Work and Pensions: London. Available at: http://webarchive.nationalarchives.gov.uk/20110120090141/http://povertyreview.independent.gov.uk/media/20254/poverty-report.pdf.

Frawley, A. (2014). *The Semiotics of Happiness: The Rhetorical Beginnings of a Social Problem*. London: Bloomsbury.

Furedi, F. (2004). *Therapy Culture: Cultivating Vulnerability in an Uncertain Age*. London: Routledge.

Giddens, A. (1991). *Transformation of Intimacy: Sexuality, Love and Eroticism in Modern Societies*. London: Polity Press.

Giddens, A. (1998). *The Third Way: The Renewal of Social Democracy*. London: Polity Books.

Harwood, V., & Allan, J. (2014). *Psychopathology at School: Theorizing Education and Mental Disorder*. London: Routledge.

Hseuh, Y. (2002). The Hawthorne Experiments and the Introduction of Jean Piaget in American Industrial Psychology, 1929–1932. *History of Psychology, 5*(2), 163–189.

Humphrey, N. (2013). *Social and Emotional Learning: A Critical Appraisal*. London: Sage Books.

Humphrey, N., Lendrum, A., Wigelsworth, M., & Greenburg, M. (2016). Editorial Introduction to Special Issue: Social and Emotional Learning. *Cambridge Journal of Education, 46*(3), 271–277.

Isin, E. (2004). The Neurotic Citizen. *Citizenship Studies, 8*(3), 217–235.

Jubilee Centre for Character and Virtue (2015). *Character, Service and Gratitude: A Working Paper*. Available at: https://www.jubileecentre.ac.uk. Accessed July 4, 2015.

Layard, R., & Dunn, J. (2012). *A Good Childhood: Searching for Values in a Competitive Age*. London: The Children's Society.

Lexmond, J., & Grist, M. (Eds.). (2011). The Character Inquiry. London: DEMOS. Available at: https://www.demos.co.uk/files/Character_Inquiry_-_web.pdf?1304696626.

Lumby, J. (2012). Disengaged and Disaffected Young People: Surviving the System. *British Educational Research Journal, 38*(2), 261–279.

McLaughlin, K. (2011). *Surviving Identity: Vulnerability and the Psychology of Recognition*. London: Routledge.

Mental Health Foundation. (2015). *Mental Health Statistics: Children and Young People*. Available at: https://www.mentalhealth.org.uk/statistics/mental-health-statistics-children-and-young-people. Accessed July 20, 2016.

Mills, C. (2014). *Decolonising Global Mental Health: The Psychiatrisation of the Majority World*. London: Routledge.

Morgan, N. (2015a). *Speech to Early Intervention Foundation Conference*, 1 Great George Street, London, February 12, 2015. Available at: https://www.gov.uk/government/speeches/nicky-morgan-speaks-at-early-intervention-foundation-conference. Accessed July 4, 2015.

Morgan, N. (2015b). 'Make Happiness a Priority in Schools, Says Nicky Morgan'. Report on Visit by the Secretary of State for Education to Upton Cross School. *The Times*, July 4.

Morris, I. (2009). *Teaching Happiness and Well-being in Schools: Learning to Ride Elephants.* London: Continuum.

Myers, K. (2011). Contesting Certification: Mental Deficiency, Families and the State. *Paedogogica Historica 47*(6): 749–66.

Myers, K. (2012). Marking Time: Some Methodological and Historical Perspectives on the 'Crisis of Childhood'. *Research Papers in Education, 27*(4), 409–442.

NHS. (2014). Mental Health and Wellbeing in England. National Health Service. Available at: https://content.digital.nhs.uk/catalogue/PUB21748/apms-2014-full-rpt.pdf.

NHS. (2015). Future in Mind: Promoting, Protecting and Improving our Children and Young People's Mental Health and Wellbeing. London: National Health Service. Available at: https://www.gov.uk/government/uploads/system/uploads/attachment_data/file/414024/Childrens_Mental_Health.pdf.

Nolan, J. L. (1998). *The Therapeutic State: Justifying Government at Century's End.* New York: New York University Press.

O'Donnell, G., Denton, A., Halpern, D., Durand, M., & Layard, R. (2014). Wellbeing and Policy. Report for the Legatum Institute. London: London School of Economics. Available at: https://www.li.com/docs/default-source/commission-on-wellbeing-and-policy/commission-on-wellbeing-and-policy-report---march-2014-pdf.pdf?sfvrsn=2.

Palmer, S. (2006). *Toxic Childhood: How Modern Life Is Poisoning Our Children and What We Can Do About It.* London: Orion Books.

Parker, O. (2016). Should Happiness Be Part of the School Curriculum? *Telegraph,* July 9. Available at: http://www.telegraph.co.uk/education/2016/07/11/should-happiness-be-part-of-the-school-curriculum/.

Paterson, C., Tyler, C., & Lexmond, J. (2014). Character and Resilience Manifesto: The All-Party Parliamentary Group on Social Mobility. London: HMSO. Available at: http://www.educationengland.org.uk/documents/pdfs/2014-appg-social-mobility.pdf.

Pett, S. (2012). The Contribution of Religious Education to the Wellbeing of Pupils. *Research Papers in Education, 27*(4), 435–448.

Pykett, J., Jones, R., & Whitehead, M. (Eds.). (2016). *Psychological Governance and Public Policy: Governing the Mind, Brain and Behaviour.* London: Routledge.

Reeves, R., & Lexmond, J. (2009). *Building Character.* London: DEMOS.

Rose, N. (1999). *Governing the Soul: The Shaping of the Private Self.* London: Free Association Books.

Seldon, A. (2015). *Beyond Happiness: How to Find Lasting Meaning and Joy in All That You Have.* London: Hodder Stoughton.

Sharples, J. (2007). *Wellbeing in the Classroom, Report on the All-Party Parliamentary Committee, October 27th 2007.* Oxford: University of Oxford.

Smith, J. (2016). Student Mental Health: A New Model for Universities. *The Guardian*, March 2. Available at: http://www. theguardian.com/higher-education-network/2016/mar/02/student-mental-health-a-new-model-for-universities.

Spencer, M. E. (1970). Weber on Legitimate Norms and Authority. *British Journal of Sociology, 21*(2), 123–134.

Stewart, J. (2011). The Dangerous Age of Childhood: Child Guidance and the 'Normal Child' in Britain, 1920–1950. *Paedagogica Historica: International Journal of the History of Education, 47*(6), 785–803.

Sunday Express. (2016). 'Sons and Daughters Need Our Help as Much as Their Mothers' Says Prince William. *Sunday Express*, June 19. Available at: http://www.express.co.uk/news/royal/681103/The-Duke-of-Cambridge-Prince-William-Fathers-Day-children-mental-health.

Suissa, J. (2008). Lessons from a New Science? On Teaching Happiness in Schools. *Journal of Philosophy of Education, 42*(3–4), 575–590.

Thomson, M. (2006). *Psychological Subjects: Identity, Culture and Health in Twentieth- century Britain*. Oxford: Oxford University Press.

Tomsett, J. (2016). *This Much I Know About Mind Over Matter: Improving Mental Health in Our Schools*. Carmarthen: Crown House Publishing.

Valentine, G., & Skelton, T. (2003). Living on the Edge: The Marginalization and 'Resistance' of D/deaf Youth. *Environment and Planning, 35*, 301–321.

Watson, D., Emery, C., & Bayliss, P. (2012). *Children's Social and Emotional Wellbeing in Schools*. Bristol: The Policy Press.

Weare, K. (2004). *Developing the Emotionally-literate School*. London: Paul Chapman.

Weare, K., & Nind, M. (2011). Mental Health Promotion and Problem Prevention in Schools: What Does the Evidence Say? *Health Promotion International, 26*: 129–169.

Wigglesworth, M., Lendrum, A., Oldfield, J., Scott, A., ten Bokkel, I., Tate, K., & Emery, C. (2016). The Impact of Trial Stage, Developer Involvement and International Transferability on Universal Social and Emotional Programme Outcomes: A Meta-analysis. *Cambridge Journal of Education, 46*(3), 347–377.

Woodhall, V. (2016). Electro-soul Artist Rosie Lowe Is Using Music to Lift the Lid on Mental Health. *You Magazine*, July 3. Available at: http://www.dailymail.co.uk/home/you/article-3656764/SPOTLIGHT-Electro-soul-artist-Rosie-Lowe-using-music-lift-lid-mental-health.html.

WHO. (2012). Depression. World Health Organization. Available at: http://www.who.int/mediacentre/factsheets/fs369/en/.

Wright, K. (2011). *The Rise of the Therapeutic Society: Psychological Knowledge and the Contradictions of Cultural Change*. New York: Academia Publishing.

Wright, K., & McLeod, J. (Eds.). (2014). *Rethinking Youth Well-being: Critical Perspectives*. New York: Springer.

CHAPTER 11

Skivers, Strivers and Thrivers: The Shift from Welfare to Wellbeing in New Zealand and the United Kingdom

Karen Scott and Annick Masselot

INTRODUCTION

Our interest in writing this chapter was in part stimulated by a thought-provoking phrase used by economists Paul Dalziel and Caroline Saunders (2014, p. 132)[1] in their book *Wellbeing Economics: Future Directions for New Zealand* in which they advocated a shift 'from welfare state to wellbeing state'. In questioning the implications of this idea, our contribution to this edition regards the relationship between national wellbeing agendas and state welfare provision. At the same time as wellbeing measurement is gaining traction on political agendas in many liberal market democracies, welfare reforms are also being implemented in line with neoliberal economic agendas (Esping-Andersen et al. 2002). Although welfare reform has been happening since the 1970s in many

K. Scott (✉)
Department of Politics, University of Exeter, Penryn, Cornwall, UK
e-mail: k.e.scott@exeter.ac.uk

A. Masselot
University of Canterbury, Christchurch, New Zealand
e-mail: annick.masselot@canterbury.ac.nz

© The Author(s) 2018   253
I. Bache and K. Scott (eds.), *The Politics of Wellbeing*, Wellbeing
in Politics and Policy, https://doi.org/10.1007/978-3-319-58394-5_11

countries to respond to new social risks (NSRs), it has intensified and changed character more recently in some countries, in part due to the 2008 financial crisis (Jenson 2009).

In order to focus our discussion, we draw on our knowledge and research of wellbeing measurement programmes and welfare reforms in New Zealand (NZ) and the United Kingdom (UK). Both NZ and UK have been pro-active at developing wellbeing measures and strategies around the same time with transnational discussion between policy actors from NZ and UK, and both countries introduced significant welfare reforms in 2012. Both have right-leaning governments: in NZ, the National Party has been in power since 2008; in UK, the coalition (Conservative and Liberal) government was formed in 2010, and from 2015 until the time of writing the Conservative Party has been in power.[2] The two countries also have broadly similar welfare regimes. However, it is not our intention to offer in-depth comparative analysis here, rather to provoke some questions regarding the potential relationship of wellbeing agendas with welfare provision policy that we feel are important for inclusion in an edited collection on *The Politics of Wellbeing* and using the two countries as case studies.

In addition, we explore wellbeing and welfare through a gendered lens by reviewing the position of solo[3] parents within these policy agendas. Both sets of welfare reforms in NZ and UK have, within their respective countries, been heavily criticised for impacting adversely on women and children, and imposing greater conditionality on solo parents, particularly those under 18 years of age. In both countries, the vast majority of solo parents are women,[4] and traditionally, the policy and societal narratives around solo parenthood have been heavily gendered (Wilson and Huntington 2006; Scottish Welfare Reform Committee 2015). In addition, we are concerned about the lack of recognition of the gendered nature of wellbeing discourses informing measurement. The general assumption that wellbeing survey questions, measurements and indicators are gender neutral may obscure important factors such as care responsibilities, which are often central to women's lives, or differently experienced by women.

In looking at welfare and wellbeing strategies in these specific countries, we acknowledge the global influences on both agendas. The interest in wellbeing is a worldwide phenomenon where many nation states and supra-national bodies are developing measures and influencing each other, as outlined by Bache and Scott (Chap. 1, this volume). There is a global flow of ideas, and to a certain extent, this can be seen as an international movement (Allin and Hand 2014; Bache and Reardon 2016; McGregor, this volume, Chap. 9). Much has been written about the rise of interest in various conceptions and measures of wellbeing around the world and the potential implications for public policy. We do not attempt to foreground this chapter by repeating what has already been set out earlier in this volume, other than to provide some brief country-specific summaries on wellbeing strategies necessary to the focus of our discussion. Similarly, welfare reform takes place within a global context of political economies where national policies are influenced by wider economics and social norms in other countries (Esping-Andersen 1996; Kingfisher and Goldsmith 2001). It is to that discussion we now turn.

THE POLITICAL ECONOMIES OF SKIVING, STRIVING AND THRIVING

The term Welfare State (notwithstanding the proliferation of debates about its meaning and application) usually encompasses a range of social provision and protections including social security, health care and education. In this chapter, we focus on social security in the form of welfare benefits to those unable to take up paid work, or who need a supplement to their income. Welfare states developed in the earlier part of the twentieth century were based predominantly on the male breadwinner model, and certainly, this was the case in NZ and UK. As the well referenced (and critiqued) typology by Esping-Andersen (1990) outlines, welfare regimes can be categorised into three broad types reflecting different histories, political economies and cultural norms. These are: *liberal* welfare states that provide social assistance (usually means-tested) but modest social insurance (NZ and UK would fit broadly here); *corporatist/conservative* models that are more focused on social insurance rather than assistance, with the church and the family as additional support (e.g. Italy); and *social-democrat* where the state takes direct responsibility for the welfare of all citizens and there is a high level of insurance and assistance (e.g. Scandinavian countries). However, these typologies have been criticised for being too static and not allowing for dramatic changes between different governments within countries, so that perhaps we should call these 'welfare-governments' (Veit-Wilson 2000, p. 6).

From the 1970s onwards, national welfare states began a transformation due to global patterns in the deregulation of wages and labour markets, and the changing nature of women's role in the family and in the labour market (Esping-Andersen 1996). A number of 'new social risks' (NSRs) for individuals caused by these changes include reconciling work and family life, solo parenthood,[5] care of elderly relatives, insufficient social security coverage and possessing low or obsolete skills (Bonoli 2005). As a result, modern welfare states are increasingly underpinning labour force participation through an expanded range of provisions such as childcare, training and so forth (Mitchell 1992).

The modernisation of welfare states to respond to NSRs has been different in nature and has happened at different times in these three types of welfare state. Bonoli (2007) argues, using OECD statistics, that early post-industrializers such as Sweden have been able to develop the most comprehensive NSR coverage and this is in part due to the timings of the emergence of NSRs in relation to the capacity for increasing welfare state spending, and also to the strength of left-wing politics and lobbying groups for women in social democrat countries. The more women in the workforce have experienced NSRs associated with their working patterns, the greater the social coverage has been. In this pattern, the NZ and UK show almost identical timings in terms of deindustrialization, expansion of female employment and changing family structures, which is around a decade or so later than Sweden, and in a different political context, with a greater reliance on market forces to fill gaps in social welfare (Bonoli 2007). For example, in Sweden, childcare provision is mainly provided by the state, contrasted with a reliance on market forces in NZ and UK to keep wages for carers low in order to provide affordable childcare. Both NZ and UK have migrated since the 1980s and 1990s towards a 'neo-liberal testbed' and a 'neo-conservative model', respectively (Mitchell 1992, p. 53; Veit-Wilson 2000, p. 6).

Scholars note the increasing reliance on a social investment model as a distinctive welfare policy paradigm in more liberal states (Esping-Andersen et al. 2002; Jenson 2009; Hemerijck 2015). The aim of social welfare is no longer to provide social security through, for example, health, pension or unemployment benefits, but to sustain the knowledge-based and service economy (Palier 2008, pp. 8–9). The social investment model puts forward the market as the primary source of well-being for the citizen. However, these perspectives recognise that market participation also might not produce sufficient employment income for all citizens. Therefore, the state is 'allowed' to intervene in the market as an investor for future returns with a view to 'building capacity' (Sen 2000). A related phenomenon, and arguably one that is needed in order to make this model work, is the increasing emphasis on 'active citizenship' within political discourses. This emphasis puts the onus on individuals to assume self-responsibility, create their own solutions to problems and manage the impact upon them from changes in society (Jensen and Pfau-Effinger 2005). In terms of social security, this has been related to an increased focus on 'activation', meaning the requirement to take steps to seek work or undertake training or personal development programmes (O'Brien and Salonen 2011). As such, a greater number—and different types of—conditions have been imposed upon welfare benefit recipients in NZ and UK, among other countries, a phenomenon known as 'creeping conditionality' (Dwyer 2004).

Similarly, new agendas in national wellbeing measures are located within a context of international political economies. New political and policy interest in wellbeing has arisen due to a number of drivers, including concerns about the failure of existing political economies in advanced liberal democracies to deal with new risks such as those discussed above, and issues such as climate change and inequality (Scott 2012). In fact, there is a growing concern that the lifestyles encouraged and supported by neoliberal economic policy are actually detrimental to citizens' wellbeing, or at least providing a diminishing return. In addition, supra-national organisations such as the EU and OECD have been influential in mobilising actions in various countries regarding the measurement of wellbeing (Bache 2013; Bache and Reardon 2016). Much has already been written about this; suffice for us to say that, in part, the impetus for wellbeing agendas came out of international concerns about the failure of economic systems to deal with growing social inequalities and concerns about GDP as a proxy measure for societal progress. However, there are concerns that new wellbeing evidence is supporting neoliberal agendas due to its focus on individual active citizenship and the promotion of self-responsibility, rather than a social solidarity model (Tomlinson and Kelly 2013; Friedli and Stearn 2015). Scott (2015) finds in her study of political wellbeing discourses in the UK under the coalition government that increased wellbeing was often synonymised with a decrease in state bureaucracy and welfare.

Following this, there are a number of ways we could interrogate the relationship between welfare and wellbeing agendas globally. Can wellbeing agendas be seen as an attempt to promote some social protection or individual resilience at a time when welfare and public services are under pressure? This is what Polanyi (2001) called the 'double movement', where increased market freedom and increased measures of social protection from market forces co-develop. Or, following ideas that neoliberalism only survives by co-opting new agendas and movements, can the new agendas of wellbeing and welfare reform be seen to be supporting each other in the preservation of neoliberal political economies? Finally, are welfare and wellbeing 'wicked problems' that are simply resistant to the application of such totalising theories? (Bache et al. 2016). Is it possible that these two agendas are being developed largely in isolation, each as a partial and at times desperate response on the part of under-resourced officials who are tinkering at the edges of a vast chasm of complexity and change? Regardless of the answers to these questions, which are bound to be contingent and context dependent, we argue that it is important that ideas of wellbeing *do* inform welfare policies; that would seem a common-sense idea, and a morally correct stance. We also argue that ideas of wellbeing need to be supported by robust evidence, which is nuanced enough to take account of social relations and everyday life, and is gender sensitive and gender specific. We now address those issues.

Gendered Perspectives of Welfare and Wellbeing

In exploring the ways that the institutional changes and innovations described above may relate to gender, we follow Jill Rubery (2014, p. 26) and recognise the 'multiple and contradictory ideologies underpinning gender relations' that continually shift over time and in different contexts. For example, ideologies supporting greater equality may co-exist with essentialist ideas of gender roles (e.g. children need their mothers at home), even within the views and everyday practices of one individual, and these beliefs may shift over the course of someone's life. As such, we highlight that this is complex terrain even at an individual, let alone societal, level. Second, gender relations are socially constructed and pervasive; they are therefore *embedded* in institutional practices and decisions and not just affected by them.

A wealth of feminist scholarship has long challenged institutional discourses and practices that normalise and preserve particular dominant gendered relations in society. Feminist scrutiny of scientific research norms (see e.g. Harding 1991; Nelson 1996) highlights not only the gendered nature of the construction of problems but also the way that scientific research is constructed to research those problems and obscure gendered effects. Nelson (1996) discusses the need for different scientific approaches for complex problems, but because more dialectical forms of knowledge are often gendered as feminine they are therefore seen as 'soft', inconclusive or unreliable in the masculine world of 'hard' science and formal logic; or, as Georgescu-Roegen (1971) terms it, *arithmomania*. This renders policy discourses incomplete because the evidence they use often does not consider gender (nor race or sexual orientation or the intersectional consequences of these)[1] as a formative category of analysis. Feminist critiques of this have largely failed to make an impact and so 'policy studies mirror prevailing power relations' (Hawksworth 2009, p. 276). This results in 'malestream methodologies' and 'malestream data' that androgenise population trends in quality of life measures (Eckermann 2000, p. 38). This androcentrism casts the everyday experiences of women as 'other', producing unintended consequences and simplistic conclusions.[6] Very often, this phenomenon goes unrecognised due to the assumption that if we can disaggregate statistics into male and female, we have adequately considered gender. This assumes, among other things,[7] that the original measure that is disaggregated is free of discriminatory assumptions and that within the indicator set there is no need for indicators specifically related to gender in recognition of different experiences and bodies.

The relevance and importance of these points will of course depend on what is being studied and measured. However, we argue that a discussion of gendered effects in society, and how indicator sets perpetuate or resist them, is not clearly apparent in the development of wellbeing indicators. As Eckermann (2000) argues (focusing on health indicators), whilst newer quality of life measures may incorporate a greater degree of sensitivity, many are based on gender-neutral assumptions about health experience. She recommends that in order to consider gender properly, we need qualitative evidence to feed into indicators that are not only gender disaggregated but also gender sensitive and gender specific in reproductive *and* non-reproductive areas of life. Otherwise, we risk simplistic and erroneous messages. For example, in a report of the 'first' NZ wellbeing survey funded by the Sovereign insurance company, researchers at Auckland University of Technology (Human Potential Centre 2013) state that based on evidence (quoting only one source) 'giving' promotes wellbeing. They incorporated a question on 'giving' into their wellbeing survey: 'To what extent do you provide help and support to people you are close to when they need it?' The responses to this question were on a scale that ranged from 0 (not at all) to 7 (completely). The results show that 'compared with males, a larger proportion of females "give"' (p. 24). In another part of the document, they state that 'For each increase in giving, there is a significant increase in flourishing' (p. 26), showing a graph where the actual rates of flourishing are almost the same for men and women and rise similarly in proportion to how much they 'give'. Yet nowhere in this report does it draw on the sociological evidence on gendered perceptions and nature of giving/care, discuss why it is that women give more in society and what types of giving they are engaged in, and what the complex trade-offs may be. Therefore, any understanding of gendered relations of care or giving seems to have been missing in formulating the question.

There is often a substantial difference between how national and local indicators frame quality of life and how local people talk about this in the context of their everyday lives (Scott 2012; Oman 2015; White 2015). This is despite the assertion that indicators have been built on extensive consultation. As Scott (2012) found in her study of participation in wellbeing measurement at local authority level in the UK, a clear omission from national quality of life indicators was proper consideration of care and the impact of caring responsibilities. This avoids any difficult discussions of how the notion of 'care' is constructed in indicator sets and how this relates to the valuing or devaluing of certain types of gendered activity in society. Gender relations are shifting and it is important to recognise different family structures, and the increasing provision of parental leave and flexible working arrangements for all, with men becoming more involved in parental care than previously. However, research shows that men and women use flexible working arrangements differently and that these provisions may actually further increase the stresses on certain women with care responsibilities whilst casting a cloak of gender-neutral invisibility over their situation (Masselot 2015).

Campbell et al. (2016) conducted a systematic review of the qualitative evidence regarding the impact of mandatory welfare to work (WtW) programmes in five countries (Australia, Canada, New Zealand, UK and USA) across five overlapping themes (domestic role, the WtW system, employment, economic circumstance and health and wellbeing). Where WtW conflicted with sole responsibility for caring due to lack of suitable childcare, caring responsibilities usually came first, which 'results in absence, financial sanctions and loss of wages' (p. 4). Although across all studies some benefits were identified, the main findings were that mandatory WtW often leads to low paid precarious employment where employment and childcare are in conflict and 'solo parents are often denied control over major life decisions and everyday routines by WtW obligations'. Contextual factors such as a lack of suitable employment and childcare, social support and welfare assistance may lead to WtW being 'counterproductive with respect to health and wellbeing' and there is evidence of adverse effects. They call for further research on the health and wellbeing of solo parents in mandatory WtW programmes.

The situation of female solo parents is not helped by changing social and political discourses, and there is some evidence of attitude change towards solo parenting, particularly targeted at teenage parents. In both NZ and UK, although public attitudes to welfare assistance for solo parents have stayed surprisingly supportive in the face of neoliberal reforms and political discourse, there is an increased support for greater conditionality linked to individual responsible behaviour (Humpage 2010 and 2015; Clery et al. 2013). Contrary to popular beliefs, which focus on the stereotype of teenage mums as a social problem, the average profile for a solo parent in both NZ and UK is a woman in her late thirties who needs temporary assistance after a long-term relationship breakdown. As Wilson and Huntingdon (2006, p. 60) argue in their review of discourses and evidence of teenage motherhood in NZ, UK and USA, the declining rates of teenage pregnancy in these countries are 'inversely mirrored by a growing preoccupation with anxiety about teen motherhood' (p. 62). They outline a contrast to half a century ago, when teenage years were considered optimum for childbirth; older motherhood has now become the norm, with associated health issues overlooked in favour of a focus on teenage mothers as part of a social or public health problem. They argue that this anxiety is linked to narratives of 'welfare dependency', reinforced through particular scientific methods, evidence and discourse that highlights bleak outcomes for both mother and child. This evidence has been consistently challenged by experts due to concerns about selectiveness on the part of policy makers and the robustness of individual studies. They argue that, in general, qualitative studies— which were hardly ever used in the policy documents analysed—paint a much more positive story in which pregnancy may enhance the life of an already disaffected teenager by allowing her to access more support and resources and giving her a purpose for re-engaging with various educational and social support mechanisms. Rather than revealing a dependency problem, this qualitative evidence gives a voice to young mothers who actively weigh up the opportunity costs of early pregnancy in a society where other opportunities seem limited (see also Cater and Coleman 2006; Alexander et al. 2010).

Welfare Reform and Women

Welfare Reform in NZ

NZ is commonly framed as an early pioneer in the provision of state welfare, the so-called 'social laboratory of the South Pacific', which, for example, introduced the first state pension in the English-speaking world in 1898. The bicultural nature of NZ has long presented challenges to equitable state provision that continues today, and early policies, using notions of 'deserving' and 'undeserving poor', disadvantaged non-Pakeha[8] New Zealanders, with applicants having to prove their moral character before a magistrate before being granted assistance (Scott 2014). In terms of the focus of this chapter, a significant reform was the introduction of the Domestic Purposes Benefit (DPB) in 1973. In recognition of changing social orders, this reform gave solo mothers the same opportunity that partnered mothers had, to stay at home and care for dependent children. This was, arguably, the first time that solo mothers were recognised as 'deserving poor' in NZ, and this was reinforced in a 1977 government report that 'no pressure should be placed on the mother of the young child to utilise child-care facilities and return to full-time employment' (Scott 2014, p. 9). During the 1990s, the welfare state in NZ underwent radical shifts under the National Government with the DPB (alongside other benefits) coming under increasing scrutiny, leading to a cut in benefit rates that resulted in an increase in rates of child poverty (O'Brien 2011). There was a resurgence in emphasis on moral values and judgements, which are permeating policy framings. Such judgments are being increasingly applied in family policy, where solo parenthood is singled out as abnormal and generating social problems requiring government action (Masselot 2015).

In 2010, a new Welfare Working Group was set up to oversee welfare reforms, chaired by Paula Rebstock, an investment economist employed by Minister for Social Development, Paula Bennett. The focus of the group was on the development of a social investment model, with Rebstock announcing: 'It's about maximising the return on the investment the New Zealand Public are making in assisting people while they are on benefit to help them get off it' (Rebstock, quoted in Holmes 2012). The aims of the group were to examine:

> ways to reduce benefit dependence and get better work outcomes; how welfare should be funded, and whether there are things that can be learned from the insurance industry and ACC[9] in terms of managing the Government's forward liability; how to promote opportunities and independence from benefit for disabled people and people with ill health; whether the structure of the benefit system and hardship assistance in particular is contributing to long-term benefit dependency. (Welfare Working Group 2011)

The final report, entitled 'Reducing Long-Term Benefit Dependency', fed into a new 'Investment Approach' to welfare in the Social Security (Youth Support & Work Focus) Amendment Act 2012 and Social Security (Benefit Categories & Work Focus) Amendment Act 2013. These instruments aimed to simplify the benefits system and, at the same time, introduce a 'stronger work focus' with work activation, greater conditionality and sanctions. These changes are considered to be 'in line with modern social norms, where it is common for both parents in a household to work' (OMSD 2012, p. 2). They are designed with the intention to promote incentives for long-term employment (OMSD 2012, p. 3), but they have been strongly motivated by an economic approach rather than a capacity approach.

A key focus was on solo parents, who are now required to be available for part-time work when their child turns five and prior to this are expected to take steps to prepare to enter the labour market. Once a child turns fourteen, there is an expectation for solo parents to be available for full-time work and to take any reasonable offer. Failure to comply may result in a 50 per cent support benefit cut. Women (not men) are provided with assistance associated with the use of long-term contraceptives. Women who give birth whilst already claiming welfare support for a first child are required to seek part-time work when the new child turns one year old, as opposed to five years in the case of the first child.

Young parents (aged 16–18) are subject to much heavier obligations than older parents, which are justified on grounds of social outcome. For example, young solo parents have their benefit controlled by a youth service provider, with automatic payment of bills and charging of a grocery card. There is an expectation that youth beneficiaries (under 19) with children are in education or training when the child turns six months or one year. They must be enrolled on budgeting and parenting programmes and their spending is monitored. The reforms have had a disproportionate impact on women and specifically Māori and Pasifika women; unsurprisingly, as 90 per cent of solo parent benefit recipients are women. The reforms have made women the target of more control (and for longer than young men) despite the claim that the reform is about making people less dependent—there are some serious contradictions in the legislation (Masselot 2015). The reforms also appear to have a unidimensional perspective that hides structural inequalities between women and men and between women. They also contribute to the devaluation of care and defamilisation of women and children relationships. The assumption is that young and poor parents, who are disproportionately women—and Māori/Pasifika women—need parenting education to make them good parents, and in fact 'good mothers' (Dobrowolsky and Jenson 2005).

Welfare Reform in UK

Like NZ, the UK welfare system is seen as an exemplar, particularly due to the 1942 Beveridge Report, which was one of the first reports to suggest that the state had a formal obligation to support its citizens through family allowances, health care and full employment. It signalled a shift away from 'Poor Law' ideas of a safety net towards the notion of positive support for all citizens. A significant precursor to the 2012 UK welfare reforms we discuss here was the introduction of welfare reforms from 1997 onwards under a New Labour government. The 'New Deals' package offered greater incentives and support to find employment alongside an increase in obligations (Beatty and Fothergill 2014). Of significant relevance to our chapter here, over the last two decades, for solo parents, there has been a gradual reduction in the qualifying age for the youngest child; once a child reaches this age the parent becomes available for work. Under the Labour government of 1997–2010, the qualifying age was gradually reduced 16 to seven.

Although one could argue that the welfare reforms under the coalition government continued this trajectory, the 2012 reforms were an intensification of the process of change that brought the biggest changes in welfare for 60 years.[10] The UK Welfare Reform Act 2012 was passed with explicit aims to simplify the benefit system and replace a number of means-tested benefits and tax credits for people of working age with Universal Credit[11]; to bring welfare more in line with norms in working life (including decisions about when to have children); and to improve work incentives:

> This is part of the process of saying there is a limit to the amount of welfare available and we need you to be positive about doing the right thing, to seek a job and to support your family.

> Iain Duncan Smith, Minister for Work and Pensions.[12]

Besides introducing Universal Credit and related measures, the Act made other significant changes to the benefits system, including: capping the total amount of benefits; restrictions to Housing Benefit entitlement for new and existing social housing tenants whose accommodation is larger than is deemed necessary (the controversial 'bedroom tax')[13]; stronger penalties for fraud and error; changes to the Social Fund,[14] including greater powers for local authorities; and a new 'claimant commitment' with increased sanctions for non-compliance. Of particular significance to our focus here, a restriction on Income Support for solo parents was introduced that lowered the qualifying age of the youngest child even further, from under seven to under five years of age. Once a child reaches five, the claimant is transferred from Income Support to Jobseeker's Allowance (JSA) meaning there is a requirement to seek work. One of the most controversial aspects of the welfare reforms that has received attention from the media and campaign groups has been the programme of reassessing people on disability benefits using the Work Capability Assessment. This has been linked, in a recent empirical study by epidemiologists at Cambridge University, with 'an increase in suicides, self-reported mental health problems and antidepressant prescribing' (Barr et al. 2016, p. 339). Additionally, the authors advise that 'this policy may have had serious adverse consequences for mental health in England, which could outweigh any benefits that arise from moving people off disability benefits' (p. 339).

The impacts of these changes on solo parents have also been severe; for example, the changes in housing benefit alone have predominantly affected this group (Rubery and Rafferty 2014). In addition, female solo parents have experienced increased stress due to benefit cuts and increased pressure to find work at a time of reduced opportunities and employment protection (Browne 2012; Rubery and Rafferty 2014).

The cumulative impact of welfare reform and public sector cuts have hit women the hardest. The Fawcett Society (2012) calls this 'the triple jeopardy' facing women: they are hardest hit by welfare reform, by austerity and public sector cuts, and are the ones most likely to fill gaps in care left by withdrawal of state services. Unsurprisingly, women's support organisations in the voluntary sector have seen a staggering rise in demand, alongside a sharp decrease in funding, with many women's services closing across the UK (Robson 2016). According to House of Commons Library statistics collected in 2012, of the £14.9 billion worth of cuts that were made to benefits, tax credits, pay and pensions between 2010 and 2012, 74 per cent of this was taken from women's incomes. Projections are that this figure will rise to 81 per cent by 2020, with solo parents around 20 per cent worse off (and this does not include the impact of public sector cuts) (Women's Budget Group 2016). The further £10 billion of planned cuts to welfare spending during 2016/2017 alone is likely to have a 'devastating' impact on women (Poverty and Social Exclusion Group 2016).

Despite repeated requests by numerous lobby groups for the government to conduct detailed gender analysis of these reforms, and despite such requirements for gender analysis being stipulated in the 2010 Equalities Act, none has been forthcoming (Women's Budget Group 2016). Nevertheless, popular TV programmes such as Channel Four's *Benefits Street* 'expose' extreme examples of teenage solo parenthood and 'welfare dependency' and not the actual impacts or trends. This is reinforced by a political narrative that there are a rising number of people who regard welfare benefits as a 'lifestyle choice' (Osborne, quoted in Wintour 2010) in the absence of any evidence to substantiate the theory that there are pervasive cultures of dependency (Shildrick et al. 2012).

Skiving, Striving and Thriving in NZ and UK

Both NZ and UK have been enthusiastic about engaging with global discussions on wellbeing and how this can signal an important development shift. The NZ Treasury, working with Statistics NZ and the Ministry of

Social Development, created the 'Living Standards Framework', influenced by Amartya Sen's work and using the concept of good growth (NZ Treasury 2012). It asserts, for example, that 'the distribution of living standards across different groups in society is an ethical concern for the public, and a political concern for governments' (p. 4). The Living Standards Framework is designed to align public policy with what matters to people and is comprised of five areas: economic growth, managing risks, social cohesion, increasing equity and sustainability for the future. It is complemented by the New Zealand General Social Survey, which now includes a subjective measure of life satisfaction. This work has included a large national consultation with Māori communities to inform the development of a separate Māori wellbeing survey (*Te Kupenga*) by Statistics New Zealand. This reflects the distinct cultural philosophies of the Māori way of living, which places greater emphasis on living in relation to others and to the environment.

The UK is often seen as one of the forerunners in developing a strategy for measuring national wellbeing. David Cameron's assertion on becoming Prime Minister that we must consider 'Gross National Wellbeing' as well as GDP (Cameron 2010) has underpinned the Office of National Statistics' national consultation regarding 'what matters' and how to measure it. From this a 'Wheel of Wellbeing' has been produced comprising ten domains of living (and 41 indicators). Four new subjective measures were included in a national survey, which measure happiness, anxiety, life satisfaction and the factors that make life worthwhile. The devolved governments of Scotland, Wales and Northern Ireland are all developing their own ideas and strategies for measuring wellbeing. An All-Party Parliamentary Group on Wellbeing Economics has been established and has carried out consultations and research on various aspects of wellbeing, including in the area of work and the labour market (APPG 2014). A new What Works Centre for Wellbeing has been set up to gather evidence to inform policy.

Discussions of these initiatives are described in detail elsewhere and it is sufficient for us to say that a great deal of activity is happening in these two countries to try to bring policy objectives in line with wellbeing evidence. However, our concern is that these streams of work on wellbeing continue to speak past current welfare reform agendas and are taking place in political environments that are ideologically opposed to state welfare. Welfare reforms have clearly had negative wellbeing impacts on various groups, including women and solo parents; indeed, some of the welfare reform measures in NZ and UK have sparked challenges from NGOs and legal bodies on the basis that they contravene human rights conventions (Hollingsworth 2015; Masselot 2015). The financial impacts of welfare reform (alongside austerity and labour market changes) have hit women as a group much harder than men (House of Commons Library 2012; Graham and McQuaid 2014; Karamessini and Rubery 2014; Scottish Parliament Welfare Reform Committee, 2015). In addition, the qualitative changes to welfare, including conditionality and sanctions, have had an adverse impact on women. The focus of welfare reforms is on work activation rather than wellbeing, with little regard for detailed analysis into the needs of solo parents, the suitability of work in an increasingly flexible and precarious labour market, the availability or affordability of child care, or the stresses of juggling competing demands (O'Brien 2011; Dwyer and Wright 2014; Stewart and Wright 2014). This is despite evidence that low-paid precarious work is sometimes worse for wellbeing than unemployment, particularly for solo parents (APPG 2014).

Although the wellbeing agenda has helped to raise awareness about the plight of people on zero-hours contracts, it seems to have had very little effect on welfare reform discourses or on policy, which are continuing to impose regressive measures upon solo parents in this respect. International evidence supports governmental statistics that sanction reduced benefit claims; however, long-term government analysis is missing (National Audit Office 2016). Where academic studies have been carried out, these show more negative outcomes of sanctions on longer term income, job quality and criminal activity: claimants are forced to move into low-paid, insecure employment and get trapped, finding it difficult to progress to better employment (Griggs and Evans 2010). Solo parents are far more likely to experience low-paid, part-time, insecure work and to move in and out of that work (Bradshaw et al. 2008). In the UK, the Department for Work and Pensions has added wellbeing measures to policy service evaluations in order to understand, for example, the impact of interventions on long-term unemployed. Whilst these sorts of evaluations are welcome, unless 'wellbeing' is gender sensitive and gender specific (and it has a long way to go as far as we can see), this will not capture the detailed transition needs for solo parents who rely on assistance for certain periods of time.

Additionally, by constructing humans as atomistic individuals and wellbeing as an individual 'package' rather than a complex set of interconnections, individual behaviours become both site of and solution to wellbeing, with interventions increasingly based at the level of individual self-development. This dovetails into agendas of 'creeping conditionality' (Dwyer 2004) where offerings of work-related education and training, and, increasingly, health and social/sexual education, become more and more obligatory. These obligations upon claimants relate increasingly to the performance of idealised behaviours as well as their eligibility to receive benefits due to their circumstances. On the one hand, there is a 'work norm' discourse being applied to people on benefits in both countries and yet they are being subjected to behaviour tests, and to conditions not applied to employed people, and with fewer resources to fulfil those requirements.

The oft-rehearsed concerns that welfare promotes dependency underpin these discursive constructions of ideal behaviours, which include attributes such as 'autonomy, independence, self–sufficiency' (Kingfisher and Goldsmith 2001, p. 714). The implication is that welfare can actually be bad for wellbeing because it may corrupt our ability to look after ourselves. This works in line with the social investment perspective, where there are shared responsibilities for the welfare of citizens: the State is responsible for ensuring that some investments are possible by providing, for instance, crèche facilities and access to doctors, whilst the citizens are responsible for investing in their own human capital. Where citizens are percieved to be at risk of not investing in their own welfare, the state may intervene; for example, it may compel young parents to attend budgeting/parenting classes as a condition for receiving their benefits. The ultimate idea is to reduce the transmission of intergenerational poverty, although there is very little evidence for this phenomenon.

FROM A 'WELFARE STATE' TO A 'WELLBEING STATE'?

In this chapter, we have attempted to raise some questions about the relationship between ideas of wellbeing and welfare, focusing on welfare reform in NZ and UK. We will end with a return to the beginning and a further thought on the notion of moving from a 'from a welfare to a wellbeing state'. John Veit-Wilson (2000) questions the usefulness of the term 'welfare state', arguing that since all modern industrial states offer some form of welfare to some citizens, there is no distinction between the terms modern industrial state and welfare state and thus the term 'welfare' has become redundant noise. If 'welfare state' is used in such a vague way, then how would we distinguish 'counterfactual *unwelfare* states' (p. 4)? His point is that in order to make some meaning out of the term 'welfare', we need to re-analyse what this means and how comprehensively different states provide and enable this, regardless of the 'ephemeral activities of short-lived and changeable governments' (p. 4). It is not enough to try to provide typologies of different welfare states; we need to make some pronouncements about what is sufficient to justify the label 'welfare state'. His main argument is that a welfare state, in order to be described as such, must provide welfare to *all* its citizens, not just some. We would like to apply the same argument to the idea of a 'wellbeing state'. As, increasingly, nation states sign up to wellbeing development paradigms and enthusiastically start measuring wellbeing, we would argue that this is meaningless noise without a full analysis of the question: wellbeing for whom?

The review of evidence outlined briefly in this chapter of the impacts of recent welfare reform in NZ and UK indicates that, certainly as a group, solo parents have been negatively affected. Under current wellbeing measurement orthodoxies, which support the same gendered *arithmomania* as many other forms of research that underpin policy decisions, we would not want a 'wellbeing state' to replace a 'welfare state', especially as the term wellbeing is even more nebulous than welfare. The concept (and measurement) of a gender-neutral idea of wellbeing is being used predominantly in an evaluative sense to measure the effects of policy largely uninformed by proper gender analysis, with the result that although women are the group most likely to suffer from welfare cuts, labour market policy and austerity policies, this is not properly understood, highlighted or considered. Women as a group have always been seen as a malleable resource in labour market policy to be deployed or restricted as needs determine (Rubery 2014). It is therefore unsurprising that women are targeted as a result of recent fiscal crises. This impact on women looks likely to continue apace and we cannot see any rescue coming from a 'wellbeing state' that largely supports a focus on positive individual behaviours which underpin discourses of self-determination in welfare reform agendas, without first understanding the pathways to such self-determination. Women, and particularly young solo parents, have been severely disadvantaged in the latest round of welfare reforms in both NZ and UK, compounded by public sector cuts and withdrawal of support services at the same time as these countries have enthusiastically supported the idea of national wellbeing. If wellbeing is consistently being undermined for a particular group of people and there is insufficient attention to understanding their needs, as we argue in this chapter, then that is not only discriminatory and fundamentally unjust but it seriously challenges, on theoretical and methodological grounds, the political claim of measuring and promoting national wellbeing.

NOTES

1. We consider the shift from a welfare to a wellbeing state to be a provocative idea and stress that our discussion in this chapter is not a critique of Dalziel and Saunders' book, which argues for a 'wellbeing state... that concentrates on activities that add value in ways that citizens cannot achieve by themselves using the same resources' (p. 135). We are indebted to the authors of that publication for many stimulating discussions.

2. It is important to note that although both countries have two dominant parties representing left (Labour Party in both) and right (National in NZ and Conservative in UK) of the political spectrum, their policies and positions are not directly comparable. For example, in 1984, when Labour won power in NZ, many commentators viewed their economic reforms as more aggressively neoliberal than those promoted in UK through Thatcherism. The NZ finance minister gave his name to a particular brand of market fundamentalism, 'Rogernomics'. It is important to understand the historical basis of the development of politics in both countries.

3. We use the term 'solo' instead of 'lone' or 'single' parent. This term is commonly used in NZ and, whilst it is not so common in UK, we feel this is a more positive term than the others. The terms lone parent and single parent have often been used in a derogatory manner to promote negative stereotypes of solo parents, particularly in certain media and political discourses.

4. In both NZ and UK, 90 per cent of solo parents are women. We stress that gender is non-binary, and we recognise the danger of essentialising when talking about 'women'. We argue in this context of welfare reform that women are still essentialised by bureaucratic systems, and we try to navigate these terminological difficulties in our critique.

5. This is how solo parenthood is usually characterised in these studies, with reference to the increased disadvantages associated with solo parenting for parent and child, evidenced by statistical instruments such as the Index of Multiple Deprivation in UK. However, we take a more comprehensive view, as discussed later in this chapter, and do not suggest that solo parenthood per se leads to disadvantage, whilst recognising it is generally associated with a higher risk of financial stress and other issues.

6. Appositely highlighted by the persistent tendency in statistical analysis to use 'male' as the 'constant' category to which 'female' is the variable, despite women being the slightly larger group within most general populations. Whilst of course this makes no difference to the outcome of the actual statistical analysis, it is a small example of androcentrist research norms, which can affect ways of thinking about population study more generally.
7. It assumes that gender is binary.
8. *Pakeha* is the Māori term for whites of European descent. It is generally viewed as a descriptive rather than derogatory term, and used to distinguish between groups in a bicultural nation.
9. Accident Compensation Corporation—A Crown service overseen by NZ government, funded largely through levies on working people. http://www.acc.co.nz/about-acc/overview-of-acc/introduction-to-acc/index.htm.
10. According to the news article on the UK Government website: https://www.gov.uk/government/news/iain-duncan-smith-welfare-reforms-realised.
11. Universal Credit is a single monthly payment for people in or out of work and replaces: Income-based Jobseeker's Allowance, Income-related Employment and Support Allowance, Income Support, Child Tax Credit, Working Tax Credit and Housing Benefit.
12. Part of a speech at Cambridge reported by the BBC. http://www.bbc.co.uk/news/uk-politics-20077758.
13. Interestingly, in the NZ Social Survey, having a spare room is correlated with higher wellbeing.
14. The Social Fund is a government scheme aimed at helping those on low incomes and in severe difficulties, to obtain grants or no-interest loans in the event of unforeseen circumstances.

Acknowledgements The authors were funded by the Knowledge and Expertise Exchange Europe New Zealand (KEEENZ) under the EU Marie Curie grant scheme, enabling academic collaboration. We are grateful to Dr Carmen Hubbard at Newcastle University for facilitating this exchange. Heartfelt thanks also to Professors Paul Dalziel and Caroline Saunders at Lincoln University NZ and to Professor Bronwyn Hayward at Canterbury University NZ for their hospitality and for many interesting and challenging conversations on wellbeing which fed into this chapter. Thanks also to Professor Ian Bache for his helpful comments on the draft of this chapter.

References

APPG. (2014). Wellbeing in Four Policy Areas. All Party Parliamentary Group on Wellbeing Economics. Available at: http://b.3cdn.net/nefoundation/ccdf9782b6d8700f7c_lcm6i2ed7.pdf.

Alexander, C., Duncan, S., & Edwards, R. (2010). *Teenage Parenting: What's the Problem?* London: Tufnell Press.

Allin, P., & Hand, J. (2014). *The Wellbeing of Nations: Meaning, Motive and Measurement*. New York: Wiley.

Bache, I. P. (2013). Measuring Quality of Life for Public Policy: An Idea Whose Time Has Come? Agenda-setting Dynamics in the European Union. *Journal of European Public Policy, 20*(1), 21–38.

Bache, I., & Reardon, L. (2016). *The Politics and Policy of Wellbeing: Understanding the Rise and Significance of a New Agenda*. Cheltenham: Edward Elgar.

Bache, I., Reardon, L., & Anand, P. (2016). Wellbeing as a Wicked Problem: Navigating the Arguments for the Role of Government. *Journal of Happiness Studies, 17*(3), 893–912.

Barr, B., Taylor-Robinson, D., Stuckler, D., Loopstra, R., Reeves, A., & Whitehead, M. (2016). 'First, Do No Harm': Are Disability Assessments Associated with Adverse Trends in Mental Health? A Longitudinal Ecological Study. *Journal of Epidemiology and Community Health, 70*(4), 339–345.

Beatty, C., & Fothergill, S. (2014). The Local and Regional Impact of the UK's Welfare Reforms. *Cambridge Journal of Regions, Economy and Society, 7*, 63–79.

Bonoli, G. (2005). The Politics of the New Social Policies: Providing Coverage Against New Social Risks in Mature Welfare States. *Policy & Politics, 33*(3), 431–449.

Bonoli, G. (2007). Time Matters: Post Industrialization, New Social Risks, and Welfare State Adaptation in Advanced Industrial Democracies. *Comparative Political Studies, 40*(5), 495–520.

Bradshaw, P., Jamieson, L., & Wasoff, F. (2008). Growing up in Scotland Study: Use of Informal Support by Families with Young Children. Edinburgh: Scottish Government Social Research. Available at: http://www.gov.scot/Publications/2008/03/12110018/3.

Browne, J. (2012). The Impact of Austerity Measures on Households with Children. Institute for Fiscal Studies and Family and Parenting Institute. Available at: http://www.theministryofparenting.com/wp-content/uploads/2012/05/FPI_IFS_Austerity_Jan_2012.pdf. Accessed February 21, 2017.

Cameron, D. (2010). Prime Minister's Speech on Wellbeing on November 25, 2010. Available at: https://www.gov.uk/government/speeches/pm-speech-on-wellbeing. Accessed March 15, 2013.

Campbell, M., Thomson, H., Fenton, C., & Gibson, M. (2016). Lone Parents, Health, Wellbeing and Welfare to Work: A Systematic Review of Qualitative Studies. *BMC Public Health, 16*, 188.

Cater, S., & Coleman, L. (2006). 'Planned' Teenage Pregnancy: Views and Experiences of Young People from Poor and Disadvantaged Backgrounds. York: Joseph Rowntree Foundation. Available at: https://www.jrf.org.uk/report/planned-teenage-pregnancy-views-and-experiences-young-people-poor-and-disadvantaged.

Clery, E., Lee, L., & Kunz, S. (2013). Public Attitudes to Poverty and Welfare, 1983–2011. Analysis using British Social Attitudes Data. Joseph

Rowntree Foundation and Natcen. Available at: http://www.natcen.ac.uk/media/137637/poverty-and-welfare.pdf. Accessed February 20, 2017.

Dalziel, P., & Saunders, C. (2014). *Wellbeing Economics: Future Directions for New Zealand*. Wellington: Bridget Williams Books.

Dobrowolsky, A., & Jenson, J. (2005). Social Investment Perspectives and Practices: A Decade in British Politics. *Social Policy Review, 17,* 203–230.

Dwyer, P. (2004). Creeping Conditionality in the UK: From Welfare Rights to Conditional Entitlements. *The Canadian Journal of Sociology, 29*(2), 265–287.

Dwyer, P., & Wright, S. (2014). Universal Credit, Ubiquitous Conditionality and Its Implications for Social Citizenship. *Journal of Poverty and Social Justice, 22*(1), 27–35.

Eckermann, L. (2000). Gendering Indicators of Health and Well-being: Is Quality of Life Gender Neutral? *Social Indicators Research, 52,* 29–54.

Esping-Andersen, G., Gallie, D., Hemerijck, A., & Myles, J. (2002). *Why We Need a New Welfare State*. Oxford: Oxford University Press.

Esping-Andersen, G. (1990). *The Three Worlds of Welfare Capitalism*. Cambridge: Polity Press.

Esping-Andersen, G. (1996). After the Golden Age? Welfare State Dilemmas in a Global Economy. In G. Esping-Anderson (Ed.), *Welfare States in Transition: National Adaptations in Global Economies* (pp. 1–31). London: Sage.

Fawcett Society. (2012). The Impact of Austerity on Women. Fawcett Society Policy Briefing. Available at: https://www.fawcettsociety.org.uk/the-impact-of-austerity-on-women.

Friedli, L., & Stearn, R. (2015). Positive Affect as Coercive Strategy: Conditionality, Activation and the Role of Psychology in UK Government Workfare Programmes. *Medical Humanities, 41,* 40–47.

Georgescu-Roegen, N. (1971). *The Entropy Law and the Economic Process.* Cambridge, MA: Harvard University Press.

Graham, H., & McQuaid, R. (2014). Exploring the Impacts of the UK Government's Welfare Reforms on Lone Parents Moving into Work: Literature Review. Employment Research Institute, Edinburgh Napier University and Stirling University. Available at: http://www.gcph.co.uk/assets/0000/4284/Lone_parents_Literature_Review_web.pdf. Accessed February 26, 2017.

Griggs, J., & Evans, M. (2010). Sanctions within Conditional Benefit Systems: A Review of Benefit Sanctions. Joseph Rowntree Foundation: New York. Available at: https://www.jrf.org.uk/report/review-benefit-sanctions. Accessed February 27, 2017.

Harding, S. (1991). *Whose Science? Whose Knowledge?: Thinking from Women's Lives.* Ithaca: Cornell University Press.

Hawksworth, M. (2009). Policy Discourse as Sanctioned Ignorance: Theorizing the Erasure of Feminist Knowledge. *Critical Policy Studies, 3*(3–4), 268–289.

Hemerijck, A. (2015). The Quiet Paradigm Revolution of Social Investment. *Social Politics, 22*(2), 242–256.

Hollingsworth, K. (2015). Judging Children's Rights and the Benefits Cap: R (SG and others) v Secretary of State for Work and Pensions. *Child and Family Law Quarterly, 27*(4), 445–466.

Holmes, P. (2012). Paul Holmes Interviews Paula Rebstock, *Scoop,* 20 May 2012. Available at: http://www.scoop.co.nz/stories/PO1205/S00296/qapaul-holmes-interviews-paula-rebstock.htm. Last accessed July 2, 2017.

House of Commons Library. (2012). *How Have Coalition Budgets Affected Women?* Available at: https://docs.google.com/spreadsheets/d/1bKckn9dl_V2j7gPoFCAcbU3Q64iN1TEO6gGIDnypihI/edit?pli=1#gid=0. Accessed July 1, 2015.

Human Potential Centre. (2013). Sovereign Wellbeing Index: New Zealand's First Measure of Wellbeing. Auckland University of Technology. Available at: http://www.mywellbeing.co.nz/mw/report/sovereign-wellbeing-index-2013-report.pdf. Accessed February 20, 2017.

Humpage, L. (2010). Neoliberal Reform and Attitudes Towards Social Citizenship: A Review of New Zealand Public Opinion Data 1987–2005. *Social Policy Journal of New Zealand, 37,* 1–14.

Humpage, L. (2015). *Policy Change, Public Attitudes and Social Citizenship: Does Neoliberalism Matter?* Bristol: The Policy Press.

Jenson, J. (2009). Lost in Translation: The Social Investment Perspective and Gender Equality. *Social Politics, 16*(4), 446–483.

Jensen, P., & Pfau-Effinger, B. (2005). 'Active' Citizenship: The New Face of Welfare. In J. Andersen, A. Guillemard, P. Jensen & B. Pfau-Effinger (Eds.), *The Changing Face of Welfare: Consequences and Outcomes from a Citizenship Perspective.* Bristol: The Policy Press.

Karamessini, M., & Rubery, J. (Eds). (2014). *Women and Austerity: The Economic Crisis and the Future for Gender Equality.* London: Routledge.

Kingfisher, C., & Goldsmith, M. (2001). Reforming Women in the United States and Aotearoa/New Zealand: A Comparative Ethnography of Welfare Reform in Global Context. *American Anthropologist, 103*(30), 714–732.

Masselot, A. (2015). Gender Implications of the Right to Request Flexible Working Arrangements: Raising Pigs and Children in New Zealand. *New Zealand Journal of Employment Relations, 39*(3), 59–71.

Mitchell, D. (1992). Welfare States and Welfare Outcomes in the 1980s. *International Social Security Review, 45*(1–2), 73–90.

National Audit Office. (2016). Benefit Sanctions. Department for Work and Pensions. Available at: https://www.nao.org.uk/wp-content/uploads/2016/11/Benefit-sanctions.pdf. Accessed February 26, 2017.

Nelson, J. (1996). *Feminism, Objectivity and Economics.* London: Routledge.

New Zealand Treasury. (2012). Improving the Living Standards of New Zealanders: Moving from a Framework to Implementation. Available at:

http://www.treasury.govt.nz/publications/media-speeches/speeches/living-standards/sp-livingstandards-paper.pdf.

O'Brien, M. (2011). Lone Parents Working for Welfare in New Zealand. *Local Economy, 27*(5–6), 577–592.

O'Brien, M., & Salonen, T. (2011). Child Poverty and Child Rights Meet Active Citizenship: A New Zealand and Sweden Study. *Childhood, 18*(2), 211–226.

Oman, S. (2015). Measuring National Wellbeing: What Matters to You? What Matters to Whom? In S. White & C. Blackmore (Eds.), *Cultures of Wellbeing: Method, Place, Policy.* London: Palgrave.

OMSD. (2012). *Paper A—Welfare Reform: Overview of Package.* New Zealand Government: Office of the Minister for Social Development

Palier, B. (2008). Présentation. In G. Esping-Andersen, B. Palier & M. Groulez (Eds.), *Trois Leçons sur l'Etat-providence*, 5–17. Paris: Seuil.

Polanyi, K. (2001 [1944]). *The Great Transformation.* Boston: Beacon.

Poverty and Social Exclusion Group. (2016). Women 'Hit Worst' by Austerity Measures. Available at: http://www.poverty.ac.uk/report-gender-tax-benefits-government-cuts-government-policy/women-%E2%80%98hit-worst%E2%80%99-austerity-measures.

Robson, S. (2016). The Impact of Austerity Measures on Women's Voluntary Community Organisations and the Response of the Women's Sector. Women's Resource Centre. Available at: http://thewomensresourcecentre.org.uk/wp-content/uploads/State-of-the-womens-sector-survey-reportMay2016-FINAL.pdf.

Rubery, J. (2014). From 'Women and Recession' to 'Women and Austerity'. In M. Karamessini & J. Rubery (Eds.), *Women and Austerity: The Economic Crisis and the Future for Gender Equality.* Abingdon: Routledge.

Rubery, J., & Rafferty, A. (2014). Gender, Recession and Austerity in the UK. In M. Karamessini & J. Rubery (Eds.), *Women and Austerity: The Economic Crisis and the Future for Gender Equality.* Abingdon: Routledge.

Scott, B. (2014). Welfare Reform: Its Impact on Women as Mothers and Workers. Thesis, Master of Applied Psychology (MAppPsy). University of Waikato, Hamilton, New Zealand. Available at: http://hdl.handle.net/10289/8719.

Scott, K. (2015). Happiness on Your Doorstep: Disputing the Boundaries of Wellbeing and Localism. *Geographical Journal, 181*(2), 129.

Scott, K. (2012). *Measuring Wellbeing: Towards Sustainability?* Abingdon: Routledge.

Scottish Parliament Welfare Reform Committee. (2015). Women and Social Security. Scottish Parliament Publications. Available at: https://www.scottishwomensconvention.org/content/briefing-papers/Women-and-Welfare.pdf.

Sen, A. (2000). Social Exclusion: Concept, Application and Scrutiny. Office of Environment and Social Development, Asian Development Bank. *Social Development Papers #1.* Manila: ADB.

Shildrick, T., MacDonald, T., Furlong, A., Roden, J., & Crow, R. (2012). Are 'Cultures of Worklessness' Passed Down the Generations? York: Joseph Rowntree Foundation. Available at: https://www.jrf.org.uk/report/are-cultures-worklessness-passed-down-generations.

Stewart, A., & Wright, S. (2014). Conditionality Briefing: Unemployed People. ESRC Centre for Welfare Conditionality: Sanctions, Support and Behaviour Change. Available at: http://www.welfareconditionality.ac.uk/wp-content/uploads/2014/09/Briefing_Unemployment_14.09.10_FINAL.pdf. Accessed February 20, 2017.

Tomlinson, M., & Kelly, G. (2013). Is Everybody Happy? The Politics and Measurement of National Wellbeing. *Policy & Politics, 41*(2), 139–157.

Veit-Wilson, J. (2000). States of Welfare: A Conceptual Challenge. *Social Policy & Administration, 34*(1), 1–25.

Welfare Working Group. (2011). Reducing Long-Term Benefit Dependency: Recommendations. Available at: https://media.nzherald.co.nz/webcontent/document/pdf/20119/Bluestar%20WWG%20Recommendations%20Report%20180211.pdf.

White, S., & Blackmore, C. (Eds.). (2015). *Cultures of Wellbeing: Method, Place, Policy.* London: Palgrave Macmillan.

Wilson, H., & Huntington, A. (2006). Deviant (M)others: The Construction of Teenage Motherhood in Contemporary Discourse. *Journal of Social Policy, 35*(1), 59–76.

Wintour, P. (2010). George Osborne to Cut £4bn More from Benefits. *The Guardian*, 9 September. Available at: http://www.guardian.co.uk/politics/2010/sep/09/george-osborne-cut-4bn-benefits-welfare. Accessed February 7, 2017.

Women's Budget Group (2016). A Cumulative Gender Impact Assessment of Ten Years of Austerity Policies. Available at: http://wbg.org.uk/wp-ontent/uploads/2016/11/De_HenauReed_WBG_GIAtaxben_briefing_2016_03_06-1.pdf.

CHAPTER 12

The Politics of the Official Statistic: The UK 'Measuring National Well-Being' Programme

Matt Jenkins

INTRODUCTION: THE NATURE OF THE OFFICIAL STATISTIC

In this chapter, I am interested in the official statistic as a social phenomenon—as a mode of interaction between humans and the world. I pose two questions: what changes when we count officially? How does the official statistic reconfigure or represent interactions between humans or between humans and the world? To address them, this chapter will examine the UK's 'Measuring National Well-being'[1] programme and one of its components, the statistics on subjective well-being (see Bache and Scott, this volume, Chap. 1). Broadly stated, its argument is that the content of the official statistic, the area of human life with which it is concerned, is less important than its form *as* an official statistic. The fact that we are counting 'well-being' configures that concept in particular ways that are reductive, alienating and express existing modes of power.

M. Jenkins (✉)
Independent Scholar, Newcastle upon Tyne, UK
e-mail: matt.jenkins@newcastle.ac.uk

© The Author(s) 2018   279
I. Bache and K. Scott (eds.), *The Politics of Wellbeing*, Wellbeing
in Politics and Policy, https://doi.org/10.1007/978-3-319-58394-5_12

Before such an examination is possible, it is necessary to sketch out a characterisation of the official statistic, which the 'Measuring National Well-being' programme will illustrate. An official statistic is an articulation of a relationship of power. Its creator, a heterogeneous and shifting web of individuals and structures attached to the state (see Painter 2006; Jones 2007; Jenkins 2016), is active in making both ontological and epistemological claims: that the statistic's object exists and does so in a particular form, and that this object can be counted. The object of the statistic has no power to resist such claims or substitute its own. Objects are passive, able, at most, to refuse to be counted yet still finding themselves caught up in the dragnet of external definition. They are characterised by the average; a non-person they have not met nor ever invited to speak on their behalf.

The official statistic is thus a particular type of engagement with its subject, which may be contrasted with alternative modes of social interaction such as negotiation, dialogue or exchange. Its ontological claim is not only that its subject exists—that it can be identified, defined and observed—but that it can be isolated: meaningfully separated from the world as a discrete object (Doel 2001). This is reductionist in two senses: it reduces the subject of the statistic by stripping away its context, interactions and complexities; and it reduces the bearer of that subject to the subject, stripping away the aspects of their existence that the statistic does not count. It does so in response to a problem of scale: while an individual can be interacted with in all their complexity, the mass of individuals is unintelligible. The need to make them intelligible belongs to those doing the counting, and not to those being counted.

Hand (2004) conceives of the statistic (official or otherwise) as having two components: the representational and the pragmatic. That is, the statistic must, in some way, represent what it counts and it must do so in a way that serves the counter's purposes. This distinction of the representational and pragmatic, however, is not clear-cut. The decision about when and what to represent, in order to establish which part of an interconnected world is to be drawn out as a separate object with its own definition, is a pragmatic one. That is, the purposes of the statistical agent precede the claims on the empirical world: representation, here the choice to interact with a subject through counting, is itself a pragmatic act (Power 1994, 1996; Hacking 1999).

These preparatory remarks should be uncontroversial; they do little more than unpack statements made by the producers of official statistics.

For example, Prime Minister David Cameron, in launching the UK's programme of official well-being statistics, expressed his hope of the programme that 'It will help bring about a re-appraisal of what matters, and, in time, it will lead to government policy that is more focused not just on the bottom line, but on all those things that make life worthwhile' (Cameron 2010, np). The aim of the statistical programme, as imagined by one of its key promoters, is to improve reality in two different ways: representationally by redefining how it is conceived ('what matters') and pragmatically how it is configured ('lead to government policy').

There is a difference, however, between the account of the Prime Minister and my own above. For Cameron, it is 'what matters' that is changed by the statistic, which is itself a neutral observation of the world. There is something in the world, 'well-being', the counting of which will lead to a shift in priorities. On my account, the statistic is creating something, 'well-being', which is one of many potential representations of things in the world. This is perhaps a mundane point, but an important one: the statistic does not record the world, but represents it. In facing the statistic, we are not facing information about the way things are, but a set of claims about how the statistic believes things are. These beliefs are formed under particular conditions and for particular purposes.

The points above are statements about statistics in general, which here will be illustrated using the UK's 'Measuring National Well-being' programme: the collection of social statistics produced by the state statistical agency, the Office for National Statistics (see Bache and Scott, this volume, Chap. 1). The next section ('Historical Precedents'), will examine the programme as a whole, showing that its form precludes any understanding of, and so any meaningful action towards, 'well-being'. The following section ('The Logic of Measurement'), contrasts this with the subjective well-being components of the programme, arguing that their form, which reduces and commensurates, restricts actions to those that are similarly reductive and limited. The effects of this will be considered in the penultimate section ('Whose Well-being?'), which considers the example of Bhutan's 'Gross National Happiness' programme and argues that the content of the statistic is less influential than its form in determining the actions that it permits. This chapter will conclude by arguing, on this basis, that an interest in well-being precludes its counting.

It should be made clear at the outset that this argument is not meant as a criticism of those who have created or championed the 'Measuring

National Well-being' programme. Rather, its aim is to highlight the politics of measurement *qua* measurement. Recognising that statistical statements are representations with a particular form and logic, it is insufficient that the normative aims of an official statistic are benign. Rather, there are always the questions of whether counting will achieve these aims or is the best way of achieving them.

HISTORICAL PRECEDENTS: WHAT'S NEW ABOUT 'WELL-BEING'?

One way of highlighting the role of the ontological and epistemological claims of the official statistic is to examine a case where the statistic fails: where there is an incompatibility between the content of the representation and the logic of its form. The 'Measuring National Well-being' programme offers a good example of this, as the claims it makes about the existence of 'well-being' cannot be fulfilled by its content. That is, this section argues that the programme fails in its representational aspect, with what passes for its definition of 'well-being' being no definition at all. Rather, the programme follows all previous efforts at considering 'well-being' in collecting discrete aspects of everyday life that do not coalesce into a single entity.

'Well-being' is not a well-formed construct. This is apparent not only in the variety of statistical conceptions that have arisen as part of the current vogue for measurement (compare, for instance, the Office for National Statistics (Beaumont 2011) with the Organisation for Economic Co-operation and Development (OECD 2013) and these with Eurostat [n.d.]), but also in the difficulty these programmes' promoters have in specifying what the 'well-being' they are counting actually is. Cameron, for example, in launching the UK programme offered 'how our lives are improving' and 'quality of life', two vague and open categories that were themselves only defined by negation, in that they were not 'economic growth' or 'standard of living' (Cameron 2010, np). By the time the ONS had finalised their set of headline measures even this attempt at definition had been given up; they described the programme as 'an accepted and trusted set of National Statistics which help people understand and monitor well-being', but one that achieved this aim through 'looking at different areas of national well-being such as health, relationships, job satisfaction' (ONS 2014, p. 52). These explanations produce a circularity: the programme to measure well-being includes measures to do with well-being.

'Well-being' is here defined into existence by the programme; it is simply what the programme counts.

The result of this approach is not a framework, but a miscellany. The collection produced is incoherent, in the sense that the statistics included have no common basis of valuation. They cannot be equated and relate to each other, except by assertion.[2] Statistics, often created for other purposes, are now asserted to be 'about well-being', and it is only this assertion which connects constructs as diverse as subjective happiness and government debt-to-GDP ratio. Happiness aggregated from the individual level and the debt of government expressed as a ratio with the summed economic activity of individuals within the nation's borders are not the same type of thing; they cannot be expressed in terms of each other. As a result, there is no way of relating their movements: we cannot say, for example, how much one must rise to compensate for a fall in the other. The argument is that there is something, 'National Well-being', that can rise, fall or remain stable, but a miscellany of non-coherent measures offers no means by which we can say how this is happening.

There is, then, a space between the ontological and epistemological claims of the programme; we cannot know about what is believed to exist using the method chosen. Such a miscellany can be contrasted with earlier efforts at social accounting, such as the 'political arithmetick' of William Petty (1899 [1690]), an attempt to understand the power of the Great British state. Here, different indicators—life expectancy, population, the productivity of land—were expressed through the uniform measure of money, making them equivalent and able to be equated. In this model it was possible to talk of 'the [financial] loss we have sustained … by the Slaughter of Men in War, and by sending them abroad into the Service of Foreign Princes' (p. 267), and of the potential gains of depopulating Scotland (p. 289), because they were expressed in the same units. Death, emigration and place of residence became 'about' national well-being because it was possible to say, using this framework, whether well-being, conceived of as a financial bottom line, is increasing or decreasing as its component measures move.

This problem of incoherence is not novel but was also experienced by the Social Indicators Movement of the 1960s and 1970s. Writing in the introduction to the first issue of *Social Trends*, the UK's compendium of the social statistics it collected at the time, the Director of the Central Statistical Office outlined the same issues:

Even on the assumption that it is possible to agree on an overall measure of health, housing, etc., the various indicators cannot satisfactorily be
combined into a single index as there is no objectively agreed weighting
system, such as the price system employed in the National Accounts, which
would assess the value of improved health against improved housing.

(Moser 1970, p. 11)

Social Trends aimed at 'drawing together, initially once a year, some of
the more significant statistical series relating to social policies and conditions' (Nissel 1970, p. 4). It was a miscellany, in the sense outlined
above. Allin, reporting critiques made during its 40-year life, notes that
there was always the question of 'What does it all add up to?' (Allin
2007, p. 51). The answer was nothing, and *Social Trends* was careful
not to claim that there was any supervening abstraction that could draw
together the disparate measures it reported. The 'Measuring National
Well-being' programme starts from the premise that such an abstraction
exists ('well-being'), but is unable to provide any means by which this
abstraction could be drawn. By assertion, its components have become
'about' well-being in the same way that many of them were once 'social
trends', but they do not together form a thing called 'well-being' any
more than together they once formed a thing called 'social trends'.
While it remains possible to act on these individual component 'well-be-
ings', there is no 'national well-being' that can be pursued here.

Without such a 'national well-being', it is hard to distinguish the
current vogue for well-being measurement either from the 'first wave'
of the social indicators movement (Bache 2013; Bache and Reardon
2013, 2016), which did not, in the main, consider itself to be concerned
with 'well-being' (the major exception being the work of the OECD;
see OECD 1973), or from all the statistics before and after that wave
that were concerned with the social. As Lepper and McAndrew, in their
report for HM Treasury, somewhat defensively observed, 'Governments
already factor well-being considerations into the overall balance of economic, social and environmental policy. Economic policy does not generally seek to prioritise growth *per se*, but as a means to higher aggregate
welfare' (Lepper and McAndrew 2008, p. 3). Similarly, the case can be
made that the very first statistical series, the *Bills of Mortality* first published in the mid-sixteenth century, were 'well-being' statistics; after all,
they sought to collate the deaths recorded in London parishes with a
view to warn the affluent of epidemics that necessitated their fleeing to

the fresher air of their country estates (Collier 1854). They exist, in an updated form, in the life-expectancy figures of the 'Measuring National Well-being' programme. While they did not claim to be about 'well-being', existing and historic statistics are concerned with aspects of what is now claimed as well-being. That is, as long as there have been social statistical programmes, there has been an interest in well-being.

As Bache and Reardon (2016) suggest, the defining feature of these two 'waves' is that they reflect state-level engagement in the idea of something larger than the sum of their component statistics. However, in the case of both 'social trends' and 'well-being', this interest is expressed largely through organisation. While both waves see the development of a small number of novel statistics, they concern themselves in the main with the re-presentation of existing statistics with their limited and specific aims. As mere taxonomic exercises, though, they do not deliver on their appeals to larger concepts: their components remain specific statistics created for specific purposes, unconnected to each other, however much they are rebadged as being 'about' something else.

In passing, it should be noted that the incoherence of the 'Measuring National Well-being' programme would not be solved if the set was adjusted to include more or fewer measures. The vagueness of the concept 'well-being' leads to a temptation to police the boundaries of the statistical miscellany, to include 'social justice' or exclude 'human capital', for instance. Such taxonomic disputes are ultimately fruitless, as the miscellany model has a much more basic problem than composition. Without a means of relating the measures within the collection, they are just a collection of measures, summing to nothing. The most they can do is provide the impression of context for each other.

The question facing us becomes a very simple one: what changes about, for example, an unemployment figure when it is re-organised as 'unemployment as a component of well-being' figure? It cannot be that it becomes any more visible: access to the statistic does not radically change when *Social Trends* is discontinued and 'Measuring National Well-being' is published in its place. It is not that the issue it describes becomes any more salient: the statistic existed because it was recognised as a problem. Similarly, the statistic was recognisable as being 'about well-being' (necessarily, to be included within the programme), so its salience has not changed. This is the reverse of the point raised by Lepper and McAndrew (2008) above: there, they argued that well-being had previously been considered but on other terms; here, other things are still being considered, but now in terms of 'well-being'. We remain where we started, only our vocabulary has altered. The effect of this shift in vocabulary will be considered below.

THE LOGIC OF MEASUREMENT: WHY SUBJECTIVE WELL-BEING DRIVES COST–BENEFIT ANALYSES

As argued above, the 'Measuring National Well-being' programme as a statistical programme fails because its ontological and epistemological claims do not align: we cannot know about 'National Well-being' through the observation of the statistics assembled. What, though, of its component statistics? In this section, I will consider the statistics on happiness and subjective well-being. These official statistics were developed specifically for the 'Measuring National Well-being' programme, so even if my argument about the programme as a whole is accepted, it may be argued that the development of subjective well-being is a positive one, allowing interventions to boost happiness and well-being. In this section I will suggest that such hope is misplaced, as the act of counting makes particular ontological and epistemological claims a feature of 'happiness' and 'subjective well-being', thus determining the ways in which these concepts can be acted on.

As a starting point, it should be noted that the official statistic is an act of alienation deriving from a structural logic of abstraction. In a very real sense, the 'nation' in 'Measuring National Well-being' is one uninhabited by people. At every stage of the data-collection process, the individual is progressively stripped away. First, their complicated internal or social life is collapsed into a single definition, such as 'employment status' or 'happiness'[3], which are homogeneous categories and thus in each instance commensurable with all other instances of the same. Then, their multiple conditions are separated from each other; 'employment' summed to feed a local or national rate, 'happiness' averaged, as if the two did not interact. Then, the averages or sums of these measures are brought together by the programme so that regularity on the grand scale stands in place of their interaction on the individual scale, in the hope of offering an overall picture of 'our progress as a country' (Cameron 2010, np). The world of meaning that the individual inhabits with the complex inter-relations of their happiness and employment status has been discarded as noise. In its place is a world of crisp regularity, ordered by causal laws, applying uniformly to all individuals.

A mechanical world such as this can offer causal relations, but never reasons. Happiness as measured can be placed in a statistical relationship with employment status as measured, but this occurs independently of any individual experience. The relation is an epiphenomenon that supervenes on experience. That is, it relates not to any actual individual, but to the mass of individuals surveyed. It is a pattern in the data, not a relationship in any individual's life. We cannot ask of the statistic why unemployment is related to happiness; such a relation is a regularity that arises from the sum of individual reasons that comprise it. At the same time, we cannot ask questions of it beyond that of the closed set of causal relations presented by the measures in the programme. We do not know, for instance, the relation between happiness and security of employment, as that second condition is not measured.

Other ways of considering subjective well-being are possible; for instance, as a mode of being in the world rather than as an output state. One way to think about this is the way in which questions of happiness are asked and answered in everyday discourse beyond the work of the statistician. The question 'How are you?' forms part of a social relation; its meaning is determined by the relationship between questioner and respondent. Sometimes it is a social nicety, a pleasantry to open up or politely side-step a conversation. Sometimes it is sincerely meant and an opening for empathic exchange. The meaning of both question and answer is not fixed by the content of either but by their structural form, their position within a lived relationship.

This bi-directional subjectivity, in which both questioner and questioned are capable of engaging with each other on the level of meaning, does not inform the statistics on subjective well-being. Instead, the model taken for the four headline subjective well-being questions is that of 'happiness economics' (Layard 2005), which attempts to extend the model of economic person, *homo economicus*, to the realm of internal life. In the same way that *homo economicus* continually strives to maximise the utility[4] received from resources expended, so the happy person, *homo beatus*, seeks in every action to maximise happiness. Happiness is made to stand in for utility. While economists previously attempted to adjudge utility through purchasing activities in the market, happiness economics reverses the process, using direct measures of subjective well-being to assess the effectiveness of purchases. In this way, it seeks to correct the failures of existing economic approaches exemplified in the critique of the GDP statistic and in the vernacular wisdom that happiness cannot be bought (Larson 1993; Cameron 2010; Davies 2015). GDP is saved by being expressible in terms of happiness; they are given the same basis of valuation, making happiness economic and economic activity happiness. Subjective well-being, which ostensibly seeks to count something other than economic activity, becomes merely another means to express such activity. This was why it was devised; subjective well-being has an economic form because it was created by economists to serve economic purposes.

The project of happiness economics is structurally identical to that of the official statistic that it informs. It is based on an abstraction which assumes that both happiness and the individuals who possess it are uniform, interchangeable and alienable. It seeks causal relations, assuming mechanistic linkages between circumstance and human behaviour. It is worth highlighting how disappointing the fruits of this project have been. Summarising 30 years of research in the field, Dolan, Peasgood and White (2006) observe that bereavement, debt, ill-health, unemployment, and insecurity all negatively impact on happiness, while having intimate relationships and seeing family and friends have positive effects (see also Seaford, this volume, Chap. 5). However, while not successfully revealing anything that sympathy, empathy and human experience had not already told us, the project has achieved a re-coding of these into the language of power. Happiness has moved beyond the realm of meaning and into a realm of expertise (see also Bourdieu and Wacquant 2001). This may be viewed as a pragmatic act (although, as argued above, this is overly pessimistic given that subjective well-being was not beyond political discourse previously), but it is one that fundamentally changes the way in which subjective well-being is articulated and so understood by those in power. Oman (2015) illustrates the difficulty the ONS had in moving from the responses made by the public, when consulted on 'What matters to you?', to a statistical conception; moving from accounts of specific interactions with their families that gave individuals joy to a generic question about overall satisfaction with family life. The nexus of meanings that the individual lives within is abstracted away to leave the general rule it is believed to express. 'Happiness' and 'subjective well-being' as acted on are now those as imagined by the statistic, incorporating its reductive logic, its belief in the homogeneity and commensurability of happiness, and its faith in mechanical relations.

The re-coding goes further than this, as happiness economics provides a way of re-valuing happiness in terms of money. For example, Blanchflower and Oswald (2004) state that 'To "compensate" for a major life event such as being widowed or a marital separation, it would be necessary... to provide an individual with $100,000 extra per annum' (p. 1373). While these authors stress that this does not mean that a bereaved person given $100,000 would regain their former levels of happiness, it is difficult to understand what else could be meant by such an equivalence. Happiness here is a uniform state, affected in the same way by money and by human relations; these are merely causal inputs resulting in a mechanical emotional output.

The placement of *homo beatus* in a world beyond meaning subject to indifferent causal laws dictates the ways in which happiness statistics can be used. For example, the methodology used by Blanchflower and Oswald (2004) when attempting to place a monetary value on bereavement has been incorporated into the Treasury's *Green Book* (HM Treasury 2011), allowing happiness to become a basis for cost–benefit analysis. In this way, the Cabinet Office (2013) reported that 'an adult learning course which improves life satisfaction has a value to those who receive it of between £750 and £950 on average' (pp. 2–3); Fujiwara (2013) reported that '[p]eople who visit museums in their spare time value this at about £3200 per annum' (p. 28) and Fujiwara, Oroyemi and McKinnon (2013) reported that 'we estimate the value that frequent volunteers place on volunteering to be about £13,500 per year at 2011 prices' (p. 1). These are not statements that could have been made without the statistic, nor could they have been made had the statistic imagined happiness differently.

One response to my argument might be to suggest that such a redescription of human experience in the language of power allows it a consideration that was not previously possible, offering a pragmatic solution to the problems of incoherence discussed in the previous section. The Fujiwara paper on museums (Fujiwara 2013), for example, was commissioned as a lobbying piece, to show that museums were not an idle frippery but that they provided tangible benefits and were a worthwhile investment. Similarly, Layard (2013) argues for easier access to cognitive-behavioural therapy, as this is a cost-effective way of ameliorating mental suffering that will bring economic benefits in terms of productivity and reduced strain on public services (see Evans, this volume, Chap. 2). This is not a consideration of the subject on its own terms, however.

Museums and mental health are stripped of their moral, historical or cultural justifications and have imposed on them an economic one. In doing so, questions around them are taken out of the realm of the democratic and passed into the realm of the technical. We can no longer ask if mental health is worthwhile, only if it is cost-effective. Further, we cannot ask whether unhappiness is justified, or whether the solution should be sought in structural conditions; the need to maximise happiness has been assumed, and cognitive-behavioural therapy will achieve this most cost-effectively.

What becomes possible when subjective well-being is abstracted from its context and becomes independent of the subjective well-being of the individuals who comprise it? It is early days in the happiness project, but Davies (2015) reports on a scheme to give job-seekers 'positivity' training, re-articulating the misery of their precarity as a personal failing to be overcome through a change in outlook. Their position at the bottom of the labour-welfare complex is taken as a neutral given, to be ameliorated through action on themselves rather than through structural changes. The meaning of their position and its role in their life are ignored; we cannot ask if their unhappiness is justified by their circumstances. It has causes, but not reasons. Happiness has been alienated from the individual, separated from their world of meanings, and converted into a norm; a target to be achieved.

Whose Well-Being? How Measurement Obscures Ill-Being

In the two previous sections, I have argued for the importance of the form of the official statistic, suggesting that the act of counting makes particular ontological and epistemological claims about its content that prove to be homogenising, alienating and reductive. It may still be argued, however, that any programme purporting to measure 'well-being' is better than none. The existence of a programme elevates 'well-being' as an aim of government and acts as a visible commitment to the promotion of 'well-being'.

This optimism is as equally misplaced as the pessimistic idea that 'well-being' was previously not a concern of government. As has been shown above, the individual is considered in the same reductive manner whether you are counting their economic activity or their well-being. Focusing on the latter does not engage with their reasons but only a restricted reading of their causes, removing them from the realm of the democratic and sub-jecting them instead to technical expertise. The change in subject does not change the power relation expressed by the official statistic but only artic-ulates it over a new domain. This is nicely illustrated by an example of a national well-being programme in practice: the Bhutanese programme of Gross National Happiness (GNH).

GNH is often held up as a trail-blazing programme, originating in advance of the Second Wave in the global North and acting as a set of priorities for national development different from those built around GDP growth (for a typical paean, see Burns 2011). It is normally pre-sented as having been first developed in the early 1970s (Ura et al. 2012) although, as Munroe (2016) convincingly argues, this is almost certainly untrue. While the concept very occasionally featured in the public pro-nouncements of the King of Bhutan from the early 1970s, there is no evidence that it operated as a governing principle until the late 1990s.

The timing of GNH's movement to the centre of government is interesting, because it follows considerable negative press generated by Bhutan's ethnic cleansing of its southern population. Starting with the Citizenship Act of 1977, a few years after GNH was supposedly enshrined as a governing principle, the ethnic Nepalese who lived in the south of Bhutan were progressively stripped of their rights (Human Rights Watch 2007). For example, the Marriage Act of 1980 out-lawed miscegenation between ethnic Nepalese and other Bhutanese, and a series of laws in 1989 outlawed the schooling of children in the Nepalese language and imposed the dress code of the ruling northern elite. At the same time, the Citizenship Act and its 1985 successor selec-tively stripped many ethnic Nepalese of their citizenship and the rights that went with it. This escalating oppression led to protests in 1990, to which the government responded by coercing ethnic Nepalese to leave the country through intimidation and violence. At the peak of the con-flict, refugee camps set up in Nepal and India held 140,000 Bhutanese refugees, a figure which, at the time, represented about a sixth of the entire population of the country (Association of Human Rights Activists, Bhutan 1994; Rizal 2004; de Varennes 2008; UNHCR 2011). While this account has been disputed (for example, Shaw 1992), the exiles were granted refugee status by the United Nations, recognising that they faced a well-founded risk of persecution were they to return home (UNHCR 2011).

Were we to accept the official line, *contra* Munroe (2016), that GNH has framed Bhutanese government policy since the 1970s, then the persecution of the ethnic Nepalese highlights the space between counting happiness in the abstract and happiness as experienced by individuals. Having a programme does not change the relation of power between the governed and the governing; the latter are still free to act in spite of the former's well-being. This is particularly pronounced in the Bhutanese case, as GNH includes measures of cultural homogeneity, such as fluency in the language spoken by the northern elite and adherence to northern cultural practices. The happiness of the nation, on these measures, has been improved by exiling one-sixth of it and enforcing cultural norms amongst those who remain.

Accepting Munroe's (2016) argument that it post-dates the ethnic cleansing of the ethnic Nepalese, however, GNH becomes a discursive tool to divert attention and repair reputational damage. 'Happiness' here is a smokescreen, suggesting a beneficent government to the outside world. By promoting happiness publicly, to the point where it sponsored a UN General Assembly Resolution on the subject (65/309, in 2011), Bhutan has developed a reputation for something other than its oppression of minorities.

In either of these cases, there is a discursive role for GNH, obscuring events on the ground by re-presenting them. This illustrates a general point that policies stem from multiple motives, but also a more specific one. When your mode of understanding a population is based on the discarding of individuals and the meanings they draw as noise, the actions which that understanding permits are similarly dismissive. While on a somewhat different scale, the UK programme includes a measure of the public sector debt-to-GDP ratio, allowing policies justified on the basis of reducing the national debt to be associated with well-being. Just as ethnic cleansing increases national well-being by improving cultural homogeneity, policies of austerity improve national well-being by bringing down national debt. In both cases, the sufferings that result are discursively (and, in the Bhutanese case, literally) excluded from 'the nation', the happiness of which occludes any individual unhappiness. The statistical form, which is based on such an exclusion—abstracting as it does from actual humans to statistically representative ones—permits this.

One further point should be noted; by badging a headline set of measures as being 'about national well-being', any statistics not included in the set become, by extension, 'not about national well-being'.

They become less visible, and harder to talk about. It is here that the motivation to indulge in boundary policing mentioned earlier arises; the 'Measuring National Well-being' programme does not talk about inequality, or excess winter mortality, or private debt. Adding these (or other of our concerns) would make the set more complete. Again, though, it should be noted that this would not solve our problem; 'well-being' would not be any more coherent, there would always be another measure we could add or take away and the set would still not add up to single concrete entity. This illustrates Sayer's argument about chaotic conceptions (Marx 1993; Sayer 1981, 1982, 2000): abstract concepts that present themselves as being concrete. The illusion of concreteness limits what we can say, but the reality of the abstractness means there is no compensatory ability to speak about anything new. Our new vocabulary re-describes and excludes, as well as enables (Bourdieu and Wacquant 2001).

Fuzzwords and the Emptiness of 'Well-Being'

This chapter has argued that the pragmatic role of an official statistic is structured by its representational logic. Put simply, the fact that a statistical programme has 'well-being' as its subject does not mean it is about well-being as lived or that it will serve well-being, and the statistical form means that it will act independently of non-statistical conceptions of 'well-being'. The miscellany of the 'Measuring National Well-being' programme's content, the reductive and economic nature of its novel measures, and its potential to mask regressive policies are all hidden by the normative force of 'well-being'. While initially indicating nothing specific, the term 'well-being' now indicates a definite set of measures to the exclusion of everything else. 'Well-being' becomes what Cornwall and Brock (2005) label a 'fuzz-word': an unimpeachable moral container that can hold otherwise unpalatable policies (see also Bourdieu and Wacquant 2001). In the same way that it is difficult to oppose 'development' or 'progress' (both of which are themselves cited by the promoters of well-being measurement as being advanced by such measurement) it is hard to challenge specific interventions that have been justified on well-being grounds. This is particularly the case when we have, as argued above, an incoherent set of measures where multiple, potentially conflicting, things are all 'to do with well-being'. Challenging austerity becomes challenging well-being; an opposition to ethnic cleansing becomes a call for less national happiness. At the same time, promoting subjective well-being becomes promoting subjective well-being as statistically imagined; mechanical, homogeneous, shorn of context.

This chapter has argued that this danger is greater than it may appear. In the first section ('Historical Precedents'), it was shown that the vagueness of 'well-being' carries through to the multi-item index, offering no guidance for policy. This was true of the statistics collected before the current vogue for well-being, and it remains true once those statistics have been re-badged and expanded. If life expectancy was lower, and relative employment, underemployment and over-qualification higher in the north of England for example, or male suicide rates higher in Wales, for another, before well-being existed, it is impossible to claim that this was not known about, and hard to claim that knowing in addition that this made people sad will lead to any great crusade to change it (Hacking et al. 2011; Gunnell et al. 2012; Rafferty et al. 2013).

The second section ('The Logic of Measurement') argued that the well-being statistics collected in the UK were ill-suited to this task anyway, embodying a disregard for the individual. The statistics' foundation on the principles of equivalence and exchangeability entail a denial of individual experience and meaning. 'National' happiness is not the happiness of anyone living within the nation, but a series of averages and placeholders that are obtained by stripping out the 'noise' of lived experience. The consequences of this were highlighted in the third section ('Whose Well-being?'). When a premise of your data collection method is that people can be discarded, it is unsurprising that an effect of policies based on such a collection is that people are.

Fundamentally, the appeal to the statistic, with its related appeals to 'objective' or 'evidence-based' policy-making, is always one that restricts the ability of individuals to negotiate on the level of meaning and which passes power to a technocratic administrative elite operating on a level of abstracted causal relations. As was highlighted when considering the uses to which the UK programme has been put, the move to abstract mechanical regularities around subjective well-being is one that denies people the ability to explain their everyday life by forcing it instead into a set of causal relations. Within the discourse of the statistic, it is not possible to talk about the value of goods and services beyond subjective well-being, for example in terms of fairness, need or desire. The most efficient well-being maximising good or service wins out, regardless of the other values that might be embodied by its rivals. Mechanising the messy world of meaning through statistics and statistical relations is an act of disenfranchisement. The person doing the counting starts with an individual, with dignity and rights, and leaves with data, to which anything may be done (Weil 1986). This act of depersonalisation allows and invites abuse.

It may be countered that this is a pragmatic response to a policy-making world in which numbers are 'hard evidence' and accounts of experience are written off as 'anecdote'. It should be recognised that this is a profoundly undemocratic world, one premised on the silencing of individual voices. In such a world we are not only faced with the question of whether or not it would be better that we expressed our concern for well-being using long-established terminology, but whether or not that terminology should be changed. The same is, of course, true for all existing statistics. It would be possible to react to the crisis of GDP, its failure to capture what 'really matters', by abandoning it. This would take some imagination, and a rearticulation of the way in which we organise socially, politically and economically. As the statistic is a response to scale, it is likely that this rearticulation would involve a devolution of policy to a level at which anecdote and discussion were possible as a basis of action. The critique of the official statistic is the critique of the society organised to require the official statistic; the failure of 'well-being' is the failure of that society. If we are interested in well-being, as I believe we should be, it is incumbent on us to imagine something better than counting.

NOTES

1. While the word 'well-being' is increasingly presented without a hyphen it is hyphenated here for consistency with the title of the ONS National Well-being Programme, which is the focus of much of the discussion.
2. In the UK context, this assertion is legitimated by reference to a public consultation. This is not the place to explore that consultation process; although I have argued elsewhere (Jenkins 2016, 2017) that this was well-meaning but ultimately inconsequential to the selection of measures. Even if this were not the case, a crowd-sourced assertion does not make the selection any more coherent than an assertion by more restricted fiat.
3. An objection could be raised here that it is the individual who chooses to collapse the complexity of their emotional life into a single figure when they agree to translate it into a number on an 11-point scale. The fact that they have answered an alienating question, however, does not make it non-alienating. The act of posing the question, interested, as it is, not in the individual's happiness but in the acquisition of an anonymous data-point-is inherently

alienating, designed to strip an emotion out of its context in everyday life and resituate it as a possession of the statistician. That the respondent is made confederate in this does not change its structure.

4. 'Utility' is very loosely defined in economic models, but can be thought of as akin to 'usefulness'. Usefulness itself is related to the aims and desires of the individual; so the theory states that a person purchasing product A rather than product B does so because they want product A more. Product A is, in this way, infused with a democratic legitimacy; an individual has endorsed it with their resources.

Acknowledgements I am indebted to Karen Scott, Ian Bache, Arezu Bari, Tessa Holland and Andrea Wilkinson, whose kind and careful attention to earlier drafts of this chapter considerably improved it. The research on which it is based was funded by the ESRC (grant number ES/J50082/1). It incorporates ideas that were worked up for the 2015 Big Ideas Project, conducted jointly by Seven Stories/The National Centre for Children's Books and the University of Newcastle. Thanks also to the students of High Spen, St John's and Byker primary schools.

REFERENCES

Allin, P. (2007). Measuring Societal Wellbeing. *Economic and Labour Market Review, 1*(10), 46–52.

Association of Human Rights Activists, Bhutan. (1994). *Bhutanese Refugees: Victims of Arbitrary Deprivation of Right to Nationality and Political Representation*. Jhapa, Nepal: AHURA Bhutan.

Bache, I. (2013). Measuring Quality of Life for Public Policy: An Idea Whose Time Has Come? Agenda-setting Dynamics in the European Union. *Journal of European Public Policy, 20*(1), 21–38.

Bache, I., & Reardon, L. (2013). An Idea Whose Time Has Come? Explaining the Rise of Well-being in British Politics. *Political Studies, 61*(4), 898–914.

Bache, I., & Reardon, L. (2016). *The Politics and Policy of Wellbeing: Understanding the Rise and Significance of a New Agenda*. Cheltenham: Edward Elgar.

Beaumont, J. (2011). Measuring National Well-being: A Discussion Paper on Domains and Measures. London: Office for National Statistics. Available at: http://www.ons.gov.uk/ons/dcp171766_240726.pdf. Accessed October 17, 2012.

Blanchflower, D. G., & Oswald, A. J. (2004). Well-being Over Time in Britain and the USA. *Journal of Public Economics, 88,* 1250–1286.

Bourdieu, P., & Wacquant, L. (2001). NewLiberalSpeak; Notes on the New Planetary Vulgate. *Radical Philosophy, 105,* 2–5.

Burns, G. (2011). Gross National Happiness: A Gift from Bhutan to the World. In R. Biswas-Diener (Ed.), *Positive Psychology as Social Change* (pp. 73–87). Dordrecht: Springer.

Cabinet Office. (2013). Wellbeing Policy and Analysis: An Update of Wellbeing Work across Whitehall. Available at: https://www.gov.uk/government/uploads/system/uploads/attachment_data/file/224910/Wellbeing_Policy_and_Analysis_FINAL.PDF. Accessed February 4, 2014.

Cameron, D. (2010, November 25). PM Speech on Wellbeing [Speech]. Available at: http://www.number10.gov.uk/news/pm-speech-on-well-being/. Accessed October 22, 2012.

Collier, G. (1854). An Account of the Metropolitan Bills of Mortality. From Their Commencement to the Present Time. *The Lancet* (19 August), 141–143.

Cornwall, A., & Brock, K. (2005). What do Buzzwords do for Development Policy? A Critical Look at 'Participation', 'Empowerment' and 'Poverty Reduction'. *Third World Quarterly, 26*(7), 1043–1060.

Davies, W. (2015). *The Happiness Industry: How Government and Big Business Sold us Well-being*. London: Verso.

de Varennes, F. (2008). Constitutionalising Discrimination in Bhutan: The Emasculation of Human Rights in the Land of the Dragon. *Asia-Pacific Journal on Human Rights and the Law, 9*(2), 47–76.

Doel, M. (2001). 1a. Qualified Quantitative Geography. *Environment and Planning D: Society and Space, 19*, 555–572.

Dolan, P., Peasgood, T., & White, M. (2006). Review of Research on the Influences on Personal Well-being and Application to Policy Making. London: DEFRA.

Eurostat. (n.d.). *Quality of Life (QOL)—Data*. Luxembourg: Eurostat. Available at: http://ec.europa.eu/eurostat/web/gdp-and-beyond/quality-of-life/data. Accessed May 9, 2015.

Fujiwara, D. (2013). Museums and Happiness: The Value of Participating in Museums and the Arts. Stowmarket: Museum of East Anglian Life. Available at: http://happymuseumproject.org/happy-museums-are-good-for-you-report-publication/museums-and-happiness/.

Fujiwara, D., Oroyemi, P., & McKinnon, E. (2013). Wellbeing and Civil Society: Estimating the Value of Volunteering Using Subjective Wellbeing Data (Working Paper No. 112). London: Department for Work and Pensions. Available at: https://www.gov.uk/government/uploads/system/uploads/attachment_data/file/221227/WP112.pdf.

Gunnell, D., Wheeler, B., Chang, S.-S., Thomas, B., Sterne, J., & Dorling, D. (2012). Changes in the Geography of Suicide in Young Men: England and Wales 1981–2005. *Journal of Epidemiology and Community Health, 66*, 536–543.

Hacking, I. (1999). *The Social Construction of What?* Cambridge, MA: Harvard University Press.

Hacking, J. M., Muller, S., & Buchan, I. E. (2011). Trends in Mortality from 1965 to 2008 Across the English North-south Divide: Comparative Observational Study. *British Medical Journal, 342,* d508.

Hand, D. J. (2004). *Measurement Theory and Practice: The World Through Quantification.* Chichester: Wiley.

Human Rights Watch. (2007). Last Hope: The Need for Durable Solutions for Bhutanese Refugees in Nepal and India. New York: Human Rights Watch. Available at: https://www.hrw.org/report/2007/05/16/last-hope/need-durable-solutions-bhutanese-refugees-nepal-and-india.

Jenkins, M. (2016). Official Statistic-making as a Social Practice: The UK 'Measuring National Well-being' Programme (Doctoral thesis). University of Newcastle, Newcastle-upon-Tyne.

Jenkins, M. (2017). Knowledge and Practice Mobilities in the Process of Policy-making: The Case of UK National Well-being Statistics. *Political Geography, 56C,* 24–33.

Jones, R. (2007). *People/States/Territories: The Political Geographies of British State Transformation.* Oxford: Blackwell Publishing.

Larson, G. (1993). The Far Side (cartoon). *Chicago Tribune,* December 29, p. 2.

Layard, R. (2005). *Happiness: Lessons from a New Science.* London: Penguin.

Layard, R. (2013). Mental Health: The New Frontier for Labour Economics. *IZA Journal of Labor Policy, 2*(2), 1–16.

Lepper, J., & McAndrew S. (2008). Developments in the Economics of Well-being. *Economic Working Paper No. 4.* London: HM Treasury. Available at: https://www.escholar.manchester.ac.uk/api/datastream?publicationPid=uk-ac-man-scw:198219&datastreamId=FULL-TEXT.PDF.

Marx, K. (1993). *Grundrisse: Foundations of the Critique of Political Economy.* (M. Nicolaus, Trans.). London: Penguin.

Moser, C. A. (1970). Some General Developments in Social Statistics. *Social Trends, 1,* 7–11.

Munroe, L. T. (2016). Where did Bhutan's Gross National Happiness Come From? The Origins of an Invented Tradition. *Asian Affairs, 47*(1), 71–92.

Nissel, M. (1970). Editorial. *Social Trends, 1,* 4–6.

OECD. (1973). How to Measure Well-being. *The OECD Observer, 64,* 36–37.

OECD. (2013). *Measuring Well-being and Progress.* Paris: Organisation for Economic Co-operation and Development.

Oman, S. (2015). Measuring National Wellbeing: What Matters to You? What Matters to Whom? In S. White & C. Blackmore (Eds.), *Cultures of Wellbeing: Method, Place, Policy* (pp. 66–94). Basingstoke: Palgrave Macmillan.

ONS. (2014). Measuring National Well-being: Life in the UK, 2014. Office for National Statistics. London: HMSO. Available at: http://webarchive.

nationalarchives.gov.uk/20160105184137/https://www.ons.gov.uk/ons/rel/wellbeing/measuring-national-well-being/life-in-the-uk--2014/art-mn-wb--life-in-the-uk--2014.html.

Painter, J. (2006). Prosaic Geographies of Stateness. *Political Geography, 25*, 752–774.

Petty, W. (1899 [1690]). Political Arithmetick. In C. H. Hull (Ed.), *The Economic Writings of Sir William Petty* (Vol. 1, pp. 232–313). Cambridge: Cambridge University Press.

Power, M. (1994). The Audit Society. In A. G. Hopwood & P. Miller (Eds.), *Accounting as Social and Institutional Practice* (pp. 299–316). Cambridge: Cambridge University Press.

Power, M. (1996). Making Things Auditable. *Accounting, Organizations and Society, 21*(2/3), 289–315.

Rafferty, A., Rees, J., Sensier, M., & Harding, A. (2013). Growth and Recession: Underemployment and the Labour Market in the North of England. *Applied Spatial Analysis and Policy, 6*(2), 143–163.

Rizal, D. (2004). The Unknown Refugee Crisis: Expulsion of the Ethnic Lhotsampa from Bhutan. *Asian Ethnicity, 5*(2), 151–177.

Sayer, A. (1981). Abstraction: A Realist Interpretation. *Radical Philosophy, 28*, 6–15.

Sayer, A. (1982). Explanation in Economic Geography: Abstraction Versus Generalization. *Progress in Human Geography, 6*(1), 68–88.

Sayer, A. (2000). *Realism and Social Science*. London: Sage.

Shaw, B. C. (1992). Bhutan in 1991: 'Refugees' and 'Ngolops.' *Asian Survey, 32*(2), 184–88.

Treasury, H. M. (2011). *The Green Book: Appraisal and Evaluation in Central Government*. London: The Stationery Office.

UNHCR. (2011). Nepal. UNHCR Global Appeal 2012–2013 (pp. 194–198). Geneva: United Nations High Commissioner for Refugees. Available at: http://www.unhcr.org/uk/publications/fundraising/4ec231050/unhcr-global-appeal-2012-2013-nepal.html.

Ura, K., Alkire, S., Zangmo, T., & Wangdi, K. (2012). *An Extensive Analysis of GNH Index*. Thimphu, Bhutan: Centre for Bhutan Studies.

Weil, S. (1986). Human Personality. In S. Miles (Ed.), *Simone Weil: An Anthology* R. Rees Trans., pp. 50–62. New York: Weidenfeld and Nicholson.

Index

© The Editor(s) (if applicable) and The Author(s) 2018
I. Bache and K. Scott (eds.), *The Politics of Wellbeing*, Wellbeing
in Politics and Policy, https://doi.org/10.1007/978-3-319-58394-5

Lightning Source UK Ltd.
Milton Keynes UK
UKHW020609231119
354076UK00005B/262/P